All the Things You Are

The Life of Tony Bennett

DAVID EVANIER

WILEY

John Wiley & Sons, Inc.

To Derek Boulton, Joe Soldo, Dini Evanier,
Andrew Blauner, Theodore Mitrani, Lenny Triola,
Nick Riggio, and Jerome H. Kogan

This book is printed on acid-free paper. ∞

Copyright © 2011 by David Evanier. All rights reserved

Photo credits: Page 56 top, 122, 213 top: courtesy of Nick Riggio; 56 bottom, 123 top, 125 bottom, 215 bottom, 296 bottom: photo by Derek Boulton; 123 bottom, 124, 125 top: photo by Ron Rolo; 213 bottom, 214 bottom, 215 top: photo by Fran Riggio; 214 top: New York Daily News; 216 top, 293, 294, 295 top, 296 top: courtesy of Mark Fox; 216 bottom: courtesy of Geri Tamburello; 295 bottom: photo by David Evanier.

Published by John Wiley & Sons, Inc., Hoboken, New Jersey
Published simultaneously in Canada

For general information about our other products and services, please contact our Customer Care Department within the United States at (800) 762-2974, outside the United States at (317) 572-3993 or fax (317) 572-4002.

Wiley also publishes its books in a variety of electronic formats. Some content that appears in print may not be available in electronic books. For more information about Wiley products, visit our web site at www.wiley.com.

ISBN 978-0-470-52065-9 (cloth); ISBN 978-1-118-03354-8 (ebk);
ISBN 978-1-118-03355-5 (ebk); ISBN 978-1-118-03356-2 (ebk)

Printed in the United States of America

10 9 8 7 6 5 4 3 2

I wanted to be one of the keepers of the flame
when it came to great music.

—Tony Bennett, *The Good Life*

CONTENTS

Introduction

Staying Real

In 1966 Tony Bennett was singing "Lost in the Stars" at the Hollywood Bowl with Count Basie's band. A shooting star shot through the sky right over his head, astounding even a jaded Hollywood audience. The next morning Bennett's phone rang. It was Ray Charles, whom Bennett had never met up to that time, calling from New York. Charles said, "Hey, Tony, how'd you do that, man?" and hung up.

In many ways Tony Bennett's life—his real last name, Benedetto, means "blessed" in Italian—has been a magical one, and some of his experiences over the years come as close to the celestial as a human life can aspire to. He has packed several lifetimes into his eighty-five years. The rebirth of Bennett generation after generation is amazing. He has never lost his sense of wonder, even as he has reached the pinnacle of a career that has kept him a huge star for more than sixty years, with sixty million record sales and fifteen Grammy Awards. In 2006 a television special, *Tony Bennett: An American Classic*, on NBC won multiple Emmy Awards. In 2009 Bennett signed a new $10 million recording contract with Columbia, the company that gave him his greatest early triumphs. His paintings have been accepted for the permanent collection of the Smithsonian American Art Museum in Washington, D.C.,

1

including his oil paintings *Central Park* and *God Is Love*, a stunning portrait of Duke Ellington with twelve red roses. The roses have a story of their own. Ellington would send a dozen roses to Bennett every time Bennett wrote a new song. The painting was the only one of his own Bennett hung in his home. When Bennett speaks about Duke, he could be describing himself: "He was very consistent about being creative all day long. There wasn't a moment that he wasn't creative. When I was in his presence, he was creating something. At all times." The love was mutual. Ellington wrote in his autobiography that "Tony Bennett is the most unselfish performing artist today."

He seems to have always been with us. He said on his eightieth birthday, "I feel like Rip Van Winkle." He fought in World War II and helped to liberate a concentration camp. He became a top star with "Because of You," which topped the charts in September 1951 and sold a million copies. He repeated that triumph in November of that year with "Cold, Cold Heart," another gold record, and again and again after that. He marched at Selma. Vittorio De Sica, one of the greatest Italian filmmakers of all time, wanted to make a documentary about Bennett's life in the 1970s. It was not surprising that the foremost Italian humanist director should be drawn to the story of the poor Italian American boy with the warm, gruff street voice, whose passionate antifascism, antiracism, and pacifism were shaped by his experiences in the world war.

Today, at eighty-five, Bennett's charm, heart, technical facility, and sincerity have never relinquished their hold on the country. He stands at five feet nine, and his blue eyes still startle. He is extraordinarily handsome for a man of any age, and his is a classic Italian profile. His speaking voice remains virile, husky, with a strong touch of gravel, hickory smoke, and the streets of New York. His mind and heart seem to wrap around every song, and his husky voice seems to personalize a song as if it were an intimate encounter between singer and listener.

He is, astoundingly, a better singer than he ever was before, more melodic, more haunting. Writing of Bennett's performance in Philadelphia in August 2010, A. D. Amorosi wrote in the *Philadelphia Inquirer*, "I've attended several Tony Bennett shows in the last 20 years, and I must report: Saturday night's sold-out Mann Center gig was his best. . . . The great triumph . . . was that, simply, Bennett never sounded finer—refined, tough, tender, more theatrical than ever, capable of crooning to the rafters without losing the nuanced phrasing he has developed."

Listening to more recent Bennett recordings, singer Ellen Martin says that "the voice is different from the young voice, but he sings beautifully and with the same feeling. It's very penetrating, thoughtful, intense, and rich. He really does stay in the moment. It actually feels live, as if he hadn't worked out in advance how he was going to sing the end of the song. Because he's so connected with these life experiences and feelings, because he touches something in himself, it touches the same in us and we relate."

There are only a handful of performers in the history of show business who rise above all the other stars because they are not only great singers but also great entertainers: Sinatra, Judy Garland, Louis Armstrong, Jimmy Durante, George Burns, Dean Martin, Ray Charles, Fred Astaire, Al Jolson, and Tony Bennett. We are talking about the kind of magic—stardust—that transcends all fashions and trends, simply magic that will endure forever.

Bennett has a level of self-awareness that is hewn out of years of struggle and triumph. Sinatra, Duke Ellington, and Count Basie are among his primary influences. He is eager to admit the impact of others on his work. He told BBC2 in 1979, "It wasn't stealing . . . it was what Stravinsky would have called 'sweet thievery.' I was inspired by what I saw and heard, which is really expressing my love for my fellow artist." He has said that Count Basie's "attitude became my philosophy: economy of line, keep it simple, keep it swingin'."

Bennett and Sinatra, his idol, both tell a story from within. Neither of them is simply performing songs; they are living them. They are entirely different, except that each can surprise and be unpredictable.

"Tony stood up, he was always driven and doing what he wanted to do," his niece, Nina Chiappa, told me. "There's that Calabrese element there. I think it's a family trait that we're very tenacious but also very sensitive." Bennett's loyalty to Sinatra is based purely on his admiration of his talent. Nick Riggio, a lifelong friend of Tony who thinks that Tony is even better than Sinatra, recalls that Bennett has always bristled at that suggestion. "Tony would get mad at me," he told me. "He'd always say, 'Sinatra invented the art of intimate singing.'"

There seems to be no trace of envy in Bennett's attitude toward Sinatra. Indeed, there is love. He is totally committed to the furtherance of the art. He wrote of Sinatra, "I look at Sinatra as a musicologist would look at Mozart or Bach or Beethoven. . . . Everything Sinatra has ever done musically . . . is a tremendous contribution to popular music because it has a timelessness to it. That is the test of art, and his music is art."

Sinatra could swing, but Bennett can swing even better. And he is open-hearted to the point that as he sings, I have sometimes visualized a glass shattering or, as the old theatrical phrase goes, "the rafters ringing." For a moment in time, we are alive as the troubadour is alive—jubilant, euphoric, joyous. Unlike the great Garland, there is no edge of hysteria; unlike the magnificent Sinatra, there is not the darkest depression. There is always a touch of hopefulness, for embedded in Bennett's philosophy is a commitment to uplifting his audience. And it is telling that Bennett tries to avoid songs with negative outcomes. He refused to sing "Didn't We" because the lyric says "We *almost* made it." "I'm not doing any song with a negative front line," he told his manager, Derek Boulton.

Judy Garland said it best a long time ago: "I remember the first time I heard Tony sing on a record years ago. I thought, That *sound*! He isn't copying *anyone*! His sound gets into your ear and into your heart."

But no one defines Tony as well as record producer and archivist Jimmy Scalia. "I hear warmth in Tony's voice, but I also hear strength. He's a belter, but he can convey a gentle song with feeling. And he's sharp. The sharpness sticks out for me because he's got such damn power that he knocks me off my chair. I mean Tony's just so in your face, he's just so there. On the money. What happens when he sings I can't find the words, my emotions run so quickly my mind can't keep up with them. But he is very warm and very gentle when he sings a love song. The older he gets, he's telling me through his experience. I would say his voice is honey with a little bit of lemon and sugar in it.

"Artists, as they rise, as they're still trying to find themselves, they're lightning in the jar. They take our breath away, whatever they do. And sometimes it comes to a point with an artist that you've not fallen out of love with them, but you've kind of plateaued with them. I loved Ray Charles, there was nothing the guy could do wrong. And then at one point Ray just kind of evened out. Everything he did I liked, but it wasn't like it kicked you in the pants. It's great when an artist like Tony is still trying to find himself. I don't think I can recall anybody else in the business, still living or not, continually trying to find themselves— somebody who really continued to plug at it and did it. With Tony the freshness is still there. Look at his body of work. At eighty-five he's still got it. And he has managed to work his voice around his age.

"Look, the voice is a tool, it's a muscle. It gets older. You have to work around it. His phrasing is always so good, so intuitive. And that's what keeps him fresh, that's what makes him real. It's hard to stay real for a long time. I remember seeing him at an affair one night in Manhattan. I'm like yelling to my wife, this guy's incredible! *He's everywhere.* He lives and breathes music. He *is* music. We've got to hold on to a guy like that with both hands."

There is Bennett the singer, and there is Bennett the painter. He has held steady to his twin vocations of music and art since he was a boy of ten drawing with chalk on the sidewalk in Astoria, Queens, while his boyhood friends good-naturedly threw peanuts at him to try to distract him.

Nothing stopped him. Throughout his life Bennett has gravitated toward living near Central Park. "I love that park," he told writer Robert Sullivan. "I always dreamed of having a place that would catch the afternoon light, so I could paint the park over and over." Today Bennett gazes from the window of his Central Park South apartment at the beauty of the park; mornings he steps outside his door with a sketch pad or easel and canvas, walks across the street, and enters the park, where he paints. He always carries the sketchpad with him, and he also draws on scrap paper, restaurant napkins, hotel stationery: still lifes and black-and-white portraits.

Bennett also paints in his fifth-floor studio, which is one building over from his apartment and which also has a majestic view of the park. His apartment, which he shares with his wife, Susan Crow Benedetto, contains memories of his musical life, including a Bosendorfer baby grand, a mandolin, paintings by his friend David Hockney, many Asian art objects, and an old Victrola.

It was not always magic for Tony Bennett. He overcame a drug addiction that almost killed him, and yet that triumph—probably the greatest victory of his life—remains a hidden story because he will not really talk about it. "He thinks it's nobody's business but his," music critic Will Friedwald told me. "I think he accentuates the positive in his own life just as he does in his music. Of course, you could argue that it would be positive to tell the world how he conquered his drug problems, but Tony obviously doesn't see it that way."

He did tell the *Boston Globe*, "I used to take pills. Uppies. Downies. Sleepies. But no more. I'm in touch with myself. I'm healthier now than I ever have been. And I've become unbuggable."

The 1970s through the mid-1980s were Bennett's blackest period. There were drugs, the decline of the record industry with the ascent of rock and roll, losing his record label (he walked out on Columbia; they didn't walk out on him), a seemingly disastrous second marriage. Peers such as Sinatra were getting older (and so, it must have seemed then, was Bennett). Where do you go? What do you do?

He went through all of that and emerged as the only singer of his generation still performing, on top, and with integrity in a compromised music world. Tony Bennett was from another world and yet he stayed afloat. Most of the stars of his period never broke through again. He did, and he has become the staple, the untouchable. He did not wane. Bennett is a teacher, a watcher, and a learner all at once. He has emerged with all the knowledge of what he went through. Not only does he have enormous musical acuity, he has the knowledge of having made it through as a survivor.

Bennett has been uncompromising, an artist who has been tenaciously true to himself. He is very wise about creativity: "There's a push and pull with the creative process. That's why I learned never to give up, even if it feels as if it's not happening the first time around. Keep going; keep plowing through it."

Bennett understands that singing and painting are isolating and lonely professions, meditative processes, but ones that grant him self-knowledge. He told Robert Sullivan, "One thing about painting is, the more you paint, the more you realize how beautiful life is. To be alive. How wonderful life is, what a gift we have. That helps you get past the bad times. Another thing that painting does: it keeps you real. It's not a board meeting; it's not eleven guys making a decision. When you're at the canvas, you're alone. And when you're painting, you're thinking about your own story. Just you.

"In fact, both singing and art are forms of meditation. People go to the ends of the world to search for calmness. Painting takes time; you're by yourself. You can paint for four hours and it seems like a minute. And in those four hours, you're facing your own story."

And perhaps because he practices more than one art form, he has a real understanding of how all the arts are related to one another.

"Joe Williams told me, 'It's not that you want to sing, you have to sing,'" Bennett explained to James Isaacs. "And I said to myself, 'You know, he's right.'" He recalled, "I used to work weekends in Astoria as a singing waiter, and I really felt that if nothing else ever happened I'd be completely happy doing that for the rest of my life."

He has the highest-quality output of any pop singer. He has won the love and admiration of the most distinguished music critics of our time: Jonathan Schwartz, Gary Giddins, Will Friedwald, Whitney Balliett, Nat Hentoff, David Hajdu, John McDonough, Terry Teachout, and Leonard Feather among them.

Jonathan Schwartz is an impassioned champion of the American Songbook and a major figure both on Sirius XM radio and WNYC-FM. He was the preeminent disc jockey at the most respected radio station in the history of popular music, WNEW-AM in New York City. "Tony's rich, textured singing has found a new level of intelligence and candor," Schwartz has written. "His lifetime of popular songs, his hundreds and hundreds of nights of performance, have shaped a vulnerable and surprising artist . . . when one of his records starts up unexpectedly, he is a conversation stopper: only Sinatra, Billie Holiday, and Judy Garland have been able to do this through their recordings. Of the four, only Tony Bennett remains, live and in person, at the top of his power, still building a catalogue for Columbia Records, an enriching gift for the 21st century."

He has somehow managed to convey a deeper and deeper sense of himself to the public and to carve out a greater awareness and appreciation of his achievements. Yet there is much more to Bennett than what is already known; it will continue to unfold in the public's consciousness, and I hope this book will contribute to that unfolding.

Dizzy Gillespie said, "Talking about Tony Bennett is the same as a finished musician playing a solo; you don't need twenty-five choruses to get your message across. I can tell you in a few words. I think Tony's spirituality is so profound in his performance that it cuts through everything superfluous, and what's left is raw soulfulness. Because his philosophy of life is so basic, the moment he opens his mouth to sing you know exactly what he is—a prince. I really feel that guy."

He is cherished, he is loved, and perhaps he knows it. There is still a vulnerability to him, a sensitivity that deepens his music and his art. He remains a student today. He practices his singing and painting every day. He produced some albums from the beginning with just a piano and a trio. Bennett would have sections in his performances where he would work entirely with his pianist, Ralph Sharon, or with just a string section, or he would work with a trio for the whole show, or with only brass and reeds. Today he could always perform and record with huge orchestras. Instead he focuses on singing only with a trio, where his voice is most vulnerable and exposed. He still sings "Fly Me to the Moon" a cappella in large and smaller halls, from Carnegie Hall to the London Palladium to the Hollywood Bowl to the Apollo Theater in Harlem.

Sinatra was the first consummate saloon singer, but Bennett was the first singer on the level of Sinatra who stayed close to an urban, New York milieu. Sinatra changed; he became a suburbanite, a habitué of Palm Springs and Vegas. Bennett has an East Side saloon sensibility; he continues to frequent the New York saloon, jazz, and cabaret scene, from Feinstein's to the Village Vanguard, from the Blue Note to Birdland, from Dizzy's Coca Cola to Arturo's to the Iridium and the Oak Room of the Algonquin. He tried Hollywood for several years, during his second marriage. He returned to his home turf, hanging out with great East Coast musicians, many of them not big stars but heroes to him: Bobby Short, trumpeter Ruby Braff, Alec Wilder, songwriter Cy Coleman, Mabel Mercer, pianist-singer Barbara Carroll, singers Sylvia Syms and Blossom Dearie, and singer-entertainer Hugh Shannon.

Bennett is the keeper of the flame; he now single-handedly represents the Great American Songbook; he is the custodian, the "believer," as composer Alec Wilder called him. He makes the songbook relevant to people who were born after Vietnam. He is the bridge from the past to the present.

We still have Tony Bennett.

He is a survivor, but more than that, in the final chapters of his life he has reached unparalleled heights. He is the last of the great singers of his generation—Sinatra, Judy Garland, Ray Charles, Louis Armstrong, Joe Williams, Billie Holiday, Dinah Washington, Nina Simone, Ella Fitzgerald, Sarah Vaughan, Mel Tormé, Ray Charles, Etta Jones, Nat King Cole, Jo Stafford, Sammy Davis Jr., Dean Martin, Bobby Darin, Lou Rawls, Jimmy Rushing, Bobby Short, Billy Eckstine, Lee Wiley, Bing Crosby, Carmen McRae, and Peggy Lee. He is the last link. Yet he has never stopped evolving and growing. Once, when a colleague praised him for his latest hit record, Bennett said impatiently, "That was the past. I look to the future!" and walked away.

The breadth and scope of his achievements are overwhelming. In 1968 *Billboard* listed fifty-eight songs that Bennett had helped to make famous in recordings. That was 1968; today there are hundreds more. Bennett has not just sung these songs; he also *owns* many of them. They are stamped on our consciousness as his. Then there are scores of fabulous, unknown, or little-known songs that are just as good as the hits. (See the Appendix: Awards, Albums, and Songs.)

The kind of music that Bennett champions has had various names: standard pop, pop standards, vintage pop, classic pop, the Great American Songbook. As David Hajdu wrote, "This type of music has survived just about every other musical development or fad in this century, from ragtime to rap, and shows every sign of continuing to flourish into the next century, just as the symphonic and operatic classics of previous centuries have survived into ours." It is music with melody that suddenly grabs us at unexpected moments, stopping us in our tracks, evoking the deepest emotions. Bennett unabashedly, aggressively is its number-one advocate. Tony regards this music with reverence; it tells a universal story with utmost simplicity.

Another key aspect of Bennett is his devotion to his Italian American identity, with its emphasis on the arts. His pride in his heritage was embedded in his youth, when he imbibed his family's love of music and art. He writes of Italian artists such as Arrigo Benedetti, Vittorio De Sica, and Roberto Rossellini that "they uplift the human spirit and make you feel like there is a great deal to live for." Nina Chiappa recalls Tony telling her when she was a kid, "Don't ever, ever be ashamed of being Italian." "He reminded us," she told me, "that the Italian heritage in the arts goes back many centuries, and that we have a tremendous history."

"From the Italians," he wrote in the anthology of Italian American writing *Growing Up Italian*, "we can learn . . . how to express ourselves. They are not frozen and frightened about every little thing or stiff-upper-lipped and reticent. They express what they feel. If they are angry, they say it. If they are happy, they express their joy. One way or the other, they are definite. . . . They are givers."

Bennett connects the artistic impulse with that sense of uplift—of generosity of spirit and optimism, and belief in the triumph of goodness in the world. Will Friedwald has referred to Bennett as the "Pangloss of pop," for Dr. Pangloss taught the title character of Voltaire's *Candide* that we are living in "the best of all possible worlds." This spirit, Friedwald writes, "finds its clearest modern-day manifestation in the music and world outlook of Tony Bennett. . . . The Panglossian spirit also influences Bennett's large-scale view of his own life and career. From the beginning, Bennett has consistently proven that by giving the world the best performances of the best songs, he can touch the hearts of all who listen to him, and through this miraculous process, both ends of the communication, both the singer and the sung to, are elevated. The more we can communicate, the more we can understand each other, and the more we pursue excellence in our lives, the better things become. . . . Cole Porter and Duke Ellington can save the world."

Bennett's uncanny intersections with history have occurred—and continue to occur—throughout his life. Whether it was because he is a walker in the city or because of his enthusiasm, his human curiosity, his watchfulness, his warmth, his responsiveness, his Italian good looks, or his talent, Bennett has had an ability to interconnect with both ordinary and extraordinary people and historic and artistic events at every stage of his life. He has always reached out and responded to the intensity of the moment. Because he has never sought the limelight in egocentric ways, he seems to pop up almost invisibly, Zelig-style, all over the map. He has always seemed to be there.

Several years ago I visited the Louis Armstrong Museum (in Satchmo's home in Corona, Queens). In Armstrong's study, there was a vivid, monochrome portrait painting of him in front of his desk so he could look at it every time he sat down. It was by Anthony Dominick Benedetto. Armstrong showed the painting to anyone who visited him. When asked who painted it, he replied, "Just a boy in the neighborhood."

And because he seems always to be there, I fear that if we don't appreciate him fully now, the loss will be that much greater and more devastating when he is gone.

We still encounter him in hallowed halls such as Carnegie Hall and the Apollo Theater and small clubs such as the Blue Note and the Village Vanguard, the foremost jazz clubs in Manhattan, or getting up to sing at revered old landmarks such as Arturo's restaurant on West Houston Street or lecturing at the Metropolitan Museum. Or painting or sitting in Central Park. On May 10, 2010, Jonathan Schwartz spoke on his radio program about a recent Sunday with Tony. "I took a walk with Bennett in Central Park. We sat on a bench. Some recognized him and some didn't. People would walk up and just tell him of the happiness he'd brought into their lives. His presence just lit up the lives of the people who happened to recognize him."

"A couple of months after 9/11, I went down to the Village Vanguard with a friend to hear the Bill Charlap Trio," Terry Teachout, drama critic of the *Wall Street Journal* and author of the Louis Armstrong biography *Pops,* told me. "Just before the first set got going, my friend saw that Tony Bennett had slipped into the back of the club, and a few minutes later he astonished us by strolling up to the bandstand and sitting in with Charlap on 'Time After Time' and 'The Lady Is a Tramp.' Those were tough times, and I suspect his impromptu appearance meant a great deal to everyone in the room. That rough-grained, utterly sincere voice of his somehow seemed in perfect accord with the battered, bruised sensibilities of a bunch of scared New Yorkers who were still getting used to the idea that it might be all right to start going out again and having as good a time as we possibly could. I've loved Bennett's singing ever since I was a kid, but I've never felt *closer* to him than I did that night."

Jimmy Lategano, a talented younger singer, recalls Bennett dropping in at the long-standing Greenwich Village restaurant Arturo's in the 1980s. Lategano stars at Arturo's on Thursday nights and works as a singing waiter there the rest of the week. "Tony came in to see Bobby Pratt, the pianist who played at Arturo's. The word was out that Bobby was dying. Bobby had been one of Tony's teachers when Tony was a singing waiter at the Nestle Inn in Astoria. Tony heard about Bobby and came to Arturo's three times in the last year of Bobby's life.

"Bobby called out, 'Tony, want to sing a song?' The place came to a hush. Everybody stopped. I'm holding the tray. Now we hear his voice. He was there physically before our eyes to see, but only when we heard his voice: it's Tony!

"Tony sang 'On the Sunny Side of the Street.' And this tells you so much about his state of mind: at the end of the song Tony said, 'The song is wonderful and it's for you.'"

Bennett's comment at Arturo's is characteristic of the ethic of service that he has always brought to his work. It has always been his operating philosophy: putting the music before himself. What the song was trying to say was more important than what he might want to say. When he gets up to sing a song, it's about the song; it's not about him.

His perception of his own gift was his ability to sense the universality of a particular song. He wanted to select songs that would communicate most effectively to the greatest number of people. That has been his mission. He has never been dismissive or impolite to fans who approach him for autographs or photographs. In fact, he thanks them for asking. In the same spirit, he is always thanking his audiences at performances. He is tremendously grateful to his audiences for their support. He has never lost his capacity for appreciation. It is important to Bennett to be perceived as someone who remembers where he came from, the singing waiter from Astoria who got lucky.

"I remember Tony singing to a mass audience in Philadelphia," said John di Martino, one of the most gifted young contemporary pianists.

"You feel as if he's singing *right* to you. You feel as if he's looking right at you. There's a million people there. And he creates that intimacy, that bond. And he makes you feel as if you've stepped into his living room. 'Welcome; come in.' How does he do that? So down-to-earth, so warm. And he has that quality of making every lyric come alive. You feel his whole life experience in every lyric. And you think about how rare making that connection is. Sinatra could do it, Judy Garland and Edith Piaf in her own way. It's a rare thing to not let the song sing you, but really sing the song. It feels as if you're hearing the lyrics for the first time."

John Bunch, Bennett's musical director and pianist for six years, died at age eighty-eight in March 2010, soon after I conducted my last interview with him. Bunch had been a bombardier in the Army Air Corps during World War II. During a B-17 Flying Fortress run over Germany on November 2, 1944, his bomber was shot down and he became a prisoner of war. He spent six months in a Nazi prison camp. A memorial was held on May 16, 2010, in his honor at St. Peter's Church in Manhattan. A two-hour concert with some of the finest musicians in the country was held. Bennett was there, in the third row. He spoke third. First he rose to sing "Who Cares?," which he identified as a Depression song that resonated today. Bennett paid tribute to John Bunch's humanity, telling a story that when Bunch was captured by German soldiers during World War II and brought to a concentration camp, he gave his last piece of food, a bit of bread, to an inmate who was being herded into a gas chamber.

Then Bennett sat down and watched the entire two-hour concert, enjoying the music and the musicians he admires so much. He could easily have left, as celebrities are prone to do after making public appearances. He remained afterward to talk with the crowd. Bennett is not a celebrity seeking to grandstand, much as he loves the limelight. He is comfortable in the limelight and also outside of it. This is someone who still partakes of the fleeting beauties of life. There is a simplicity about Bennett that he clings to: it is the refusal to clothe and shield himself in the garments and bastions of celebrityhood that would prevent him from continuing to experience real life, with its surprises of joy, charity, appreciation, inspiration, and redemption. For that was the scene at St. Peter's Church that evening.

Bennett is also a political creature, but not of Hollywood-style politics. He is not cocooned in Beverly Hills. His artistry, his commitment to his music and his painting, and his political commitment to brotherhood, equality, and peace have remained constant from the early years to the present. One of his favorite quotes is from Arthur Miller: "The tragedy of America, is that we don't believe in anything other than money. We don't believe in tradition because we're still young, yet. In other words, we're still immersed in a gold-rush mentality, rushing towards anything that makes money." He told Will Friedwald, "It's like what the Chinese say about paper money, 'The rats eat it.' The rats eat it! There are things that are more than money. Integrity is more important than money, and as a society, we're just beginning to learn that."

Bennett was recently asked to sing the "The Star-Spangled Banner" at halftime at the Super Bowl. He refused, and said he refused to sing war songs. He sang "America" instead. Eric Comstock, the gifted singer and pianist, recalls attending a Bennett concert in 1986 at the (now defunct) Atlantis casino in Atlantic City. "He closed the show— it was his encore—with a multimedia presentation of his paintings while he sang 'This Is All I Ask.' Every painting was arranged to illustrate the lyric. When he came to 'Stars in the sky make my wish come true before the night has flown,' the stars spelled out 'peace.' And when he sang 'And I will stay younger,' there was a photo of him in the present day and then while he did this cadenza, 'I will stay younger . . . I will stay younger than spring,' he got younger and younger. Through the eyes in the photos, you could just watch the face change until he was a baby."

A friend of Sinatra, Count Basie, Duke Ellington, Louis Armstrong, Billy Eckstine, and many other great artists, Bennett is an establishment icon and they are all gone. His friends also include Donald Trump, Bill Clinton, and Mario Cuomo, but he is still not a commercial animal. He is inevitably frailer today; he walks more slowly. He relishes the iconic status he has achieved. Still, he walks alone without an entourage or bodyguards through the beautiful Manhattan streets he adores, usually with his little dog Boo in his arms, alive to the moment and responsive and accessible to strangers. He remains a solo act. He is probably one of the most beloved figures of our time, perhaps as much loved as one of his idols, Jimmy Durante. Durante, like Bennett, showed only the sunny side of his life.

Jimmy Scalia told me, "Bennett's songs remind me of home. Safe. The wine, the pasta. It's a weird thing. Sinatra was like a relative but distant, because he was higher up. Tony was always like a cousin, he was home. So when I think of him, I have a warmer feeling." Scalia recalled meeting Bennett in 2008, when Bennett and Phil Ramone were up for Grammies for *Duets*. "He's the real deal," Scalia said. "He's flesh and bone; you can touch him; you can hear him still. He's the only one. He's here, and he's here for a reason. When I see him, there are many things I see in a flash. As soon as I hear his name or hear his voice: Italian American. One of the people who carries the torch of the Great American Songbook. And a painter, too. And a very warm fella. Because he didn't have to pay me any never mind."

In writing this book, I concluded that the only accurate, fair way to approach Tony Bennett was primarily through his art, although I have not glossed over his rough edges and tough times. You can find flaws in any human being without the redeeming qualities that an original artist brings to our lives. Bennett has remained true to that art through thick and thin. He has sacrificed for that art, and he has been bold and fearless in holding fast to it. Frank Sinatra was right from the beginning when he said that Bennett "has four sets of balls." He is not a sentimentalist at heart. Jonathan Schwartz told me, "When you think of the things he's seen—when you work in nightclubs, you experienced the worst of human behavior. And he has. And being a musician, I mean he's really seen all this crap. I wouldn't call him a cockeyed optimist. I would call him a realist and a man who loves his music."

I think that Bennett may love singing more than any singer who has ever lived. The great singer Joe Williams said that onstage Bennett still looks like a little boy, he's so eager for the praise. Danny Bennett said of his father, "He is one of those people who has to do what they do. He will die singing."

And he will stay real to the end.

One of the central themes of this book is that the dimensions of Bennett's real accomplishments are still inadequately known. That seems a paradox in the light of his fame, his popularity, the ubiquity of his presence on the American entertainment scene. But the truth is that he has a body of work whose breadth is awe-inspiring. There are scores of great Bennett records that are out of print and little known— records that, in addition to the many favorites that are heard every day all over the world and collected in his four-CD set *Fifty Years*, definitively establish the magnitude of Bennett's achievement—an achievement that puts him on the same level as Frank Sinatra. In addition, there are his magnificent concerts, which present Bennett at his peak. Some of these concerts—most notable of all is the 1964 concert at the Sahara Hotel in Las Vegas—are absolutely breathtaking. None of them except his 1962 Carnegie Hall concert and one concert with Count Basie has ever been issued on recording. They are still in the vaults. There are at least thirty Bennett albums that are not in print, many of them unknown to the contemporary public.

Still, even while conceding the unavailability of much of his work, the reasons for the underestimation of Bennett remain somewhat mystifying. After all, Bennett has been fully appreciated and honored by scores of critics who have written of him with depth and insight.

Three of these critics have also touched on the reasons for Bennett's simultaneous fame and relative obscurity, as compared to Sinatra and others. "Because Sinatra achieved a kind of cult following that nobody else has," Gary Giddins, a preeminent jazz critic, biographer of Bing Crosby, and author of *Visions of Jazz*, *Satchmo*, and *Weather Bird*, told me. "I mean, there are so many discographies. And because he was such a dreadful guy in so many ways. The hundreds of people I interviewed about [Bing] Crosby, almost all of the musicians had also worked with Frank, would make the comparison that Frank had his entourage and you couldn't walk over to him and everybody was terrified of him in the studios. Bing came in all by himself and walked over to you and knew the names of your kids and that kind of thing. Like Tony. Sinatra, I think, in part because he was a guy who was always front-page news, with his lovers and his wives and punching reporters out and all that stuff—the drama sort of added to it. And, of course, Sinatra is Sinatra. I mean, he's a magnificent singer. He also, I think, understood how to make the records distinctive one from another.

So that they really stood out in a dramatic way. Which is not always true with Tony's records."

Bennett is a singer who, unlike Sinatra in the desperate loneliness of many of his greatest recordings, never sounds defeated. He will hold on. When he sings "What a Wonderful World," he somehow means it without skirting life's many cruelties and betrayals and horrors. Perhaps he means it because he is thinking of the song's greatest interpreter, Louis Armstrong. Tony ends it by saying quietly, his voice almost breaking with feeling, "You were right, Pops."

Jonathan Schwartz has spoken of the difficulties of locating within all the hundreds of albums that have been issued by Sinatra the key and central songs of his career—the wondrous songs that Schwartz plays every weekend on his radio programs. That is even more of a grievous problem with Bennett. Will Friedwald, citing the magnificent early Bennett albums on Columbia, wrote that after 1962, when rock and roll dominated the record scene, Bennett albums began to lose their identity, and what resulted sometimes was "the directionless mishmash of quality and crap."

All this would change in 1986, when Bennett returned to Columbia and recorded several masterpieces, beginning with the album *The Art of Excellence*. But there was a floundering period of some years when Bennett albums, even with beautiful tracks throughout, lost their coherence. They were mainly compendiums. Friedwald speculated that if Columbia had continued to burnish Bennett's career by producing conceptually interesting packages, as Sinatra did with the superb artistic help of Nelson Riddle, the result might have been far different.

Perhaps Sinatra's extraordinary and dramatic career was a contributing factor in overshadowing his equally extraordinary *paisan*, Anthony Dominick Benedetto. Sinatra also shined in movies, and Bennett did not. Sinatra learned to dance well, too. Bennett was initially awkward onstage for many years. And above all, Sinatra represented volatility, danger, and drama. Perhaps there was something of the metaphor inherent in J. M. Synge's great play *The Playboy of the Western World* in the Sinatra/Bennett saga. Synge depicted a gentle soul who gained the respect of the community when they thought he was a murderer. Sinatra was not a gentle soul, but he was not the villainous figure he portrayed in his life, either. Ironically, Sinatra's bad-boy image earned him far more public adoration than Bennett's good-boy image, as in Synge's play. And yet both have the toughness as well as the vulnerability they spotlight or deny.

Bennett does not push his masculinity. He shows his love. For Bennett it is not unmanly to love an audience and show it. Sinatra, because he showed such aching vulnerability, pain, and loss in his music, seemed to feel he needed to be the snarling tough guy once he stopped singing. As personalities, Sinatra hides his vulnerability; Bennett hides his toughness.

Tony Bennett was, and is, a shooting star. To Jimmy Scalia, to Jonathan Schwartz, to all of us who love him, he is family, he is home. And he is magic. As Ray Charles asked, how did he do it?

1

Beginnings

"I was a poor kid," Tony Bennett told music writers David Hajdu and Roy Hemming in *Discovering Great Singers of Classic Pop*, "like everybody in New York in the Depression, but there was great hope, skyscrapers were going up, and everybody felt we were going toward something great. It was a unique era, and it all still lives in the music that came out of that time."

Recalling that period in an interview with David Frost in 1967, Bennett also defined it as a period of sharing and egalitarianism: "It was the Depression, a time when we were all very hungry. There was a great camaraderie. Everybody was helping one another out." There is a rueful longing in his words, a sense that something was lost in the periods of affluence that came later.

That sense of hopefulness infused the early years of Tony Bennett, who came from a warm and loving family Duke Ellington described as "wonderful optimists."

Tony Bennett's paternal grandfather, Giovanni Benedetto, grew up in the village of Podargoni, above Reggio Calabria. The family were poor farmers, producing figs, olive oil, and wine grapes. His mother's family, the Suracis, also farmed in Calabria. Neither side of the family could read or write.

In the 1890s a widespread blight caused thousands of farmers, among them the Benedettos and the Suracis, to leave Italy. Bennett's family was part of the mass immigration of southern and eastern Europeans to the United States between 1880 and 1920. Eighty percent of that immigration came from southern Italy—the Mezzogiorno—and Bennett's family came from one of its provinces, Calabria. The south was generally looked upon with contempt by other Italians as an area of shiftless criminal elements, while the north was perceived as comprised of enlightened, conscientious, hard-working citizens. As the north of Italy reached a high level of industrialization, improving the life of the peasants, the south continued to suffer from poor wages, high taxes, widespread unemployment, usury, deforestation, and soil erosion. Drinking water was scarce; cholera and malaria epidemics were widespread.

There was a severe economic depression in 1887, followed by volcanic eruptions of Vesuvius and Etna that completely destroyed many villages. More than two million Italian men, women, and children would immigrate to the United States, primarily from the south, and by the 1920s there was an Italian population of five million in America. The passage by steerage across the Atlantic was horrific. The immigrants huddled together, lying in piles of blankets and rags. They arrived at Ellis Island exhausted and drained, but still hopeful.

In America they faced discrimination and prejudice, as they were viewed as an inferior, dark-skinned people. There were fierce debates about their racial classification. Italian American musicians such as violinists Joe Venuti and Eddie Lang (born Salvatore Massaro), writes Patrick Burke in his book *Come In and Hear the Truth: Jazz and Race on 52nd Street*, were widely regarded as "in-between people," those who ranked above African and Asian Americans but below whites in the hierarchy. The National Origins Quota system, which was instituted in 1924, decreed that "Italians were nonwhite with respect to immigration restrictions but were white for purposes of naturalization." This stigma persisted for many years. "Italian-Americans such as [singing star] Louis Prima were still perceived as racially indeterminate by many Americans in the 1930s," wrote Burke.

"The Americans," wrote Napoleone Colajanni in 1909 in his book *Gli italiani negli Stati Uniti* (Italians in the United States), "consider the Italians as unclean, small foreigners who play the accordion, operate fruit stands, sweep the streets, work in the mines or tunnels, on the railroad or as bricklayers." A large majority of Italian Americans were confined to a very low rung of the economic ladder.

Three thousand unskilled Italian laborers in New York State alone toiled in work camps for mining, quarrying, railroad, and lumbering crews, facing nightmarish conditions. Michael La Sorte wrote in *La Merica* that "the work camp immigrants came close to becoming the new American slaves of the post–Civil War era. Workers were held as prisoners in some camps; the only means of freedom was to escape. They had no protection of any national jurisdiction; only the laws of the camp applied. Living and working conditions were among the most primitive and oppressive that any immigrant group endured in America during those years."

In downtown New York City, Mulberry Street, the first and largest of the country's Italian enclaves and the destination of the Benedettos and the Suracis when they came to America, was described by Jacob Riis in his classic 1890 study *How the Other Half Lives*: By day, he wrote, "it was a purgatory of unrelieved squalor," and at night "an inferno tenanted by the very dregs of humanity where the new arrivals lived in damp basements, leaky garrets, clammy cellars, outhouses and stables converted into dwellings." The Italian, he wrote, "comes in at the bottom and he stays there." The windowless railroad tenements were cold, dirty, and dark. Most had no hot water. None had bathtubs or electricity.

Outside the ghetto, Italians faced deeply embittering prejudice and opprobrium. "A day did not pass that the Italian was not vilified in one manner or another," wrote Michael La Sorte. "The Americans laughed at his speech, his clothes, his customs, and where and how he lived. Such treatment caused Italians to be wary of all Americans." To many Americans, Italians were guineas, wops, dukes, dagos, tallies, macaronis, or spaghetti benders. In his classic study of Italian American history *Blood of My Blood*, Richard Gambino wrote of a typical raid in Chicago in 1909 when 194 Italian Americans were arrested. "The police charged en masse into Little Italy and collared anyone who appeared to be suspicious," wrote Gambino. "When the authorities were unable to produce any link whatsoever between the prisoners and crimes, the police reluctantly released all 194 men. In many cities these tactics designed to keep the Italian immigrants in line created a state of open hostility between police and Italian-Americans."

In the face of such discrimination, Italian American families such as Tony's slowly, determinedly, with character, grace, fortitude, culture—and always music—set about creating new lives of dignity and honor.

Tony Bennett's maternal grandparents were the first of his relatives to travel to the United States, in January 1899. His grandmother was one month pregnant with his mother, Anna Suraci. The ship entered New York Harbor after three weeks crossing the Atlantic. The family went to a five-story tenement building (still standing) at 139 Mulberry Street (near Mott and Hester streets) in New York's Little Italy. Tony's mother was born the following September.

Most of the Benedetto family arrived in the early 1900s. In 1906 the family sent for Tony Bennett's paternal grandmother and father. His father and grandmother sailed for America on a steamship with Italian immigrants from the south of Naples on April 2, 1906. Two days later a volcano erupted from Mount Vesuvius south of Naples. A huge tsunami rolled toward the ship, but tragedy was averted as the captain gained control.

The Benedettos also settled in Little Italy but soon escaped the claustrophobic ghetto when grandfather Antonio Suraci moved the family to Twelfth Street, between First and Second avenues, and started a wholesale fruit and vegetable business catering to pushcart owners. Tony's grandfather worked from dawn until late in the evening. He gave his wife all his earnings, which she hid in a trunk under the bed.

By 1918 his father's sister Antoinette and her husband opened a grocery store on the corner of Sixth Avenue and Fifty-second Street and lived in an apartment above it. His father worked for them and moved into a spare room.

On November 20, 1919, Tony's mother and father, who were first cousins, were married. His father continued to work in his uncle's grocery store, and the married couple lived at his uncle's apartment.

Tony's maternal grandparents, the Suracis, moved to Astoria, Queens, and purchased a two-family house at 23–81 Thirty-second Street. He recalls that his grandmother had a goat and chickens and a huge garden. Just a few minutes from Times Square on the elevated subway, Astoria was almost farm country in those days. Soon the rest of the Suracis and the Benedettos moved to Astoria, and the house on Thirty-second Street became the center of family life for many years. Tony's parents followed the path of his grandparents and opened up a grocery store of their own in Astoria. Soon their first child, Mary, was born in 1920, and John Benedetto Jr. (Giovanni) was born in 1923. The children lived with their parents in the apartment above the store.

In 1923, soon after John was born, Tony's father became ill and began to deteriorate rapidly. His father would be sickly from then on, and it became too difficult to keep running the store. He was soon unable to do any physical work. Tony's parents sold the store and moved to a four-room apartment in Astoria, a railroad flat, above a candy store. The apartment was heated only by a coal-burning stove.

Tony was born on August 3, 1926, at a time when his father was already becoming gravely ill. He and his brother slept on a pull-out couch in the living room in the chilly cold-water flat. The family gravitated toward the kitchen, close to the warmth of the stove, where they socialized, ate, and played cards.

With his father increasingly incapacitated, Tony's mother found work as a seamstress in the garment district. She worked through the day, then came home and took care of the children. Tony and his brother and sister would wait for their mother at the subway because she brought piecework home from the factory to earn extra money; in the morning they would walk back with her with the dresses to the subway. His mother earned a penny a dress. As weak as his father was, he helped Tony's mother with the alterations on a sewing machine in the corner of the kitchen.

As his father's health continued to deteriorate, his paternal grandmother, Maria Benedetto, came to live with the family. She took care of the children while Tony's mother was away at work. She died when Tony was five, but Tony's grandfather Antonio Suraci also lived with the family. He was a large man with red cheeks and a white beard, and Tony did one of his first sketches of him sitting on the stoop smoking his pipe.

There was little heat and no hot water, but there was love in every crevice of that chilly railroad apartment. Everything revolved around the family. For a brief time—until Tony was ten—Bennett's father played a critical role in his young life, essentially shaping his moral character and his fate as a singer and an artist. John Benedetto had an artistic soul. An innate poet and humanist who loved art and literature as well as music, he would read to his children from the classics, such as *Of Human Bondage*. Bennett told Whitney Balliett, "I remember my father was a beautiful man, who was much loved by his family and friends. He had an open, warm voice, full of love and melody. He was a very poetic, sensitive man. . . . I vividly recall being cradled in his giant arms until I fell asleep. Even to this day when I think of my father, I see the 'huge' man of my earliest memories. His arms were strong and his hands were big and his eyes were deep, dark, and soulful. He used to sit on the front stoop of our house and sing a cappella to my brother and me in the gentle, sensitive voice I can still hear. He loved Italian folk songs. He derived tremendous pleasure from singing to anyone who would listen." One of the songs Tony's father sang to him was "My Mom," an old Walter Donaldson song that can be found on Bennett's 1998 album *The Playground*.

It was after his father's death, when he was ten, that Tony learned of a legend about his father. In his hometown of Calabria, his father would go to the top of a mountain and sing, and the whole valley would hear it. It was his father who inspired his love for music.

Like so many little Jewish and Italian boys of his generation, Bennett was initially inspired by Al Jolson. Tony's father loved show business and took him to see Al Jolson in *The Singing Fool*—the talkie in which Jolson sang "Sonny Boy"—when Tony was three years old. "I was so excited by what I saw," he told Whitney Balliett, "that I spent hours listening to Jolson and Eddie Cantor on the radio. In fact, I staged my first public performance shortly after seeing that movie. At one of our family gatherings, I went into my aunt's bedroom and got her makeup. I covered my face with some white powder in an . . . attempt to imitate Jolson. Then I leaped into the living room and announced to the adults, who were staring at me in amazement, 'Me Sonny Boy!' The whole family roared with laughter. I loved that attention." Tony also imitated Eddie Cantor singing "If You Knew Suzie."

He was bitten early by the show business bug. Tony's uncle Dick, one of his mother's younger brothers, had been a tap dancer in vaudeville and was working in a Schubert Broadway theater box office. He introduced Tony to the magic of show business. He emphasized that talent was not enough for a performer—that empathy and warmth were essential qualities to be a successful entertainer. His uncle brought Tony backstage at the theater to watch Maurice Chevalier rehearse and introduced him to the singing of Bing Crosby. Tony would be greatly influenced by Crosby over the years. He also would tell Tony about vaudeville stars Harry Lauder, James Barton, and Bill Robinson. His uncle would stress how hard these troubadours worked, developing their acts over the years on the Keith vaudeville circuit that stretched across the country. Their goal was the legendary RKO Palace Theater on Broadway and Forty-seventh Street in Manhattan, the mecca of vaudeville. If you were a hit at the Palace, your career was made.

Tony's uncle Dick provided the spark for his love of show business, but his father instilled in Tony an awareness of human differences and diversity, a sense of compassion. People were to be judged not by the color of their skin but for what they were. His father spoke to him with reverence of Mahatma Gandhi and Paul Robeson. John Benedetto was a sky-watcher. Sitting on the stoop on a star-filled night, his father indicated a star that was close to the moon. Tony feared the star might crash into the man in the moon. His father made a lesson of it. He told him that the moon and the stars were millions of miles apart, and that things were not always as they seemed to appear. His father said that Tony needed to study and to ascertain the facts of situations and not hasten to quick judgments.

John Benedetto's frailty, sensitivity, humanism, and compassion toward others would be powerful factors in shaping Tony's character. There is no doubt that Tony deeply identified with his father, who had such great compassion for human suffering.

"They were a very close-knit Italian family," musician Eugene Di Novi, who has known Tony since 1950, told me. "Tony would absorb the rich Italian heritage of music throughout his childhood." On Sunday the family—his mother and father, aunts and uncles—came to his grandparents' house and cooked all morning. The joyous vibrations of those Sundays would stay with Tony throughout his life. The family had picnics in Astoria Park or at his aunt's house, and after dinner the uncles took out their guitars, banjos, and mandolins. The adults made a circle around the children, and their uncles played their instruments. Tony's father sang Italian folk songs. Then the children entertained the adults with songs by Cole Porter, Jimmy Van Heusen, and Irving Berlin. Mary was the mistress of ceremonies and the announcer. Tony's brother, John, was the star, with his operatic voice, and Tony played the comedian. Then the three children—Mary, John, and Tony—put on improvised shows, acting and singing for their aunts and uncles.

Tony recently elaborated on those Sundays to journalist John Lewis: "'They would clap like this'—clapping a steady beat with his hands—'and we would sing for them. We couldn't wait until Sunday to be with all the relatives. . . . I realized, this is natural, the way it's supposed to be. There was never a touch of loneliness, never a thought of what's going to happen to me. It's funny that, in the middle of deep poverty, it was the warmest time of my life.'"

Tony played stickball and roller hockey, and ice hockey in winter. Once he fell through the ice. He was afraid to let his mother know, so he built a fire and poked his clothing through it to dry. At eight he sang "Ida" in a local parish and was the prince in *Snow White.* He raised pigeons on the roof and played in the Astoria Pool, where synchronized swimmers performed to Glenn Miller's "Moonlight Serenade."

An Italian kid in a predominantly Irish neighborhood, Bennett had his nose bloodied more than once and learned how to handle himself with his fists. He was an altar boy for four years, and told David Frost in a 1967 interview that while his religious faith had taken a more spiritual direction, his early religious training "has made me keep the faith."

In those early years, it was Tony's brother, John (Giovanni), three years older, who was considered the serious singer in the family. He was called the Little Caruso. He received formal singing lessons, studying bel canto singing. He was chosen to sing in the children's choir of the Metropolitan Opera, did solo spots, and sang on radio. But Tony, who loved opera but preferred pop songs that suffused him with happiness, sang, too, but in the church choir and at the show for children run by the local Catholic church.

It had been Tony's uncle Frank, who was the commissioner of libraries in Queens and knew Mayor LaGuardia, and Tony's teacher at P.S. 141, Mrs. McQuade, who arranged for him to stand side by side with Mayor LaGuardia as he cut the ribbon at the opening ceremony of the Triboro Bridge in 1936. Tony was ten years old. It was shortly before the death of his father. Tony was the mascot of the parade from Queens. He led the throng of people across the bridge singing "Marching along Together," singing along with the crowd and with Mayor LaGuardia. Bennett invoked for writer Chet Flippo the feeling of hopefulness and optimism of that day, and the way that experience made him become a performer. His innate generosity and desire to serve people had already found its outlet. "My mother put me with Mayor LaGuardia cutting a ribbon on the bridge and *all* of New York City was walking behind us. Mayor LaGuardia and the whole city walking the length of the bridge. You talk about carnival in Rio or Mardi Gras in New Orleans—those were nothing compared to that day. Maybe it's my own youthful imagination now, looking back at it, but it was a *spectacular* day. Everybody was singing, the *whole* city was singing and they were *up*. Highly idealistic about the future. And Mayor LaGuardia was patting me on the head and I saw everybody feeling so good and I just said, 'I'd like to do this the rest of my life, make people feel that way.' It really was indelible for me."

It was a bright moment in a darkening time.

Tony's father continued to weaken until he was almost bed-ridden. His condition, which originated in a rheumatic heart, was not understood in those days, and he must have suffered from not understanding what was causing his deterioration. He had developed a phobia about being seen in public, and passed out at Mass. He was unable to ride the subway or be among crowds. He couldn't climb stairways and, finally, could not even leave the house. He hated his confinement. Even the touch of the bedsheets was unbearable because of the aching of his body. His lungs filled with fluid, and he found it difficult to breathe. Sometimes he was rushed to the hospital in the middle of the night.

Soon he was in a semiconscious state. Tony sat beside his father's bed in the darkened hospital room holding his hand. Within a few days he and his family arrived at the hospital to find the doctor waiting for them. He told them that John Benedetto had died of congestive heart failure. He was forty-one years old. Tony wept.

In the midst of this sorrow, Tony went through another traumatic time that unmoored him. His father's brother Dominick wanted to take some of the pressure of raising three children off his sister-in-law Anna, and decided that Tony should come to live with him and his wife upstate in Pyrites, a small working-class mill town about fifteen miles from the Canadian border. The arrangement would last nine months. Dominick owned a general store and farmed. He meant well, but he did not relate positively to Tony, who was still mourning the death of his father and disoriented from being separated from his mother. Dominick yelled at him constantly and made him sleep on the floor.

It was not an entirely negative experience, since Tony enjoyed his first exposure to nature and ice skating on the St. Lawrence River. He enjoyed an unprecedented sense of freedom and the open spaces, the expanse of trees, lakes, and rivers. He went to school with Dominick's children and sang in the school play, where he was a hit with the parents. Still, it was a deeply unhappy and unsettling period for him, and it left permanent scars.

A family friend recalled that "Tony's very hotheaded. Always has been. And you know why? Because of the time he went to live outside of Buffalo with his uncle. He's talked about this in other interviews; it's come out in dribs and drabs, but not all of it. He missed his mom and family terribly. He was very close to his brother, John. He followed John around all the time. And that experience made an indelible impression on Tony. Just the fact that he was away from his mom really hurt him. The separation caused a void in his life.

"Tony's brother, John, was a bon vivant, very outgoing, worldly wise. We went to many of Tony's shows together. He was a good singer and a great guy. John was everything Tony isn't. He was a little bit of everything. He opened a beauty parlor in Long Island; he made wigs, too. Dabbled in black-market stuff, you name it. Tony is the most insecure person you'll ever run into. He can cut you off. He does it all the time. Never anything physical. He doesn't believe in it. Tony is a peace activist because of his experience in the war and always will be. With a temper. He's not gonna start a fight with anybody. But he turns like a worm. A lot of people, when they get to know him, learn of that childhood separation from his mother and see how deeply it affected Tony: how fearful he is that everything is going to be swept away. Remember, he was a Depression-era baby. Always looking over his shoulder. Never trusting. I don't know his trusting too many people for a long period of time. Nobody. I don't know anybody."

Upon returning to Astoria from Pyrites, Tony found that to save money, his family had moved to a smaller, less expensive apartment. His sister, Mary, stayed home to take care of Tony and his brother while his mother worked in the factory, and Mary would be a surrogate mother to the boys for many years. Tony had begun to sing in local Astoria dives before his father's death, mainly to "clown around" with friends. When his mother went to work in the factory, he really wanted to help, and eventually found a job singing in a small tavern.

During the day, alone for many hours, Tony began to draw, sketch, and cartoon more seriously. He wrote in his memoir, "I found, even as a kid, I'd draw or paint away and all of a sudden, it was my own little creation. I was shocked by it, in a way. I'd say, 'Look at that. Look at that thing I made.'"

His introspectiveness led to an initial shyness with girls. Tony was an intensely private person from the beginning, and has remained that way. He is not prone to talk about personal matters. Asked by David Frost in 1967 if he romanced girls as a boy by singing to them, he replied, "Well, I always thought about them. I still do."

"But when you took girls out for the first time," Frost persisted, "did you woo them with songs?"

"No. I do that now," he quipped.

"Can you remember your very first girlfriend back in Astoria?" Frost asked.

"Yes," Tony replied.

"What was she like?"

He paused. "That's very personal."

"Do you remember things about her?"

"She actually encouraged me to go into music," Tony said.

That was the end of the exchange.

It is likely that Tony's acute sensitivity stemmed originally from the artistic personality, depth, compassion, and suffering of his beloved father. His optimism, tenacity, and determination came from his mother. There are endless stories of Tony's mother's goodness, vibrancy, strength, and love of life. She believed in him unconditionally. She also had excellent taste and style, imbuing in her son an appreciation of excellence in art and music. "She had very high values and morals," remembers Tony's niece Nina Chiappa. "She was very loving. She was an incredible cook and seamstress. She sewed all of my mom's clothing and our draperies and bedspreads—everything, with beautiful quality material. She just had a beautiful sense, a very high sense of style."

"Many guys say this about their mothers," Tony said in *Growing Up Italian*, "but my mother was really quite exceptional. After my father died, she worked in the garment center as a seamstress and then came home to look after the house and kids. . . . I realize she was a tremendous motivator and *very, very* clever about life. She had an artistic way of handling people, and this included us kids. It was subtle."

One of Bennett's enduring memories, one that has served as a marker in the way he has approached his music, is his mother's refusal to work on a cheap or badly conceived dress. He recalls seeing her get angry only about having to work on a bad dress. To him his mother's attitude meant: work with the best and never compromise. He would find himself subconsciously turning down every bad song that came his way. He realized later that he learned about refusing the second-rate from her. He noted that "Many years later, when producers and record companies tried to tell me what type of songs to record, in the back of my mind I could see my mother tossing those dresses over her shoulder."

A devastating memory was seeing his mother getting her thumb caught beneath the sewing needle as she worked on a dress at home at night. It passed through her thumbnail and into her flesh, and she screamed out in pain. She would often work at the factory until nine or ten at night. Helping his mother was one of his strongest motivations in forging a career. Tony resolved he would make enough money so that his mother would never have to work again. He told his sister, "I'm going to make it for Mom if for nobody else." Her salary was based soley on the number of dresses she made. He found it painful that his mother was working such long and hard hours for such thankless, excruciating work.

There was still joy in that poor household, even after Tony's father died. His mother, a widow at thirty-six, had a love for people. The house was bustling with relatives and friends. Anna would cook for as many as eighteen people a week in addition to working at her job. Long afterward, in 2010, Nina Chiappa told me that Anna Suraci Benedetto as a young girl "was very much into music and dancing. She told me that when the organ grinder would come by the neighborhood, the kids would all follow and she would be dancing in the streets. She was a very lively, happy person."

Tony had another loving maternal presence in the household: his sister, Mary. "Mary was almost more like Tony's mother," said author Will Friedwald, who worked with Tony on his memoir. "Because Tony's mother was out there making money. The one who really took care of the kids was Mary. She was a very warm Italian earth mother type." "His sister, Mary, idolized Tony," an anonymous source said. "She was as proud as can possibly be."

Nina Chiappa recalls that period when she and her parents lived with Tony's mother in River Edge, New Jersey. "My grandmother and Tony were very close. I mean, she adored him. Of course, she loved all of her children. But, of course, Tony was a special person to everyone in all of our lives. And still is."

"Tony's mother was a lovely lady," Tony's former contractor, saxophonist, and lifelong friend Joe Soldo told me. "She was just like Sinatra's wife, Nancy."

Still, it was tough love that his mother sometimes administered. "My mother used to hit me round the face with a wooden coat hanger every morning before she went to work before I did anything wrong," he told Glenys Roberts in the *London Daily Mail* of December 21, 1996. "She used to say: 'That's just in case you do.'"

Bennett in his youth was anchored by his family and by the informality and liveliness of Astoria's immigrant population. Astoria was a traditional community of row houses with working-class Greek, Polish, Italian, Irish, and Jewish families. It is situated between the Triboro and Hell Gate bridges in Queens, and it looks back across the East River toward the majestic Manhattan skyline. Today, it still has a feeling of community, with scores of ethnic restaurants and shops. Its closeness to Manhattan, its vibrancy and unpretentious hometown feel still make it viable to aspiring young people. With its relatively low rentals and bustling vitality, it is popular with actors, musicians, and stand-up comics—just as it was when Tony took the N subway (with twenty cents in his pocket for lunch) from Ditmars Boulevard into Times Square in the 1930s. Tony has kept his love for Astoria throughout his life, returning often to visit the school he formed with his wife Susan, the egalitarian Frank Sinatra School of the Arts just blocks away from where he grew up. Astoria helped to shape his feeling that ordinary working people had qualities of honor, beauty, decency, and humanity in their lives.

"The finest place to live," Bennett told *New York Times* reporter Corey Kilgannon on one of his frequent visits back to Astoria in 2009. "I've been all over the world—Paris and Florence and Capri—and yet I come back here and I like this better than any place I've ever lived." The neighborhood, wrote Kilgannon, "seems to transport him back in time to when he'd stare longingly at the shimmering skyline of Manhattan across the East River. It was only a 15-minute subway ride away, but to a young Anthony Dominick Benedetto . . . it loomed large and distant like Oz."

"When you'd see this big city, you'd say, 'Boy, someday wouldn't it be great to become famous in that great city there?'" he said, standing where Astoria Park meets the East River and overlooks the skyline. He pointed out to the reporter Riccardo's by the Bridge catering hall and said, "I worked as a singing waiter there."

From the beginning he listened and watched carefully and picked up nuggets of beauty wherever he found them, and soon enough he realized they could be found everywhere—on the streets, in the classroom, in the scuffle of everyday life. He took theatrical lessons from Mae Homer, who also had taught Eddie Bracken and Judy Garland. In high school he had a music teacher named Mr. Sonberg, who would bring a Victrola into class and play Art Tatum records. It was while listening to Tatum (whom he has admired throughout his life) that Tony decided to become a singer. And from the start, he was intrepid when it came to standing up for what he loved. Harry Celentano, who went to school with Bennett and became a bellman at the Algonquin Hotel, recalled those days for Whitney Balliett: "Tony used to sing 'God Bless America' and 'The Star-Spangled Banner' in assemblies, and when he was a little older he'd go into places out there like the Horseshoe Bar and the Queen of Hearts—this quiet, shy little kid—and get up and sing all by himself. Some of us would go with him, and he'd stand there and sing 'Cottage for Sale' like a soft Billy Eckstine. We didn't take him seriously, and we'd shout and throw peanuts at him, but he never batted an eye. But he was also into art then. He would play hooky and draw these huge, beautiful murals right on the street with chalk. Mothers and children would stop and watch, and they were amazed. Then we'd come along and play football over the mural, and that was that."

By the time he was twelve, Tony was known as a caricaturist of his classmates and teachers at P.S. 141, and he was as fond of drawing as he was of singing. He was drawing a mural on the sidewalk using chalks his mother had given him when a man stood over him and said, "That's pretty good." James MacWhinney, a junior high art teacher, added, "I like what you're doing, son." He offered to help Tony with his art, and invited him to go to the park on Saturdays, where he water-colored, and offered to help Tony learn. Tony loved those weekly outings. They would become lifelong friends. MacWhinney would be one of the first of many mentors in Bennett's life, people who deeply cared about him and reached out to him because they saw his potential and because he was so responsive to their offers of help.

He sang whenever and wherever he could. The *New York Times* reported in an 2009 article about Bennett's regular returns to Astoria that Luke Gasparre, eighty-five—a bar patron at the Italian restaurant

Piccola Venezia, where Bennett hangs out at his own corner, its shiny metal plate reading TONY BENNETT CORNER—brought over a photo from his junior high school class of 1942 with Tony smiling at the camera. Gasparre remembered working with Bennett in a local nightclub when they were teenagers. "Right under the El," he said to Tony. "I tap-danced and you sang." In reality Tony wanted to be an artist before he wanted to be a singer. He would make his decision about singing when he came home from the service. He had initially thought he would become a commercial artist. His sister recalled in the documentary *Tony Bennett: The Art of the Singer* that "When they formed the band in Germany with the other enlisted men, that's when I remember Tony saying he'd decided that when he came home, he really wanted to be a singer; remember even in elementary school, he was drawing those pictures on the sidewalks, and he was always able to just knock off a cartoon in no time flat. Long before he even went into his music."

But he always sang. Bennett had his first professional singing job at thirteen, at a Saturday night get-together at a Democratic club in Astoria, and soon he was singing at clubs by himself. His first paying gig came about when, on a dare, he demanded a trial engagement from the owner of the Pheasant Tavern in Astoria, which later became Ricardo's and is still functioning today. He impressed the owner with his loud, piping voice that drowned out the orchestra and was hired for fifteen dollars a week and all the rolls he could eat. He waited on tables, and afterward he would come out and do the show. Tony's mother came to see him. He was learning the trade. He took the bus on weekends to sing in Patterson, New Jersey, to earn extra pocket money. He sang to the clank of dishes, the tinkle of goblets, the scuffling of chairs, and the flirtations of men and women all around him. He learned how to project his voice, vary his volume, how to break through the babble around him. He got the knack of seizing an audience the moment he stepped onstage and holding on to them, and he learned how to deal with hecklers. According to Mary, when he received requests for songs he didn't know, he would rush into the kitchen and the other waiters and kitchen help would coach him on the songs.

Tony drew people to him, not only with his conspicuous talent, but also because he was so appreciative of those who reached out to him and helped him. He was, moreover, extremely deft at utilizing that help. And there is no doubt that he cared about people, saw them in their complexity, suffering, and yearning. He viewed them from the perspective of the artist, never with condescension.

There was always music in the Benedetto household. "In those days you didn't buy a record just for yourself," he told the BBC. "I mean, we were told that if you buy a record, make sure that everybody in the house likes it. So we ended up with Caruso records."

Tony soon received his first theatrical training. He enrolled in a dance school in Astoria run by a British woman named Mae Homer. He learned how to tap-dance while singing and how to perform in front of an audience.

Before graduating from junior high school, Tony had applied for admission to the High School for the Performing Arts, the most prestigious public school (and the setting for the movie *Fame)* in Manhattan for aspiring artists and musicians. He was turned down. His best friend, Rudy De Harak, then suggested that he apply to the High School of Industrial Arts. Tony had met Rudy in 1938, when Tony's family had moved again, to a housing complex called the Metropolitan Apartments, where they rented a comfortable four-room apartment at a reasonable rent. Tony and Rudy had gone to P.S. 141 together. Rudy became very close to Tony's family, as well; the two boys were drawn together because of their love of jazz and drawing. De Harak would become a famous graphic designer, exhibited internationally and in the collection of the Museum of Modern Art in Manhattan, as well as a very prominent recording engineer.

"I was lucky, in a very incongruous way. I couldn't pass the test," Tony told the BBC. "I was dejected. I wanted to go to this great school that had a wonderful reputation. Roosevelt at this time, this wonderful Roosevelt, he created industrial schools because we were pulling ourselves up by our bootstraps. And so they sent me to an industrial arts school [the High School of Industrial Arts]. And I regretted it for years and years until I ran into my great friend Everett Kinstler, the foremost portrait painter since John Sargent. He had gone to the same school. And he changed my whole mind. After many years of my regretting, feeling sorry for myself, he says, 'That's the best.' He said, 'First I [went to] Music and Art (the other famous public school for aspiring artists). And the minute I went there, the first thing the teacher said to me was, 'Don't worry about technique; just paint what you feel.' He said, 'I just closed my book. I didn't feel anything.' He told the teacher, 'I'm only fourteen years old; I don't have a clue what I'm supposed to be feeling. I wanted to learn technique.'

"So he switched to the Industrial Arts school. He made me realize many years later that it was the best thing that ever happened. Because all I did was study how to make stained glass windows, how to do silk screen, how to do lithographs, sculpturing, painting, photography. So I had this wonderful experience of [learning] technique. Because you finally end up realizing that the only way to become a very formidable painter is the study of patience. Duke Ellington started out as a sign painter. A sign painter is forced to just be exact and concentrate on what you're doing. You just can't be dreamy doing it; you have to really make sure it's right. So that's a good discipline." He became grounded and resolute.

"[My high school] was way ahead of its time," Bennett said to Whitney Balliett. "I studied music and painting, and they'd work it so that you didn't have to be there every day, so long as you did your work. You could go over to the park and sketch trees." During that period, Tony rented a room for nine dollars a week in the old Metropolitan Opera House. He could not help but be affected by living in the building where Caruso and Tetrazzini sang. But he also was being influenced by jazz.

The school would let Tony and the students stay out for days with the provision that they come back with four days' worth of paintings. His teacher, Mr. Sonberg, strongly encouraged him to become a singer. Tony and three friends from school organized their own vocal quartet. Frank Smith and Tony practiced singing all the time. Frank Smith kept time by pounding on his desk so passionately that his fingers bled. The school helped to form Tony, although the surroundings were spartan and dilapidated. One time, part of the ceiling fell down on the desks while Tony was out to lunch. He might have been killed.

(Those unsafe conditions in high school helped shape his vision of the beautiful school he would create for struggling students in the very same community more than half a century later, the Frank Sinatra School of the Arts.)

The basic lesson he absorbed at that time was that all art is technique. The great drummer Louis Bellson taught him, "If you want to understand free form, you must first learn form before you can be truly free to experiment. You can't successfully break the rules until you learn what rules you're breaking."

Coupled with that awareness was an understanding that the creative process was not an automatic thing; there was always that push and pull. Tony learned never to give up, even if things felt hopeless. You had to persevere, keep trying, keep plowing through it. Things would eventually coalesce. Amid the meanderings, uncertainties, and distractions of youth, Tony always knew what he wanted to do.

"My boy wanted to be a singer," Tony's mother said in *The Music Never Ends*. "He used to tell me, 'Mom, someday I'll be a big singer and I'll buy you a big house.' That sounded good, but I kept on sewing."

"I used to catch all the bands at the Paramount and the Strand," Bennett told *Billboard* (November 30, 1968). "I *lived* the bands. I'd go hear Count and Duke and Benny and Lunceford and every band you can name. Sometimes I'd come back two or three times a week, and stay for two or three shows a day. The biggest thing for me, half my life, was waiting for a movie to end and hearing a drummer test his skins behind the curtain or in the pit, and little scraps of musicians' laughter floating out, and seeing the bandleader's feet showing under the curtain. Then the curtain would open, or the elevator stage would come up out of the pit, and the band would be playing 'Cherokee' or 'Blue Flame' or 'Let's Dance' or 'Uptown Blues' and I was in heaven."

By the time he was fifteen, Bennett had discovered the three singers and entertainers who would most inspire him for the rest of his life: Frank Sinatra, Jimmy Durante, and Louis Armstrong. Bennett saw Sinatra, who had recently left Harry James's band to sing with Tommy Dorsey, perform at the Paramount Theater in New York. He stayed for the entire seven shows Sinatra gave during a day. In a tribute he wrote for *Life* magazine, Bennett recalled, "It was my brother, an aspiring opera singer, who told me at the very beginning: 'There's this singer, a singer of popular songs. He's really magnificent. His name is Frank Sinatra, and you have to check him out.' So I went to see him at the Paramount. . . . Tommy Dorsey was like the Wizard of Oz. He'd have Jo Stafford, the Pied Pipers. He had Ziggy Elman on trumpet and Buddy Rich on drums, all for the admission price of 65 cents. Every one of them would stop the show cold, but when Sinatra hit the stage, he topped them all. No one could follow him. The audience's reaction was pandemonium. You couldn't get near the Paramount when he was there.

"I was 14 years old. It was still during the Depression, and my mother and father had said that if we were going to buy a record, it would have to be one that we'd all enjoy. My family insisted on quality, so all we listened to was Caruso until Sinatra records slowly started to find a place in our home. My favorite record of his is still one of those early ones, 'Weep They Will.' It's wonderful. I love so many of his songs, but to me it's the best Sinatra record ever. The first lines are 'Weep they will, will the lads down the street / When they find that you're promised to me.' He did that wonderfully."

Before Sinatra, for Bennett it had been Bing Crosby, who invented intimate singing. From Tony's perspective, Sinatra went much deeper, went inside himself, expressing exactly how he felt. He was reliving the experience as he sang, and was expressing what was inexpressible for much of his audience. Sinatra's achievement was startling and unprecedented, erasing the divisions between the artist and the audience. He communicated stories more vividly and beautifully than any singer had ever done before.

Soon after, he got his chance to visit the number one nightclub in the world, the famous Copacabana. And there onstage was Jimmy Durante, with his teammates Lou Clayton and Eddie Jackson. There was no warmer and wilder performer in the world than Durante, whose trademark routine including making fun of his large nose and staging a calculated riot on stage of slapstick, chaos, attacking the piano, moving, jumping, and running around. Durante had been a singing waiter (a path Tony would follow later) in Coney Island along with Eddie Cantor and Georgie Jessel. Durante's "Inka Dinka Doo" and his famous sign-off, "Good night, Mrs. Calabash, wherever you are," endeared him to the world. He never lost his common touch, the same feeling of accessibility, warmth, and unpretentiousness that Tony has. Tony went backstage that night and met Durante in person. Durante intuited Tony's sincerity, admiration, depth of appreciation, and genuine enthusiasm (as would so many others who opened up paths to Tony throughout his life) and talked to the young man about his own start in the business and about the legends whom Tony idolized, from Fanny Brice and Jolson to songwriters George and Ira Gershwin, Cole Porter, and Rodgers and Hart. Tony never forgot Durante's lamenting the changes in Broadway theater toward more serious fare. Durante said sadly, "That's when everything went psychological!"

"Oh, he was the best," Tony told the BBC. "There was never a better performer in the United States than Durante. No one can imitate him. He was a complete individual. He created a musical circus. The energy on that stage: it never stopped for an hour. You were spent at the end of the hour. You'd say, 'What happened?' I loved Jimmy."

Tony was unable to stay in high school to graduation. He dropped out at sixteen to help his mother financially. The family had moved to a larger apartment in Astoria. Tony's mother was still working in the factory, and he felt he wanted to contribute to the upkeep of the household. He worked as an elevator operator, in a laundry, as an usher at the Ditmars Theater, as a page in a library returning books to shelves, as a copy boy for Associated Press. None of these jobs worked out, and he started singing at amateur shows in clubs. He won many of these amateur nights and began to think that perhaps he really could become a professional singer. He became a singing waiter. "I just didn't want to work unless I was singing," he told writer Robert Sullivan. "I'm proud of my intuition, that I stuck with it. With my dad having died, everyone was pleading with me to take this job or that to help out. I wanted to sing."

Bennett liked being a singing waiter very much. It was the first job he had ever enjoyed. He often said then that he would like to be well known, but that if he remained anonymous, he would still want to be a singing waiter for the rest of his life.

These experiences and events converged to shape him into the singer he would become. They had grit and poverty in them, family love and deep emotion, the learning of stagecraft and show business savvy, all kinds of mentors and wise teachers, solid training, common sense and practical education, suffering and yearning, and an immersion in good music and the arts. And he was an excellent learner. He would soon hear the honeyed sound of Stan Getz and decide to replicate it, and by the time Duke Ellington counseled him to also "put a little dirt in it," he was ready for that, too, because of his hardscrabble life experience.

The mix resulted in one of the sweetest, most authentic and reassuring musical sounds ever heard. Bennett may have a "smiley face" image today, but his music and his personality were shaped by hard, serious, and constant struggle and sacrifice. As a result, he would never settle into complacency and a comfortable niche. He has always been evolving and searching. In 2007 Everett Raymond Kinstler, the portrait painter to whom Bennett had apprenticed himself many years before, could still say of him, "Tony loves skill—he loves craftsmanship; he appreciates it. He has grown tremendously artistically. But he's still a student. He's still hungry." In the same year, his son Danny Bennett told Margaret Turoff of *AARP Magazine*, "He worries about falling into the same routine. That's his advice. Always follow your passion, your heart, your dream. Don't say something is impossible."

There is such a direct line leading from the young Tony Benedetto to the Bennett of today that it appears that the thread has never been broken. He has always felt blessed by knowing what he had to do and what he wanted to do. That feeling grew stronger with each year. For Tony, it was always the journey instead of the arrival.

In 1940 he was playing amateur nights in every borough of the city and working as a singing waiter at the Pheasant. A booking agent (whose name is lost to memory) witnessed him singing on an amateur night, saw his promise, and got him his first professional engagement at the Piccadilly Club in Paramus, New Jersey, in 1941. He was fifteen. Thinking Benedetto was too long and ethnic a name (and too hard to remember) for nightclubs, Tony picked the performing name of Joe Barry. (Later it became, for a time, Joe Bari, which was the name of both a province and a city in Italy.) The bandleader at the Piccadilly, Earle Warren, had played alto saxophone with Count Basie and sang tenor. Tony was very nervous, but Warren assured him he would do fine. He was a hit at the Piccadilly, and he began to think that a career was beckoning.

"I knew Tony just as a guy from Astoria that used to come around the city," said composer Eugene Di Novi. "So I'd see him. I'd meet him on the train, Hanson's drugstore on Broadway, just around. There was a place named the Dog House in Long Island City. It looked like a dog house from the outside; it was shaped like one. Tony doesn't remember this, because I reminded him. He used to come in there. I remember him coming in one night and singing.

"He was just a very affable guy who liked the music. He was doing all kinds of other gigs too, designing jewelry. The guys knew him and he came around. And he made it known that he wanted to be a singer."

Since Germany's invasion of Poland in 1939, the ominous signs of war were everywhere. On December 7, 1941, the Japanese attacked Pearl Harbor. Tony sat with his family around the radio and listened to FDR declare the date as one "which will live in infamy."

America was at war.

2

A Young Man's Initiation

Other singers have served in wartime, but it seems that among the popular singers of his generation, Tony Bennett was one who not only took part but also fully understood the nature of why he was fighting and what war symbolized about the human condition. He served for only a short time, and as he told the BBC, "I was one of the replacements after the Battle of the Bulge. So it was really just clean-up time. But there was still strafing and, you know, danger. And it lasted a couple of months." Still, it was war, and he reacted with acute sensitivity and empathy to the suffering all around him. He may have served in the infantry briefly and was mainly engaged in mopping-up operations in France and Germany, but he was deeply seared by the experience of war and emerged from it with a profound repugnance for violence, bigotry, hatred, racism, and fascism. That awareness would follow him throughout his life and define many of his actions on behalf of equality, tolerance, and human dignity. While he may have hated the military, he served with honor and showed courage both in the war and earlier, upon induction, in refusing to tolerate unfair treatment because he was an Italian American.

The advent of the war cast a darkening shadow over normal life for a young man of fifteen. In 1942 Tony's brother John was drafted into the air force and stationed in Blackpool, England. Tony turned eighteen in August 1944 and received his draft notice on November 2. Whatever the truth of the reasons for Frank Sinatra's exemption from service, there is no doubt that, fairly or unfairly, his reputation suffered during the war from his nonservice. There was never any question of Bennett's willingness to serve. (Sinatra was declared 4-F until 1945, when he was reexamined and declared 2-AF, disqualified because of a punctured eardrum and because he was "necessary for the national health, safety, and interest.")

While the Italian community had been split in the 1930s between the anti-Fascists and the pro-Fascists, as soon as Mussolini declared war on the United States, there was a mass defection of pro-Mussolini Italian Americans from the Fascist cause. That defection was so significant that although the Italian immigrant population in 1941 included more than 600,000 Italians who were not yet American citizens, only 250 were interned by the Department of Justice at the start of the war as potentially dangerous aliens. A presidential executive order of the Roosevelt administration in October 1942 exempted all of the non-citizen Italian population (except for the interned 250) from the restrictions imposed on other aliens of enemy nationality.

Tony was inducted almost immediately and sent to Fort Dix, New Jersey, and on to Little Rock, Arkansas, for six weeks of boot camp training at Fort Robinson. It was the final stage of the war. Tony was to be trained to be an infantry rifleman. For Bennett, the military was hatred at first sight, although he never doubted for a moment the necessity of fighting the Nazis. He detested the army for what he saw as the brutalization of the men as well as the level of bigotry. One sergeant ruthlessly harassed Bennett from the start because he was Italian.

Bennett fought back, refusing to be humiliated, and was penalized severely for his rebellion. The sergeant would constantly scapegoat him, and during a bivouac mission he accused Bennett of marching too slowly. He hit the top of Bennett's helmet with his crop and screamed at him. Bennett took his knapsack off, threw it away, and walked the seven miles back to camp by himself. As a result Bennett was put on KP duty for a month and assigned to cleaning Browning automatic rifles. The other soldiers were granted leave to go into town on weekends, but Bennett was restricted to the barracks. When he was finally given leave, he went home to Astoria. The depth of his anguish and revulsion toward army life and the abuse he had endured can be measured by what happened next. When he reached his house and saw his waiting mother standing there at the door, he fainted in her arms.

Bennett was processed through the Le Havre "repple depple" replacement depot, a holding area for those soldiers who had recently arrived. He was assigned as a replacement infantryman in January 1945 to the Seventh Army, 255th Infantry Regiment of the 63rd Infantry Division, a unit filling in for heavy losses after the Battle of the Bulge. Bennett was startled to discover that replacements were not prepared in advance, but were expected to learn the rules of combat and the modes of survival in the heat of battle. Many of the replacement troops had inadequate training and no combat experience and had never fired a gun except in basic training. More than half the replacement troops that Bennett was a part of became casualties within the first three days on the front line.

Amid the horrors of the war, Bennett kept his sanity by finding moments to practice the other art form he loved: painting. "There was a guy who was on the line with me in Germany," he told Robert Sullivan, "and he said to me later, after the war, 'Do you remember when we were in those trenches, with the bombs coming at us and everything? Remember what you were doing?' I said, 'No.' He said, 'You were sketching all the time.'"

"I can't imagine Tony in the war," his sister, Mary Chiappa, recalled. "It's a good thing that he came in at the tail end. Because he's so sensitive about people. Fortunately he came in after the Patton invasion of France. His troop went in and did what they called flushing out towns. They would go in, pick a house and set up headquarters. I can't picture him with a gun: not only during the war, but even before that, ever having any such feelings."

He moved east across France and into Germany by March 1945. Bennett went straight to the front line and called it a "front-row seat in hell." As the Germany Army retreated, Tony's company went through bitter fighting in freezing winter weather, hunkering down in fox-holes as German 88 mm guns targeted them. Air battles raged above, with the roar of airplane engines and the swirling sound of bombs. There were artillery battles all around, with shells bursting every-where. He watched his buddies die right beside him and expected he would be next at any moment. Shrapnel flew and hot metal strafed the Americans. Tony recalled his first night on the line, when he dug his foxhole and then, exhausted, passed out on the ground before he could even get into it. When he woke, his face and body were completely covered with snow and he was totally disoriented. The men had to secure the surrounding area with booby traps and set up communi-cations lines back to the command post. He would lay in a freezing foxhole, sometimes for sixteen hours, watching and listening for the enemy. Mornings on the front line he would see the dead soldiers and dead horses. He would never forget the horror of war.

At the end of March the men crossed the Rhine and took part in town-to-town, house-to-house fighting to clean out the remain-ing German soldiers. They occupied Germany and had driven back the German Army. Tony prowled on night patrol in the disputed forests of southern Germany. The company's numbers had been severely depleted, and Tony was among the few men left when they met up with the rest of the 63rd Division.

In the midst of this horror at the front, there was one bright moment: Tony and thousands of other GIs were pulled off the line to see Bob Hope, Jane Russell, Jerry Colonna, and Les Brown's orchestra perform. Bennett was enthralled by the show. It had a significance far beyond that moment, for it made him realize just how much an entertainer could give to people at times of need and crisis, that a laugh or a song could be the greatest gift. Bennett has often said that he feels that Bob Hope saved his life that day, and the lives of thousands of other soldiers, by uplifting their spirits. During the first week of April the men crossed the Kocher River and by the end of the month reached the Danube.

As terrifying as his war experience had been so far, his final experi-ence of the war would be the most devastating of all, and it would be ingrained in his consciousness forever. Tony's last official mission was the liberation of Landsberg, a concentration camp in Bavaria thirty miles south of Dachau. He would never forget the ravaged, starving faces and blank stares of the prisoners as they wandered aimlessly around the campgrounds. The American soldiers immediately provided food and water to the survivors, but they had been brutalized for so long that they could barely comprehend what was happening. Tony and the other soldiers learned that all of the women and children had been killed before they arrived and that half of the remaining adult survivors had been murdered the day before.

The 63rd Infantry Division was recognized as a liberating unit by the U.S. Army's Center of Military History and the U.S. Holocaust Memorial Museum in 2000.

Writing of the liberation of Landsberg that Tony had taken part in, the division chaplain, Colonel Herbert E. MacCombie, gave an account that has been preserved in the Texas Military Forces Museum. "I visited the concentration camp at Landsberg. It was at this camp that Hitler had been confined after the failure of his putsch in 1923. It was here he wrote *Mein Kampf* in 1923. When he rose to power he turned the prison into a concentration camp for his enemies.

"As I came into the courtyard I saw a great pile of what appeared to be skeletons. On closer approach I found that they were not skeletons, but the bodies of men and women who had been literally starved to death.

"In the buildings we found beds in tiers, about five deep, one above the other. On many of the beds were located the charred remains of prisoners. When they knew our troops were arriving, the keepers of the prison set the building afire with the prisoners still chained in their bunks.

"I personally handled gold wedding rings that had been stripped from the fingers of their victims. I also saw the gold fillings that had been forced from their teeth. The stench was terrible.

"It was a horror that will remain with me forever. Nearby Germans said they did not know what had been going on. The stench of the place was enough to arouse the suspicion of any normal human being."

Dachau included 123 subcamps (Landsberg was one of them) set up in 1943 when factories were built near the main camp to use the forced labor of the Dachau prisoners. A battalion of the 63rd Infantry Division was ordered to search for subcamps in the Landsberg area. Soldiers of the 63rd Infantry Division liberated seven of the eleven Kaufering subcamps on April 29 and 30, 1945. While these camps had already been partly evacuated and the prisoners marched to the main camp at Dachau by the Nazis, hundreds of weak and sick prisoners had been left behind to die.

In his book *Americans and the Liberation of Nazi Concentration Camps*, Robert H. Abzug wrote of the testimony of the Allied soldiers who liberated Buchenwald, Dachau, Belsen, and other concentration camps, and the reactions of horror, guilt, shame, and fear provoked in the soldiers about witnessing such atrocities: the piles of dead, mass graves, crematoriums, and ghostly survivors. "The GI could not really escape the reality before him. He might invoke every inner defense, but it remained just a defense against an overwhelming environment that he could not escape, one that might haunt him forever."

Abzug writes of the 71st Division of the Seventh Army at Dachau; the division had liberated the subcamp of Gunskirchen, the destination for transports of Hungarian Jews. The army published a small pamphlet with a narrative, photos, and drawings to convince the world of the actuality of their experience. It was simply unbelievable, incomprehensible, and the soldiers felt a compelling need to convey what they had seen.

Captain J. D. Pletcher wrote, "As we entered the camp, the living skeletons still able to walk crowded around us, and, though we wanted to drive farther into the place, the milling, pressing crowd wouldn't let us. . . . Every inmate was insane with hunger. Just the sight of an American brought cheers, groans, and shrieks. People crowded around to touch an American, to touch the jeep, to kiss our arms. . . . The people who couldn't walk crawled out toward our jeep."

Abzug writes of the difficulty the soldiers faced in communicating to an incredulous world what they had seen. They encountered disbelief, disgust, and silence. As a consequence, many reacted with silence themselves, keeping within them buried memories that riled their dreams and still gave them nightmares. "Only as they got older," Abzug noted, "and looked back upon the important events of their lives did the encounter with the concentration camps begin to loom large."

When the soldiers returned to the States, most of them would share "a revulsion for human cruelty and a vigilance and fear concerning the rise of totalitarianism and political violence."

Tony Bennett passionately shared those feelings, and they have remained a powerful, abiding aspect of his personality and his character. He could not forget what he had seen. He would write of the war that "it was a terrifying, demoralizing experience for me. I saw things no human being should ever have to see."

When the war was over, Bennett had to remain in Germany as part of the occupying U.S. Army, since he had served only four months. The 255th Regiment was stationed in the town of Mosbach. He was assigned to Special Services, the section of the military responsible for entertaining the troops. His assignment to the 255th Regiment band came after an officer overheard him singing in the shower and told him about the band. Tony approached one of the musicians and asked if he could audition. He was chosen for the band's vocal quartet.

The band traveled around Mosbach entertaining the troops, and was then moved to the town of Kunzelsau and then to Seckonheim. In Seckonheim a pianist named Freddy Katz joined the band and would become a lifelong friend of Tony's. Tony also met future director Arthur Penn, who was head of the Soldiers' Show project.

His first meeting with Penn was in Wiesbaden, where the new unit was started. Penn was deeply impressed with Tony's singing and cast him in a free-floating, imagined, and spontaneous version of *On the Town*. (Penn had no script, no score, and no sheet music.) The musicians just played records or V-Discs (twelve-inch 78's that held up to 6½ minutes of music) and the piano player would learn them by ear. And so Tony found himself cast as one of the leads in a show that would, in its real version, feature onscreen his future friend and hero Frank Sinatra. The show ran for months in the opulent Wiesbaden opera house, which had not been destroyed in the war.

Tony was back in Mannheim at Thanksgiving 1945, and there he would experience a devastating incident that made a permanent impression on him. It further intensified what would turn out to be his lifelong commitment to fighting racism.

On a lonely walk through the flattened city, he ran into a buddy from New York, Frank Smith, who had been part of his vocal quartet at the High School of Industrial Arts. Tony was exhilarated and filled with happiness to find a familiar face from home, and invited him to a holiday service at a local Baptist church. Tony was allowed one guest at a Thanksgiving dinner and asked Frank to join him.

What followed was a nightmare of almost surreal proportions, a display of insane cruelty and bigotry. As the two young soldiers reached the lobby leading to the mess hall, a sergeant ran up to them and screamed. Tony was so stunned he couldn't comprehend what was going on at first. Then he understood: Frank was black, and the mess hall was only for white servicemen. Discrimination and segregation in the U.S. Army were still in effect during World War II, even in a war against the most barbaric, racist, and murderous regime of the twentieth century. The sergeant took out a razor blade and cut Tony's stripes off his uniform, spit on them, and threw them on the floor. He said, "Get your ass out of here! You're no longer a corporal; you're a private again!" Tony was a victim of a sergeant's hatred and bigotry, but even worse was his empathy and sadness for his good friend Frank.

Tony was reassigned to Graves Registration. The bodies of soldiers who had not been properly buried because of the ongoing battles had been wrapped in the dead soldier's own mattress bags and buried in common graves. Tony's job was to dig up the dead bodies and rebury them in individual graves.

It was a very embittering experience, the climax to what had been for Tony anger and rage with the military way of doing things. Despite all he had been through, it was still a violation of innocence, a wake-up call about the way things were. He was stunned that he and Frank were being punished for being friends while serving their country during a world war against racism. All it meant to the sergeant was that Frank was the wrong skin color. It would take Tony years to recover from the incident, and he would never forget it.

But of course the bigoted sergeant was not representative of the entire army. Once again, Bennett's unique qualities of character drew rescuers and friends to him, as they would throughout his life. A Major Letkoff heard of the ugly incident and came to Tony's aid. He reassigned him to the American Forces Radio Network in Wiesbaden. And that rescue, coming at the very moment when he was sunk in total despair, would be momentous in Tony's life.

Tony was assigned as chief librarian for the 314th Army Special Services Band of the European Theater. The band was led by Warrant Officer Harold Lindsay "Lin" Arison, who wanted to put together a top-notch American pop-jazz orchestra to play in occupied Germany to entertain American GIs still stationed there. First-rate players were enlisted, including trombonist and orchestrator George Masso (who would later play trombone for Jimmy Dorsey and become a composer) and sax player Dick Stott. When Lin heard Tony sing, he included him in the band as one of four vocalists in the show.

The band broadcast weekly from the Wiesbaden Opera House on a show called *It's All Yours* over the Armed Forces Radio Network. There were guest stars from the USO such as Bob Hope and Paulette Goddard. The band itself had a remarkably modern, sophisticated sound under the direction of George Masso, playing swing and dance music as well as the popular songs of the time. It included fifty-five musicians. Later, with the addition of Jack Elliott in 1946, bebop was added to the mix. Tony was assigned blues and rhythm songs and novelties. It was a heady time and wonderful relief from the wartime years; there was plenty of booze, girls, and a taste of pot, too. But for Bennett, as always, it was the exposure to a wide range of music—the musical freedom—that meant the most to him. He could sing whatever he wanted to. He took away from that experience a life lesson that he never has lost sight of: it is a critical mistake to underestimate the taste of the audience. That would become Bennett's credo, his stress on artistry, not commerce. He listened to Sinatra on V-Discs and heard Nat King Cole for the first time and loved him. It was a revelation.

He sang "Body and Soul," "On the Sunny Side of the Street," and above all, "St. James Infirmary." It was the song he got the most requests for and the one he sang constantly, and it is the only vocal of his with the band that is extant.

Listening to "St. James Infirmary" today, preserved on a sixteen-inch radio transcription and on cassette, is an amazing experience. Bennett sounds fully hatched; the record doesn't show its age. He sounds more like the Bennett we know in his prime than he does in the first Columbia singles that followed later and brought him success. Keeping in mind the muted, casual, light, emotionless, and effete sound of the crooners of that day, it is even more extraordinary to hear what sounds like a modern, thoughtful, interpretative voice—a contemporary voice—coming out of the mists of time on a scratchy V-Disc. This was no Rudy Vallee or Guy Lombardo drone. This was the real thing.

There is no evidence as to whether Bennett saw Frank Sinatra's 1945 film *The House I Live In* while he was in the service. There can be no doubt that whenever he did see it, that historic film in which Sinatra lectures young people on the meaning of racial equality and democracy had a profound impact on him, since it so completely jibed with his own convictions and beliefs. Coming, as it did, from an artist—and an Italian American—who already had captured his deepest admiration, it must have been a revelatory moment in his life.

Tony finally sailed home on the SS *Washington* in August 1946. He was honorably discharged on August 15 as a private first class, and came into New York Harbor a few weeks later. He had fought honorably for his country. He had experienced firsthand some of the horror and carnage of a bestial, terrifying period of the twentieth century. His experiences with war and with bigotry had shaped a philosophical viewpoint he would hold to with tenacity and determination. He would tell writer Laurie Henshaw in the early 1970s, "I'm a humanist, I think that's the simplest way of putting it. I am antifascist, antiwar, antiviolence of whatever kind. The destruction, it's all so heartless and pointless. I'm a great supporter of world citizenry—break down the barriers and let everybody go where they will. Nationalism is such an awful thing. Why can't we realize that there's enough for us all to go round if only we share it fairly? Life is a beautiful thing."

Gordon Burns, in the British *Radio Times*, asked him if he would support his sons if they decided to evade the draft, and he said, "All the way. In fact, I'd say that's exactly what I've brought them up to do.

I've taught them to hate war like me. I was an infantryman for three years myself and I know exactly what goes on. Pablo Casals once told me that people in our positions must use our influence to combat the politicians who the people no longer trust."

He had experienced critical growth and change as an artist and had felt the exhilaration of singing with major musicians on an equal basis. He was lucky; he was a man swept away, transfixed by music, and music beckoned to him as a career he could excel at—be the best at. There was music, and there was painting, too. He would do it all. He was appreciated, and soon he would be loved.

He stood on the ship looking at his beloved Manhattan shining in the distance. And those who knew him and loved him most were waving at him and crying now. His mother and aunt stood waiting on the dock. "I was all grown up, and I was home."

Tony at age one.

Tony at age nine.

Tony back from the war,
with his mother, 1945.

Tony surrounded by fans at the Paramount Theater, 1947.

Tony is kissed by his mother and sister on his birthday.

Family Album . . .

Happy Birthday to Tony Bennett

Joe Riggio (Nick Riggio's father), Bobby Riggio (Nick's brother), and Tony, in 1958 at a benefit Tony performed to fund research for Cooley's anemia victims. Bobby suffered from the disease and subsequently died at age twenty-seven from its effects.

Tony Tamburello and Rudy Van Gelder, legendary jazz recording engineer, in the 1960s.

3

"I Was Lost,
I Was Drifting"

In his notes for the beautiful song called "I Was Lost, I Was Drifting," which was included in his autobiographical *Astoria* album, Tony recalled its context: "I always relate the song to a time when I was returning from World War II. . . . It was a time of soul-searching, and the task to become a civilian once again was not easy. Where to start, where to go. I was truly adrift."

He was now certain he would make singing his career, and his mother supported his decision. "I know that when he came home from the service," Mary Chiappa would remember, "my mother felt she would have to help him. I remember her saying to me that if this is what he wanted, instead of sending him to school to pursue a formal education, this was just going to be in place of what parents normally do for their children. I remember her leaving money on the dresser for him for the day, because every morning he would go into New York, knock on people's doors, that kind of thing, for his first big break. And he would not take most of the money. He would take twenty cents, because she was a widow and she was working, he felt really badly about taking the money. He would use five cents for the subway to go and five cents to come back. The reaction of the whole family was that if this was what he wanted, we were all going to support it, and we all did. My brother John and I formed his first fan club, answered fan mail and that kind of thing."

He had a foundation to build on. He had immersed himself in greatness from a very early age, and he knew it instantly when he encountered it. As Robert Sullivan wrote, "He had lived in the worlds of music and art for a good while even by 1945. He could hear that Art Tatum was the greatest of all jazz pianists, and Louis Armstrong and Duke Ellington were among the foremost musical titans of all time."

He lived at home and looked for work.

And always people were drawn to him—important, key people, those whose talents he admired. He took the twenty cents from the dollar his mother left for him every day and went into Manhattan, looking for a job and haunting the jazz clubs lining Fifty-second Street. He tried to spend ten cents instead of twenty; he knew how much his mother had sacrificed working as a seamstress to give him the money. He saw most of the greatest jazz musicians in the world up close; he hung around all night, and sometimes he was allowed to sing. He sang nights for a few dollars at grungy local Astoria clubs. He also polished his performing and communication skills by performing at benefits for army and navy hospitals, learning what songs the soldiers and sailors would want to hear.

He became very close to Fred Katz and his brother Abe when he returned from the war. Tony had met Fred when the 255th Regiment Band was re-formed in Germany after the war. Tony was the singer and Fred was the pianist. Fred also played the cello and later became a well-known musician in the jazz scene in Manhattan. Abe, first trumpet at the Metropolitan Opera, taught Tony how to breathe.

Tony's best friend was Jack Wilson, a poet and aspiring songwriter, whose family lived next to Tony's in the Metropolitan Apartments, and they hung out with future screenwriter and director Abby Mann. Both boys wanted to make it in the music business. They listened to big-band records and scat-sang the solos on street corners of Astoria, sometimes receiving dimes from onlookers. Tony taught Jack about painting and drawing, and Jack instructed Tony in poetry.

The boys went to see Sinatra, Tommy Dorsey, Glenn Miller, Bob Hope, and Red Skelton. They traveled to Harlem to the Apollo and Savoy theaters to see Billie Holiday, Count Basie, and church choirs. Jack loved bridges and spoke about them as routes to the world beyond. The two dreamers watched the barges and ships sail by in the river and imagined traveling across the seas once they became successful.

It was Jack Wilson who introduced Tony to Abby Mann. The two aspiring artists would meet on Central Park South and imagine how wonderful it would feel to dwell in one of the elegant buildings beside the park. Tony lives in one of those buildings today and has rarely strayed from the Central Park area and milieu. Wilson became Tony's first manager when he began to sing in small clubs.

According to writer Joe Mosbrook, Cleveland guitarist Fred Sharp and his wife, Iris, were living in Astoria at the time and saw Bennett—then called Joe Bari—sing at the Shangri-la at Queens Plaza under the El. They were impressed with his voice and invited him to have a drink at their table. Tony told them that he had written a song called "Satan Wears a Satin Gown" and was looking for a well-known singer to perform it. Sharp told him that he and his wife were friends with Frankie Laine, who was then appearing at the Paramount Theater. Sharp suggested that Tony bring his song to Laine. Bennett went backstage and sang his song for Laine. In his autobiography *That Lucky Old Son*, Laine recalled listening to Tony and responding, "What do you need me for? You sing great!" Laine recorded the song, and Fred Sharp and his wife became friends with Bennett, playing and singing together a few times.

Childhood friend Bobby Margillo remembers Tony from those years. "He was Joe Bari then," Margillo told me. "He came from a very, very poor family. There was like a trestle bridge that went from Long Island to the Bronx, and he lived in that area. He was singing in all the joints in Astoria. I worked together with him; I was a singing waiter at the Nestle Inn, a Mafia joint, underneath the Hell Gate Bridge. This Nestle place was just a joint; it wasn't a high-class place. When the train came over, the whole damn place used to shake. About every two hours. He had to stop singing because you couldn't hear anything. Tony was nineteen. He was getting $37.50 for singing

Friday and Saturday nights. He always sang one song without the microphone, just as he does today. Oh, what a voice. He had an old tin microphone.

"Tony always had a maroon jacket and a black pair of pants. That's all he ever had. He was so bashful and quiet. Onstage he just loved to sing. He's not much of a talker, you know. He was just the opposite of Sinatra as far as personality. Very mild. Four of us: Rosie the hatcheck girl, another guy, me, and Tony used to imitate the Ink Spots. This Rosie used to give Tony a goose every time he came to the high note [to make his voice higher]. We talk about that when we see each other after all these years. He was very bashful with women, you know. His whole life was singing.

"I said to him, 'We'll write a letter to *Arthur Godfrey's Talent Scouts* show.' So we got a letter together and we sent it. About a week later, somebody got shot in the Nestle Inn and they closed it down. I didn't see him for about six months. One day I turned on the TV and watched *Talent Scouts*. It comes down to the last contender. And it was Joe Bari. That's when they had the clapometer. He got 102. But there was one more contestant. She sang and she got 104. Rosemary Clooney.

"When we talk now I say, 'Do you realize you sang before kings and queens?' He started laughing. Very shy laugh. Tony never forgot me. That man . . . it's unbelievable. Only in America could that be done. Rags to riches. I call him the Astoria Kid. He likes that. He loves Astoria. Put Astoria in your title; he'd appreciate it."

There were many rejections, and for years he couldn't find real work as a singer. His first real break was that night at the Shangri-la, the time Fred and Iris Sharp heard him sing. The trombonist Tyree Glenn heard him singing at the bar and invited him to come up and sing with the band. "He got me up on the stage," Bennett told the BBC, "and I sang. I had no idea he was one of Louis Armstrong's guys and played with Duke Ellington and everything. He's part of the history of jazz." Tony was hired, and the job lasted until Glenn joined Duke Ellington's orchestra. Then Tony worked wherever he could, at the Venice Gardens in Astoria, as a singing waiter at the Red Door and the Pheasant Tavern, all in Astoria. The big time seemed distant and unrealizable, but as always, he kept plugging.

He knew that in addition to honing his craft in clubs, he needed to study music and learn how to develop his voice. "I enjoyed that experience [of singing over Armed Forces radio] so much that I said I'm going to stay in show business, or try to, when I come back," he told the BBC. "Well, as Studs Terkel from Chicago said, that was the good war. And as we came back, they gave us the best teachers. To this day I can't believe what a wonderful education was afforded me as a result of being a GI and coming back. They made sure that everybody was able to make up for the loss of education. And they gave us the American Theater Wing, which became such a good school that it became the Actors Studio." It was at the school that Tony studied the Stanislavsky method of acting.

Tony studied with Pietro D'Andrea, who taught him bel canto singing, and with Mimi Spear, also a bel canto teacher and vocal coach for popular songs whose studio was right on Fifty-second Street, the center of the jazz world. As he sang in her studio, he looked down at the awnings from her brownstone, at the names of all of the musicians playing on the street: Tatum, Basie, Shearing, and Getz. She had coached Helen O'Connell and Peggy Lee. He told Mick Brown of the *London Daily Telegraph* that Spear gave him sound advice: "She advised him not to imitate other singers 'because you'll just be one of the chorus,' but instead to listen carefully to the jazz musicians. . . . Bennett strove to emulate the 'beautiful honey sound' of the sax player Stan Getz and the chopped phrases of the pianist Art Tatum."

He applied the techniques he learned at the American Theater Wing and from Spear to his singing. Like an actor, he thought autobiographically as he sang, as if the lyrics described an experience he had gone through. He described what the dance band era had been like to Mick Brown as a period "when a singer was regarded as just another instrument in the orchestra, their vocal style determined by whichever dance step the band happened to be playing." "So if they were playing a foxtrot," Bennett said, "a singer would take a long line. . . ." He snapped his fingers and began to sing, dragging out the syllables. "There was a moooooooon out in spaaaaaace, but a cloud drifted over its faaaaace. . . . But Art Tatum would change the tempos, chop it up, and I liked that. You couldn't take a long line the way Tatum did it. You'd have to find songs that lent themselves to that style. And what that did was make you tell stories and dramatize songs."

And then there was Stan Getz. "Getz had this kind of honey sound which was wonderful," Tony told Joanne Kaufman of the *Wall Street Journal*, "so I started imitating that sound with my voice."

He was criticized by other musicians for singing too dramatically, for being a "mad singer." Singing dramatically was proving a hindrance to getting hired; Bennett was not passing any auditions. In addition to his singing waiter jobs, he worked as an elevator operator at the Park Sheraton Hotel (but couldn't get the knack of stopping evenly at a floor; he stopped either above or below it), copy boy for the Associated Press, and grocery store clerk.

As he developed his craft and studied Tatum, Basie, Charlie Parker, and the early beboppers, singing for him came to mean improvisation, surprise, doing the unexpected, as well as nuance and feeling. He was literally stunned when he first heard Parker play; he had never heard anything like it. He ran out of the club and threw up on the street.

He hung around Fifty-second Street but never officially sang on any stage there. But he witnessed the greatest artists and was deeply impacted by them, including Billie Holiday. "Not because she was 'singing jazz,'" he said. "She was singing Billie. She was singing her life." And there were many who were recognizing his potential. Long afterward, the composer Alec Wilder reminded Tony how they had met. Wilder would always hide in the closet when Tony was studying with Mimi Spear. Many others were paying attention, too. Pianist Barbara Carroll invited Tony to sing with her at La Cava on Fifty-second Street. He sang for free drinks and experience. Comics Milton Berle and Jan Murray had heard him sing and arranged for Tony to perform once at the famous nightclub Leon and Eddie's so that agents could come in and discover him.

He kept on singing. He didn't get paid, but he performed at the Chantilly in Greenwich Village and all over Queens and Manhattan. He was a singing waiter in Astoria, just as Sinatra had been a few years before at the Rustic Cabin in New Jersey. During the day Tony hung out with the other aspiring singers and comics in the Broadway area around Forty-ninth and Fiftieth streets, at the B–G Bottomless

Coffee, Hanson's drugstore, Hector's Cafeteria, and Charlie's Tavern, and near the Forty-seventh Street Horn and Hardart Automat, the RKO Palace, Jack Dempsey's Restaurant, and the Colony Record Shop. "I used to see Tony at Hanson's drugstore," composer Johnny Mandel told me. "Tony was just a young, wide-eyed guy who was just starting out. But he was always the same person, just always great. He's the same guy you always see. And he always wanted to do things that were interesting, like good music. He used to hang with the musicians. He liked musicians. He wasn't interested in the money part of it at all."

Jack Wilson was Tony's manager at this point, and the boys hung out with Freddy Katz a lot. Freddy was working as a pianist and an accompanist and got a big break when he was hired by Lena Horne. Katz also was playing piano for Vic Damone. According to Damone's autobiography, *Singing Was the Easy Part*, Damone's manager was Ray Muscarella, who also would work with another important singer, Jimmy Roselli. Muscarella was a show business promoter connected to wiseguys, including "Buckalo," whose real name was Anthony Ferra. Ferra ran the East Harlem Mafiosi and at one point was also Jimmy Roselli's manager.

"Tony Tamburello [Bennett's vocal coach and closest friend] told me," Derek Boulton recalled, "that Tony B was started by the Capone family, Lou Capone. Bennett never told me that himself at all." Tony dropped Jack Wilson as his manager when Muscarella auditioned Tony in late 1948 and became his manager, which included giving him financial backing. Tony's friendship with Jack Wilson was ruptured as a result. Jack Wilson spoke to Tony privately and said, "You realize, don't you, what we're talking about here? You're making the wrong move." To make Tony get the point, Jack slapped him hard in the face. Tony tried to explain to him that he'd been struggling for so long, surviving on ten cents a day, that he couldn't turn Muscarella away.

"So Ray Muscarella became Tony's manager," Boulton, who managed Tony from 1970 through 1974, recalled. "But Muscarella was a wine salesman. In other words, if you bought the wine, you got Bennett. Look, you had to go through them to get work because they controlled the booze. I remember I was with Tony one day when he got the news that Ray Muscarella was dead. And he jumped in the air with joy and hit his head on the ceiling."

"There have been a lot of what we called 'dirty money' singers," Johnny Mandel told me. "Jerry Vale, Al Martino, Don Cornell. That was what we called them. Tony was one of those. That's how he started out. But you know, I think that jazz is probably the only American art form, truly, that originated here. And I think that without the 'big boys,' without the rackets, jazz would never have had a place to survive or be nurtured, and who knows if jazz, if the Jelly Roll Mortons or the Louis Armstrongs would have survived. And this is no reflection on Tony. Matter of fact, these guys loved what he did.

"Because it was always the whorehouses in New Orleans," Mandel continued, "and then it moved up to Chicago and Kansas City, both wide-open towns. And everybody had to work for them. And they liked entertainers and they liked musicians. If you didn't fuck with them, they wouldn't fuck with you. As long as you took care of your business and didn't think about theirs, they didn't mess with you. Without them, jazz wouldn't even have had anywhere to develop, there was no place to nurture it. Every big city had their clubs. And they were all run by the wiseguys. They're the only ones that knew how to run a club and to look the other way at the right time.

"I don't think jazz would exist, or many other show business arts for that matter, cabaret; people like Streisand, when they developed, had to play these places like the Bon Soir. Bette Midler. The people who backed the big musical shows in the twenties: same thing. All that money came from there. I mean some of the biggest hoods in the world bankrolled those shows that Fats Waller wrote. And they were better to work for as long as you didn't fuck with them: don't pay any attention to what they were doing and any of the extracurricular stuff. Frank Sinatra would get really upset with somebody slamming the 'boys.' Those are the only guys who knew his name when he was really dying in the early fifties. They helped him when no one else would. He didn't forget it. And he was right.

"And they loved the music! You can't get that from a corporate person. They're cold fish usually. They have a cash register in their heads. Look at Jimmy Roselli: they cried when he sang. They'd shoot you, but they'd cry. Even if they shot him, they'd mourn over him. I just don't enjoy people with no blood in their veins."

"Tony wasn't cut out for the Mafia," Bobby Margillo told me. "He was brought up to be responsible and shy." It would be manifestly unfair to criticize Tony Bennett for any dealings he had with the Mafia. Although he wanted nothing to do with them, they were simply impossible to ignore or escape. When he had his chance later to get away from them, he took it, and paid massively for the opportunity. (Even then, they kept trying.) But when he was starting up, he would have been turned away at the opening gate if he had fought them. He was constitutionally unsuited for them; he had a sensitive, artistic, and contemplative nature even as he was ferociously ambitious and tenacious about his music.

The issue of the Mafia has always rankled Bennett because he knows it defiles and distorts the image of the Italian American, exaggerates the small criminal element within the community, and encourages a stereotype that has become deeply ingrained in the American psyche. As far back as the late 1800s, historian Richard Gambino writes in *Blood of My Blood*, Americans were debating "whether Italian Americans were somehow all disposed to criminality by their genetic endowment or cultural inheritance." Gambino has noted that the stereotype of Italians as violent, cunning, and criminal "grates against every nerve ending in the Italian-American ego, which desires respect and honor. Instead not only are they ignored and ridiculed, but they are also held in contempt."

Of course Italians were engaged in organized crime, but their number was comparatively small. As Martin Scorsese put it to Clint Eastwood, "The reason I used [Tony's] 'Rags to Riches' as the opening for *Goodfellas* was instant memory of where I came from and who I knew. I just made a picture about people I knew growing up around me. It didn't mean that everyone was like that. I was aware of that power around me. But I was more aware of the Italian-American who was, like my mother and father, going to the garment district every day trying to earn a living. They were not involved with these guys. But you lived amongst them."

The wiseguys controlled the clubs all across the country, from the Copacabana in New York to the 500 Club in Atlantic City, built by Marco Reginelli, a Mafia underboss from Philadelphia, run by his successor, Angelo Bruno, and fronted by Paul (Skinny) D'Amato. The truth was that the mob made you or destroyed you, as Jimmy Roselli would learn when he defied the wiseguys and was banned permanently from performing on the West Coast and his records were taken out of the jukeboxes.

Muscarella hired coaches and arrangers for Tony; a publicist, Sidney Ascher; and a record promoter, Paul Brown; and he arranged for him to appear on the *Arthur Godfrey's Talent Scouts* radio program. (Bobby Margillo's letter may have had its effect, as well.) The program, like its predecessors the *Major Bowes Original Amateur Hour* and the *Ted Mack Amateur Hour*, was a very early and tame version of the *American Idol* type of amateur- and rising-talent competitions of today.

Eight months later Jan Murray, who had heard Tony and Rosemary on the Godfrey show and who starred on a television show of his own called *Songs for Sale*, invited them to appear on his program together. Tony also appeared on the *Robert Q. Lewis* TV show as Joe Bari. He was still scrambling. He sang club remotes together with future song publisher Eddie Deane on WOR Radio in New York City, recording from the Manhattan Yacht Club, the Knickerbocker Yacht Club, and the Riviera Yacht Club.

Tony's first record, a 78 rpm, was made in April 1949 under the name Joe Bari for a small record company owned by Sy Leslie called Leslie Records. It was produced by George Simon, head jazz writer for *Metronome*. Bennett recorded an Italian novelty number, "*Vieni Qui*," and Gershwin's "Fascinating Rhythm." The recording session was held at the New York Decca studios on Fifty-seventh Street where Crosby, Satchmo, Woody Herman, and many other greats had recorded. The record is now impossible to locate, and even Bennett's copy disintegrated in his hands in the 1960s.

Ray Muscarella was a real help to Tony in those early years. He prevailed upon a lawyer named Jack Spencer to reach out to the composer Hugh Martin. Bennett went over to Martin's apartment with the demo recording of "The Boulevard of Broken Dreams." Martin responded by saying, "This kid is another Martha Raye." (Raye was known in those days as a first-rate jazz singer, not the slapstick comedienne she became.) Martin's reaction was a promising sign of what was to come. These were still the scuffling days, but there was no doubt about it: Bennett was slowly but surely making his way.

Shortly afterward, Pearl Bailey became one of Tony's many rescuers over the years. It happened during the time he was working days as an elevator operator. She spotted Tony's talent at an audition and insisted to management that Tony appear on the bill with her at the Greenwich Village Inn. (It was an all-black cast; Tony would be the only white performer.) She was so convinced of Tony's potential that when the owner was reluctant to hire him, she said, "Either this boy stays on my show, or I'm not playing here." It was Ray Muscarella who made the initial connection. What followed was a dizzying series of events that moved Tony out of obscurity to almost instant fame. Bob Hope was in the audience one night to see Bailey. After watching Tony sing, he beckoned to Bennett to come over and talk with him. Hope said, "Come on, kid, you're coming up to the Paramount and singing with me."

Backstage at the Paramount Theater, Hope asked him what his name was, and Tony replied, "Joe Bari." Hope said the name was too affected, and asked him what his real name was. Tony told him it was Anthony Dominick Benedetto, and Hope said that it was too long for a marquee. He suggested Americanizing it and calling him Tony Bennett. Hope said something else that Bennett, the constant student, would remember always. "He said, 'Show the public you love them,'" Bennett recalled in his interview with Joanne Kaufman.

Within a few hours after that meeting, Bennett was singing at the Paramount, one of the most famous theaters in the world, before a huge audience. (Hope had to introduce him twice; Tony, nervous as hell, did not recognize "Tony Bennett" as his name the first time.)

When Bennett finished singing, Hope said to the audience, "Well, I was getting tired of Crosby anyhow!"

Bennett wired money home soon after and ended his mother's seventeen-year stint in the dress factory.

He had virtually debuted at the top. The Paramount Theater at Forty-third Street and Broadway was the mecca of Times Square.

A thirty-six-hundred-seat theater in the palatial neo-Renaissance style, it was to the younger generation what the legendary Palace had been to the older. The greatest stars appeared there, including Benny Goodman, Jack Benny, Tommy Dorsey, Martin and Lewis, and biggest of all, Frank Sinatra.

After the Paramount engagement, Hope took Tony on a brief six-city tour. In Hollywood he introduced Tony to two of Tony's idols, singer Margaret Whiting, who would become a lifelong friend (she now lives one block from his house), and Bing Crosby.

Things moved swiftly from then on. Tony had recorded a demo disc in October 1949 with Tony Tamburello at the piano; the demo included Harry Warren and Al Dubin's "Boulevard of Broken Dreams" and "Crazy Rhythm." And again, it was Ray Muscarella who helped Tony: he sent the disc to Mitch Miller. Miller, who had just become head of the pop singles division of Columbia Records, had heard about Bob Hope's discovery. He listened to the "Boulevard of Broken Dreams" demo. Without meeting Tony, Miller immediately signed him to a contract with Columbia in April 1950. Tony was twenty-three years old.

"I remember Tony breaking out as a singer then," singer Stan Edwards recalled. "Tony became my idol, what I would have wanted to be. His voice was totally unique; what matched the uniqueness of his voice was his style. You couldn't trace the influences. You really couldn't. You didn't hear Frank, or Dick Haymes; it was *Tony*. It was as if he was born with a style and wasn't influenced by anyone other than himself. And he had an embracing warmth and an earthiness."

It was during this time that Tony got together with Tony Tamburello, who had worked briefly with Frank Sinatra in 1946. Arranger Marty Manning brought Bennett to Tamburello's office in 1949 to prepare a new act.

"My husband, Tony," Geri Tamburello said, "was working in the John Quinlan studio [Quinlan had been Sinatra's voice coach, and Tamburello was Quinlan's pianist], a vocal coach studio where opera singers, Broadway stars, and pop singers came for coaching. One day three [Mafia] backers came in with three male singers to audition. One of them was Tony Bennett. The head guy asked which one should they put their money on. My husband said, 'Take the banana-nose.'"

This was the noxious, debasing atmosphere in which Bennett had to make his way if he was going to make it, and he had to do it with a smile. Tamburello, a genuine artist himself, understood who he was dealing with and was not trying to insult Bennett; he was helping him. He knew the language of the wiseguys. In fact, Bennett had a handsome, long Italianate face with a strong nose and a wide, warm grin that crinkled his affectionate hazel eyes under curling black lashes. That look endures today. His smile—after every song—creates a glow on the high points of his face and a look of love and perpetual wonder, at what he is doing. His appearance was in sharp contrast to the bland looks of the crooners of the day, and it was captivating to audiences.

Ironically, considering that shaky beginning, Tony Tamburello, a brilliant composer, pianist, and musician, became a huge presence in Tony's life; he was Tony's best friend, piano accompanist, occasional recording supervisor, auditor of new lead sheets and demos, and vocal coach.

A key to understanding Bennett is his choice of Tamburello as his most trusted friend. Their tight friendship spanned forty-five years. Tamburello achieved legendary status in the music industry for his daring, sense of humor, irreverence, and musical acuity. "He was one of the most helpful with Tony's career," Derek Boulton told me. No one would be closer to Bennett than Tamburello until his death. Bennett loved his artistry, spontaneity, and sense of humor. He compared him to a Fellini character and called him his musical conscience. They worked very closely together over many long hours on songs and arrangements, and Tamburello was instrumental in finding songs for Bennett to sing and record.

Tamburello operated out of a large old dry-cleaning truck during those scuffling years and gave vocal lessons in the truck. He placed a little spinet piano in the back and built a staircase for his students to climb in and out. Tamburello painted a sign on the side of the truck that read "Fresh Fish and Music."

"Tony T was a fixture at our house in River Edge," Nina Chiappa, Tony's niece, remembered. "He was a great guy. I took piano lessons from him. He was unique and he was a lot of fun. He was close to Tony for many years. He was close with our whole family. And he was a funny guy. He liked to laugh a lot, and he kept us laughing. I remember many times around the dinner table laughing with Tony T."

"Tony T [and Don Murray] also had a record label called Horrible Records; I think it was a registered label," Rudy Van Gelder said. He laughed fondly at the memory of Tamburello. In fact, everyone I spoke to about Tamburello smiled or laughed. Tamburello and Murray used the name to express their opinion of the 1953 music scene. "Horrible Records" was written in electric-shock typeface on a bilious green label, with the legend "If It's a Horrible Record, It's Bound to Be a Hit."

"He coached a distinctive singer with a beautiful sound named Beverly Kenny," Van Gelder said. "We did her demo here: 'Snuggle on Your Shoulder.' This was around 1954. He was a wonderful musician; that was the basis of the whole thing [his friendship] with Tony Bennett. Tamburello had an old car that had been a yellow Checker cab. He always bragged that he never washed it. He had that kind of self-deprecating humor. He had the cab for years. He did all these wacky things. We were laughing all the time.

"Tony T recorded a woman singer who booked herself into Carnegie Hall—she was rich—and he recorded her. She was totally tone-deaf. She had no idea of pitch. It was just horrible. And yet she got to be popular because people would come and laugh at her because she sounded so funny. He recorded her on Horrible Records. A singer who couldn't sing. That's the kind of thing he did.

"When Tony T came here, the police knew he was here. They knew his car. And him. They followed him right to my driveway, which is set back from the highway. They were on the lookout for him. They asked me why he was here. It wasn't just one time. They were watching him."

Those who met Bennett in those years were struck by his sensitivity and gentle sense of humor. "I remember very well the day I met Tony Bennett," recalled George Avakian, the legendary jazz producer who helped establish the 33⅓ LP as the primary format for the recording industry, ran Columbia's jazz division, and is responsible for essential albums by Louis Armstrong, Duke Ellington, Miles Davis, Errol Garner, and Dave Brubeck. "He had just signed the week before with Columbia. 1950. I bumped into him in the hallway. He introduced himself and said he had just signed. He was in to see Mitch Miller, who signed him. He had to wait a few minutes, so I invited him to come sit in my office, which was next door. I took a liking to him right away, because he seemed to be a very straightforward kind of person and a little bit shy. One of the nice things about him was that he didn't talk about himself at all. He spoke of the opportunity, of course, and how he was grateful and hoped that something would happen. So I wished him the best of luck and never realized we would be friends for the next fifty years or more.

"I also remember with great amusement that he was wearing a top-coat. I think it was in the spring, and it was a black-and-white her-ringbone coat with a gray look to it. I said, 'Gee, that's a nice-looking coat.' And he said, 'Well, I got it real cheap.' And he held out the lapel and showed there was a very bad misweave. So we had a big laugh over that. He had no inhibition about talking about it. He wasn't ashamed of it. He knew perfectly well that he was somebody that didn't have much money, and he was starting out and he had managed to buy a rather good-looking job cheaply. And even though it had a flaw, he didn't hide it. I didn't even notice it until he told me about it. But that's the kind of guy he was. He could laugh at himself. He stayed that way."

The first major news story on Bennett, written by Rube Dorin, appeared in the May 25, 1950, *New York Morning Telegraph* and was headlined "Hope's 'Find' Making Mark":

Into the swim of male vocalists jumps Tony Bennett, a neat, serious looking young man who carries with him the distinc-tion of having been discovered and yanked from comparative obscurity by none other than Bob Hope. And from the looks of things the young gentleman will make decidedly more than a pebble-splash.

Hope caught Bennett one night when he was singing at the Greenwich Village Inn during the fairly recent show which starred Pearl Bailey. The star took a shine to him and the next thing Tony knew Hope had him up on one of his Paramount stage shows, then dragged him off on a tour. . . .

A cross between a tenor and a baritone, Bennett has already recorded for Columbia and his platters of "I Wanna Be Loved" and "Boulevard of Broken Dreams" are in the bestseller class. He's appeared at the Club Charles in Baltimore, the Pittsburgh Copa and on a number of television shows, including Robert Q. Lewis'. Mitch Miller at Columbia Records sees Bennett sky-rocketing before the year is up. . . .

Bennett's background is not unusual with a single twist. Parents (especially fathers) have never been known to encourage singing careers. Tony's father explicitly wanted him to become a singer and hoped for it all his life. That was OK for Tony, too, who would sing at any opportunity—church socials, community sings and the like. . . .

Out of the Army, he was doing a number at the studio of a friend, Ray Muscarella, who is Vic Damone's sponsor and manager. Muscarella immediately signed him to an exclusive contract and his first big stop was the Village Inn engagement.

Tony lives in Astoria with his mother, a brother and a sister. His father died when he was 9 [*sic*]. His uncle, Dick Gordon, was a dancer who played the Palace and other local spots and who furnished the major inspiration and drive for Bennett.

Personal preferences in singers? We get an answer from Tony that's refreshing and unhackneyed. Not Vic Damone, or Perry Como, or Frankie Laine or any of the other boys.

"I get a kick out of the way Fred Astaire sings," he claims.

Fred Astaire—Tony would include him today in any list of his favorites. Tony's consistency, over the years, like his tenacity and his integrity, has never wavered. He pointed this out himself to Robert

Sullivan in 2007: "I think what I was saying about music in 1950 is what I'm saying now. I've never tried to follow a fashion." And he once described himself as "the fighter who never took a dive." The direct line from 1950 to 2011 is a clear one.

It was 1950 — half century. Tony was twenty-three, and the bells were starting to ring for him.

4

An Alarm Clock in Church

Tony's first recording date at Columbia was April 17, 1950, and the first song was "Boulevard of Broken Dreams." He actually finished the record on a second date, April 20, along with "I Wanna Be Loved." The song is melodramatic, overly emotive, full of purple passion, a faux tango, and Tony gives it an abundance of vibrato, but his raw power and emotion still broke through. "'Boulevard of Broken Dreams,'" George Avakian told me, "was an extraordinarily good example of how to phrase a song, get the message across." Marty Manning conducted the orchestra, and Frank Laico, the engineer on that session, would stay with Bennett for the entire first twenty-one years he was at Columbia (Bennett would be back later). The recording dates took place at a beautiful old church on East Thirtieth Street that Columbia had purchased and turned into a recording studio. Tony recorded there through the late 1960s.

Bennett was asked by an interviewer if he had any advice for young singers. "Use your own voice," he answered. "Depend on your own particular sound to carry yourself to popularity. It doesn't mean anything for a singer to make a splash for a record in which the real selling factor is not him but the tune or some gimmick." The record became a moderate success and allowed Tony to begin traveling on the road for the first time, hitting Boston, Philadelphia, Cleveland, Wilkes-Barre, and Buffalo, honing his craft. He took the great guitar player Chuck Wayne with him on these trips, sometimes following performers such as Billie Holiday and Art Tatum. He also joined Rosemary Clooney on a TV summer replacement show called *Songs for Sale*, a talent contest for aspiring songwriters hosted by Jan Murray, which was broadcast first on CBS Radio and soon simulcast on CBS-TV. Tony and Rosemary were hired for a CBS radio show of their own, *Steppin' Out*, with a quintet led by the fine pianist Johnny Guarnieri. It was broadcast five nights a week.

Tony returned to the recording studio on July 14, 1950, with arranger-conductor Percy Faith, whom Mitch Miller had brought to the label, to record a tedious religious song called "Our Lady of Fatima." The song reeked of bells and incense, and it didn't get anywhere. Eleven more singles were released between July 1950 and January 1951 to little effect. They included "Let's Make Love," "I Wanna Be Loved," "I Can't Give You Anything But Love," "Just Say I Love Her" (one of the great Neapolitan classics made famous by Jimmy Roselli—Tony also sang in Italian here), "Sing You Sinners," "Kiss You," "One Lie Leads to Another," "Don't Cry Baby," "Once There Lived a Fool," "Beautiful Madness," and "Valentino Tango." Columbia was getting nervous and gave Tony an ultimatum. They would give him a final recording date and if none of the songs he recorded were successful, they would drop him. "Because of You" came out of that recording date. Recorded on April 4, 1951, at the church on Thirtieth Street, "Because of You" hit the charts, reached number one on June 12, 1951, and remained on the charts for thirty-two weeks, ten of them as number one. It sold more than a million copies. The song was almost an accidental choice. (The other song Bennett recorded that day, "I Won't Cry Anymore," is also one of his finest early recordings, one that easily stands the test of time. It also reached the top twenty.)

"Although Bennett's first record for Columbia, 'Boulevard of Broken Dreams,' went well enough," *Newsweek* wrote on October 1, 1951, "succeeding efforts failed to catch fire. 'I tried everything,' Bennett says, 'from being a race singer to trying to do a Mario Lanza song. Then we decided I would just sing honestly and sincerely.' With 'Because of You,'" *Newsweek* continued, "the new formula worked."

Percy Faith had searched through a batch of sheet music on his desk, grabbed a song at random, and said off-handedly, "Well, let's do this one." It was "Because of You." Written by Dudley Wilkinson and Arthur Hammerstein, uncle of Oscar Hammerstein II, more than ten years before, the song had languished on the shelves until Tony recorded it. The senior Hammerstein was eighty-two years old when he had a hit of a lifetime. Faith gave Bennett good advice that day that may have made a critical difference in the fate of the record. Instead of singing overdramatically, as he had been doing, Percy said to him, "Just relax. Use your natural voice and sing the song."

"Because of You" haunts the listener today; it is an evergreen. To hear it now is to wonder why it never dates, why it is never boring, why it stays inexplicably fresh. It certainly struck a chord when it came out: Jimmy Scalia's father, Anthony Scalia, remembers hearing it when he was in the marines. A former trumpet player, he was stationed in South Carolina in 1954. "I used to go on liberty in South Carolina," Anthony Scalia recalls. "This restaurant we went to had a jukebox with Tony Bennett on it. We played 'Because of You' over and over. I used to sit there for hours. I got a bacon, lettuce, and tomato sandwich. Finish that. Get another one, and played the song over and over again. I'd just sit there. They'd say, 'Why don't you play something else?' I don't know why I loved it so much. It just stuck with me. It was the rasp. The raspiness of his voice. It wasn't pure. It was something like Louis Armstrong. It was genuine. Beautiful, yeah. So I kept playing it for these people in the restaurant, and I would look at their faces. To me it looked like they were saying, 'Please go home. Get out.' Keeping the Italian heritage alive in South Carolina."

Jimmy Scalia's father was not alone. Although Columbia didn't have much confidence in the record, and it didn't immediately get played much on the radio, it got traction on jukeboxes. Record executives may not have seen its potential, and disc jockeys may have ignored it, but thousands, soon millions of people loved it and it began to build incredible momentum. "Because of You" followed the highly unusual route of first finding acceptance on jukeboxes rather than on radio. Then listeners started to call disc jockeys and demand that the song be played. To his amazement, Bennett heard the record playing everywhere, on the radio and blaring from speakers in front of record stores.

"Because of You" has a yearning to it, a deep sincerity, soaring intensity, emotional forthrightness, passion, simplicity, and warmth—everything that Bennett brings to his music. And there is also the rare intimacy, the closeness and accessibility of Bennett. Alec Wilder wrote of Tony's singing, "There is a quality about it that lets you in. Frank Sinatra's singing mesmerizes you. In fact, it gets so symbolic sometimes that you can't make the relationship with him as a man, even though you may know him. Bennett's professionalism doesn't block you off. It even suggests that maybe you'll see him later at the beer parlor." And all of this was there at the beginning. The song is so resonant that its life goes on and on. I have listened to it hundreds of times, and like the later "San Francisco," I can never get enough of it.

And then there is the pure "Italian" quality of the voice, whatever that means to the listener or the critic. But it is there. Perhaps it can be defined as getting to the emotional core, whether it be joy, anger, spontaneity, love, ecstasy—warmth. We know it when we hear it.

Italian singers of the 1950s were among the most popular performers on the scene, especially ballad singers. Music critic Arnold Shaw maintained in 1952 that their musical arrangements were characterized by an "undercurrent of swirling strings, woodwinds, and light rhythm," "a pasta of Neapolitan bel canto and pseudo operatic singing." Those he had in mind in this less than laudatory description included Sinatra, Dean Martin, Tony, Jimmy Roselli, Connie Francis, Bobby Darin, Louis Prima, Sergio Franchi, Al Martino, Mario Lanza, Frankie Valli, Jimmy Darren, Jerry Vale, Perry Como, Don Cornell, Vic Damone, Frankie Laine, Johnny Desmond, Buddy Greco, Lou Monte, Toni Arden, Julius LaRosa, and Alan Dale.

But Tony, like Sinatra, Martin, Darin, Prima, LaRosa, and Roselli, was certainly no "pasta" singer. (Nor, for that matter, were Como, Damone, Vale, Greco, Francis, Desmond, Valli, and several others.) He was a total original. He listened carefully to the lyric, he improvised it like a jazz singer, he related it to his own experience, and he touched the heart.

Tony was not only competing with other Italian singers but also with a magnificent roster of other contemporary singers, including Peggy Lee, Dinah Washington, Judy Garland, Ray Charles, Nat King Cole, Ella Fitzgerald, Lou Rawls, Jo Stafford, Dick Haymes, Sarah Vaughan, Barbra Streisand, Ernie Andrews, Bobby Short, Bill Henderson, Doris Day, Johnny Mathis, Al Hibbler, Arthur Prysock, Mel Tormé, David Allyn, Etta Jones, Johnny Hartman, Joe Williams, Nina Simone, Herb Jeffries, Rosemary Clooney, Della Reese, Dakota Staton, Louis Armstrong, Margaret Whiting, Etta James, Billy Eckstine, Steve Lawrence and Eydie Gorme, and Lena Horne.

"For two decades Crosby ruled," music critic and Bing Crosby biographer Gary Giddins wrote, "and all the crooners were casual baritones. Bennett was a tenor and 'casual' was not in his makeup. He was more of a shouter, related to Leoncavallo and Puccini. Lacking operatic chops and timbre, he nonetheless sang ballads Pagliacci-style, as if his life depended on it. But he also had more than a touch of Manhattan bop in his soul, and his jazz-infused swingers paraded raw emotions with a hipsterish elan—even the high notes radiated a husky, hustling, local-boy temperament.

"At a time when Italo pop meant the lean homey Sinatra of wartime, the lassitude of Como or the light ballads of Damone," Giddins continued, "Bennett's zealous, sometimes melodramatic assault on the pop charts had the effrontery of an alarm clock in church . . . making an emotional connection, taking listeners by the lapels and shaking them up."

In a conversation with Robert Sullivan, Tony himself admitted his early tendency to overdramatize his singing: "I was always loud, and always very dramatic. Back then, I was too much. The guys in the band would say to me, 'Hey, kid—what're you trying to do? Calm down.' But see, Ella had told me to sing to the balconies. And also, I was nervous and I couldn't control myself."

Gary Giddins elaborated to me in 2010 on his early impressions of Tony: "The thing that I think really separated him from everyone else from the start is the operatic quality of his singing. Sinatra is often referred to as a master of a kind of American vernacular bel canto. But Tony seems to me to be almost this operatic tenor without portfolio. When you listen to his early recordings, what balls to be choosing things like 'Boulevard' or even 'Because of You' and singing them with that kind of bravura. I mean, no one else was doing that. Even Sinatra, as different as he is from Crosby, there was a sense of understatement, laid back, being cool. Saving up your chops for the high note when you needed it.

"Whereas Tony came on like gangbusters. And I loved those early records of his. I listen to them a lot. There's nothing else like them. The farther you get in time, the more you realize that of all of those Italian singers, there's nobody else [but Bennett] who attacks a song that way. The emotion is amazing. I always find that I totally believe the lyrics."

Soon Bennett was everywhere. He served as Perry Como's summer replacement host on the *Kraft Music Hall* show in 1951, appeared for the first time on the *Ed Sullivan Show* on September 23, 1951, and made his New York nightclub debut that year at the prestigious Ben Maksik's Town and Country Club in Brooklyn. He sang to jam-packed crowds. Tony appeared on the cover of the then leading music/jukebox-industry trade paper, *The Cash Box*, on June 30, 1951, along with Mitch Miller and jukebox entrepreneur Harry Siskind.

Many of his records were hitting the charts at the same time. His rendition of the Hank Williams song "Cold, Cold Heart" followed on May 31, 1951, and it quickly topped the charts, racking up a sale of two million. Bennett hadn't wanted to record it. It was the great Jerry Wexler, later of Atlantic Records, who introduced Mitch Miller to Hank Williams and to "Cold, Cold Heart." The song, writes Gary Marmorstein in *The Label*, "was begging [in Miller's ears] to be recorded in a non-country setting. The singer he finally pushed it on was as non-country as they came." Bennett told Miller he didn't want to sing cowboy songs, but Miller insisted: "Listen to the lyrics." According to Marmorstein, Tony "hated it." Bennett actually changed his mind later and realized that Miller had been right about the song—especially when it became a huge hit.

Bennett also recorded a haunting version of "While We're Young" on the same recording date. Tony was becoming the hottest singer in the country, and followed up with "Blue Velvet," which also went gold. A glance at the *Billboard* music popularity chart for New York in 1951 (the charts for the other major cities are very similar) shows the company Bennett was in during the years just before rock and roll would come to dominate the charts. It was actually a fairly distinguished list, with a few exceptions. Bennett was on top with "Because of You," followed by Rosemary Clooney's "Come on-a My House," the kitschy song she was forced to sing by Mitch Miller and always detested. The number three slot was accorded to Nat King Cole for his fine recording of "Too Young," and Tony Martin was fourth with "I Get Ideas." Les Paul and Mary Ford's recording of "The World Is Waiting for the Sunrise" was number five, Frankie Laine was sixth with "Jezebel," and Mario Lanza was in the seventh slot with "Loveliest Night of the Year." Rounding out the list were Dinah Shore with "Sweet Violets," Guy Mitchell with "Belle, Belle, My Liberty Belle," and Tony was back again at number ten with "Cold, Cold Heart."

Jim Lowe, who was a leading disc jockey at WNEW-AM for many years, recalled his first impressions of Bennett. "I first met him in 1950 while I was still in Chicago radio at WMAQ and WBBM, and I came to New York and WNEW in 1954," Lowe told me. "He was so different as to call immediate attention to himself. I knew his was a voice to be reckoned with, but it was so unusual. He wasn't in the big band, crooner mold we were so used to. It was operatic. I grew up listening to big bands records at my grandfather's music store back in Missouri. My frame of reference was Sinatra and other singers with Tommy and Jimmy Dorsey and Glenn Miller. And as a personality, again he was a different-looking person. He was different in every way from what we had been used to. He was a groundbreaker. It took me a while to adjust to him, and then I realized what a treasure, what a force he was, and of course continued to be. Once I got him, I knew he was here to stay and that he was going to be an influence unto himself.

"He was very tenacious. He wouldn't take no for an answer; he wouldn't take yes for an answer. It wasn't enough. He just kept coming at you. Ultimately he wore down the nonbelievers one by one. Somebody should tell him, 'Tony, you won.' He kept right on going, plowing new territory. And he loved to sing. If you ran into him on the street, he'd almost sing for you. And he was very congenial to talk to, no pretense. He was very appreciative and accessible. He was an easy star, a hands-on star. He didn't change that much vocally over the years; I think everybody changed around him. He made us change, made us pay attention. So different, and so not in your face but in your ear. He took no prisoners."

Phoebe Jacobs, publicist and vice president of the Louis Armstrong Educational Foundation, met Tony on Fifty-second Street in the jazz clubs. "I met him with Chauncey Olman, who represented Pearl Bailey. Tony was very shy. He had an appreciation for everything that was good and beautiful. And he was like a sponge; he would soak up everything around him. I think that created the whole person. In those years it was like Tony won an amateur night with Major Bowes. He was dear and a wonderful young performer."

Those who met Tony Bennett in those years recall how high his standards were and how deeply he loved and understood good music. Composer and pianist Eugene Di Novi saw Tony again in 1950. "The link was actually a great man named Billy Exiner, who was a drummer and a guru to a generation of musicians and singers," Di Novi told me. "He was a drummer with the great Claude Thornhill band that led into what they call the birth of the Cool: Gil Evans and all of that. Billy was a big father figure to Tony and to me. Tony was tight with him, Tony Tamburello, Joe Soldo, and Ernie Calabria, who played guitar for Harry Belafonte for years.

"When Claude's band broke up, Billy Exiner went to work with Tony. And Billy said, 'Come over to the Paramount Theater; we're there with Ray McKinley's band.' And Billy got me in with Tony, whose piano player at the time was Jack Medoff. When Jack left in 1952, I joined Tony after the Paramount engagement. By then he'd already had a number of hits. See, I think the most important thing about him is the fact that he always had great respect for the musicians. He knew what was good. A lot of the singers, to tell you the truth, didn't. Some of the other Italian singers had no idea who Billy Exiner was or Gil Evans or Bobby Hackett or Count Basie or Duke Ellington.

"Tony just loved this stuff; loved doing it. And that was so infectious, you know. That was the quality that made him last through all of the garbage years of music to come. He knows how to live in that world. He can tell the story, man; that's what it's all about. He gets into it and he reaches a lot of people. He just loves doing it.

"He did what all good musicians do," Di Novi continued. "They don't let you know about it, but they're always studying. And he listened. He listened to the right people in the beginning—I mean the guys who were good who nobody knew about. David Allyn probably had the best sound of anything I ever heard. I first heard Allyn because Tony had a record of his. Tony listened to the phrasing of Crosby, Sinatra, and Astaire. He listened in a way that all people do: you take what you want and do it your way, but that's where you learned. He was doing that right from the beginning. Because he idolized them from the start, you know. He understood them as performers. If you're smart: because those guys, Durante, Armstrong, communicated, man.

"We played New Orleans together, Florida, Vegas. We played the El Rancho in Vegas when there was a dirt road outside, that's how long ago it was.

"The thing is, certain singers are so great they appeal to both the commercial world and to the real music world, like Peggy, Lena, Sinatra, Nat Cole—and Tony. Tony was the real thing. Because he appealed to everyone, which is a gift that God knows how you get that. But those singers are the only ones. We're talking about people who had it all. Mel Tormé was a masterful singer, and Tony's not as good a jazz singer as Tormé was. But Mel never reached people like Tony did. I think other artists know that Tony has an understanding of what they do as well, whether it's the musicians or Cary Grant, or whomever he meets. They know that he digs what they do, he understands what they do. I mean he understands the *related* fields to music. He's always observing and studying; that's the important thing."

Those high standards set Bennett on a collision course with Mitch Miller. Bennett had problems with Miller's choices, even though they would turn out to be hits: "Blue Velvet" and "Rags to Riches." "Solitaire," the B side of "Blue Velvet," also hit the top twenty. "Bennett chafed under Miller's authority and often stood up to him,"

Gary Marmorstein wrote. Bennett felt debased by some of Miller's commercial choices of songs for him, but he also was quick to grant Miller's abilities and in later years softened toward him. "Actually he was pretty good to me," Bennett told James Isaacs later on. "I mean, we had to fence at one time, but he understood me."

Bennett's gripe with Miller was that he wanted to sing only the great songs, not kitsch. While Tony had mixed feelings about Miller, Sinatra detested him. Sinatra never forgave Miller for asking him to sing "Mama Will Bark" with Dagmar and other kitschy songs. Miller actually loathed rock and roll as much as Bennett did. A classical oboist, Miller had turned to pop music in 1947 and became an A&R man at Mercury Records, first finding the song "Mule Train" for Frankie Laine, and producing Patti Page and Vic Damone. He switched to Columbia in 1950 and turned it into the most successful pop label. He launched Tony, Mahalia Jackson, Johnnie Ray, Rosemary Clooney, the Four Lads, Johnny Mathis, and Jerry Vale.

"I noticed a unique quality in his voice," Miller told *Billboard* in 1968. He went on to express it a little indelicately. "You know, Tony has always 'smelled of the city' to me; I've always thought of him as the voice of the city streets. Whereas Sinatra is the voice of the city indoors.

"In those [early] days," Miller continued, "I was lucky: I was the only musician in control of an A&R post. Other producers listening to country and western records couldn't hear past the singers—the scratchy voices of the country and western singers. Jerry Wexler, who was then at *Billboard*, put me onto Hank Williams. He played a record by Williams for me and said, 'Listen to this guy. He's fantastic!' And I heard the *song*, not just the singer. It was Hank Williams's 'Cold, Cold Heart.'

"I played the record for Tony. He looked at me and said, 'You want to turn me into a cowboy, don't you?' He tried it anyway, and we did take after take, because that particular song depended on simple singing, not dramatic emotion. After a number of takes, he got closer and closer to what it needed and finally he got right into that groove.

"If I were A&R-ing him today? Well. I say this only with love for Tony. Every hit song was a fight with Tony. It's like he was ashamed to have success with a hit. It was too easy a way. So today I'd give him a variety of songs, but only songs that are to the heart. He's a heart singer. When he loves a song, that's it. Tony's a man of unflagging ideals. Many times, I have to say, his ideals hurt him a little, professionally. He can get off it long enough to stay popular with the masses, but he never deserts it [his ideals]. You notice every time Tony has a hit record, he goes back to jazz! No, it doesn't hurt him professionally. Even when he's between hits he does capacity business wherever he sings."

Many years later, Bennett, in a reflective mood, talked about a different aspect of his conflict with Miller to Robert Sullivan: "Miller wanted me to do one ballad after another. Ralph Sharon [his pianist] said, 'Make sure you do some jazz.' Ralph knew how much I loved jazz. He knew that, really, I'm a jazz singer. In this commercial world, they put me in the traditional pop category, because, well, I'm white and Italian, which makes it tough to be seen as a jazz singer. But if you asked me what I was, once I'd learned how to sing, I'd say 'a jazz singer.'" In truth Bennett is an "everything" singer. He is eclectic and bold in his choices and no music is really alien to him.

"The fifties [for Bennett] are shown as a montage of contradictions and close calls with compromise," wrote Will Friedwald. "Bennett the crusader for class at first gains and then loses the advantage over Bennett the cog in the Miller machine." Bennett had an ambivalent relationship with Miller, but Miller was helpful to him in many ways. "With Miller guiding him through his Columbia sessions and strong arrangers writing for him," Marmorstein wrote, "Bennett was a dependable hit maker, even when he sang over the top. . . . Of male singers who began to record only after the advent of the LP, Bennett became the most essential to the label." The verdict may be mixed on Miller, but as Marmorstein noted, "Miller could be a despotic master, shaping the voices and careers of young singers. But he also sensed what would communicate with an audience. . . . He could savage young singers but also salvage their careers."

Bennett gave an interview to the BBC in 2002 in which he rendered a balanced and more forgiving assessment of what the interviewer deemed "the Mitch Miller problem."

"Well, everybody puts him down," Bennett answered. "I always laugh at that, because I've not had a hate relationship [with Miller]. . . . It was the age of my trying to compromise and make things work when you first start out. . . .

"He wanted us to make records that . . . were timeless. Yes, he did little ditties, but in the meantime he had Doris Day, Rosemary Clooney; he was in the stable of Duke Ellington and Count Basie and Errol Garner. . . . He made sure we had the best engineers and the best musicians. And the records were made very well. He had Jo Stafford: beautiful, beautiful singer. And Rosemary Clooney's 'Tenderly' and Errol Garner, you know making all those great records. But [Miller was cautious with me] because he was getting such severe criticism from Sinatra. To the day Sinatra died, I would be a bit of a rascal. One time I just said 'Mitch Miller' to him and he just blew his stack. I mean, he went into a rage. You couldn't even mention his name. . . . That would ruin the whole night. Everybody was having fun until that moment." Bennett laughed again.

When Mitch Miller died at age ninety-nine in August 2010, I sat down again with Will Friedwald to discuss the Bennett-Miller relationship. He recalled that the first time he ever met Bennett in the early 1980s, they talked about the Sinatra-Miller conflict. "At that point Tony was a bit more guarded about Mitch," Friedwald recalled.

> He didn't want to say anything bad about him. You can't talk about that relationship without one guy saying something bad about somebody. Obviously they can't both be right. Tony really seemed to be at a loss as to what to say. If he said something in favor of Frank it would be knocking Mitch. And vice versa. I could tell he was struggling. It's like you had two close friends who were fighting each other and you had to pick sides. He was really confused. An hour later, he called me. And he said, "The more I think about it, Mitch really wanted Frank to do lousy songs. That's really what their conflict was." So he had to bite the bullet and say it. As he got to know me better over the years, or Mitch was out of the picture, Tony got more comfortable talking about what had happened between him and Mitch. It's like

everybody says: what Mitch wanted to do, and what Frank and Tony wanted to do, were two different things. Mitch just wanted to go for the hits, whatever it took to get there.

Before Mitch, pop music was in the hands of the bandleaders. And they had certain ideas of quality and standards. And Mitch was a musician, too. But he really wasn't invested in pop music the same way they were. There were no second-raters among anyone who led a band. All the star bandleaders were really great musicians.

And when Mitch came in, it was like a whole new thing. The idea emerged that the producer was as important as the artist, the song, or the material. In other words, you could have a singer and a song, and one guy would produce it, and the record would go nowhere. But Mitch would take the same combination: the same singer, and the same song, and what he would do to it would make it a hit. And that's like a world where the producer is all-important.

After the swing era, it's no longer big bandleaders that are running the show. Sinatra's vision was that the artist would be in charge. That the artist knew what songs would work for him, and to that extent, Sinatra was a direct extension of Tommy Dorsey, who was a performing artist himself, but who called his own shots, ran his own show, had his own publishing house. And that was a direct extension of that view that it was the performer who knew what was best for them. And Mitch Miller's vision was that the producer be in charge.

So that really was the conflict between Mitch and Frank. I really don't think that it was about songs per se. Sinatra, when he really thought it would behoove him he would do a song he didn't like. He did "Strangers in the Night" and he hated it. He did "My Way" and he hated it. Actually that's one thing that Danny [Bennett] said to me, that this was essentially the difference between Tony and Frank. Tony took that even further. Danny pointed out that Tony would never do a song that he hated even if he thought it would be the biggest thing ever. He always said he didn't want to do a bad song, especially because it might become a hit. And then he would be stuck singing it forever.

Because he could see Rosemary Clooney hated "Come on-a My House" and she had to sing it every night of her life no matter how much she hated it. Sinatra was forced to do "My Way" every night because of the crowd reaction. Tony would never do that. That's kind of the essential difference. He took what Sinatra had done and extended it. There were really times when Mitch pressured Tony to do terrible songs, too. And they were hits. Sometimes not. A good example is "In the Middle of an Island." But there were also some dumb songs of Tony's that weren't hits, like "My Pretty Shoo-gah" and "Cinnamon Sinner." They're pretty lousy.

Essentially the dynamic was that Mitch was just trying to do pop hits, and Tony and Frank were trying for art. Tony certainly followed Frank's idea that the artist had to be in charge. He was enabled to do it because Sinatra set the example. That empowered him. When Sinatra was doing it, it was pretty much unprecedented. Even Bing Crosby didn't pick most of his own songs.

So Bennett was even going further than Sinatra in that respect. He was really trying to take charge of his own destiny.

So it really wasn't a fight over songs. It was a fight for control, particularly in Sinatra's case.

Friedwald paused and said, "Tony resents everybody that claimed to be his producer or his manager. Because he feels they're taking credit for his own achievements. It was his own artistic destiny and he was in charge and he knew what he wanted to do. But he says he outlasted eight or so producers—he's got the number down. I remember when I was working on his memoir with him, somebody told me he'd been Tony's manager and I'd say, 'So and so, who was your manager.' Tony would say [doubtfully], 'He said he was my manager.' To him these guys are taking credit for what he did."

"Hearing these early [Bennett] recordings," Bennett's accompanist Ralph Sharon wrote many years later, "one can sense the gradual but meaningful influence that certain key figures in the music business were having on Tony. He was given advice and encouragement by such giants as Duke Ellington and Count Basie, and he was thrilled with the playing of the piano genius, Art Tatum, and the saxophone of Lester Young. In fact, any fine jazz musician, no matter the instrument, found a warm spot in his heart. So with Tony, from the early beginnings, the natural musicianship was always there and was fostered and nurtured through the years by the finest musicians, arrangers, and conductors."

Bennett was booked into the Paramount Theater as the headliner beginning September 19, 1951, at a weekly salary of $3,500. (He'd made $37.50 a week in Astoria not long before.) He was sharing the bill with the great Louis Prima and Keely Smith. What ensued was glorious pandemonium, rivaling Sinatra's tumultuous first appearances at the theater. The grinding schedule was exhausting. Again, Ray Muscarella performed yeoman service. His wine trucks were wired for sound and formed a parade from Little Italy in Manhattan uptown to the Paramount playing "Because of You." The trucks got louder and louder as they drove up Broadway and reached the Paramount. Muscarella also hired skywriters to announce TONY BENNETT: NEW YORK PARAMOUNT across the Manhattan skyline.

The schedule was grueling: Bennett did seven shows a day at the Paramount. He was numbed at the end of the night. He would fall into bed in a faint, wake up, and show up again at nine-thirty in the morning to start all over again.

But there were the girls; girls everywhere, pleading with him, touching him, throwing their keys on the stage. David Patrick Stearns, music critic for the *Philadelphia Inquirer*, told me that while Sinatra was considered the sexier singer, "It isn't as if Tony Bennett wasn't sexy; I mean he is. When he was young and first hitting and really hot, my mother-in-law told me she went to see him at the Paramount. The girls were going nuts and he was going, 'Come on, girls, come on up, I'm ready.' His attitude was 'Hey, bring them on; fine with me.'"

Bennett was soon learning the benefits—and drawbacks—of success. "When I had my first record hits, in the early fifties," he told Whitney Balliett, "I suddenly found myself with an entourage, most of them takers. And I didn't like it. Maurice Chevalier was doing a one-man show here around then, and all he had was a piano and a hat, and that made me realize I was off on the wrong foot."

But the momentum was unstoppable. It culminated at the end of the year with *Cashbox* naming Tony male vocalist of the year. In January 1952 he returned to the Paramount at four thousand dollars a week, appearing with the DeMarco Sisters, the Step Brothers, and comics Joey Adams and Al Kelly. *Time* magazine dubbed him "Idol of the Girls." Despite the pandemonium of the Paramount shows (some of it willfully induced by Muscarella), Bennett's fundamental seriousness and earnestness came through in an interview he gave *Time*: "This isn't the kind of singing I want to do. I can go out on stage and crush them every time—they'd stand on their hands for me. But I don't like being sensational that way. If I could sing the way I like to sing—naturally—I'd be a better entertainer. It'll take from six months to a year to get the right arrangements and the right songs, but that's what I'm going to do."

The 1950s was still a time of intense racism permeating show business, with black singers forbidden to occupy rooms in the hotels they were starring at and prohibited from entering the front entrances of hotels. Bennett can best be understood in the light of his intense hatred of racial prejudice, a hatred intensified by his close friendship with many black artists and his witnessing the humiliations they were constantly subjected to.

Nina Chiappa, Tony's niece, remembers how often Tony talked about these matters with her and the family when she was growing up in River Edge, New Jersey, and that, in fact, the entire family shared that understanding. "Tony was really so antiracist in a period of American history when that wasn't the popular thing to do," she told me, "and I took a lot away from that in terms of just being inclusive toward all races, being able to respect people for what they are, regardless of what color their skin was. Growing up in an all-white suburban neighborhood, that wasn't popular, either. It was, I would say, unusual in my life that I had a lot of exposure to different cultures and a wide acceptance of that. It left a deep impact on me.

"It wasn't just civil rights. Our family had strong political beliefs, being Democrats, supporting democracy. Tony used to tell us about his experience in the army when he invited his black friend Frank Smith to Thanksgiving dinner. And he used to tell us about performing, too, how the blacks had to go through separate doors and sleep in different places when they were on the road together, and how that was not right. I mean, he was passionate about that, as well. I would say he was passionate about everything he believed in. My mother, Mary, was the same way. She had a passion for history. She was very knowledgeable and could speak intelligently about historical and political events. That was one of her great interests in life. For the little education that they had in those days, I think a lot of our family was very highly intelligent in that regard. They read on their own and learned and studied independently, and continued that way always."

Bennett expressed his feelings about the corrosive nature of bigotry in a recollection of his close friend Billy Eckstine, the most popular male vocalist in the country between 1949 and 1952. Eckstine was more successful than Sinatra or Crosby in those years, with twelve top-ten hits on the charts. Eckstine's ascendant career came crashing down when *Life* magazine ran a photograph of him in 1950 surrounded by a bevy of adoring white women. In Bennett's opinion the photograph destroyed Eckstine. "He ran into a lot of bigotry," he told music writer David Hajdu, "because *Life* magazine did a double-page of him in the middle of a whole bunch of white girls just swoonin' all over him. There was a big circle, like a beehive, around him, and in those days, it was so ahead of its time. You know, now it would be a normal thing. It was such a complete shock that that one photo hurt his career. It changed everything—before that, he had a tremendous following, and everybody was running after him, and he was so handsome and had great style and all that. The girls would just swoon all over him, and it just offended the white community.

"He was magnificent," Bennett said. "I can't believe how underappreciated. He was a great romantic, he was a gentleman, and he loved life. There wasn't an ounce of Uncle Tom in him at all. He was the beginning of a whole new 'this is who I am, and if you don't like it, you can fuck it.'"

Bennett told Hajdu that he called Eckstine after the singer had suffered a stroke and was dying. "We had a lot of great moments,

especially in the early pioneering days of Las Vegas, and right when he
was dying . . . I was on the phone with him and reminiscing. We had
so much fun swingin' through Vegas in those early days—with a lot of
gals, you know—a lot of beautiful nights. I told him, 'B—remember
when Frank Sinatra and Dean Martin used to tell their press agents,
"Sneak up and find out what Tony Bennett and Billy Eckstine are
doing, and put in the paper that we're doing that"?'

"He could barely talk, and he said, 'Don't forget, T—it's just you
and me. It's just you and me, T. Now it's just you.'"

"Tony can just cut off the bigots beautifully," Derek Boulton
told me. "He knows how to handle it. He can knock a guy out with
one punch. He always felt as I do, that racism should never get in
the way of the arts. He didn't want that nonsense in his life. He got
very upset at Baron Hilton when he canceled Cassius Clay, who was
supposed to appear with Tony. Hilton didn't want Clay to be the
opening act in Vegas. He said, 'I know you've got the right in your
contract, but I don't want him there.' At that moment Count Basie's
agent called me up. 'We've got a problem. Basie's promoters have
gone broke. Do you think you could ask Tony to take Basie?' I told
Tony the situation. Tony told me to set it up. So we went in with
Bill Basie. You don't want black people, you've now got seventeen
of them!"

"Tony was influenced by Sinatra on civil rights," Will Friedwald
said. "Certainly Sinatra was doing that even when Tony was a soldier. Sinatra filmed *The House I Live In* about racial equality in 1945.
I wouldn't say he got it from Sinatra. But certainly it was something
that was encouraged by Sinatra."

Tony's burgeoning success enabled him to do the one thing he'd
been most committed to from the first: freeing his mother from her
backbreaking jobs as a seamstress and her financial struggles and give
her a beautiful home of her own. He purchased a house for her at
76 Valley Road in River Edge, New Jersey, and it became the center of
Benedetto family life for many years to come. Sadly, as soon as the pres-
sures were off and she no longer had to work, the burdens of a lifetime
of physical labor began to overcome her, and she became seriously ill.
Tony's sister, Mary, and her husband, Tom Chiappa, moved into the

house with her and took care of her. Nina, the Chiappas' daughter, would be born in this home.

Father John Morley—or Father Jack, as he is affectionately called— has been the family priest for more than fifty years. He told me that he met Tony through Tony's mother, Anna, who was a parishioner at St. Peter's in River Edge, where Father Jack was a parish priest. "Tony would bring a live band and perform for free, and as a result of this we became close friends. When his mom passed away, I performed the funeral Mass, as well as for his sister, Mary, more recently."

With his mounting success, Tony was on the road constantly now, playing Miami, Cleveland, Buffalo, Washington, D.C., and Chicago, where he costarred at the Chez Paree with Sophie Tucker, the "Last of the Red Hot Mamas."

Tony was appearing at Moe's Main Street in Cleveland in 1951 when a beautiful young woman, Patricia Ann Beech, came to the club with a date. She was sitting ringside, and Tony spotted her from the stage. She was overwhelmed by Tony's singing, and insisted on meeting him—and he was overwhelmed with her beauty.

He called her the next day, and they went out. She told him she was attending the Cleveland Institute of Art and was a big jazz fan. When he left Cleveland, he called her every day, and he saw her when he played near Ohio. He soon convinced her to move to Manhattan, where he could see her constantly. By the start of 1952, he was the biggest-selling recording artist in the country. When Patricia arrived in Manhattan she headed straight for the Paramount Theater, where he was appearing. She was astonished to see hordes of hysterical bobby soxers surrounding the theater and clamoring for Tony.

Taking her by surprise, Tony proposed to her from the stage of the Paramount on New Year's Eve. It was a momentous beginning. Ray Muscarella was upset by the prospective marriage and tried to sabotage it. He felt it would hurt Bennett's image with the young girls who adored him. Tony and Patricia were married at St. Patrick's Cathedral on February 12, 1952. A special detachment of policemen was on hand to keep the crowd of five thousand fans, mainly girls, in line. Thousands of people milled about on the street. In a stunt arranged by Muscarella (and that Bennett did not appreciate at all), two thousand female fans (it was Lincoln's Birthday and they didn't have school) gathered outside the cathedral in black veils to mourn the wedding. The "jealous" girls blocked Patricia's way up the steps and tried to prevent her from getting to her own wedding. She struggled up the steps through the crowds, trying to reach the cathedral. Patricia was unremittingly hostile toward Ray Muscarella after that. It was the beginning of the end of Bennett's relationship with Muscarella. Tony's sister, Mary, would take over as Tony's manager in 1955.

Tony and Patricia first settled down in an apartment on Riverside Drive and Eighty-sixth Street, and later in Riverdale, New York. He now owned a Lincoln Capri, six tuxedos, six single-breasted suits, and ten sports shirts. Tony continued playing on the road much of the time, at Copa City in Miami with Sophie Tucker and at the Loew's State Theater in Cleveland. Patricia traveled with him. A sculptress, interior decorator, and artist, Patricia (whose nickname was Sandy) seemed like a perfect mate for Tony.

"Patricia Bennett," Derek Boulton said, "made things with her hands. She was into arts, did sculptures, ceramics, painting, photography; she was ideal for Tony. Like Sinatra with Nancy senior. The one that stuck by you."

"She was a lovely lady," Geri Tamburello remembered. "She is. I met her first in 1959. They were happy. We used to be up at their house often, in Englewood Cliffs, New Jersey. Tony had a studio downstairs and the two Tonys would go down and work with the music and the singing. Then they'd come upstairs. Patricia had a piano in the living room. My husband would play. It was a Frank Lloyd Wright–designed house.

"The neighborhood was mountainous and hilly and very picturesque. They bought a plot that had one street, and it led up to their house. The street's name was Next Day Hill. You went up this very steep driveway to their property. They had the house and the garage right there on the flat level. And the house was built down the side of the hill. They had a tree house for the boys. And a pool and a tennis court. Actually the sketches I still have by Tony are sketches of their yard: pictures of trees and bushes, black ink and brush, in Japanese style."

Tony opened in Las Vegas for the first time in April 1952, starring at El Rancho. He had many record successes that year, including "Congratulations to Someone," "King of Broken Hearts," and a powerfully emotive song, Bennett at his best, "Have a Good Time," about a lover ruefully wishing his lost love a good life without him. He also did a cover of Al Martino's "Here in My Heart," but Martino owned that one song, and good but unheralded versions of "I'm Lost Again," "Sleepless," "Stay Where You Are," and "Anywhere I Wander." Bennett had another huge hit in 1953 with "Rags to Riches," an uptempo big band record, again arranged by Percy Faith with a bold and brassy sound with a double tango in the instrumental break. It was number one for eight weeks and a gold record. Bennett hated the song initially, but Miller insisted he sing it. He grew to like it in time. On top of the number one spot for "Rags to Riches," Tony took the third spot as well with "Stranger in Paradise."

By 1954 there were more than two hundred thousand members in the USA Tony Bennett Fan Clubs and additional clubs based in twenty other countries. When he appeared again at the Paramount in 1955, the September 18 *New York Daily News* reported that he was literally besieged by his eager fans when they pinned him against the stage door. When doctors examined him they found that he had broken small blood vessels in his throat. The following day Bennett tried to sing above the "screams and moans and hoots" of his fans, but as a result of the incident at the stage door, his voice was no longer able to rise above the noise. "Even with the mike turned up," the newspaper wrote, "the strain was too much. He lost his voice on the second night and had to cancel the engagement. The doctor he consulted told him that he had better not even whisper for a week."

When there was a newspaper strike in New York in 1953, Broadway producers and composers pleaded with Mitch Miller to allow Bennett to record one of their songs. This would be "Stranger in Paradise" from *Kismet*. They pressured New York radio stations to play Bennett's record again and again weeks before the musical's opening. The record hit the charts in November and reached number two on the charts in December—just when the musical opened on Broadway.

From that point on, producers came to Bennett constantly, and he was receptive to them if he liked their music. He was not the first: other singers had been having hits with new show tunes for years, including Sinatra, but Bennett certainly played a part in Columbia's success with cast albums. In 1956 Jule Styne came to Bennett with "Just in Time," the song featured in his forthcoming show *Bells Are Ringing*. Columbia said that if Bennett were to record the song, Columbia must have the rights to the entire cast album. From then on the cast albums of Broadway shows followed upon Bennett's recording of one song from a show.

Goddard Lieberson, musical director of Columbia, had always had a major interest in musical theater. Hearing of the imminent production of *My Fair Lady*, Lieberson increased Columbia's involvement in the Broadway scene further. He persuaded William S. Paley, head of Columbia, to invest some of Columbia's money in the show. *My Fair Lady* was the biggest hit in the history of Broadway up to that time. Columbia made a fortune with the original cast album, becoming the biggest-selling cast album of all time. And finally, the producers of the show sold the movie rights to Warner Brothers for $5 million. As a result of Lieberson's role, when *My Fair Lady* opened on Broadway on March 15, 1956, Lieberson became president of Columbia Records by June of that year. Cast albums became the foundation of the Columbia catalogue. As Bennett's hit records piled up, he began to play Las Vegas, opening at the El Rancho in April 1952. He would soon play the Sahara, the Dunes, the Riviera, the Sands, and Caesars Palace.

Bennett speaks of the ascending peaks (and some of the valleys) of his career during these years in his autobiography *The Good Life*, but he is largely silent about his marriage with Patricia. A curious impersonality sets in, a sense of many lacunae, of feelings and memories withheld, especially for a person of such passion, churning emotions, and intensity as Bennett. His career entirely takes center stage. He gives scant details, yet from all indications the marriage was a very loving relationship for some time. "It was a very loving Italian family," Derek Boulton recalled. Tony skips over personal details almost instantly and moves on to the success of his next records.

Tony scored another huge triumph in October 1953 when he starred for the first time at one of the most famous nightclubs in the world, the seven-hundred-seat Copacabana. He was joining the company of show business immortals. The Copa became the home of Sinatra, Nat King Cole, Sophie Tucker, Sammy Davis Jr., Joe E. Lewis, Lena Horne, Billy Daniels, Bobby Darin, Martin and Lewis, Louis Prima and Keely Smith, Ted Lewis, and Ella Fitzgerald. Tony was reaching the top.

Named for a resort hotel in Rio de Janeiro, the club had been created by gangster Frank Costello. It had been run since its inception in 1940 by Jules Podell, a former bootlegger with a police record, who originally fronted for Costello. "Tony was always under the impression it was controlled by the Jewish mafia," Will Friedwald told me.

Bennett was on the road practically all the time by 1953, traveling with his musicians, Danny Stevens, a radio promotions man from Columbia, and Dee Anthony, his new road manager. When Eugene Di Novi left, Bennett chose as his next accompanist the superb guitarist Chuck Wayne. Bennett liked the soft, intimate sound that a guitar brought to the music.

Tony relates a story about his enamored fans in his memoir that points to his uncanny ability to perceive the comedy or pathos of his experiences and consciously utilize them creatively and transform them into art. (To put it another way, Bennett seems to have been everywhere and done everything). He had been shadowed and virtually stalked, but in an innocent way, by two squealing, besotted teenage girls who followed him everywhere. They even persuaded a landlord to lend them an unoccupied office space that faced directly into Bennett's dressing room for a month. In 1954 Bennett filled in one day for newspaper columnist Dorothy Kilgallen and wrote of his experiences with the two girls, Molly and Helen. The column inspired a comic novel by Nora Johnson, *The World of Henry Orient*. That was not the end of it. The novel was adapted for a memorable film starring Peter Sellers as Tony—Henry Orient—and then made into a Broadway musical with Don Ameche titled *Henry, Sweet Henry*.

Tony had two more hits on the top ten in 1954, "There'll Be No Teardrops Tonight" by Hank Williams and "Cinnamon Sinner," an R&B number. There were other recordings that year that were unfairly neglected, including "Funny Thing" and "Please Driver," as well as a number of standard singles, including "My Heart Won't Say Good-bye," "Until Yesterday," "Take Me Back Again," and an ersatz calypso number, "My Pretty Shoo-gah."

Tony and Patricia were overjoyed in 1954 to learn that she was pregnant, and moved to a larger apartment in Riverdale, New York, with stunning views of the Hudson River and the New Jersey Palisades.

Some of the happiest moments in the Bennett marriage occurred with the birth of their children. D'Andrea, their first boy, was born in 1954. Patricia was twenty-two and Tony was twenty-eight. Patricia had wanted to name the baby "Andrea," and Tony decided to put a "d" in front of it in honor of his singing teacher, Pietro D'Andrea. But then Tony had heard Patricia constantly calling the baby Danny. The resonant sound of the name touched him and he then recalled Art Tatum playing "Danny Boy" at a nightclub years before. "One time at Moe's Main Street in Cleveland," Bennett told James Isaacs, "[Tatum] was playing 'Danny Boy.' It was St. Patrick's Day. The whole audience was crying. It was the most beautiful that I could ever remember. That was so strong I named my son Danny." Tony was determined to keep the baby with them while traveling on the road—"I didn't want to miss a day of my son growing up"—and so the parents traveled with their baby.

Daegal, their second boy, was born in October 1955. The Scandinavian derivation of that name means "day." Patricia now decided to stay at home with the two boys. That may have been a critical mistake. The marriage began to unravel with Tony away from home so frequently. Tony attempted to rescue it by moving the family to Englewood, New Jersey, where he built the house designed in the Frank Lloyd Wright style. The house did not solve their problems. "I remember very well Tony saying, 'The sight of one pubic hair could sink a battleship,'" Derek Boulton, who became Bennett's manager in 1970, recalled.

5

Rock and Roll
Is Here to Stay

The change came in 1955," Tony told journalist Chet Flippo in 1980. "No, it wasn't just Elvis. All of a sudden, everybody was impressed by Detroit and the idea of obsolescence. Before, in the days when Goddard Lieberson [who would soon change his tune] was running CBS, he had a very ethical philosophy. He told every artist, from the top classical artist to the lowest pop artist, 'If you make a record, make it last, make a record that will last forever.' I would hire—and Mitch Miller would hire—the finest musicians. There were from fifty to seventy men on each record. We really gave full performances, and we never left the studio until the record was just right. As a result of that, the records made the catalogs and they still sell today just like current records. I get the same royalties now as I did in 1950. That's because the albums hold up, they don't sound old-fashioned, they don't sound dated.

"But in 1955 it changed. . . . They didn't want records that would last, they didn't want lasting artists, they wanted *lots* of artists. It became like a supermarket; go with the next, the next. So they started discarding people like me and Duke Ellington and Leonard Bernstein. The marketing guys took over. It took a big walk away from melodic music. It suddenly became very unprofessional to be professional. Which was very neurotic."

The change did start in 1955, but for Bennett it didn't actually become acutely threatening until about 1966, when Columbia Records, under the direction of Goddard Lieberson, Mitch Miller's boss, began to take rock and roll much more seriously. (Miller relinquished his role as director of pop music at Columbia in 1961.)

In 1954, "Sh-Boom," a rock-and-roll song recorded by both a black group, the Chords, and a white one, the Crew Cuts, had become the fifth-best-selling song of the year and the first rock-and-roll hit. In 1955, twelve of the year's top fifty hits were rock-and-roll songs. Bill Haley and the Comets' "Rock around the Clock," which was featured in the film *Blackboard Jungle*, went to the top of the charts and sold some fifteen million copies by the late 1960s, becoming one of the best-selling records of all time. "Itsy Bitsy Teenie Weenie Yellow Polka Dot Bikini" was a big hit. Rock and roll was here to stay.

Rock and roll also signaled a youth rebellion against the sexual and social status quo that would affect sexual behavior as well as race relations. From 1956 to 1960 black artists such as Chuck Berry, Ray Charles, Little Richard, Little Willie John, Fats Domino, the Platters, and Sam Cooke rose to fame and fortune. White singers, most notably Elvis Presley, borrowed black styles and utilized them to catapult themselves into the ranks of the new icons. And white rock-and-roll singers such as Presley, Jerry Lee Lewis, Buddy Holly, and Pat Boone were sometimes far more popular than the original black artists. Presley's blend of rhythm and blues, rockabilly, and country-and-western music garnered fourteen consecutive gold records from 1956 to 1968.

The musical transformation taking place was cultural, social, and political, but it was economic as well: the baby boomers had enormous buying power. Record sales soared. Annual revenues climbed from $219 million in 1953 to $277 million in 1955, reaching a staggering $600 million in 1960.

For a while, the older music survived side by side with rock and roll. In 1954, Sinatra was declared top male singer by *Billboard*, most popular vocalist by *Downbeat*, and singer of the year by *Metronome*. Bennett continued to sell, but nowhere near as well as he had. By 1955 the ballad singers were already beginning to lose their hold on the public.

Record companies, artists, composers, and musicians gradually moved to the West Coast, where Tin Pan Alley regrouped on Sunset Boulevard. As Bob Dylan would soon sing prophetically in a little club called the Gaslight in New York City's Greenwich Village, "The Times They Are A-Changin'." Gerald Early wrote in *One Nation under a Groove* that the changes in public taste included "a movement away from the Tin Pan Alley–type popular songs of the Berlin-Gershwin-Arlen ilk to a music that was more obviously and overtly influenced by, and openly mimicked, black rhythm and blues." In addition, there was "a shift away from middle-aged or mature-sounding Italian male singers as kings of the popular roost toward white southerners, adolescent Jewish songwriters, and blacks as the trendsetters in popular music, a major ethnic shift that had a profound impact on the culture at large."

Within a few years, the impact of rhythm and blues had totally transformed American popular music, and Tin Pan Alley was displaced as the music center of the universe. Nevertheless, despite the changes in American musical tastes, Bennett continued to produce superb music for Columbia. He did sell records, but sales were no longer strong enough to make the charts. His 1957 recording of "Ça, C'est L'amour" was Bennett's last appearance on the charts in the 1950s, and would only reach twenty-two, missing the top twenty. The changes did not affect Bennett's productivity or stubborn determination to keep singing what he considered good music, but their effect on his career was taking its toll. Bennett was booed off the stage at the Paramount Theater in 1956 just a few bars into "Stranger in Paradise." It was a devastating moment, a startling sign of the great divide between generations that was taking place.

Tony knew there was a lot of money to be made in rock and roll, but for him it was a question of the value of enduring art. He wanted to do only his best, and he regarded every record as being like his own thumbprint or photograph, one that he would have to live with always.

The story abroad was more positive. "Stranger in Paradise" was number one on the charts in Great Britain in 1955, and Bennett traveled there for the first time with his guitarist Chuck Wayne in July for a two-week tour, including the Empire in Glasgow and the Empire in Liverpool. Although Bennett did not appear in London on that first trip, his love for the British—and their love for him—were kindled on the trip and would grow in fervor each year.

Bennett closed out 1955 without a hit record in the States. He had recorded ten songs, including the outstanding "Close Your Eyes" and "May I Never Love Again," as well as "It's Too Soon to Know," "What Will I Tell My Heart?," "Punch and Judy Love," "Don't Tell Me Why," "How Can I Replace You?," "Tell Me That You Love Me," "Come Next Spring," and "Afraid of the Dark."

It was during these years that he forged a close working relationship and friendship with a classic saxophonist, Joe Soldo, who would double as his contractor. "I met Tony B through Tony Tamburello," Soldo recalled. "Tony T and I went to the same school in Newark, New Jersey. I'd go to his house and he'd play the piano and I started to play saxophone. Then Tamburello had met Tony Bennett at that audition at the John Quinlan studio and had said, 'This is the guy.' I met Tony Bennett when I was playing on the last big radio network show on NBC, *The Big Show* with Tallulah Bankhead. Tony B was so interested in music. He was all about music. That's the thing that impressed me so much. I didn't know then about lyrics; I never would listen. I didn't know the lyrics of songs. But then later, when I really got to appreciate it, I understood the way Tony tells a story. That's his big thing, just like Frank Sinatra, with whom I also worked.

"The most tender moment I remember playing with Tony at the Copacabana was when Tony sang Kurt Weill's 'Lost in the Stars.' We had a regular dance band and a harp. And it would be blackout, and there would be a spotlight on the floor. And he'd keep pointing to the spotlight. The whole first part of it was just him and the harp. And then in the last chorus we would come in. And even though it was the Copa, it was quiet. You could hear a pin drop. Well, people loved it. He's a master storyteller. That's what Tony does! When he said, 'Before God made the sea and the land . . .' you don't have to go and be in love with your voice. Tell the story. He's a master storyteller.

"At recording dates, Tony would not want to do anything more than once or twice. Only one or two takes. So you had better make sure you played everything right the first time. Because Tony would go in a booth with us and Tony Tamburello and we'd listen. And he'd say, 'Okay, let's do one more.' But the one that he would choose, even if there was a slight mistake with the band, he'd say, 'No, no, this is the one I want to use.' Because he was happy with what he did, and it was worthwhile for the small errors the band made, it didn't make much difference. We did most of those takes at Thirtieth Street, that old church, and Frank Laico was the mixer. Wonderful days. This was during the sixties.

"I saw him in concert at Cosa Mesa just a couple of months ago. I couldn't get over it. I mean it was a standing ovation for every number. There were young people and middle-aged people and old people. And they really went crazy for him. It's amazing. And when you think about it, he is the last one going. The only one. This guy Michael Buble has a nice sound, a great sound, but the act is so slick. The way he wears his hair, it's all premeditated. You know, Tony was never like that. Frank was never like that. Rosemary Clooney, Dean, Steve Lawrence were never like that. All of the big stars, there was something true about it. It was truthful."

Bennett has written and spoken often about his reverence for Frank Sinatra, and how he would sit through all seven of Sinatra's performances in one day at the Paramount when he was a very young man. He added to his memories of Sinatra in a piece in *Vanity Fair* in August 2009. He recalled that he was nine years old when he heard Sinatra's voice on the *Major Bowes Amateur Hour* on September 8, 1935. First it was Sinatra's jaunty confidence that impressed him: "In response to Major Bowes' booming query 'Who will speak for the group?,' Sinatra piped up, 'I will. I'm Frankie. We're looking for jobs—how 'bout it? Everyone that's ever heard us likes us.' Even Bowes had to chuckle." Later, when Sinatra joined Tommy Dorsey's orchestra, "I was amazed at how Frank, from studying how T.D. played, learned to extend his breathing, which gave him better vocal control and the ability to sing two or three sentences before taking another breath. That subtle and elegant nuance kept a listener hanging on every word, captivated the imagination, and caused his fans, myself included, to swoon. I couldn't believe anyone could sing that lovely."

Mary Chiappa had recalled how deeply Tony admired Sinatra from the time Tony was a teenager. "I would see the girls swooning and putting up Frank's picture on their lockers, and I was explaining to Tony how I thought all this was such silly nonsense. Tony said to me, 'Come here. I want to explain something to you.' And he put a Sinatra record on the phonograph. And as he played it, he explained the different things that Sinatra was doing with that song. And from that day on, Sinatra's also been one of my favorites. And that's how I learned about Sinatra. And Tony must have been about sixteen or seventeen at the time. So he really had that feel for good music."

When Bennett was about to appear again as Perry Como's summer TV replacement on NBC in 1956, he was anxious about how he would perform. In a characteristic, nervy gesture he sought out the advice and guidance of Frank Sinatra, whom he had never met before. "I was nervous as all heck," he told Robert Sullivan. "Sinatra was over at the Paramount, and I decided to visit him backstage. A friend of mine warned me not to go because Sinatra had a reputation for being tough. But I took a deep breath and showed up at his dressing room. The Sinatra I met was quite different from the one I expected. Sinatra was wonderful to me. I asked him, 'How do you handle being nervous onstage?' He said, 'It's good to be nervous. People like it when you're nervous. It shows you care. If *you* don't care, why should they?' And then he told me to stay away from the cheap songs. It was great advice. I've followed it since."

That encouragement helped Bennett to achieve success as Como's summer replacement. Como was pleased with him and invited him back three years later to star on a thirteen-week series, *Perry Presents*. It was Bennett's first extended exposure on television. Bennett appeared with more ease on other shows in the following year, including several appearances on the *Steve Allen Show*.

Something in Anthony Dominick Benedetto touched Sinatra. Bennett was special to him. There was the talent, of course. But Sinatra must have been taken aback by the young, fledgling *paisan's* willingness to take a chance and approach him and confess his vulnerability, and probably he was impressed, charmed, and disarmed by it as well. Bennett was a learner and a listener from the start. He remains so today. He worshiped great artists and he was genuinely grateful for their help. Sinatra could be brutal, but when he respected talent he could be generous and kind as well.

Bennett later recalled in *Vanity Fair* the time in the early 1970s when he was playing Las Vegas and was invited (with Ralph Sharon) to join Sinatra and saxophonist Vido Musso for dinner after his show. They all met at a small Italian restaurant and "Frank reflected on his life . . . the ups and downs . . . the amazing path he'd traveled from that evening with the Hoboken Four in 1935 to becoming 'King' of the entertainment world. Toward the end of the evening Sinatra said, 'Before we go, I'd really enjoy it if you and Ralph could perform a song.' And in this small room, late in the evening, with Frank Sinatra sitting only a couple feet away, and inspired by our time together that night, I sang a Jerome Kern song. It was a moment I will never forget: 'Yesterdays / Yesterdays/ Days I knew as sweet / Sequestered days . . . Sad am I / Glad am I / For today I'm dreaming / Of yesterdays.'"

"Sinatra was generous toward Tony," composer Johnny Mandel told me. "Very much so. Sinatra was generous toward anyone he respected. If he respected you, he didn't give you any shit. He was wonderful to me. What you saw was what you got. He didn't say one thing to you and another thing behind your back. Which I always respected." Whatever Sinatra initially felt about Tony's approaching him at the Paramount, a friendship—apparently one that was usually at a distance but genuine—was soon forged in that encounter. Tony often said that if Sinatra loved you, he loved you for life.

"If he said I was his best friend, that was it," Tony told the BBC. "One time at Radio City Music Hall he had me sitting next to his wife, Barbara, in the audience. He said, 'The gentleman who is sitting next to my wife I don't have to worry about [his stealing her]. He's not only my best friend in show business. He's my best friend period.' And then I found out from some of the people that worked with him that he told him, 'I never had a brother. But if I had a brother I'd like it to have been Tony Bennett.' We just got closer and closer."

Contrasting the two men, Will Friedwald, who had collaborated with Tony on his memoir, authored the classic *Jazz Singing*, and wrote the musical biography of Sinatra, *Sinatra: The Song Is You*, told me that

"Sinatra never really felt like talking about things or explaining things. I guess he felt that the music itself said it for him. I think Sinatra was an extreme example of somebody who actually had the opportunity to go to high school and college and just didn't. I think Sinatra to a vast degree always felt inferior intellectually to people who had been to college and higher education. He was borderline jealous of that. I think that's a big reason why he gave so few interviews because he didn't want to be perceived as inarticulate or 'some dumb Italian.' He really wasn't comfortable in any kind of academic situation.

"Tony is very articulate. He's always a mensch, he's always trying to expand. He's constantly growing. He's a work in progress. When he did interviews (he hasn't in recent years), he was very expressive and he knew what he was saying. He's a natural talent. But as an artist, and also as a human being, he's very much a carefully constructed person, in the sense that he had a lot of stuff stacked against him. He had to drop out of high school to support his family during the Depression. And because of that, I think he tends to not give himself enough credit in terms of his own intelligence and his articulateness. He doesn't realize that in terms of music and also in terms of a larger cultural understanding, he's very, very sharp. And it's not something that was handed to him. I mean everything that he knows and everything he has was something that he worked really hard to get."

Loyalty—and unmistakable, genuine admiration and love—have marked Bennett's relationship to Sinatra as well. In a 1998 tribute to Sinatra in *Life* magazine, revised and reprinted in 2008 (accompanied by one of Bennett's fine paintings of Sinatra), Bennett wrote, "He just drove everyone insane with his talent. . . . We all looked up to him, and he made us feel we were all in it together. . . . Years ago, Frank used to go to Matteo's in L.A. and Patsy's here in New York, and he'd always be the center of attention, the one who made the place come alive. And to this day, in those restaurants, his great friends still show up every Sunday night, and I swear they're waiting for Sinatra to come in. He's the guy who gave us all something to live for. . . .

"When I think of Sinatra, I think of the way that Laurence Olivier depicted Hamlet. He was Everyman. He ran the gamut of emotions. Sinatra conquered every aspect of his world, the entertainment world.

He was the two masks of the theater—the comedy, the tragedy. . . . Sinatra leaves behind a legacy of music, a legacy that will live forever. Five hundred years from now, people will still be listening to his recordings, watching his films, and they'll say, 'There was only one Sinatra.' And that's not an opinion, it's a fact."

There still hovers in Bennett's tone at age eighty-five a sense of hero worship toward Sinatra that might seem baffling in the light of Bennett's own monumental career. Yet, as writer John McDonough told me, "Tony Bennett came of age in the 1930s and men like Count Basie, Astaire, Crosby, and Sinatra were his musical gods. And to the extent that he had any contact with them, he treasured every moment of those contacts. And even though he became a great star himself, in effect a kind of peer of Crosby—I mean Crosby was still performing when Tony was at the peak of his early career. Even though they were peers in the mind of listeners and the audience, Tony Bennett himself would find it very difficult to consider himself a peer of Bing Crosby or Frank Sinatra. They were more like father figures to him, I think. They were more like the pathfinders that he followed."

It would be Sinatra who, after all, would crown Bennett as his successor in 1965. And Sinatra said similar things at other times about Bennett. Chet Flippo remembered Sinatra introducing Bennett by saying, "Tony's gonna come out now and he's gonna tear the seats outta the place for you. Because he's my man, this cat. He's the greatest singer in the world today, this man, Tony Bennett." And when they were alone (in 1957), Sinatra said something else to Bennett that was both a real insight and a loving benediction: "You can only be yourself," he mused. "But you're good at that."

Paradoxically, it would be Jonathan Schwartz, who loves Sinatra above all other singers and writes and speaks of him with great depth and feeling (and who sometimes still speaks of Sinatra in conversation in the present tense), who would offer a more mixed evaluation of the relationship between Sinatra and Bennett. "I think Frank took advantage of Tony," he told me. "Tony's very vulnerable. And when Frank sees that, if he's of a mood—and I've seen him to do it to other people, too—both famous and not famous. And it's revolting. And of course in a social situation, if Frank leaves. . . . For example, there was a table at the Waldorf. The entertainment was to be Mel Tormé. Of all the singers, I knew Mel the best. And it was Mel who told me this story. He was backstage and someone said, 'Sinatra's leaving.' And Mel looked up in the corner of the curtain and he saw Sinatra get up and Tony follow. Now I'm just a hundred percent sure that Tony felt terribly about that, that he was empathizing with Mel. That's my guess. I never brought the issue up with him. But Mel told me that Frank walked out and Tony followed. I'm very careful not to play tricks on Tony: Sinatra-like tricks. I think that Tony's a very gentle man. And I don't think he's totally confident of Tony Bennett. Sometimes when he gets huge applause, you'll see an expression on his face that says, 'Oh, I don't believe it. My God.' Well, I believe [that expression] is real. And this would be after a forty-one-song performance that was just impeccable."

Bennett offered a moving and ruminative coda to his own assessment of Sinatra when he died in May 1998. Robert Sullivan wrote of Bennett sitting in the upstairs room at Teodora, an Italian restaurant in Manhattan, and reminiscing about Sinatra. "Bennett sips red wine," Sullivan wrote, "and considers what the world will be like without his friend. For himself, it will be a lesser place, Bennett says. But for those who loved Sinatra from afar, 'there will be no void.' He gazes out the window and endeavors to explain.

"You see, it's not that way with musicians. They leave behind the music, which will live forever. We'll never lose Sinatra."

"Bennett pauses, then continues: 'I'm reminded of the day Gershwin died. One of his best friends was told about it, and he just stared. 'Gershwin died,' he said. 'Gershwin died?'

"And then he said, 'I don't have to believe that.'"

Assessing the personality differences between Sinatra and Bennett, Will Friedwald told me, "Sinatra grew up alone as an only child in an era where there were no Italian families that had only one child. Every Italian family had nine children. Sinatra always felt the need to have people around him. Elvis was the same way, and he wasn't even Italian. He always felt he was less than something if he was alone, from what I gather. Tony has never had that problem. Tony is perfectly happy by himself. He never wanted to have an entourage. He once said he doesn't like to have a lot of flunkeys or yes-men hanging around. When I was close to him some ten years ago, he walked his dog by himself, he takes out the trash. He might have a maid come in and dust, but he pretty much takes care of himself. He never had like a mansion. When he raised kids he had a house in Englewood, New Jersey. Never had to have sports cars. Doesn't even drive. Not like a speedboat or a private plane or any of that stuff. He has a very nice apartment with Susan. But that's about it. It's not lifestyles of the rich and famous."

Friedwald sees Bennett only occasionally now. "I run into him a few times a year," he told me, "and he's very warm and friendly. He's a very nice man. He's a very good man, a very intelligent man. Tony is just amazingly sharp. I never really knew Benny Goodman, but he reminds me of what people say about Benny. Tony has this tendency to focus so intensely on the music that he's not paying enough attention to other things. It's really such a strong, strong focus. And he believes the best stuff will be successful. I mean, who was the best singer of all time? Frank Sinatra. Who was the most successful singer of all time? Frank Sinatra. It's not like Sinatra was starving in an alley somewhere. Ella Fitzgerald: the best singer and also the most successful. Tony has this inherent belief that things that the people like are usually the best. The people that you remember as living legends, really are, generally speaking, the best. Even in contemporary music that's still true—the bands that are the most popular are ultimately the best rock-and-roll bands, like the Beatles and the Rolling Stones." Friedwald paused. "There's so much I love by Tony Bennett," he said simply. "I love everything. For a long time my favorite was the *Movie Song Album*. But I love *When Lights Are Low. Tony Sings for Two. Hometown, My Town*."

"When I did *Satchmo*, my documentary about Louis Armstrong," Gary Giddins told me, "I interviewed Tony on camera. We go to his apartment. And he looks great; he's got the chair picked out and he knows where the cameras should go. But it wasn't until we looked at the footage afterwards that I noticed he had a vase behind his right shoulder on the table. And new flowers in it. And it wasn't until we all looked at the playback that we realized that the color of the flowers exactly brought out his eyes and the suit he was wearing. It was *so* professional. Dave Brubeck, other people helped [with the documentary], he wasn't the only one, but he certainly was the biggest star who wanted to. But the other thing is, if you watch the film, Tony's *brilliant*. Everything he says. And not only what he says, but the way he says it. He knows how to sell an anecdote. He's got this great smile that basically is sort of like the punctuation. And what he says is very profound. He really understands Satchmo's place. He really has an understanding of popular culture. And the same thing when I interviewed him about Bing [Crosby] privately. The things he said about Bing were just really shrewd and smart."

The mid-fifties were difficult years to navigate for Bennett. He parted from Ray Muscarella in 1955, replacing him with his sister, Mary, who took over the management of his career. Bennett was grateful to Muscarella for some of the genuine support and help he had given him when he most needed it, but he didn't feel he had his finger on the pulse of his career; "I wanted to have more control over my own destiny." He negotiated a generous agreement with Muscarella that gave him 10 percent of his income for the following five years.

Still, it was not so easy to get the Mafia entirely off his back, although he resisted stubbornly. In 1956 there was "an offer he couldn't refuse" for obvious reasons—reasons every singer in the business well understood. Bennett sang for three thousand guests at the wedding reception for Bill Bonanno, son of Mafia boss Joseph Bonanno and a major figure in his father's Mafia "family" at the time, and Rosalie Profaci, niece of one of the leaders of one of the other five New York families. "It was just a gig for Tony," Derek Boulton said. There was nothing unusual in Bennett's agreeing to sing for Bonanno. Italian American singers were often coerced by the wiseguys into singing for them; there were numerous instances, including Sinatra, Dean Martin, Vic Damone, and Jimmy Roselli.

"Bennett never seems to have sought the kudos or vicarious power that came through fraternizing with gangsters," Mick Brown wrote in the *London Daily Telegraph Magazine* in 2006. "In her autobiography, Judith Exner, who enjoyed the singular distinction of being the lover of Sinatra, John Kennedy, the notorious Mafia boss Sam Giancana, and— so Exner claimed—Bennett himself, alleged that Bennett was prevented from working for some years because 'he wouldn't follow orders.'

"His [Bennett's] eyes narrow slightly when this is raised, but his smile doesn't falter. That, he says, is 'not true at all. Maybe they knew about it, but I didn't know about it.' It is true that he knew Giancana and worked at a nightclub he owned in Lake Tahoe, and one in Mexico City—'although I didn't know he owned that. But nobody ever tried to put pressure on me to do anything I didn't want to do. Only the record companies wanting me to sing some junk they thought would sell.'"

"In the '50s," Will Friedwald wrote, "while fighting for a foothold in the commercial music industry, Bennett was importuned to divide up his output. His workaday business consisted of making singles releases of purely commercial intent: current songs with a fair shot at the hit parade, recorded with string orchestra and choirs. Simultaneously, Bennett satisfied his artistic urges with long-playing albums of pure creativity, with small jazz groups and older tunes selected strictly for their musical value."

The first of these albums, and one of Bennett's greatest triumphs of the midfifties, was the jazz-oriented *Cloud 7* (although there had been a ten-inch album, *Because of You*, released earlier), which was issued on February 2, 1955. In the context of the musical times, *Cloud 7* was a miracle of good taste and sound judgment, and it was the start of his gradual transition from singles artist to album artist. Tony had pushed Columbia to allow him to do a jazz-inflected album that was not merely a long-form collection of singles. He told Nat Hentoff in the June 16, 1954, issue of *Downbeat* that "I want to make an album where I just blow . . . a very relaxed album of standards away from the commercially stylized records we've been making. I want to make it with the right musicians . . . the way the jazz sides are made."

Cloud 7 remains one of Tony's favorites today. Bennett had pleaded with Miller and everybody else at Columbia to allow him to record a full-length jazz album and they finally relented. Later he recalled more details of that experience in an interview he gave to James Isaacs on June 24, 1986. "We were almost kicked out of the studio," Bennett remembered. "We were treated like you know, they treat rock-and-roll kids. They just said, 'These guys are crazy.'. . . [Mitch Miller] allowed me to do it. He didn't go for it. Chuck Wayne [the great guitarist] kind of put that whole album together, the arrangements and everything. . . .

Oh, I was nervous. . . . But, you know, years later Miles Davis told me that 'While the Music Plays On,' from that album, is his favorite song of mine. . . . Bobby Pratt, a wonderful piano player and trombonist, [brought it to me]. I used to sing that song in the club in Astoria . . . with [tenor saxophonist] Al Cohn, and Bobby Pratt was the piano player." He began the album in August 1954. One of Columbia's first twelve-inch long-playing records, *Cloud 7* was a "concept album" with a clear thematic center. Bennett gathered some of the best musicians on it, including Gene di Novi on piano, Al Cohn, alto saxophonist Davey Schildkraut, drummer Ed Shaughnessy, and, most importantly, Chuck Wayne. Wayne had formerly been with the Woody Herman band and an original member of the George Shearing Quintet.

Cloud 7 was recorded in August and December 1954, and released in February 1955. It was not a best seller, but a critical and artistic success of the highest order. It remains fresh and alive to this day. There are just seven musicians on most tracks: guitar, tenor sax, alto sax, drums, trumpet, bass, and piano, all playing with an understated grace.

The record begins with Bennett humming along to "I Fall in Love Too Easily," and then he begins singing the song with a graceful melancholy. What is astonishing about the song—and the entire album—is the similarity to the way Bennett sings today. What is fortunately missing is what Will Friedwald referred to as "that easily parodied early Bennett voice, which lisps, quivers excessively, and acts unsure of certain vowels." By remaining faithful to his original intentions, he has maintained a consistency of sound over sixty years. The songs, too, are among the songs he sometimes sings today, from "While the Music Plays On" to "My Reverie," "My Heart Tells Me," Old Devil Moon," and "Darn That Dream." The Bennett of this first album is no stranger to us; it is the Bennett we all know now, singing with simplicity, deep emotion, precise phrasing, and storytelling acumen. It was, from the start, as Ralph Sharon put it, "a voice with an identifiable sound, with a mature and compelling style."

Tony concluded 1955 with another album, *Alone at Last with Tony Bennett*, basically a collection of his successful singles, including "Sing You Sinners," "Somewhere along the Way," "Since My Love Has Gone," "Please Driver," "Stranger in Paradise," and "Here in My Heart."

Bennett's next album, *Tony*, appeared on January 14, 1957. With orchestrations by Gil Evans, Neal Hefti, Don Costa, and Marion Evans, it remains today one of the many glories of his catalog. The motif is romance, and the songs are lovingly chosen and beautifully rendered, including "It Had to Be You," "I Can't Give You Anything but Love," "Always," "Love Walked In," and two of his masterpieces, "I'll Be Seeing You" and "Lost in the Stars." The album is simply as fresh and beautiful today as when it was first recorded.

Assessing these early albums, Will Friedwald noted, "The only Bennett albums that work as well in toto as the classic Sinatra and Tormé albums come from the pre-'San Francisco' period, beginning with the small-group session *Cloud 7* (1955) and continuing up to the magnificent *Carnegie Hall* (1962) double set." Four albums from the early period win the prize as Bennett's best, two very small band sets with Ralph Sharon—*Tony Sings for Two* (1959) and *When Lights Are Low* (1964)—and two orchestral packages with Burns—*Hometown, My Town* (1959) and *My Heart Sings* (1961).

Ralph Sharon joined Tony in late 1956 as his accompanist after Chuck Wayne's departure, and it would be a fateful collaboration for many years to come. "Ralph Sharon, I sang with him for many years," Bennett said, "and he never played a wrong note for me, right through the years." Sharon had been born and raised in England, where he studied with George Shearing. He played at small clubs after the war along with Shearing, and at age twenty he was the original pianist with the Ted Heath Orchestra, England's leading big band. Shearing wrote in his autobiography, *Lullaby of Birdland*, that "He [Sharon] always played so well I wondered why he needed me, but he obviously thought he did."

Sharon had never heard of Bennett when he met him. He was dubious; he was a jazz musician and Bennett was a pop singer. "So I was skeptical," he recalled to journalist Dale Bridges. "I met this guy and he sang a few things and I played a few things. I thought, 'This guy sounds pretty good.' At the end, Bennett said, 'How'd you like to come with me?' I said, 'Come with you where?' He said, 'Everywhere.'" They were together for forty years, and the association would have an enormous impact on both of them. It was Sharon who urged Bennett to abandon the saccharine strings usually accompanying his ballads and to move into a more intimate jazz approach.

"Les Brown, who played with Tony in the Bob Hope engagement, heard Tony very, very early," Will Friedwald recalled. "He told me that Ralph Sharon was the one who was really able to help Tony with intonation. Not that he had bad intonation before, but really, in terms of pitch. I mean you can't listen to his records and hear him sing flat or anything. But Ralph was the one who really got him the intonation."

"I'm not bragging or anything," Sharon told Les Tomkins in 1988, "but it's true that I got Tony into jazz. He'll say that himself. I said, 'Why don't you do something with a jazz feeling?' and he found a whole new audience, and a whole new way to sing and phrase and to present himself. Now he couldn't be without it. The great thing is that it's returned to him—jazz musicians really look up to him. People like Miles Davis, Dizzy Gillespie, and all the great players are very highly approving of what he does."

"Ralph is sort of the other half of Tony's large body of work," John McDonough said. "Ralph was the musical foundation for Tony's singing," pianist George Shearing told me. "He had it all: sensitivity, touch, a well-grounded knowledge of music theory, and a sense of loyalty. Tony was, indeed, very fortunate in having Ralph onstage with him. Ralph enhanced his singing and total performance." Sinatra had Nelson Riddle, and while Sharon was not an arranger, in some ways he did for Bennett what Riddle did for Sinatra: he contributed a musical underpinning that enhanced Bennett's singing in a magical way.

"Ralph Sharon just had to hit a few notes for me to know he was the piano player for me," Tony wrote in his memoir. "Hooking up with Ralph was one of the best career moves I've ever made. No one understands me more than he does . . . he really knows how to perform with a singer or a soloist. He doesn't show off like a lot of other guys, playing lots of extra notes or fancy runs. After all, it's the emotion behind the music that's important. It takes a special person to support a performer and make him look good." The first collaboration with Sharon would last ten years; it was resumed later, and continued through 2000, when the relationship ended, apparently for good. With

Sharon's emphasis on a more intimate sound, Bennett often played now with just a trio of Sharon, Billy Exiner on drums, and Don Payne on bass.

Bennett's first recording session with Sharon was singing a song he really hated, "In the Middle of an Island," by Nick Acquaviva and Ted Varnick. The song was forced on him by Mitch Miller. Miller's commercial instincts, at least, were sound. The record hit the top ten. Bennett had the solace of having Ralph Sharon in his corner, urging him to diversify and to do the unexpected. "You can have six hits in a row," Sharon told him, "but if you keep doing the same thing over and over, the public will eventually stop buying your records."

"Ralph said to me, 'Make sure you do some jazz,'" Tony told Robert Sullivan. "Ralph knew how much I loved jazz."

Bennett told *Billboard* in 1968, "I prefer the way the jazz artists work, and this is one of the things I've learned over the years from guys like Bobby Hackett. The way you feel it is the way it comes out, and it's never the same way twice. That's the way I like to sing, as if I just picked up the lead sheet for the first time and the tune struck me. It's the same way a jazz combo wings it, following the melody line. As they say, 'playing in between the notes.' You never have to ask jazz musicians to play with more feeling. That's what they're most concerned with."

Sharon and Bennett decided to make a major jazz statement in Bennett's next album. The result was Tony's triumph, *The Beat of My Heart*, which Tony recorded throughout 1957 and released on December 9 of that year. Will Friedwald calls it "the hippest of his small-jazz group records," in which Bennett and Sharon formulated the unique concept of an album of standards that paired Bennett with six major jazz drummers on different tracks. Bennett recruited an extraordinary group of jazz stars for the album, including Nat Adderley, Milt Hinton, Al Cohn, Chico Hamilton, Jo Jones, Kai Winding, Eddie Costa, Herbie Mann, and two major Latin American artists, Sabu and Candido. He won an expanded audience of jazz fans with this album, earning him the title of pop-jazz vocalist.

"Ralph Sharon was responsible for that [album]," Bennett told James Isaacs. ". . . When we did [the album], all of a sudden I acquired this whole new audience. Everybody said, 'Hey, wait a minute, this syrupy singer with strings can sing jazz.' . . . *The Beat of My Heart* really substantiated my career. From that moment the jazz audience accepted me. Not as a jazz singer, necessarily, but nobody says, 'What is this guy doing at a jazz concert?' Bill Evans and I did the opening Carnegie Hall concert at the Newport Jazz Festival one year. So [the album] showed that I wasn't just a ballad singer anymore. I wasn't predictable. That album gave me that famous word that Johnny Carson loves so much, 'longevity.'" Probably the outstanding cut on the album was "Lazy Afternoon," from the Off Broadway show *The Golden Apple*, lyrics and music by John Latouche and Jerome Moross, with Bennett accompanied by John Pisano on guitar, James Bond on bass, Chico Hamilton on drums, and Sharon on piano. It is Hamilton who dramatically creates the tropical, humid, torrid, and sensuous atmosphere of the song.

There were many fun times with Sharon, as he could be something of a prankster. The late Dee Anthony often told of the time when Tony was playing the Mogambo on the West Coast in the late 1950s, and Judy Garland was in the audience. Sharon found Tony's drummer, Billy Exiner, in the kitchen crushing croutons. He solemnly suggested to Exiner that when Tony sang "God Bless the Child" and reached the line "Rich relations give you crusts of bread and such . . . you can have your fill," Exiner should take the crumbs and just throw them out to create an effect onstage.

Tony was deep into the song, and when he sang "Rich relations give you crusts" the crumbs came falling down. There was dead silence. Tony looked as if he was going to have a fit. But Judy Garland started to laugh—that wonderful laugh of hers—and the whole place broke up with laughter. And Tony broke up. And he looked right at Ralph.

Bennett returned with great success to the Copacabana in February 1957. Writing in the February 20 *New York Journal-American*, Gene Knight said that Bennett was "a vastly improved showman. What I like especially about Tony is that he doesn't waste time cracking wise, nor explaining what he's going to do. He just goes ahead and sings the best he can. Bennett is an agreeable singer when he croons (although I think he occasionally [emphasizes] the beat too much).

He's capital when he hits the high register with plenty of volume. And he's excellent when he snaps into a rhythmic number.

"Then he has the audience clapping hands in union, sometimes even singing with him. But it's better he shouldn't dance. . . . He begged off with them yelling: 'More, more!' Could have sung all night for this audience, judging by the applause . . . because this Tony Bennett, he is a crowd-pleaser."

"I got involved with Tony doing his first act at the Copacabana," arranger, orchestrator, and composer Marion Evans recalled. "When he opened at the Copa in the early 50s, I did eighteen arrangements [for his act]. I also wrote several that turned out to be very big records for Tony. One was 'One for My Baby.'

"Tony had an incredible sixth sense about the kind of things he should do and the way he should do them. Other people would try to get him to do things a certain way and he just wouldn't do them. I remember one time at the recording studio we had an elaborate introduction and big orchestra. Tony looked at me and he said, 'I don't need all that to sell a record.'

"I put Tony on the same level as Sinatra. He just has a total natural voice. And he's got wonderful ears; he's got wonderful musical instincts." Evans learned that Bennett insisted on improvisation: "Tony liked to do things where you would actually have to follow him. I'm standing, I'm looking at him eyeball to eyeball. I'm conducting the orchestra. In most cases everybody sort of goes along; you feel where the next downbeat is coming from. You can usually hear because they're holding a vowel, and as the singer starts to close the vowel, you sense that's where the next consonant is going to be. So you go for the next downbeat and usually everybody goes along together. But one of the things I quickly learned about Tony was that if I anticipated that, I could be wrong; he wouldn't necessarily be there. He was going to do it his way. In his mind, the way he wanted to sing the lyrics and the music was that everybody else had to follow along.

"So I learned quickly to wait until he said the next word, then I gave the downbeat. So I wound up literally following him. Every time Tony would do a song, he would do it differently. And you could not anticipate when he was going to sing the next word. You just could not do it. Tony got to where he liked to do a lot of things out of tempo with the orchestra. That's the way he is. And I can't say he's wrong. Because as Frank said, he did it his way. And he just has a total natural voice. And he's got marvelous ears; he's got wonderful musical instincts."

Evans alluded to an erraticism that many musicians experienced with Bennett. "He can be really spacey. He can be very different on Tuesday than he was on Monday. But he's a very nice guy. But you could be talking to him and he'll be on a subject you never heard of; like how the hell did we get there? I mean sometimes he's a pain in the ass to work with. He's like off the cuff: 'Let's take that out!'

"'Take what out, Tony?'

"'You know, that stuff. Take it out.'

"'What the hell are you talking about?' Then you take it out and he says, 'I don't like that. Put it back in.' If you know him well, you can usually get a sense of what it is he doesn't like. But he can't tell you. He can't say 'Take the B flat out of the third trumpet;' he has no idea about that. You have to sort of monitor it. And if you know him real well, you get a sense of what's bothering him.

"Once he said to Torrie Zito [Tony's accompanist for many years], 'No more minor chords.' André Previn wrote a book with that title when he was at MGM. Irving Thalberg was the head of the whole operation and he sent an interoffice communication to the music department and said that effective immediately the music department will no longer use minor chords. That's probably where Tony got it from.

"But when it comes to performing, he's a *great* performer."

Entering the ninth year of the decade that had first launched him, Bennett had already staked out a unique space for himself as a truly innovative, defiant (with a winning smile), indefatigable, and courageous artist who held his ground and refused to betray the musical heritage he loved. "It is very rare," said Nat Hentoff, "in popular music for an artist over a long period of time to have remained true to himself and kept growing within that integrity. Tony Bennett is such a rarity." He was becoming a transcendent artist. And he had fulfilled his dream of making the transition from singles artist to album artist. He had adhered so fiercely to his goals that, Will Friedwald writes,

"Bennett made a ceaseless apostle for 'the tradition,' never missing an opportunity to wave the flag for hard-core jazz, from Louis Armstrong to Miles Davis, on the one hand, and the Broadway showbiz world of Merman, Garland, and Durante on the other, with the jazz-pop faction of big bands and their singers running down the middle, all interacting in Bennett's own music."

Tony concluded 1958 with two fine albums, *Blue Velvet* and *Long Ago and Far Away*, arranged by Frank De Vol, and a compilation of hit singles, *Tony's Greatest Hits*. But he would finish out the decade with two smashing achievements in recording. First he fearlessly took on the Count Basie orchestra and produced his first landmark collaboration with Basie, *In Person! Tony Bennett, Count Basie and His Orchestra*, recorded on November 20, 1958, and then he conceived the amazing *Hometown, My Town*, recorded on July 13, 1959.

It had been a dream of Bennett's to perform with Count Basie and Duke Ellington. Tony made two albums with Basie. The first album would be recorded live at the Latin Casino in Philadelphia, with orchestrations and arrangements by Ralph Sharon. During a recording session Basie turned to his band, pointed at Bennett, and said, "Anything this man wants, he gets!" Bennett was stunned. The personal and professional relationship with Basie would last for twenty-five years to the end of Basie's life. One of Bennett's favorite lines is the one Basie uttered to him when Bennett asked him whether he should change his basic style. "Some of my friends were trying to sing rock," he told Robert Sullivan, "and I didn't know what to do. Basie told me in that sly, wise way of his, 'Why change an apple?'"

Bennett and Basie opened at the Latin Casino on November 28, 1958, and the album *In person! Tony Bennett, Count Basie and His Orchestra* was released in early 1959. Al Ham, the producer, was dissatisfied with the concert's being recorded in mono when stereo recording was finally available, so the album was rerecorded in the studio in stereo, with manufactured crowd noise and applause to give it a live feel. According to Bennett, Ham placed the audience applause in the wrong places and the result was a mess. Bennett has remained partial to a second album he recorded with Basie, in 1961, for Roulette Records, *Count Basie/Tony Bennett: Strike Up the Band*.

Nevertheless, the first Bennett/Basie album is a gem, with great performances of "Just In Time," "When I Fall in Love," and two absolute standouts— a wild, totally original "Firefly," by Cy Coleman and Carolyn Leigh ("Wants none of that noon glow; she starts to shimmer when the sun goes down . . .") that lasts exactly one minute and thirty-six seconds. Bennett rips into this swinging two-beat number with joy and gusto in a semi-Dixieland style, Frank Wess performing the flute fills behind Tony's vocal. Bennett literally re-creates the dancing firefly in front of your eyes. "Lost in the Stars," by Kurt Weill and Maxwell Anderson, is the song of a black minister when he learns that his son is guilty of a crime. Bennett sings it hymnlike with great depth of feeling.

Bennett was thrilled to be working with Basie. Louis Bellson had described Basie's band and Ellington's band as the two pillars of jazz. Bennett quoted Bellson, "Basie is the earth and Ellington is the universe."

Harry Belafonte was present many times when Bennett sang with Basie, and told Clint Eastwood, "No white man ever stood in front of a black crew and sang with more credentials and belonging."

Asked about some of the short tracks on the Basie album, some of them not much more than a minute, Bennett responded, "Well, if a song is well written, why do it twice? . . . I mean, that's it. It's not like a novel that goes on for a thousand pages before you find out the butler did it. If you have 'These Foolish Things'—a tinkling piano in the next apartment, right away you get it, this whole story that people can identify with. They all understand that." ("Somebody asked Jerome Kern about 'Lovely to Look At,'" Jonathan Schwartz told me. "It's a short song, shorter than the usual. Someone asked him why that was. And Kern said, 'That's all I had to say.' And I would apply that to Tony as regards many of his songs.")

The album, like *Beat of My Heart*, helped to accomplish what he had sought for years: the recognition of the sophisticated jazz audience. Soon after Bennett came up with a stream of quality hit singles: Cy Coleman's "The Best Is Yet to Come," Johnny Mercer's "I Wanna Be Around," "The Good Life," "Watch What Happens, and two songs by Leslie Bricusse: "Who Can I Turn To?" and "If I Ruled the World."

Bennett had ended the decade with the astounding *Hometown, My Town*, a symphonically expnded jazz-pop fusion arranged and orchestrated by Ralph Burns. It was released on July 13, 1959. Will Friedwald dubs it "Bennett's most Sinatra-Riddle-like effort . . . opening up each of the six songs to 'Something Cool'-like proportions." The album is a musical portrait of New York City with extended performances of six songs that describe life in Manhattan on a conceptual level. Whatever conventional traditions Bennett had broken with thus far—including being the first singer to make an album mostly with percussion instruments in *The Beat of My Heart* —nothing could have prepared his audience for this album, which breaks so many rules and is surely one of the greatest triumphs of his career.

Hometown is a collection of six superb songs that fit together as if into a suite. The best of them, "Penthouse Serenade," by Will Jason and Val Burton, experiments with song form itself, being more than six minutes long and a masterpiece. The song, like all the others, has a long vocal by Bennett followed by longer instrumental portions and jazz solos, with Bennett's presence floating over it, more verses, and specially written melodies and lyrics framed by a rich, lush orchestral sound. "Penthouse" frames the album with its vivid depiction of a romanticized Manhattan ("Picture a penthouse high in the sky . . . with hinges on chimneys for stars to go by"). It is impossible to think of the album without identifying it with that one song, but all of the songs reflected a New York mood even when they did not refer directly to Manhattan. The album also includes "By Myself" by Arthur Schwartz and Harold Dietz, "The Party's Over" by Betty Comden, Adolph Green, and Jule Styne, "Our Love Is Here to Stay" by the Gershwin brothers, and Johnny Green and Edward Heyman's "I Cover the Waterfront." All of the songs were recorded at the church on East Thirtieth Street in Manhattan on November 3, 4, and 6, 1958. Far less known today than Bennett's ode to San Francisco, it will endure as a quintessential tribute to New York City and as a great work of musical art.

Bennett fully understood the implications of what he was doing. He had told Ralph Burns, "This was to be an album with no limitations." That is a perfect definition of what he accomplished. This was not to be an album with three-minute pop tunes. Bennett often talks of the atmosphere of musical excitement that filled Manhattan in the late 1950s and early 1960s, the influx of brilliant musicians such as Al Cohn, Urbie Green, and Zoot Sims, who came off the road and were working in the city. *Hometown* was meant to symbolically capture that New York scene. Bennett took it all in. He was an appreciator. He loved them all, and they came to love him.

But with the dominance of rock and roll, his records were no longer on the charts. However, due to his television and radio appearances and the grueling and "long and winding road" of his nightclub appearances around the country, his records were still in the black, and Columbia, for the moment, was allowing him the freedom he needed.

The sources of Bennett's inspiration for *Hometown, My Town* are characteristic of the modus operandi of his entire career. He is a witness, observing the creative ferment of his time and the artists and musicians whom he deeply loves and studies and aspires to be like. That creative ferment, for him, is linked to the magical, lyrical, pro-creative qualities of New York City. And he is a totally committed participant, as well. He strives to do his best work at all times, trying to stretch, to grow, to give everything that is in him, to proceed with absolute integrity no matter what the cost.

"He is not a commercial animal at all," Jonathan Schwartz told me. "Yes, he loves to sell records. It makes money, puts bread on the table. But what it does is afford him the privilege of continuing to record. That is most important to him. To get his voice down on the record on these songs."

And so he created this magnificent album with no limitations.

Tony at the London Palladium, 1970.

Tony at Alice Tully Hall, Lincoln Center, New York City, 1972.

Tony in Las Vegas, 1972.

Tony at the Las Vegas Hilton, 1972.

Tony in Las Vegas, 1972.

Tony and Count Basie at the Las Vegas Hilton, 1972.

Tony and Derek Boulton, Tony's manager, in Las Vegas, 1972.

6

Out of the Commonplace into the Rare

In the early '60s," Will Friedwald wrote, "Tony Bennett ascended out of the commonplace and into the rare. That's an exaggeration. Earlier, Bennett's constantly developing combination of soul and smarts had already put considerable distance between him and his competition. But only in this period did Bennett land in the pantheon of the immortals, the Sinatras, the Fitzgeralds (either Ella or F. Scott) and the Armstrongs."

David Hajdu and Roy Hemming echoed this assessment. By the turn of the decade, they wrote, Bennett started refining the style that would distinguish him for the rest of his career. "Bennett was employing a range of vocal textures and techniques rarely used in his big, full-bodied performances under Mitch Miller," they stated. "He began letting more throat and head tones through, coloring his voice with natural character: there was some of the rasp that would practically consume his tone twenty-five years later. He manipulated his range, adding tension by stretching far above his natural baritone.

126

His phrasing became more conversational, betraying his admitted debt to Mabel Mercer."

Bennett had recorded one classic album after another in the 1950s: *Cloud 7*; *Tony*; *The Beat of My Heart*; *Hometown, My Town*; *Tony Sings for Two* with Ralph Sharon; the two Basie albums. *Tony Sings for Two* ventured boldly in at least two directions: it featured only Tony and his pianist, Ralph Sharon, and it included one of Bennett's trademarks: the art of brevity.

During those years, Bennett made his first, long-awaited trip to Italy, appearing with Count Basie. "The first time he went to Italy," Marion Evans told me, "they didn't know who Tony Bennett was. They didn't know who Count Basie was. And when they said he was a singer, they were looking for a Pavarotti, you know. So the band comes out and Tony starts singing, and boy, they just barely got out of the town alive. They were throwing rocks and everything at him. They wanted to hear Puccini. Later on, of course, he was loved."

Bennett's output, as it would be for fifty and more future years, was simply astonishing. He continued to produce singles for the jukeboxes, but with the albums he had entered a different and higher realm. The commercial 45 rpm format hobbled and constrained him; it kept him from singing "without limitations," as he had put it to Ralph Burns. One can only compare the uninspired single of "Firefly" with a goofy background chorus (recorded August 11, 1958) to the alive and vibrant "Firefly" (recorded November 28, 1958) of his first Count Basie album to see how Bennett flourished when he was free to let his creative instincts take flight.

Yet with the advent of the 1960s, Bennett soon was matching the excellence of his albums with splendid singles that found their way to honored places on his albums. The list is dizzying: "The Best Is Yet to Come," "I Wanna Be Around," "Till," "Put On a Happy Face," "Tender Is the Night," "The Good Life," "Spring in Manhattan," "This Is All I Ask," "True Blue Lou," "Limehouse Blues," "Don't Wait Too Long," "When Joanna Loved Me," "A Taste of Honey," "Who Can I Turn To?," "If I Ruled the World," "Fly Me to the Moon," "The Shadow of Your Smile," "I'll Only Miss Her When I Think of Her," "The Very Thought of You," "Keep Smiling at Trouble," "For Once in

My Life," "A Fool of Fools," and "Yesterday I Heard the Rain" among them. And, of course, "I Left My Heart in San Francisco." Some of these got lost and await their place in the pantheon: "True Blue Lou" is an old-time music hall romp in the "My Gal Sal" vein that has delight and mischief in it. "A Fool of Fools" is a belter that raises the rooftops. (It was written by Joe Meyer and Mann Curtis, two old-timers. Meyer, who was seventy-four at the time, was the composer of "California, Here I Come," "My Honey's Lovin' Arms," and "If You Knew Susie.") "Limehouse Blues" is done with aching tenderness and slowness, burnishing the lyrics in a totally original and unique way. His new albums were superb as well: *My Heart Sings* and *Mr. Broadway*.

Bennett was a bull; nothing stopped him. He just never gave up or gave in; he kept swimming against the current no matter the cost.

And the cost was considerable in those years. The Beatles appeared in 1964 and "the musical world," said Stan Martin, who was with New York's WNEW-AM in the 1960s, "was never the same again." The Beatles had nineteen singles in the top forty of 1964. By then some of the major singers, including Della Reese, Dakota Staton, Johnny Hartman, Steve Lawrence and Eydie Gorme, and Kay Starr, were beginning to lose major-label contracts. The only Italians in the top forty were the young Dion and Bobby Darin. This did not make the veteran Italian balladeers extinct: they still had their major niches and they still sold records. But it was a new world, and Bennett's record sales continued to decline. There were fewer hit singles, and his album sales were disappointing. Columbia was not pleased, and he knew it.

Bob Taylor, who was a programmer at WNEW-AM when the music industry was undergoing these seismic shifts, noted that "good singers like Steve Lawrence and Vic Damone weren't becoming big like Sinatra and Nat 'King' Cole, and it was not because of lack of voice. Music just changed." Despite a cultural sea change, some of the traditional ballad singers were continuing to break through. Sinatra, Dean Martin, and Sammy Davis Jr. were not suffering—nor were Darin or Louis Prima. Nor, for a time, was Bennett. "Keep in mind," Bob Taylor said, "Tony Bennett came out in the 1950s and made it, and he's one of the finest singers of all time. And he's still going."

Still, the early 1960s started falteringly for Bennett. He appeared in a stage revival of *Guys and Dolls* in Chicago, playing the role of Sky Masterton. He had his eye on Broadway in those days, and had previously appeared at the end of the 1950s in a revival of *Silk Stockings* in Kansas City.

"Before his really big hit 'I Left My Heart in San Francisco,'" wrote Will Friedwald, "he had drawing power enough to be granted the chance to do a few art records, and for a few years Columbia borrowed the Sinatra/Capitol pattern of making commercial music for singles while putting the classier stuff on LPs, so many of Bennett's first twelve-inch releases contained exclusively standards. Several also used adventurous jazz and small-group settings, and one (*Hometown, My Town*) went so far as to experiment with song form itself. But Bennett had to pay for the opportunities to make these. 'Before I recorded "San Francisco,"' he said several years later, 'I was advised to try out all sorts of tricks and gimmicks. Songs were offered to me which were supposed to be surefire, but they weren't my style.'"

Yet the 1960s would soon prove to be boon years for Bennett. He was successfully navigating the rounds of the TV shows, including a fine appearance on the *Steve Allen Show* in 1960. Accompanied by the Ralph Sharon Quintet and featuring soloist Bobby Hackett, Bennett did dynamic versions of "Just in Time," "Mam'selle," "Lullaby of Broadway," and "This Could Be the Start of Something Big." On "Mam'selle" (which he does beautifully on his *Tony Sings for Two* album with Ralph Sharon), he cedes a long section of the song. He doesn't sing the lines "Your lovely eyes seem to sparkle just like wine does / No heart ever yearns as much as mine does for you." Instead he just has the spotlight on Bobby Hackett, who plays a magnificent solo (as he does on Bennett's immortal recording of "The Very Thought of You," perhaps the slowest version of that song ever recorded; Bennett is relishing the song and giving space to Hackett).

Bennett starred on three episodes of *77 Sunset Strip*, made a guest appearance with Danny Thomas on *Make Room for Daddy*, and appeared many times on Hugh Hefner's *Playboy after Dark* and *Playboy Penthouse*. Appearing with Louis Bellson, Tony sang "It Don't Mean a Thing" and "Watch What Happens" and dueted with Joe Williams on "I've Gotta Be Me," "What the World Needs Now," and "Rags to Riches."

Early in 1962, two self-created miracles happened for Bennett: a concert and a song. The concert came about because of Sid Bernstein, who would soon bring the Beatles to America. It is commonly thought that the huge success of "I Left My Heart in San Francisco" catapulted Bennett to Carnegie Hall, but in Sid Bernstein's telling, although the song had already been released, it had reached about eighty on the charts and fallen off. It was the Carnegie Hall concert that jolted the Columbia Records brass into really promoting the song. Bernstein had just joined the General Artists Corporation (GAC), second only to the William Morris Agency for representing major talent. Bennett also was a member of GAC. "From the time I was a kid," Bernstein told me, "I was a sucker for pop singers. Tony became my longtime favorite. And I watched him. I knew him from the street, from the Brill Building, Hanson's, from the neighborhood. I don't know if I shook his hand more than once or twice. It was only a handshake, a wave. He didn't know what a fan of his I was. Then he comes up to see me in 1961. He said, 'I read in *Variety* that you were joining GAC.'

"I was like a private there; he was telling me like I was one of the big shots. He takes me to lunch and he said, 'I'm leaving the agency, I'm leaving my lawyer, I'm leaving my accountant.' He was even leaving his wife, Sandy One [Patricia]. Despondent. A down moment. He tells me he hasn't appeared on the *Ed Sullivan Show* in three years. The agency is still getting him jobs at nightclubs, saloons where they serve dishes while he's on the stage. 'There's no respect,' he tells me.

"Everybody in the restaurant recognizes him. Yet he's feeling like a real has-been. We finish lunch. He says, 'Sid, what do you think?' Here I am a private. What do I think? He must have had an opinion of me, I don't know how. I hadn't done much that was notable yet. I did do the Newport Jazz Festival the year before; that was probably it. I said, 'Tony, let me think about what you said.' My favorite singer, and I'm a real softy. I'm feeling real bad for him. Leaving his wife. Young girl who probably was a big fan of his. She fell in love with him. Because he had a *shteger,* a way about him. Young women could fall in love with a crooner. Not a bad-looking guy. With an awful wig. I'm so upset for him. So despond[ent]. I'm sad. And I'm thinking. Tony said, 'Sid, I'd like to talk to you again.' I said, 'Tony, let me give it some thought.' He said, 'I'd like to come and say hello to you again. I'll come by at six.'

"I was so upset with him that during the day I called this guy from Austria, Jewish guy who escaped Hitler and became the promoter at Carnegie Hall for current acts. Felix Grossman. He said, 'Sidney, I like you very much. But the man hasn't had a hit lately. Nobody will come.' He turns me down. I then call Bill Drummond, who started the Forest Hills concerts. 'Sid, he's had nothing for years. Forest Hills is twelve thousand seats. How are you going to fill it?' I can't convince him. I call Bill Gallagher, who takes care of Tony at Columbia. He says, 'He's a pain in the ass; get him off my back. Hasn't had a hit in years.'

Tony arrived at six. Bernstein acted from instinct, as he would do with the Beatles, whom he'd never seen when they arrived in the States. He told Tony that he wanted him to play Carnegie Hall. Since he was no longer a promoter, but an agent, he was not allowed to do promotions. Bennett would have to finance the concert. He assured Bennett he would get his money back.

Bennett was intrigued, and asked Bernstein what it would cost. Bernstein said it would only involve deposit money for Carnegie Hall: two thousand dollars. Bernstein had credit for posters and would print large numbers of them. He would take out ads in the three big New York dailies. But he stipulated that he wanted three hundred tickets—the Carnegie Hall seating was 2,836—to give away to everyone working at Columbia Records: the mailboys, the operators, the switchboards. He wanted to give them two tickets each, one for their boyfriends or girlfriends. He would scale the prices for the rest of the tickets so that Tony would come out even.

"He gives me the check for the two thousand," Bernstein said. "He didn't need a check for the posters or the advertising, because of my credit. The billing went to me. I'm a personable guy. You don't realize that? I didn't loan him the money; I got the okay."

Bernstein booked Carnegie Hall, picked a June date, and went to work. He had the posters printed and placed the ads. He priced the tickets low. Bernstein and his future wife, Geri, went to every Italian neighborhood, including Westchester, putting up posters.

"Sniping: putting them up on the wall," he explained. Tony wanted comic Henny Youngman to open the concert. Youngman, a friend of Bernstein's, signed on. "I got a small orchestra," Bernstein said. "And I'm sniping." The posters and ads started having an effect, especially with Italians. "The old man, Nat Poznick, at Carnegie Hall was known as the dean of box offices. I used to bug him every day. 'Any sales?' Finally he says, 'I think you're going to have a sellout. It's slow but it's very steady.'

"Tony comes out," Bernstein recalled. "He gets a roar from the crowd. All Italians. Nobody yells 'Hey, Tony!' like an Italian does. I'm sure there were a few Jews and blacks, too, who liked him. He sings like there's no tomorrow. The next day the reviews break. He calls me up. 'Sid, you're not gonna believe it. I just got a call from the *Ed Sullivan Show*. They want me on the program.' So my bosses gave me a raise. Because Tony stopped bugging them about a release. 'Sid,' they said, 'he was going to leave us. From now on when we get bookings, you'll handle them.' So I became what's called the responsible agent for Tony Bennett. I got him out of saloons. He was doing concerts now. So I've done my job. Now they paid attention to the record of 'San Francisco.' The record shoots up and becomes what it is today.

"A couple of years later: I'm broke. I'm now married; I have a kid. Maybe 1965. We're still friends. Rarely do we speak. I go to Tony: 'I want to do a concert with you,' I said. 'What will it cost me?' Tony said, 'Sid, get me a good band.' To me a good band was someone like Count Basie. I get Tony Count Basie. Sold out. Tony's a star again. After the show I go backstage to pay him. We had not discussed the money yet. I think I made about eight or ten thousand after all expenses. I'm responsible to Tony, Basie, and the ads, of course. I said to Tony, 'What do I owe you?' He said, 'Sid, what are you talking about?' I said, 'I owe you money. I did well tonight.' 'Sid, I didn't ask you for money. I asked you to get me a good band.' It cost me zero. My mother was crippled; I moved her out of the Bronx for that money, took her down to the Village where I lived, next door, got her a full-time nurse." Bernstein paused and said, "Tony. Not a dime."

Tony played Carnegie Hall on a summer night on June 19, 1962, and made musical history. The program was staged by director Arthur

Penn, whom Tony had met in the army, and Broadway director Gene Saks. The musicians included Ralph Sharon, Candido (who played a mesmerizing solo in the middle of the nine-minute-long spiritual "Glory Road"—suggested by Tony Tamburello—that climaxed the concert), Al Cohn, Frank Rehak, Sabu, Billy Exiner, Eddie Costa, Bobby Rosengarten, Joe Soldo, Kenny Burrell, and Nick Travis. Tony Tamburello coordinated everything. "I put everything I'd been studying for the last twenty years into practice for that show," Tony wrote. Tony warmed up for the concert by jamming every night in Chicago on Rush Street in different clubs with Jon Hendricks of the jazz vocal trio Lambert, Hendricks, and Ross. Tony's mother and whole family were in the audience that night; it was the greatest night of his life, and it would turn into his greatest year—thus far.

"That was the night Tony Bennett became Tony Bennett," Jonathan Schwartz told me. "From there on in, he was a novelist rather than a short story teller. A short story teller is someone who makes hit records. The Carnegie Hall concert album *Tony Bennett at Carnegie Hall* (August 24, 1962) is a 'novel.' He sang forty-four songs. There are a couple of little mistakes on it which I once brought to his attention, and he said, 'No, I just wanted to put it out the way it happened.' Which is typical of him. For example, when he sings 'All the Things You Are,' the line should be 'trembles on the brink.' Tony sang 'lingers.' I remember questioning that because I cherish that lyric. And he sang it incorrectly. And he made a joke and said, 'Maybe because I was so nervous I didn't want to sing 'trembling.' It was near the top of the show, perhaps the second song. That was his answer, which is so charming and good. It's funny even if it's not true, you know."

"I played at his Carnegie Hall concert and I was the contractor on it," Joe Soldo told me. "He gave me a full list of jazz players that he wanted for that album. But Tony was the kind of guy who liked musicians so much, he'd be walking down Broadway and see somebody, a trombone player. And the player would say, 'Hey, Tony, I read that you're going to do a Carnegie Hall concert.' 'Yeah,' Tony would say, 'call Joe Soldo and he'll put you on.' Meanwhile, Tony had already given me four trombones. He'd already given me the whole band. But that was the way Tony was. He loved all of the players. He didn't want to say no, that the whole band was hired. So I would get calls from these guys: 'I saw Tony, Tony said I could do it.' He was very warm.

"Oh, man, that concert was so exciting. He was so good then. I mean his first special at Carnegie Hall! It was wonderful. His career opened up so much.

"We played the Waldorf, and he made sure that we had a room to ourselves that was one of the full hotel rooms and that there was liquor there for the guys. He did the same thing at the Copacabana. The Copa had the Hotel 14 next door, a kind of run-down place. But we all had a room there, too. Because the people at the Copa hated musicians, and we didn't even have a place to change. Tony did that. The music stands at the Copa had a flat kind of top. During the last show, Tony had the waiters bring champagne to us. They came with glasses, put them on all of the tops, and served the band during the show. That is the way he was. He really loved the musicians."

John S. Wilson reviewed the June concert at Carnegie Hall in the *New York Times*. The review was distinctly a minority opinion, for it was highly critical of Bennett's singing abilities. The positive part of the review was more focused on Bennett's showmanship, style, performance, and execution than on his singing voice. It was hardly a rave, but somehow it added up in the end to grudging approval. "Tony Bennett," Wilson wrote, "a singer with the sharply curved profile of a genial Punch puppet, last night at Carnegie Hall gave a deft demonstration of how to achieve a great deal with very little. The voice that is the basic tool of Mr. Bennett's trade is small, thin and somewhat hoarse, but he uses it shrewdly and with a skillful lack of pretension. In most cases he talked his songs as much as he sang them. And, except for a very occasional climactic change of pace, he made no effort to sustain notes, allowing his accompanying orchestra to fill in large areas where his contribution was only token. Yet on this seemingly shallow basis, Mr. Bennett managed to construct an extremely effective performance. His program, made up of what he calls his 'saloon songs,' the songs he customarily features in his nightclub appearances, was unusually well chosen, ranging in time from the decades-old 'Toot Toot Tootsie' to several selections from *Little Me*, a musical that opened in New York last week. Mr. Bennett also drew judiciously from the works of Cole Porter, Jerome Kern,

Richard Rodgers, Irving Berlin and Harold Arlen. The program moved swiftly and with a keen sense of pace, for Mr. Bennett rarely lingered over a song for more than a verse and chorus, and offered a constantly changing variety of moods. Polish was in evidence everywhere, a clean precision of the orchestra conducted by Ralph Sharon, Mr. Bennett's pianist, in the simple but effective lighting and in the easy manner in which Mr. Bennett first warmed up his audience and drew it to him. Listened to objectively, Mr. Bennett is not much of a singer, but he is a first rate entertainer with a thoroughly professional presentation."

Whatever Wilson's reservations, they were not shared by almost anyone else. The night was a huge triumph. Bennett said he told himself, "'That's it.' It was like going to heaven."

The other triumph that year changed Bennett's career forever. The story behind "I Left My Heart in San Francisco" by now is legend. Ralph Sharon originally shared it with British journalist Les Tomkins in 1988: "I had two friends in New York [George Cory and Douglas Cross] who used to write songs—some of them were children's songs that were published for schools and things like that. They did have one tune that Pearl Bailey recorded years ago. But they kept showing me these tunes [to show Tony] that I'd look at and say, 'Well, this is very nice, but it's not the kind of thing for Tony.' One day they gave me a song, and I didn't even look at it. I put it away in a [clothing] drawer and forgot all about it.

"About a year later, we were going on a tour, and I was looking through a drawer for some shirts, pulled this sheet out, and it said, 'I Left My Heart in San Francisco.' So I thought, 'Well, we're going to San Francisco; I'll just put this in my case.' I still didn't look at it.

"We got to Hot Springs, Arkansas, which is in the middle of nowhere; I took a look at this song, played it, and said to Tony, 'It might be a good idea to do a song like this when we're in San Francisco.' I played it for him, in the saloon bar of the hotel. There was a bartender standing there, and he said, 'If you record that, I'll buy it!' So we thought, 'Well, that's good.' And Tony performed the song in San Francisco, and it was very well received.

"But he thought, and I thought, too: singing a song like that in San Francisco is just asking for applause, but it's just a hometown song.

Tony was still with Columbia at the time, and the local man came in; he said, 'You know if you record that, you're guaranteed at least good sales here.' It took a few months to finally record it, and it was done as a B [the less important] side.

"Mitch Miller said [indifferently]: 'Well, you know if you want to do that, throw it in.'" The A side was 'Once upon a Time,' which was a very pretty song from a Broadway show called *All American*. Bennett was positive that 'Once upon a Time' was the surefire hit. Well, that [was how it happened]; it was put out. I called these two fellows [the composers] and said, 'Tony's just recorded your song.' They went crazy. But it took two or three years for it to actually hit. What happened was other singers picked it up and started singing it and then it became a worldwide hit [for Tony].

"It's Tony's signature tune now, and everything else. Yet it was a complete accident. If I hadn't looked for that shirt in that drawer, it would never have happened."

"The important thing," Bennett wrote in retrospect, "was that I loved the song, and that meant more to me than how well it would sell in one market or another."

Arranger Marty Manning recast the song for a recording, and it was recorded at the church on Thirtieth Street on January 23, 1962. Requests came pouring in from all over the country for the song. The momentum was gradual, as Sid Bernstein pointed out; Columbia did not spend much money promoting it.

Tony received a call from Goddard Lieberson, who prophetically said, "You're never going to stop hearing about 'San Francisco' for the rest of your life. As long as you keep singing, you'll be singing this song." The song won Bennett his first two Grammy awards in 1962 for Best Male Vocal Performance and Record of the Year and became a gold record; it remained on the charts for twenty-five months, although it never reached number one. Ultimately it would become the biggest record of his entire career, selling more than two million copies.

"It was the kind of record that can float an entire career," wrote Gary Giddins. "It did not crown the charts; it just hung around forever. . . . The power of Bennett's perfect verse-and-single chorus on

'I Left My Heart in San Francisco' is derived not from an image of little cable cars climbing halfway to the stars, but from the uninterrupted emotional arc that builds gradually from an appealing melody (stroked by a hokey piano obbligato) to an ascension so juiced with its own fervor that when it's over you feel as though you've been on a trip, and it wasn't to San Francisco. Still, Bennett believes in—or makes us believe that he believes in—those little cable cars."

It was clear that night at Carnegie Hall that the song had an indelible impact on audiences. "When he did 'San Francisco,'" Mary Chiappa would remember, "the people just cheered and cheered and kept calling again, more, more of 'San Francisco,'" but Tony didn't hear that. So he only did it the one time. But they wanted it to be sung again. They were practically standing on their heads. I mean, they just got up and stamped their feet. But my mother was upset. When the audience was like that, she'd say, 'Oh I wish they'd stop, he's so tired, you know. I don't want anything to happen to him.' Little did she realize that this was what the artist was looking for. But that was her reaction: she was just so concerned that something would happen to Tony because he was overworked and overtired." Mary would laugh at this memory. "At the Copa, the same thing. My mother would say, 'Why don't they stop applauding that poor boy? He's exhausted.' I would try to explain to her. But she would never buy that.

"Another time, when they had just refurbished Carnegie Hall, the manager came to Ralph and said either get him off the stage or let him come out and sing, because these people are going to wreck the hall. They were standing on their seats and they were stamping their feet. So they did call Tony out again, and that was so exciting."

The song made Bennett a citizen of the world. He expressed his feelings about it in a 1978 interview with Jonathan Schwartz that appeared in *Business Week* (January 8, 2007). Schwartz recalled asking him in 1978, when they stood on the roof of the Sahara Hotel in Las Vegas, "What do you think when you're asked to sing 'I Left My Heart in San Francisco'? Isn't it tedious?" Tony was standing there in a terry-cloth robe and red slippers.

"You've got to understand," he said. "To be recognized, identified, all over the world. I never get tired of it."

"What do you think about when you're singing?" Jonathan Schwartz asked.

Tony smiled. "I sing the song. I go right along, until I came to the word 'love.' That's where I put an emphasis. On the word 'love.'"

San Francisco was an exquisite city waiting for a song to happen. There had been Judy Garland's "San Francisco," a surefire belter, and Carmen McRae's "I'm Always Drunk in San Francisco," but few other songs. Jolson had sung "California, Here I Come." Chicago had Sinatra's "My Kind of Town" and "Chicago"; New York had dozens of songs, including Bennett's "Penthouse Serenade," "I'll Take Manhattan," "Every Street's a Boulevard in Old New York," Sinatra's "Autumn in New York," "How About You?" and Jolson's "Give My Regards to Broadway." (Soon it would have Sinatra's "New York, New York" and Billy Joel's "New York State of Mind.") Vermont had Ella's and Sinatra's "Moonlight in Vermont" and Paris had "The Last Time I Saw Paris" and "April in Paris," most especially Louis Armstrong and Ella Fitzgerald's magnificent duet. The cities alone conjure romance, adventure, and beauty, and when a song emerges with a lovely melody and lyrics to evoke them, the public is eager to embrace it.

I have listened to the song perhaps hundreds of times over the years, and never, for a moment, tire of it. It stops me in my tracks every time. That is surely the experience of many millions across the world. Bennett, who once put too much melodrama into his singing, had learned to rein it in long before this recording. Here he is perfectly modulated, his passion slowly building, the crescendo an outcome of all that has come before. He sings simply one verse and one chorus, and the song echoes and resonates in the mind and heart forever. We see that beautiful city, with its steep, hilly streets, the bay, the Golden Gate Bridge, the waterfront, the cable cars, North Beach, as he sings. We bring our own rich associations to it. Then it is a song about longing and love, about having a place that symbolizes a home to return to, and to have the object of our longing waiting there for us. And that longing is about a first love, the perfect love, the one we hold in our hearts. And then, of course, there is Bennett's depth of feeling and his incredibly soulful, embracing voice, the voice that seems to be speaking directly to us as a friend. It is a voice that, as Jimmy Scalia has said, does not keep us at a distance, as Sinatra's majestic voice does. We are one with the singer. To put it simply and truly, as Jimmy Roselli did in writing of Bennett, Bennett's "is the warmest voice ever."

"In one part of the world," Willis Conover wrote in *Billboard* in 1968, "the song means even more. Recent reports from Vietnam say it is the song of this war. Soldiers sing along with Tony's record on a jukebox or record player or on the radio. Their eyes fill. One by one, their voices drop out. They never finish the song. By the time Tony's voice reaches the line 'When I come home to you, San Francisco,' every soldier is too overcome with emotion to continue. Tony ends the song alone."

"That song," wrote Jonathan Schwartz, "has given Tony entry into castles, White Houses, opera houses, theaters anywhere, people's homes, grand banquets. That song, there it is, those words and that sound, is written in his eyes: Entry to the world, said Tony Bennett."

"Everybody got sick of 'I Left My Heart in San Francisco,'" Gary Giddins told me, "because it was played every three minutes. You just couldn't get away from it. It was like Armstrong's 'Hello, Dolly!' It was like—enough! But when I go back to that record now, that seems to be one of the great masterpieces of the three-minute single. I mean all Tony does is sing the verse and *one* chorus! Sometimes he sings less than that. But the thing about 'San Francisco' is that he sings this one chorus and it's like a perfect glide up to the climax. I just never tire of it now. And also Ralph Sharon's little vamp he came up with. It is so perfect."

Bennett traced his feeling for San Francisco back to his beloved father. He told writer Robert L. Doerschuk that when he was a young boy, his father told him that "there are only two real cities in the United States: New York and San Francisco." Bennett said that "I always had a kind of sadness that I didn't have a father [anymore]. I guess that got into the feeling of the recording."

San Francisco celebrated July 9, 1962, as "Tony Bennett Day," and Mayor George Christopher presented Bennett with the key to the city and a lifetime pass for the tollgate of the Golden Gate Bridge.

In the early 1960s, Bennett also was appearing on many of the major television shows, including *Burke's Law*, and more sessions of Hugh Hefner's *Playboy's Penthouse*. He was a guest on Johnny Carson's

very first *Tonight* show, on October 1, 1962, along with Groucho
Marx, Joan Crawford, Mel Brooks, and Rudy Vallee. He would be
Carson's most frequent guest in the years to come. But the highlight
of 1963 was Bennett's appearance on *The Judy Garland Show*. The
program began with Bennett doing a bluesy version of his great music
hall song "True Blue Lou" and going on to "Lullaby of Broadway"
and "Kansas City, Here I Come." Then Garland appeared in all her
majesty, and the two dueted on "When the Midnight Choo-Choo
Leaves for Alabam.'" These moments transcended regular show
business pizzazz: Bennett's eyes were lit and dancing as he watched
Garland's every move and were full of admiration for her. He was
thrilled to be there. No singer has ever expressed more appreciation
and generosity for other singers than Bennett; this was a truly loving,
magical moment, and it culminated in Garland and Bennett dueting on
"I Left My Heart in San Francisco." At one moment Garland briefly
caresses Bennett's face with one hand, and it often appears that he will
sweep her up in her arms and embrace her, or she will do the same to
him. They finally embrace at the end.

Bennett has often said that along with Sinatra, Durante, and Louis
Armstrong, Garland was one of his major artistic influences. He had
first met her in 1958 when he was performing at the Ambassador
Hotel in Los Angeles and she came backstage. They became friends,
and Garland was often in the audience when Bennett sang, and had
cited him as one of her three favorite singers (alongside Sinatra and
Peggy Lee). She told Willis Conover of *Billboard* that Bennett "was
the epitome of what entertainers were put on earth for. . . . I think the
world needs Tony Bennett as much as I need to hear him. He was
born to take people's troubles away, even for an hour. He loves doing
it. He's a giver. He is Tony Bennett, and there isn't any resemblance
to anyone else. There's just one, and everybody had better appreciate
him." Bennett noted in his memoir that the Rat Pack—Frank, Dean,
Sammy, and Peter—had snubbed Garland once when he and Garland
ran into them because of her drug problems.

There was another incident with Garland in which the generous and
caring side of Sinatra surfaced. Bennett was opening at the Waldorf-
Astoria, and just before showtime he received a call from Garland.

She was crying, and told him she was at the St. Regis Hotel and a man was beating her up. Bennett called Sinatra in Florida. According to Bennett, Sinatra said he would call him back in fifteen minutes. Shortly afterward the stage manager told him there was another call from Garland. Bennett called her back. Garland told him that there were "nine hundred cops" downstairs and five lawyers in her room. Sinatra called him back and said, 'Is that all right, kid?'"

"My Tony [Tony Tamburello] worked with Judy Garland," Geri Tamburello told me. "Both Tonys were close with Judy. I remember a very emotional moment for them, for my Tony and Tony Bennett. Judy was onstage at some concert. I wasn't there at the time. But she fell and kind of crumbled. Tony T and Tony B were close up, first couple of rows. She's looking right at Tony B and Tony T, and she's saying, 'Help me. Help me.' Somebody ran out from the wings and helped her stand up. The two Tonys couldn't have gotten up on the stage anyway. My Tony told me how that felt."

Bennett and Tamburello had become deeply entwined. Bennett benefited from Tamburello's great musical gifts and he relished his friend's irreverence and devilish sense of humor.

"Tony Bennett always said that Tony Tamburello taught him to be a mensch," Will Friedwald recalled. "He meant that he was the one that first showed him what a good arrangement was like, what a good song was like. But Bennett is always giving credit that way; I think that was something that he would have done anyhow. Tamburello was a genius, a wild, crazy guy. But he was *ubatz* [nuts]. He was a great character. He had this wild humor. He found this Italian police officer in Englewood and made a record of this guy singing and he was listed on the album as 'Al Dente.' Tony did this other really strange kind of novelty song called 'The Sound of Worms.' It's kind of a strange sixties novelty that sounds like somebody was smoking lots and lots of pot. And it's just about the sound of worms. It's so far out and bizarre. It might have been Tony T himself singing. Doctor Demento still plays it on his radio program."

"Yes, Tony recorded 'The Sound of Worms' and another song called 'Rats in My Room,' both written with Tom Murray," Geri Tamburello confirmed. "Tony recorded 'Worms' himself and accompanied himself on a calliope. That was at Pop Records. His partner and backer there was Frank Pasqua.

"My husband was with Tony for forty-five years. They were friends above all; that was the attraction, plus the musical knowledge. My husband coached him. Tony Bennett thought very highly of my Tony. I have a couple of paintings he did of my husband. And I have a sketch he made of my Tony's back sitting at a piano wearing one of those plaid mountain shirts. They were close through thick and thin. Tony's marriage breakups: my husband was there practically every day. They were brothers. They had the Italian bond; and the families, we knew each other. Tony B's mother was a typical Italian mother. He was very good to her, and to his sister and brother-in-law, Tom Chiappa."

In 1962 and 1963, Bennett recorded four albums: *I Left My Heart in San Francisco*, *Tony Bennett at Carnegie Hall*, *This Is All I Ask*, and *I Wanna Be Around*. Ernie Altschuler produced the albums, and among the arrangers and conductors were the best in the business: Ralph Burns, Don Costa, Dick Hyman, Marion Evans, Frank DeVol, and Neal Hefti. The top engineer, Frank Laico, recorded most of the albums.

In 1962 President Kennedy, for whom Bennett had campaigned, invited him to sing at the White House with the Dave Brubeck Quartet. He also sang later in the year at the White House with Count Basie. Bennett went on to tour South America, appearing at the Copacabana in Rio de Janeiro. He met João and Astrud Gilberto on the beach, and later they introduced him to the music of Antonio Carlos Jobim.

During this time Bennett and Patricia decided to end their first separation and attempt a reconciliation. Bennett moved back into the house in Englewood and was able to spend time with his children, Danny and Daegal.

Bennett was voted tenth favorite male vocalist with DJs in 1963. *Billboard's Who's Who in Popular Music* for 1964 listed a discography of American chart-toppers between 1948 and 1963. Bennett was cited three times for the number one position: "Because of You" and "Cold, Cold Heart" in 1951 and "Rags to Riches" in 1953.

Bennett had a cascading series of hits in the 1960s, Cy Coleman's "The Best Is Yet to Come," Johnny Mercer's "I Wanna Be Around,"

Alec Wilder's "I'll Be Around," and Sacha Distel's "The Good Life" among them. "I Wanna Be Around" originated with two lines written by Sadie Vimmerstedt, a woman in Youngstown, Ohio, who had never written a song in her life. The lines were "I wanna be around to pick up the pieces / When somebody breaks your heart." They sounded to her like the lyrics of a Johnny Mercer song, and so she mailed them to Mercer with a letter addressed to "Johnny Mercer, Songwriter, Los Angeles California." Mercer did like her two lines, and proceeded to write the song and ask Bennett to record it, which he did in October 1962 with Marty Manning arranging it and conducting the orchestra.

Mercer gave Ms. Vimmerstedt 50 percent of authors' royalties to the song, enabling her to retire and to travel around the world. She made many radio and television appearances as a result of the song's success and the novel way it had originated. Mercer related in an appearance at the 92nd Street Y in Manhattan in 1971 that he received a letter from Vimmerstedt saying that her success had exhausted her: "Mister Mercer, I'm tired. I've gotta get *out* of show business!"

Bennett followed up the song with *The Many Moods of Tony* and his first trio record, *When Lights Are Low*, with Ralph Sharon, Hal Gaylord on bass, and Billy Exiner on drums. These albums included songs that became classics: "Don't Wait Too Long," "Spring in Manhattan," "I'll Be Around," and "Limehouse Blues" on *Moods* and "Ain't Misbehavin'," "Speak Low," "It Had to Be You," and "It Could Happen to You" on *Lights*.

With Carnegie Hall, "San Francisco," and a bevy of hits and one triumph after the other, despite the winds of musical change swirling about him, Bennett's career soared through the 1960s. He was now a major concert artist as well as a nightclub performer, touring forty weeks of the year, including eighteen weeks in Las Vegas.

But the touring and heavy concert schedule still left room for his passionate commitment to civil rights and his close friendships with so many black musicians and artists. Bennett was inspired by two figures in the early 1960s: President Kennedy and Dr. Martin Luther King Jr. Bennett met with King and corresponded with him. A week after the inauguration, Frank Sinatra reassembled a group of celebrities for a five-hour tribute to King at Carnegie Hall. Bennett appeared alongside Sammy Davis Jr., Count Basie, and many others. The participants raised $50,000 for the Southern Christian Leadership Conference.

Bennett was very shaken by the assassination of JFK in November 1963 and by the militancy of the 1960s. He found it hard to conceive of the injustice and discrimination that still existed in the United States. He followed Dr. King's struggles with intense concern, and did everything he could to help the movement. Bennett not only did what he could, but he often did it anonymously, never seeking headlines or thanks.

Bennett first toured England in 1961, when he starred at the Pigalle Theatre and Restaurant. He was moved by the warmth and generosity of the response he received from the British. The *London New Record Mirror's* Jimmy Watson (April 22, 1961) wrote that "Smoothly professional, confident and merely terrific was London's Pigalle niterie's latest American star import when Bennett opened his four-week season at the club last Sunday evening. . . . All this success couldn't have happened to a nicer fellow. . . . Witnessing a Tony Bennett show, you can feel his own enjoyment in his work coming across the footlights. And you can also tell that this is no act hashed up just for the occasion."

Bennett had seen the Beatles early on at an underground club in Cologne, Germany, and had been particularly impressed with Paul McCartney. Bennett had said, "I knew he was sprinkled with stardust the moment I saw him walk onstage. You know, with some people in show business—a certain few stars—a magic shines through their every move, whether they're performing or not." Bennett returned to the Pigalle in 1965 and the London Hammersmith Theatre, where he attracted seven thousand fans, and appeared on a major television program in 1964 for BBC1, *Tony Bennett Sings*. He starred at the London Palladium in the Royal Variety show in November 1965. Singing for the queen of England was an honor, but probably the greatest kick for Bennett was sharing a dressing room with one of his idols, Jack Benny. Bennett sang "If I Ruled the World" at the command performance.

"I produced *Tony Bennett Sings* for the BBC in 1965," Yvonne Littlewood told me. "It went out live with Tony, an orchestra, a trio with Bobby Hackett, and Annie Ross as the guest singer. Then we met up again with a series on BBC2 in 1967, *Tony Bennett Meets Robert Farnon*. Then he suddenly wanted to do something just with piano with Torrie Zito, and we had a string quartet as well as his group, instead of an orchestra. Later we did a show of the week, Tony with the London Philharmonic in 1972 at Albert Hall.

"I have such respect for Tony that with all the changes of style of music, he still stuck to his guns. It's like my friend Duke Ellington once said to me, 'There's just good and bad music.' One appreciated Tony most for his singing voice, ability, and his honesty in his approach to music. He was a genuinely honest and true person in himself; I mean that came through. He always looked as though he was happy to give pleasure to people listening to him.

"I think Tony's rather shy in many ways. But I think that was part of his attraction really. He was never 'in your face.' You felt comfortable with him. When Tony was here with his book, I remember queuing up for his signature. He almost fell off his chair. He said, 'You don't have to queue up.' He greeted me like a long-lost sister. I've got his penned drawings that he gave me. He's a real artist at heart.

"He was very professional. He didn't want anything too complicated. His voice is one that, when you hear it, you know who it is. There are a few people like that. This is what makes them special. What you notice with singers as they get older is that they don't have the sustaining power in holding the notes as long as they used to be able to. It's still there, but essentially what they lose one way they gain in maturity. It doesn't mean that they're any less attractive. And Tony can do a cappella. When an artist can do that, it's very special. There's not too many people that can sing a capella anyway, even in their youth."

Back in the United States, Bennett dealt with the Beatles' invasion by continuing to find hits with quality songs: Jack Segal and Bob Wells's "When Joanna Loved Me," Leslie Bricusse and Anthony Newley's "Who Can I Turn To," and Newley and Cyril Ordanel's "If I Ruled the World." They were featured on more Bennett albums in 1965: *The Many Moods of Tony* and *Songs for the Jet Set*. Still, it was impossible to ignore the presence of rock and roll, which was big business now (Columbia had signed the Byrds and Paul Revere and the Raiders) but to Bennett seemed a kind of insanity. He struggled to find songs that would break through the rock juggernaut "like a blade of glass through asphalt."

Bennett appeared for the first time in a major film role in *The Oscar* in 1966. Playing a sidekick and press agent with the multicultural name of Hymie Kelly for a ruthless, sociopathic actor (Stephen Boyd), Bennett managed to generate sympathy as a weak-willed, guileless character, but it was a hapless role in a terrible film. The film had marvelous actors—Elke Sommer, Milton Berle, Eleanor Parker, Joseph Cotten, Ernest Borgnine, Edie Adams, and Jill St. John—but everyone should have stayed home. It is really hard to evaluate Bennett's potential as an actor on the basis of such a movie (more than anything, he appears to be drawing upon an aspect of himself, and he does it credibly), but it is safe to guess that he was not besieged with more offers. He never made a feature film again. "Maybe September," the movie's theme song written by Percy Faith, had a better fate, surfacing on Bennett's beautiful *The Movie Song Album*, a collection of film themes contributed by several major arrangers, and Bennett later rerecorded it for his first album with Bill Evans.

The Movie Song Album was produced by Ernie Altschuler, who also was Bennett's musical director on the album. Bennett contacted the original composers and orchestrators of the songs and asked them to conduct their own songs for the album. Bennett had recently received two wonderful new songs by Johnny Mandel—"The Shadow of Your Smile" (written with lyricist Paul Francis Webster) from the film *The Sandpiper* (which would become one of Bennett's lifetime hits) and "Emily" from *The Americanization of Emily*—and asked Mandel to serve as his musical director on the album. He asked Al Cohn to do scores on "Smile," "The Second Time Around," and "The Trolley Song" with a tenor solo by Zoot Sims. Tony asked Neal Hefti and Quincy Jones to arrange and conduct their songs "The Pawnbroker" (from the film of the same name) and "Girl Talk" (from *Harlow*), and Luiz Bonfa to play guitar on his songs "Samba de Orfeu" (from *Black Orpheus*) and "The Gentle Rain" (from *The Gentle Rain*). *The Movie Song Album* has remained Tony's favorite over the years.

According to Gary Marmorstein, Bennett was impatient with Columbia for not pushing "Maybe September" sufficiently and claimed that Sinatra was urging him to switch to Reprise, Sinatra's new record label. Bennett told Columbia that he was seriously considering the offer, and told Columbia executive Billy James, "If I see fantastic action on Tony Bennett then you'll have a happy cat on your hands. . . . Columbia has a habit of laying on heavy promotion as you're leaving the label, to convince you to stay . . . but I need it now, and it'll help the movie if they see I am a major recording artist."

Bennett's hard luck with this film was offset by meeting a young woman named Sandra Grant, who would become his second wife. Derek Boulton recounted to me that Bennett's marriage to Patricia really ended when she called his hotel and Sandra answered the phone. That was the point of official separation.

There would be no movie career in Bennett's future, but meanwhile in his own métier, he was exceeding himself not only on recordings, but even more in his live performances. Bennett had given the performance of his life in a historic concert at the Conga Room of the Sahara Hotel in Vegas on April 4, 1964. It would be the greatest concert of his career up to that point, and even today it ranks as perhaps one of the three or four finest live performances he has ever given. As great as Bennett is on recordings, he is sometimes even greater onstage. The energy and love of the crowd ignite his passion, and he uncovers depths of feeling and rises to new heights that must rival any of the most unforgettable moments in popular music history. There was a reason that the most gifted artists—Garland, Sinatra, Fitzgerald—recognized in him the heights they themselves had scaled: he is a kindred spirit.

Columbia had wanted a live album, but, inexplicably, the Sahara concert has never been released. Thanks to Tony's devoted friend Nick Riggio, I have a tape of it that captures it in its glory. It is one of the most celebratory and joyful concerts ever recorded. What is also instructive about the concert are the ways in which Ralph Sharon shines as Bennett's accompanist. Sharon cooks on every number, embellishing Bennett's style in the most unobtrusive but resonant way. He is a quiet star to Bennett's moonglow.

Bennett begins with "The Moment of Truth" (which was his title for the concert) and goes on to "Sing You Sinners." He varies his performance, talking a lyric here and there, he scats, he underscores a word that illustrates its meaning: "Wherever there's music, the devil *kicks*." He sings and talks "Put on a Happy Face," varying rhythm and intonation, and again, jumps on a word to give it vividness: "*Slap on* a happy face." He segues into Berlin's "Always."

Bennett's rendering of "I Left My Heart in San Francisco" is soulful and lovely, and is done differently than any other version of it I have ever heard him do. He caresses certain words; when he sings "high on a hill," he goes up and down the scale on "hill" as if he's walking that hill in San Francisco, and he does the same thing with the "sea" that follows "blue and windy," conjuring the sea as he conjures the hill. The effect is of Bennett floating through the magical city. He goes on to combine the song, as he has done ever since, with "I Wanna Be Around," that revenge tune that contrasts perfectly with the soaring spirit of "I Left My Heart." One is reminded of Duke Ellington's advice to Bennett "to sing sweet but put a little dirt in it." Bennett segues back to "San Francisco" for a great windup. He continues with "It's a Sin to Tell a Lie" and a slow and sad "Ain't Misbehavin'," a slowly swinging "One for My Baby," and "The Rules of the Road." On Ellington's "In My Solitude," Bennett twice combines the title with the three-word song title, "Love Look Away." He sings "Solitude" slowly and contemplatively until he reaches "Bring back my love." At this point he starts to shout, growl, and swing, culminating in the lyric "I know that I'll soon grow mad."

Bennett has a ball with "This Could Be the Start of Something Big." You know that you're in the company of a great singer when you suddenly hear a lyric you've listened to for years as if for the first time—you *really* hear it. Did you ever notice this lyric: "You're dining at 21, and watching your diet, declining a charlotte rousse, accepting a fig"? I bet you haven't. At least I hadn't. Bennett concludes with a big windup, slightly altering the lyric to "This could be the start of something *grand*."

Bennett goes on to sing "Mam'selle," and, for the first time, "When Joanna Loved Me."

Bennett then sings a very funny, tongue-in-cheek parody of "Rags to Riches" written by Ralph Sharon that begins:

Now just because my name is Tony
Some folks expect Italian songs [cheers from the audience]
And though I'm fond of macaroni
I know where it belongs.

Bennett goes on in the concert with "Once Upon a Time" and, in a tribute to Al Jolson, a wildly swinging, superb "Keep Smiling at Trouble." He then sings "The Show Must Go On," "Lullaby of Broadway," and a remarkable, slow, wistful version of "Chicago," quite unlike anyone else's, the syllables drawn out, reverent and jazzy.

Then all hell breaks loose. Milton Berle hits the stage: "I don't want to bore you with a lot of wonderful material." For a moment he speaks straight: 'I've never heard Tony Bennett sing better than he sang tonight . . . we witnessed one of the greatest performances tonight," but then goes on to tackle the band: "They don't play slow, they don't play fast, just sort of half-assed." Danny Thomas pops up, too: "There'll be no room up here with these two noses . . . you are look-ing at two of the bravest performers; neither of us had our noses fixed." And finally there is Mickey Rooney, meeting Tony for the first time and saying, "There's electricity in this room because of your singing." Referring to his money woes, Rooney says, "People have this question: How short is he? Well, I'm about three hundred thousand short, that's what I am."

Tony concludes with a new song from Johnny Mercer, "Whatever Happens," a fast, swinging version of "I Left My Heart," and a reprise of "The Moment of Truth."

History was made that night in 1964, but the record of it still awaits release.

The death of Nat King Cole in 1965 was emotionally wrenching for Bennett. He took part in a memorial for Cole that was presided over by Sinatra at the Dorothy Chandler Pavilion in Los Angeles. Bennett had seen many instances of racism regarding Cole, Ellington, and many other great black musicians. It was particularly galling to him to see that men he regarded as geniuses subjected to such inhuman treatment. He was enraged by it and could never temper his indignation. He had once visited Cole in Miami and invited him to join him for dinner at his table. Cole explained that he wasn't allowed in the dining room and that Bennett would have to visit him backstage.

When Bennett performed with Duke Ellington at the Americana Hotel in Miami in the mid-1950s, the hotel held a press party, but Ellington was not permitted to participate. In addition, Ellington and his orchestra could not stay at the hotel they performed in, but were consigned to a rundown motel in a poor section of the city. And of course Bennett would never forget the treatment of Frank Smith on Thanksgiving when he was serving in the army. These things went beyond politics for him. They were an affront to the human condition. Derek Boulton recalled that later, when Boulton managed Bennett in the early 1970s, he was still so angry over these conditions that he told Boulton never to book him in the South. He also refused to ever perform in apartheid South Africa.

When Harry Belafonte came to Bennett and asked him to take part in Dr. King's march against discrimination in Selma, Alabama, Bennett was ready. It was time. "Tony went at a moment's notice, because he was very much for the civil rights movement," Mary Chiappa would recall. "It was very important to him. He could never understand people being racists. I mean, to him everybody—didn't matter what the color of their skin or their nationality or their religion—if they were good people, that's who he loved."

Bennett's decision to take a stand for black rights in Selma was the logical culmination of a long-standing commitment on his part to human rights and equality; Bennett would engage in that struggle with passion and determination. It was not surprising that Vittorio De Sica had been drawn to him as a subject for a biographical documentary film. (It was to be called *Two Bits* but it did not materialize.) Bennett's activism was squarely in the great tradition of Italian humanism and antifascism that included many great Italian film directors and screenwriters, some of them pioneers of neorealism—Vittorio De Sica, Roberto Rossellini, Luchino Visconti, Gianni Puccini, Bernardo Bertolucci, Federico Fellini, and Giuseppe de Santis; novelists and prose writers ranging from Ignazio Silone, Cesare Pavese, Alberto Moravia, Giovanni Verga, and Vitaliano Brancati to Carlo Levi, Giuseppe Berto, Elsa Morante, and Primo Levi; and, most significantly, the courage of Italian rescuers of Jews during the war. Bennett had seen the genocidal outcome of racism in Nazi Germany; he had put his body on the line; he had not flinched from battle. He hated war fiercely; he came out of World War II a pacifist. Yet he had never tried to avoid the battle that was necessary to protect civilization.

Bennett proudly identified with the Italian character, and eloquent evidence of that character came with the high survival rate of Jews in Italy during Mussolini's reign and Nazi occupation. As Susan Zuccotti wrote of Italian rescuers of Jews in *Italians and the Holocaust: Persecution, Rescue, Survival*, "Italians did bend the rules, and saved lives. Italian nuns bent the rules of their orders, and allowed outsiders, even men, into their secluded cloisters. Italian priests ignored the laws of their land and, occasionally, the instructions of their superiors. Bankers some-times did not report Jewish bank accounts; innkeepers did not report unusual guests; landlords did not report unusual tenants; villagers did not report newcomers. . . . In the face of an obviously contrasting real-ity, no one could tell them that the war was not lost, that fascism meant glory, or that Jews were their enemy. Supreme individualists, skeptics, and realists, they thought for themselves, and they knew better.

"In many cases after the war," Zuccotti wrote, "non-Jewish Italians who had saved Jews, when asked about their motivations, were annoyed and even angered by the very question. 'How can you ask me such a question?' one man inquired. 'Do you mean to say that you do not understand why a devout Catholic like myself had to behave as I did in order to save human beings whose lives were in danger?' . . . Most Italians disliked the war, fascism, and the Germans. Most Italians were not anti-Semitic." Yet, Zuccotti cautioned, Italians were not angels: "Most Italians did not aid Jews. . . . In the last analysis, we must acknowledge that the non-Jewish men and women who rescued Jews during the Holocaust were exceptional people, different from the average." Yet, to Italy's eternal honor, the survival rate in Italy was high thanks to those rescuers, and their behavior cannot be fully explained out of the context of their Italian character.

Bennett emerged from the war with a gravitas and a social awareness that few of his peers shared on such a profound level. He could never forget the suffering he had seen. It deepened him as a human being, as a singer, and as a painter.

And there is no question that his model in this regard, not only for his singing, was Sinatra. Sinatra, as author Stanley Crouch wrote, "was a man who seemed absolutely free of ethnic or religious bias. It wasn't that he didn't love being an Italian-American; it was just that he didn't love it so much that he couldn't like or love anybody from a different background."

"Tony told me the stories of his experiences [with bigotry] during the Second World War," Harry Belafonte recalled for the documentary *The Music Never Ends*. "What was interesting to me was the indignation and the rage that Tony expressed. . . . He brought that spirit of the Second World War into our vision of the America of the future."

Speaking to Arsenio Hall in 1992 about the march on Selma (*Jet,* April 6, 1992), Bennett recalled that "everybody was warning one another that you have to watch it. There were a lot of people against it. When Harry Belafonte told me to go down there, I asked him why he wanted me to go. And he explained to me there were many black bodies that were never reported. There were many, many that were tortured and killed. . . . there were a couple of hundred people that were never reported. It was genocide. And it had to stop. It happened in our country, in the United States. It had to stop."

The three Selma-to-Montgomery marches that took place in 1965 were the political and emotional peaks of the civil rights movement. Bennett participated in the third march. They originated in the voting rights movement in Selma, Alabama (the town where Alabama's White Citizens Councils had been founded), formed by local blacks who organized the Dallas County Voters League (DCVL). In 1961 the population of Selma was 57 percent black, but of the 15,000 blacks old enough to vote, only 130 were registered, fewer than 1 percent of the black population. Blacks were blocked by state and local officials, the Ku Klux Klan, and the White Citizens' Council.

At the start of 1963, SNCC organizers attempting to start a voter registration project had been beaten and almost killed by Klansmen.

Thirty-two black schoolteachers applied to register to vote and were immediately fired by the all-white school board.

The Sixteenth Street Baptist Church in Birmingham was bombed on September 15, killing four adolescent girls about to lead the annual Youth Day service. "Seconds later," historian Taylor Branch wrote, "a dazed [hysterically sobbing] man emerged clutching a dress shoe from the foot of his eleven-year-old granddaughter, one of four mangled corpses in the rubble."

On October 7, 1963, more than three hundred Dallas County blacks lined up at the voter registration office in Selma for "Freedom Day," a model for the upcoming Freedom Vote in Mississippi. Only a few of the hundreds in line were permitted to fill out the voter application, and most of the applications were denied.

The Civil Rights Act of 1964 declaring segregation illegal was signed into law by President Lyndon Johnson on July 2, 1964. Despite the law, Jim Crow was still in effect. Attempts by blacks to integrate Selma's movie theater and a hamburger stand were again blocked, and blacks were beaten and arrested. On July 6, John Lewis led fifty blacks to the courthouse on registration day. The sheriff arrested them instead. On July 9, Judge James Hare issued an injunction forbidding a gathering of three or more people who were sponsored by a civil rights organization. It was illegal to even talk about civil rights or voter registration in Selma. Public civil rights activities were banned.

At this point, with white resistance intensified, the DCVL called on the assistance of Martin Luther King Jr. and the Southern Christian Leadership Conference, which encouraged many civil rights leaders to participate in the struggle. The Selma Voting Rights Movement officially began on January 2, 1965. Dr. King addressed a cheering mass meeting of seven hundred people in Brown Chapel in defiance of the injunction. It was his idea to march from Selma to Montgomery, the capital, to demand that blacks be given the right to vote.

Voter registration drives and protests in Selma and adjacent counties were immediately expanded. On February 16, 1965, there was a nighttime civil rights demonstration in nearby Marion. A protester, Jimmy Lee Jackson, a twenty-six-year-old pulpwood worker and the youngest deacon at St. James Baptist Church (who had applied for the vote five times without success), was murdered by an Alabama state trooper while trying to protect his mother and grandfather in a café to which they had fled while being attacked by troopers. Jackson had been part of a group of demonstrators who were fleeing fifty state troopers. When his mother was beaten to the floor, Jackson lunged to protect her and the troops shot him. Jackson died on February 26. Dr. King preached at Jackson's funeral at Brown Chapel on March 3, and approved the march on Montgomery to begin on Sunday.

The first march, infamously known as "Bloody Sunday," occurred on March 7. Six hundred civil rights marchers were brutally attacked by the police with billy clubs and tear gas as they crossed the Edmund Pettus Bridge. The second march took place on March 9. Dr. King led almost twenty-five hundred marchers to the bridge. One of the protesters, a white Unitarian Universalist minister named James Reeb, was attacked and beaten with clubs. He was turned away from Selma's public hospital, which refused to treat him, and he was taken to another hospital in Birmingham, two hours away. He died on March 11.

It was the third march, in which Tony Bennett participated, beginning on March 21 and lasting five days, that actually made it the fifty-one miles to Montgomery. Among those who marched were Dr. King, John Lewis, Rabbi Abraham Joshua Heschel, Ralph Bunche, Rabbi Maurice Davis, and Fred Shuttlesworth. Protected by two thousand soldiers of the U.S. Army, nineteen hundred members of the Alabama National Guard under federal command, and scores of FBI agents and federal marshals, the marchers walked through pouring rain, camping at three sites in muddy fields, and reached Montgomery on March 24 and gathered at the Alabama state capitol building on March 25.

Bennett was among those in the forefront of the march.

Thousands of marchers reached the campsite at the City of St. Jude, a Catholic complex outside of Montgomery. A "Stars for Freedom" rally was held, with Tony, Harry Belafonte, Peter, Paul and Mary, Sammy Davis Jr., Nina Simone, and Frankie Laine performing.

On March 25 twenty-five thousand people marched from St. Jude to the state capitol building, where Dr. King gave his historic speech "How Long? Not Long." Billy Eckstine (who walked with Tony on the march route), Sammy Davis Jr., Leonard Bernstein, and many others took part. As Bennett marched, memories kept coming back to him of twenty years before when he and his buddies fought their way into Germany. The feelings seemed similar as he observed the cold hostility of the white state troopers. He and Billy Eckstine were genuinely frightened.

On another night Bennett sang several songs at a show put on for the marchers. There was no stage available, but a local mortician donated eighteen heavy wooden coffins for the entertainers to use as a stage. Tony and Billy Eckstine shared a room in a bedraggled hotel along the route. When Tony and Billy left, Viola Liuzzo, an Italian American woman and mother of five who had come to Alabama to support the marchers, drove Eckstine and Bennett to the airport. Later they learned that she was murdered by bigots on her drive back to Selma.

One of the songs that Tony sang that night usually had a different meaning, but as he has observed, there is sometimes the incongruity of songs fitting occasions for different reasons than the ones the composers had in mind in creating them. Tony sang Jule Styne's "Just in Time" as a way of expressing how he felt about the timeliness of the march and the need for justice to prevail. He was very proud to have been able to take part in the march.

He could never understand why anyone should suffer because of the color of his or her skin. Tony would express it as simply and genuinely almost as a child might, a child who had not developed a tough skin and the ambiguous, compromising coloration of adulthood. Tony still had a touch of that ingenuous, sensitive child within him.

There was a lighter moment on the march for Tony. One of the people he met on the march took him by surprise: Sinatra's right-hand man and bodyguard Jilly Rizzo. Tony looked up in surprise and there was Jilly. He asked Rizzo what he was doing there. Sinatra had sent him. Rizzo took out a pair of brass knuckles and said he had them in case anyone did anything "funny."

Despite the tragedies and brutalities that took place, the marches were not in vain. On March 15, 1965, President Lyndon Johnson had presented a bill to a joint session of Congress that would ultimately pass and become the Voting Rights Act. Speaking in front of Congress, Johnson spoke the most significant words of the movement: "We shall overcome." On August 6 the bill became law. Tony treasures the letter of thanks he received from Dr. King.

Soon after the march Carmen MacRae approached Bennett with a 1921 vaudeville song, a lullaby called "Georgia Rose," which was about a black woman singing to her baby as she rocks him in his carriage: "Don't be blue because you're black." The song engendered controversy at Columbia, which tried to shelve it. "Bennett thought at first," Gary Marmorstein wrote, "that the NAACP had complained about its patronizing lyrics, then later gathered that the label didn't want to alienate record buyers in the Deep South. Bennett, who'd worked to promote civil rights throughout his career, could be accused of misjudgment but not of paternalism." Tony recorded a new arrangement of it by Ralph Sharon in June 1966 and it appears on his great album *A Time for Love*.

There was a great moral and ethical victory on March 15, 1965, with the passage of the Voting Rights Act, and on April 23, there was a personal victory for Bennett, one that was perhaps the greatest moment thus far of his life. A man stepped up and, transcending the traditional rivalries of singers, from the high authority of his position as the greatest popular singer in American history, invoked that authority on behalf of another man. Frank Sinatra told *Life* magazine, "For my money, Tony Bennett is the best singer in the business. He excites me when I watch him. He moves me. He's the singer who gets across what the composer has in mind, and probably a little more."

It came from the singer Tony admired more than any other in the world, from a fellow Italian, and from a man whose devotion to civil rights inspired him while he was on the battlegrounds of Nazi Germany and ever since. "That quote changed my whole life," Bennett has often said.

It did change his life, but typically, in a different way that it would affect many other men. It did not inflame his ego or cause him to relax his efforts. On the contrary, he was more determined than ever to live up to Sinatra's statement. Danny Bennett has spoken of the anxiety and challenge those words inspired in his father. "Tony took that to heart," Danny said in *The Music Never Ends*. "He wasn't like, Ooh, that's nice. He took that as a huge responsibility. Talk about carrying the torch. . . . He said, 'Wow, that's just a lot to live up to.'" Bennett was moved, chastened, determined. He looked upon Sinatra's words as a great honor, but a responsibility as well. He felt he would have to apply even more discipline and technique to his singing. What more could he do to justify that praise?

7

Good-bye to All That

Tony Bennett's halcyon days at Columbia began to darken in the period bracketing 1965–67," wrote Gary Marmorstein. "He was still making one remarkable album after another but, like a weather vane spun around by the wind, the label's energies were pointing in a new direction."

At first it had been a matter of give and take, Will Friedwald wrote, "in this particular relationship of artist and corporation. Usually Columbia wanted Bennett to sing something more 'commercial,' and usually Tony wanted to sing something more 'artistic.' For most of their 21 years together, Columbia—represented by a parade of producers that began with Mitch Miller—and Bennett had managed to find a happy middle ground, and satisfy the desires of both sides of the equation. The overwhelming majority of Bennett's recordings can be described as being both art music and pop music. 'But I always had the sword out,' Bennett says, 'I was always fencing.'"

But by the end of the 1960s, Friedwald wrote, Tony "was being pressured by his record company not just to sing 'commercial' songs, but essentially to sing rock and roll. . . . For every triumph of good music, the philistines landed another six blows: the British invasion, flower power, the rise of the rocksinger-songwriter, folk rock, heavy metal, and Astrud Gilberto. The boom fell in the aftermath of the Beatles' and Clive Davis's rise to power at Columbia; Bennett had been lucky enough to generate enough sales momentum, not only to keep going in the face of changing tastes, but also to land a couple of lesser hits like 'If I Ruled the World' and 'Maybe September.' Though his concert attendance would never slacken, by 1969, Bennett had cause to worry about his recording career." Goddard Lieberson, Columbia's president, had visited Los Angeles in the fall of 1965 and, despite what had been his long-standing resistance to rock and roll, been intrigued by the omnipresence of country-inflected rock music bursting out on Sunset Boulevard. Even though Columbia's big sellers were still Andy Williams and Percy Faith, he could not help but note the impact of Simon & Garfunkel and Bob Dylan.

"By the beginning of 1966," Marmorstein wrote, "with Lieberson having another year and a half to go in the president's office, the label was waving its arms out of the warm, easy-listening surf that had once been so inviting—[Percy] Faith, [Ray] Conniff, [Paul] Weston, etc.—and had since turned to riptides." Most of "the guys who made this music didn't write their own songs, weren't compelled to say much about politics or society, and most condemning of all, kids didn't want to dance to their records. . . . To the ears of the largest record-buying demographic, [they] sounded out of touch. The label flailed for a while."

"Poor Tony Bennett," Friedwald wrote, "was left standing there with a stupid look on his face, wondering what in hell was going on. . . . Simply put, the record industry as Bennett had known it in 1952 no longer existed. In Bennett's time, record labels had endeavored to sell as much of their product as possible, by fair means but often by foul. Eventually the decision was made to eliminate choice on the part of the artist as well as the consumer. As tenor saxist Lew Tabackin once said in describing playing in sessions for Motown Records, 'Everything had to be interchangeable. When one of the girls [the Supremes] would act up, they'd replace her with a new one and no one would know the difference. There was no room for jazz [i.e., individuality] in their thinking.'"

On the surface Bennett's career was on a level plateau, with sold-out concert appearances and numerous TV appearances, including many on the *Ed Sullivan Show* in the late 1960s. Tony appeared with Count Basie on one occasion, singing "On the Sunny Side of the Street," "San Francisco," "Wanna Be Around," "Don't Get Around Much Anymore," and "The Lady's in Love with You." On another appearance on the show, in 1968 with Woody Herman, Tony sang "Lullaby of Broadway, "Moment of Truth," "Who Can I Turn To?," and "For Once in My Life." In a third appearance, with Woody Herman, Tony sang "Get Happy," "Hushabye Mountain," and "There Will Never Be Another You" (with a solo by Zoot Sims).

On one of the many *Ed Sullivan Show* appearances Bennett performed with Duke Ellington on Easter, 1969. This miniconcert, with Duke at the piano, was so spectacular, so euphoric, and so infectious, it seemed to explode the TV screen and the plastic contours of the Sullivan format. Bennett began with a song Ellington had recently written for him "[Making That] Love Scene." He went on to do a lovely version of Ellington's "Solitude," giving it a soft ending on "bring back my love." His rendition of "What the World Needs Now" (with the words "No, not just for some . . . but for everyone") were rendered not as an easygoing waltz but as the political statement Bennett intended it to be. His concluding song, "People," arranged by Torrie Zito, was simply astounding, full-throated and heartfelt, subversively turning the song's platitudes into a passionate political anthem. Duke Ellington sprang up from the piano and hugged him.

Bennett's precarious situation was compounded by the separation from Patricia. Christmas 1965 had been lonely and sad for him. He spent the holiday in a room alone at the Gotham Hotel, feeling depressed and isolated. He missed his children, Danny and Daegal, terribly.

It was on that Christmas Eve that a rescuer had come to his aid, as would happen again and again in his life. He suddenly heard music, and looked around his room to see where it was coming from. He checked the TV and the portable tape recorder. Nothing was on. The music seemed to be coming from the hallway. Bennett opened the door and saw a choir singing Burton Lane and Alan Jay Lerner's "On a Clear Day

You Can See Forever." The choir was Duke Ellington's. Ellington was performing a concert of sacred music at the Fifth Avenue Presbyterian Church, and his drummer, Louis Bellson, had told him of Bennett's situation. Ellington, who had forged a close relationship with Bennett by then, sent the choir to Bennett's hotel to give him a moment of joy on the holiday. The experience reaffirmed Bennett's belief in the goodness of humanity, no matter how painful the circumstances.

Bennett's friendship with Ellington, whom he revered, was one of the most sustaining relationships in his life. Ellington's creativity has been a lifelong inspiration to him. Bennett had first seen Ellington and Ethel Waters together at the Capitol Theater on Broadway when he was a teenager.

Bennett clearly has tried to model himself on Ellington. Traveling with him on the road over the years, he was struck by the consistency of Ellington's creativity. No matter the circumstances, Ellington was always creating. Bennett learned from that. Ellington had told him, "Do two things instead of one." That advice also moved Bennett toward taking his painting as seriously as he took his singing. The eternal student, Bennett watched and listened and remembered. He'd always loved painting, but now he came to understand that it required the same deep level of commitment as his singing. The friendship of Tony's sister, Mary, with Duke's sister, Ruth, had further consolidated a relationship that soon extended to the entire families.

Another experience shaped Bennett's view of Ellington. A salesman in a record shop in Britain had asked Tony if he knew who had composed more music than any other composer in world history. Bennett said no, and the salesman replied, "Duke Ellington." It was a significant piece of information that Bennett stored in his memory, one he was certain was unknown to most of the world. For him it was evidence of how little credit some of the great creative minds received in the United States, although he was convinced that in time an awareness gradually came to people, an appreciation for the geniuses in their midst.

On an afternoon in Boston at the Somerset Hotel, Bennett had one of those unforgettable epiphanies that have occurred again and again in his life. On a beautiful sunny afternoon, he sat with cornetist Bobby Hackett in Tony's room. Hackett said that he wished they could take part in a jam session. The phone rang. It was Duke. He was downstairs in the lobby. He said he had written a new song and wanted to play it for Tony. Tony conveyed the unbelievable news to Hackett, and both of them went down to the lobby, where a piano happened to be with Duke seated at it.

It was a terrible piano—eight notes on the whole middle C were missing—but Ellington started playing on both sides of the middle C. And playing. Playing every song he'd ever written. He played for an hour with intensity and total absorption. Bennett glanced at Hackett and saw that he was weeping.

Phoebe Jacobs observed the relationship between Ellington and Bennett. "I knew that Tony had substance abuse problems," she said, "although nobody thought of him as a druggie. No one accused him or thought badly of him. People appreciated him, loved him just the same. But I believe that Ellington was almost a healer for Tony. Because Ellington himself was such a regal, spiritual human being. And without being a Svengali, with his attention and genuineness, he healed Tony. I think Tony liked himself better. Ellington was Tony's mirror. Tony never really had great self-esteem. I think Tony saw himself in the way Ellington treated him, and that gave him a positive energy about himself."

At first the process of change at Columbia seemed gradual, and Bennett was intensely busy. On May 3, 1966, he starred in his first TV special, *Singer Presents Tony Bennett*, for NBC; the program was produced by Al di Scipio and directed by Gary Smith and Dwight Hemion. Bennett had requested of di Scipio the latitude to do the show the way he wanted to, without artificial dialogue or filler—to just sing and have artistic autonomy. The show feels exactly that way except for the klutzy dated sets that look as if they came out of the dinosaur age. Ralph Burns was musical director, and the classic soloists included Candido on "The Moment of Truth," Milt Jackson on "Lost in the Stars," Bobby Hackett on "Because of You," Buddy Rich on "Fascinating Rhythm," Gene Bertoncini on "Quiet Nights of Quiet Stars," and flutist Paul Horn and his quintet on "The Shadow of Your Smile." Emile Charlap, music copyist for the program, told Willis Conover, "There was no confusion. Everyone felt it was like going to a party, and Tony was the happiest of all. You know, some people's claim to status would be, like, 'I had lunch with the president today.' Tony's claim to status would be that he went out and had a drink with Zoot Sims, or some other musician he likes."

The band also included the great saxophonist Frank Wess (still often playing with Bennett today), Joe Soldo, Gerry Sanfino, Sol Schlinger, Bernie Glow, Ernie Royal, Joe Wilder, Richie Kamuca, Tommy Flanagan, Sol Gubin, Al Derisi, Urbie Green, Dave Carey, Jimmy Buffington, Urbie Green, and Quentin Jackson. Some of the program was taped in a studio, but several scenes were taped outside of it. Bennett sang "Just in Time," "Once Upon a Time," "A Taste of Honey," and of course "San Francisco," with rear-projection shots of Bennett actually wandering around San Francisco. Another segment was taped live at the shore. While Bennett was sitting on a rock jutting out on the Atlantic, a huge wave knocked him over, providing a funny, spontaneous moment.

In an article in *Holiday* that year titled "The Mature Mr. Bennett," the noted music writer Nat Hentoff wrote, "The rough exterior with its inner core of sensitivity is part of a vintage American tradition that endures in Marshal Dillon, the Bogart cult, Spencer Tracy at Black Rock, Lee Marvin anywhere, the mythology of Miles Davis." Hentoff referred to the younger singers of the time who "have greatly energized and democratized American music, but very few of them can sing ballads that are not taut. . . . [Bennett] takes kids who think meaningful singing began with Bob Dylan and makes them suddenly feel there must be some kind of social significance in 'I Left My Heart in San Francisco.'" He concluded, "It is true that [Bennett] sells illusions, but like equally perishable wine, some illusions are much more satisfying than others. And since a certain amount of illusion is necessary to sustain 'real life,' Tony Bennett, like all superior entertainers, is a valuable man."

Hentoff told Conover that after writing the article, he received a note from Frank Sinatra: "He was glad, he told me, that I'd given Bennett the credit he deserved."

In another memorable appraisal of Bennett years later, Hentoff wrote, "It is very rare in popular music for an artist over a long period of time to have remained true to himself and kept growing within that integrity. Tony Bennett is such a rarity."

Important changes were taking places in the musical lineup behind Bennett. Bennett's gifted drummer Billy Exiner was forced to leave the band due to ill health in 1966. Exiner had shrapnel in his back from an injury in World War II that caused him great pain, and he had become addicted to morphine. The drug had not affected his playing, but he also became afflicted with Berger's disease, a circulation disorder that crippled the limbs. He was forced to undergo the amputation of one leg. Bennett kept him on the payroll, unable to play, for the rest of his life. Billy Exiner died in 1985.

It was at this time that Bennett formed another of his most enduring musical relationships. Ralph Sharon had decided to join Hugh Hefner's new club in San Francisco in the spring of 1966 as musical director, and Bennett and Sharon parted for a time. Tommy Flanagan became Bennett's accompanist after playing for Ella Fitzgerald for many years, but it was agreed that he would stay for a limited period, so Bennett needed someone on a more permanent basis. Bennett had seen pianist John Bunch playing in Buddy Rich's big band at a Hollywood jazz club called the Shez and was enormously impressed. He asked Bunch to become his new musical director. It would be an auspicious choice, one that enhanced Bennett's work for many years, from 1966 through 1972. When I met Bunch and his wife, Chips, several times shortly before he died at age eighty-nine in 2010, he was still close to Bennett.

"It was 1966," Bunch remembered,

and Tony came in one night and Buddy asked him if he would come up and sing. He didn't have his own piano player, so I played the piano for him. I knew the tunes he wanted to sing, even the arrangements. I didn't meet him that night. Several months passed. The phone rings. Danny Stevens, Tony's road manager in those days, said Tony Bennett would like to know if you'd be interested in playing for him. I never thought I could ever do anything like that. I had never even played for singers very much.

I figure if he wants to talk, maybe I should talk to him. I was very reluctant, though. I knocked on the door. Tony appeared. I was very nervous to meet him. I immediately told him I wasn't very experienced during this kind of work. He said, "Well, the job is yours if you want. The next gig is going to be at the Copa. I happen to like the conductor of that band. You watch him; see if you can't learn a lot from him."

My very first gig with Tony was before the Copa. It was with Count Basie. Well, I was absolutely a nervous wreck. Tony gave me the piano conductor parts, and he gave me his records of all the tunes that he was going to do in his act. Anyhow, I got through that pretty well, and then we did the Copa job and by that time I felt I'd learned quite a lot.

Tony always treated me great. He's very sensitive for a star. But you know, the longer I worked for him the more it got to be kind of nerve-racking as the years went by. He was changing the pace of his tunes. I felt like his slower tunes were getting slower and his fast ones getting faster. He never said anything to me about it, but it just felt like he wanted them faster and slower. And when we did a record, it was with the guy who wrote the arrangements for the record, quite often the conductor. So I learned from like Torrie Zito, Marion Evans, Robert Farnon. You just watch a man, you know. My first album with him was *Tony Makes It Happen*. Marion Evans was conductor. They say Tony's evolved into a jazz singer. But even on that very first record I made with him, he sounds just as much a jazz singer then as he does now.

His taste in orchestration has always been absolutely the best ever. I don't know of any singer that's consistently insisted on good musicians writing music for him, good songs. He's a man of his own mind. There's nobody ever like him.

I also had the responsibility of finding some songs for him. People found out what my job was and they'd send them to me. I'd be inundated, a whole roomful of them piled up in the office, waist deep. He was very slow about making up his mind to record a song. Sometimes I'd go to his apartment. On his piano there'd be an original song by some prominent songwriter. And I'm thinking, what kind of chance does this guy have against Johnny Mandel written just for Tony in mind? We'd go over this tune again, and again, and again. A year later, it would still be on the piano. I'd say let's go over that song again. Sometimes, maybe two years later, he'd have somebody write a wonderful arrangement for a big orchestra for the song and finally record it. Took him that long to decide, or maybe not decide. On the other hand, he'd get tunes he'd want to do right away. Always a perfectionist.

He'd always try to get the audience to appreciate instrumental music. He'd find out the name of the tenor saxophone player, because some of the songs had saxophone solos. He always announced, when the guy finished the solo, maybe only eight bars, Tony would say his name, a nice hand for so-and-so. And he always told the maître d' at Caesars Palace, "Make sure the pretty girls are up front, at ringside." I think he felt it was impressive in case cameras were around, or it made him feel good. He could be strange, too. You know, putting your finger on your nose with an orchestra usually means to start from the top again in a rehearsal. He thought the musical director was making fun of his nose.

Ella Fitzgerald and Billy Eckstine were real favorites of mine, I loved the both of them. But when they got to be even in their sixties, you could hear age in their voices. You never heard that in Tony. It's amazing. He's got a lot of guts. I really admired him very much. I don't even know any opera singers that have lasted anywhere near into their eighties singing. He told me this: he still studies singing and art. So he knows how to breathe right. It's a classical approach he uses. You breathe from the stomach. So he doesn't get tired the way most singers do. That's the way he is.

They talk about Tony's comeback. All I know is every place he played was always sold out. The only time I remember that it wasn't was when they had the damndest blizzard in New York. We were working the Waldorf. The place was half full. And you know what he did? He put on a better show for them than he would normally. He added some tunes. He said that anybody who had the nerve to show up in that weather deserved a better or longer show. Isn't that amazing? Because many singers would have done absolutely half of a show. They wouldn't have given all that: "Oh, what a drag; now I'm gonna have to go home in the snow."

He was a big star by 1950. There were other stars then, coming up and making records. And he's the only one that has lasted anywhere near that long. Some of them were forgotten in twenty years. But I became very nervous working for Tony over the years on that job. When I started with Tony he had a manager, a road manager, a contractor that took care of arranging for the performances in every city we played months and months ahead of time. That was Joe Soldo, who was a wonderful sax player himself. And he had Tony Tamburello, who rehearsed with him, just the two of them up in the apartment. So I didn't have to do any of that and I didn't have to worry about the music.

But little by little, those people left and nobody was replaced. And I started doing more and more, and more and more and more, whew! It really got to jar on my nerves. I guess that's why we broke up. Because I sort of told Tony off one day. He seemed awfully uptight at a rehearsal. Actually it might have been my fault because I hired the wrong guys for the rhythm section. But we didn't talk about that. I just made that remark, and that was the end for me. I told him he seemed nervous. I was probably the one who was nervous. And boy that's the mistake of your life! We got through the gig all right, but later he remembered that incident. He'd give me a strange look after the shows, like happy but unhappy. We went to play the Hollywood Bowl. Sixty pieces. The concert came off brilliantly. People cheering, gigantic audience. Very heartening for me. I came off and I said to Tony, "Pretty good one." He just walked away from me and I thought, this is the beginning of the end. He never had done anything like that before. It was just the final few weeks [he held the grudge]. Most of the time it was great. Shortly after that I got the news from Derek Boulton. That was it.

There was one incident—I've seen this with other singers and it's really embarrassing to have it happen on the stage. The orchestra conductor starts the tempo off wrong and the singer turns around and says, "Stop the music." Tony did that once to me, just a couple of years before I left. And I was shocked, of course. And he was right: I didn't have the tempo quite right. But after it was over he came straight to me and said, "I've really got to apologize to you." And he did. He said, "You know, I had two glasses of wine before the show, and I should never drink like that before I perform. That's an awful mistake on my part." That's the difference between him and many other people. I just think many great performers wouldn't do that [apologize] even if it was the wrong tempo.

Tony's not a schooled musician at all, but he had these almost psychic gifts. There was the time one string on the piano was out of tune. I tried not to hit it when I found out because I knew that would really throw him, particularly on a ballad. I guess I must have hit it anyhow, and I'm thinking, oh, my God, he's going to say something about that. Okay, the curtain closes and he comes running out onstage again. I thought he's going to give me hell for not having the piano tuned right. But he just says, "The piano hasn't been tuned very well, has it?" Then he goes to the piano and he picks the string that's out of tune. Now I don't understand that. I could never have done it. It would be uncanny for a piano tuner to find those actual strings that were off. I don't know. That is the most mysterious thing. Just on his way off the stage he picked the string. I held my head. Some of the guys in the band were still packing up and they'd seen that. They were all talking about it: "Do you know what he did?" He found that very one note, that one string.

And the things he thought up! He suggested that he do a tune that Charlie Chaplin wrote, "Smile." In the middle of the show, all the lights would come down. He would have just a very tiny pin spot on his face. The orchestra would start the intro. Then suddenly the film *Modern Times* would come up behind the orchestra. A big full screen. And it would be that scene with Charlie Chaplin as the tramp with Paulette Goddard. She was crying; she was a little girl then. It was all of course just pantomime. Then he patted her and said, "Come on, come on, let's take a walk." And they were walking on down the road, the two of them together. Tony had a lot of crazy ideas like that and people would say, "Oh, no! We can't do that! That can't be done!" Another idea he had was during his song "Firefly." He had that strobe light. The stage was completely dark at the beginning of the song. He would start singing the intro, and all of a sudden that strobe light went on that flashed fifty times a second. And he'd do a pantomime like a clown.

But what Tony did for my mother! About four years into my relationship with him, he found out that my mother had had a terrible stroke. She was still living in Tipton, my hometown in Indiana, and I had her in a nursing home. I was, of course, out on the road a lot of the time. Her best friend called me one day and said, "You've got to get her out of there. They're not taking good care of her. You've got to do something about it."

So I'm telling this story to somebody. Tony must have heard me. He didn't say anything. A few months passed. We're doing Pearl Bailey's TV show with Jimmy Durante out in Hollywood. Before that we had done a benefit in Chicago for a nursing home on the west edge of Chicago, called Villa Scalabrini. We were backstage at the Bailey show during a break, having lunch. Just out of a clear blue sky, Tony told Jimmy about my mother and the situation I was in trying to find a decent nursing home.

Tony says, "Why can't we get her into that nursing home for Italians and Catholics?"

Jimmy said, "Oh, I'll make a phone call."

So it was all arranged, although I'm not Italian or Catholic. Then I go to see her at the home and check up on her. Oh, it was the most wonderful place. They were so nice to her and so good to her. And this was all because of Tony.

Whatever his ongoing problems with Columbia and Clive Davis and the spiraling decline of his marriage, the latter half of the 1960s continued to be a prodigious period for Bennett. He recorded a beautiful album, *Tony Makes It Happen*, with one splendid song after another, a swinging "Old Devil Moon" and Robert Farnon's evocative "The Country Girl" among them. He began "On the Sunny Side of the Street" with a sudden shout of "*Grab!*" [your coat and grab your hat] that still reverberates over time, and he did outstanding versions of "A Beautiful Friendship," "I Don't Know Why," and "She's Funny That Way." He had done one outstanding album after another in the preceding period: *If I Ruled the World*, *When Lights Are Low*, *The Many Moods of Tony* (which featured the premiere of Jack Segal and Bob Wells's "When Joanna Loved Me," a song that would become a Bennett evergreen), *This Is All I Ask*, and *I Wanna Be Around*.

His work with Farnon was a source of deep gratification to Bennett, but he had delayed it for many years. It had come about because of Tony Tamburello. "Tony T was a great fan of Robert Farnon," Derek Boulton recalled. "I invited Tony T to dinner one night. He arrived at the restaurant, and I'm sitting there with Robert Farnon. Tamburello walked in the door and tears streamed down his eyes. Because he idolized and saw the genius in Robert Farnon. Tony sat down and cried. There was a lot of emotion in him. Like Tony Bennett. That is the Italian character."

Recording with Farnon was one of the memorable events of the late 1960s for Tony. A remarkable example of Bennett's perfectionism and modesty can be seen in his behavior with Farnon. His reverence for Farnon was so deep that even though he had met him in 1952 and Tony Tamburello had found a house for Farnon next door to Tony's mother in River Edge, New Jersey, Tony had not felt he was ready to record with Farnon yet. Farnon had wanted them to record together immediately. Bennett had told Farnon that he wanted to develop more as an artist first, and thought he'd have to wait about twenty years before doing an album with him. He actually did wait fifteen years, from 1952 to 1967.

When they finally did record together, the beautiful result was *Snowfall: The Tony Bennett Christmas Album*, released on November 6, 1968. Farnon contributed an original song he'd written with his brother Brian, "Christmasland." Farnon and Bennett taped six tracks in New York and four in London. Columbia and its new president, Clive Davis, were indifferent to the album and hardly promoted it, a situation that Bennett had been encountering and agonizing over for a long time.

"For Once in My Life" had been his last hit single, and it seemed to Bennett that by 1967 Columbia was ready to get rid of him.

Bennett had an intense love affair with the gifted British jazz singer Annie Ross of Lambert, Hendriks, and Ross in those years. Now appearing regularly at the Metropolitan Room in New York City, Ross spoke of Bennett to me. "Things were hot and heavy," she told me. "It was a loving relationship. I had great respect—and I still do—for Tony as a singer and as an interpreter of lyrics. And he was thoughtful. He had a great sense of humor. We laughed a lot. Especially about music. He would get jokes that only another musician would appreciate. And since I have always thought like a musician, it was great. Because you could say something that no one else would get, but he would. And we had great times.

"Oh, I know where we met! At the Paramount Theater. He was doing a stage show with the Step Brothers. I went backstage. And he was like a shy child. I mean he was really shy! He was a good Catholic boy. Those teenagers [besieged him]. He was a really nice man with a gorgeous voice. He was sweet. He was lovely. And he was very hot-tempered.

"He spoke of his family a lot. He told me about when he was a kid, and being in the church. And wanting to sing. He took care of his family. He's very Italian. There's an acute sensitivity to him. And a vulnerability.

"I think Tony has a kind of innocence. He could still, when I knew him, be impressed by artists. And he always liked to paint. He was kind. And he was quick to promote other people. I think that's common in really great artists. And he's grown as an artist. It's the interpretation that is so valuable. And he can really interpret a lyric. That only comes with experience. He's like wine. He gets better. I've watched him go out and wrap an audience around his finger.

"It was actually my idea for Tony to record with Bill Evans. Because I could sense qualities in Bill's playing that would jibe with Tony. They were both very sensitive. Bill was a tormented man. He had made his mind up to a certain way of thinking. And you couldn't dissuade him. I'm sure it hurt Tony. In his self. To not be able to help Bill. Tony has a very deep feeling for people.

"Generosity of heart: that's what music is all about. Tony embodies that. We had very happy memories. Rather, I have very happy memories."

As ground was shifting under Bennett's feet, Clive Davis, his nemesis-to-be, was named president of Columbia in the aftermath of the Monterey Pop Festival in the summer of 1967. But "even before . . . the label's priorities were changing," wrote Gary Marmorstein, "due to a large extent to Davis's influence and to that of Bill Gallagher, who didn't care for rock but was finding it much easier to market. The staff meetings that used to be about Mathis, Conniff, and Bennett were now about the Byrds and Paul Revere and the Raiders. Bennett felt neglected."

And he was expensive. "He was incapable of insincerity," Marmorstein wrote, "an asset that in pop circles would come to be viewed as a liability." His perfectionism cost. Marmorstein writes of job sheets on a new Bennett album recorded in 1968: "The session, held at 30th street . . . began at 8 p.m. . . . and ran to 11 p.m. Forty-five musicians were paid $65 each, with extra pay to the arranger and music copyist, plus rental, cartage and piano-tuning fees. The session cost $4,745—all for three hours' worth of recording. With Clive Davis toting up numbers and openly favoring rock-oriented groups that didn't require forty-five musicians per session, it's no wonder such recordings would soon vanish—even at Columbia." (While Bennett was expensive, so were the electric guitar pop bands that were doing an enormous amount of overdubbing and racking up huge expenses in studio time in the aftermath of *Sergeant Pepper's Lonely Hearts Club Band* and *Bridge Over Troubled Water*.)

Bennett survived the 1960s at Columbia because he made money for the company. "That Tony Bennett never recorded a Paul Simon song isn't unusual," Marmorstein wrote. "Simon's lyrics often lack the love interest or the general wistfulness so endemic to the saloon ballad Bennett specialized in. Through the sixties, though, Bennett remained the quintessential Columbia Records artist: dependable, profitable, often taking musical risks. . . . He usually had Ralph Sharon accompanying him, and [producer Ernie] Altschuler delivered, in addition to Marty Manning, the best arrangers and conductors in the business: Don Costa, Dick Hyman, Frank De Vol, Ralph Burns, Marion Evans,

Neal Hefti, Bennett's favorite engineer. Frank Laico, who first got a job as a clerk at a recording studio after delivering groceries before World War II, recorded most of these albums. During this period Bennett took on a whole new folio of signature songs, including Alec Wilder's 'I'll Be Around,' Sacha Distel's 'The Good Life,' and Johnny Mercer's 'I Wanna Be Around.' . . . In contrast to Sinatra's readings of ballads like these, which tended to plumb them for their wee-small-hours anguish, Bennett's interpretations usually let a few sun rays slant through. The Bennett narrator could be crushed but remained hopeful."

Clive Davis had been an accountant, and later an attorney who had previously been head of business affairs for Columbia. A harbinger of what was in store for Bennett can be foreseen in a meeting in early 1968 that Davis described in his autobiography, *Clive: Inside the Record Business*. He had invited the famed Broadway composer Richard Rodgers into his office to listen to new Janis Joplin tapes. He played Joplin's version of "Summertime" and waited for Rodgers's reaction. Rodgers was silent. Then Davis played "Piece of My Heart." Rodgers requested that Davis stop the tape. "If this means I have to change my writing," he said to Davis, "or that the only way to write a Broadway musical is to write rock songs, *then my career is over*." Rodgers stormed out of the office.

Bennett was embittered that Columbia had for the first time put a person in charge of the company without any musical background. Davis's insistence that singers record only rock and roll, and that only rock and roll was commercially viable, further infuriated him. On top of this, Davis's favorite kind of singer was the "middle-of-the-road art-ist" who was willing to do "covers" of already existing rock hits—in other words, imitate what had already been done by other singers in the hope of getting a piece of the action—leftovers. Bennett was offended and humiliated by what he regarded as a philistine's approach to the art form he loved and cherished.

Davis wrote in his autobiography (which Will Friedwald calls "the *Mein Kampf* of the music world"), that "as we approached the second half of the decade, the decline in middle-of-the-road momentum became noticeable. . . .Top Forty was becoming almost exclusively rock-oriented. Broadway writers were writing fewer and fewer hit songs. Tony Bennett's great streak in the early sixties, which had included 'I Left My Heart in San Francisco,' 'I Wanna Be Around,' 'If I Ruled the World,' and 'Who Can I Turn To?,' was now in jeopardy. New vitality was needed."

Bennett, of course, disagreed. He saw no reason to do second-rate music. Bennett cited two tracks he'd recorded with trumpeter Bobby Hackett on his album *A Time for Love*, "Sleepy Time Gal" and "The Very Thought of You" (when he'd appeared again in London on BBC with Hackett and one hundred musicians, one of the programs produced by Yvonne Littlewood), as "the best recording session" he'd ever had with Hackett. And he was right.

Bennett was traumatized by the situation at Columbia during the time the label purchased the Fender musical instrument company in January 1965 for $13 million. The Fender purchase might have been one of many factors in the artistic decisions Columbia made. Fender made the electric basses and electric guitars that were the most popular and widely used instruments of the Woodstock generation. A coalescence of the musical marketplace took place during the Vietnam War as the antiwar movement became massive and nationwide. It had its anthems and its poets—Bob Dylan, Jimi Hendrix, the peaceniks, and the hippies. For the first time it seemed as if the record industry could do no wrong; all of these records were going gold. The record companies associated rock-style electric instruments with economic success. It made sense to Columbia to purchase a musical instrument company, since they were promoting these instruments with the product they were selling and saw no reason why they should not profit from it.

At the same time that this was going on, Bennett and the other "middle of the road" Columbia artists were being isolated and marginalized. As the most talented and unique artist among them who still commanded sales and audiences, Bennett could ultimately survive; others, who had basked in the limelight for many years, suffered far more. But he felt humiliated at the same time that he despised the artistic direction Columbia was taking. And more than humiliation, he felt rage. His aesthetic beliefs—beliefs that he adhered to with fervor and passionate conviction—were on the line. Bennett's stance was a heroic one: he was determined to oppose the powerful commercial forces that might have destroyed him. These pivotal events were decisive in shaping Bennett's total aversion to the musical scene that would soon commandeer the entire industry.

"A year before I left the gig," John Bunch related, "Tony lost the contract he'd had with Columbia for years. They were fighting all the time; he refused to do crap. I always admired him for that, because he was really going against the grain. And going against the popularity of that music. He stood up for his musical tastes."

The Mafia continued to cast a shadow over Bennett's life in the 1960s, particularly because of Tony Tamburello. Tamburello made a serious mistake in dealing with the boys: he tried to rip them off. The date has never been clarified, but it was a close call. "The John Quinlan [vocal coach] studio, where Tony Bennett first auditioned, was run by the wiseguys," Geri Tamburello recalled. "All the singers came there; it was very popular. There were threats from these guys, and we were afraid. They threatened to hurt my husband's hands. We went underground, my husband and I. I don't know that Tony B was involved."

Marion Evans remembers versions of the incident that Geri Tamburello is unaware of. "They did a job on Tony T so bad," Evans said. "Actually it was his fault really. He had an office in the same building as Tony B at 200 West 57th Street. Tamburello started coaching other people. He had a little side business. And they had taken in a lot of money. 'The boys' had put up the money for this. And Tony T took the money and went to Italy, I believe. He said he'd pay it back. But you know, they took a dim view of that."

The definitive version seems to come from Derek Boulton. "Tony T told me that he'd forged the signature of one of the wiseguy backers on a check," Boulton said. "The check required two signatures and he forged the other one. A big check. They beat him up for the check he forged." Boulton recalled that Tamburello recovered from his injuries.

The way Geri tells it, "My husband, through the stress of the situation, developed a back problem. He was really down for over a year. He had sciatica in both legs. He was in pain. It was very rough. He kept writing. We had a piano in our apartment. He had a covered hassock to rest his legs on. He was leaning over that on the floor and would reach up with one hand and hit a chord occasionally or play a few notes with one hand. Then he was writing on the floor. He had the score paper near the hassock. He's writing on the floor, he's playing with one hand. And he wrote twelve compositions. He put an athletic bar in the doorway and used to hang from it. One day he was hanging there and his back slipped into place."

Sometime in the late 1960s, Bennett sought and received an advance from Columbia of $600,000, which he used to sever any relationships with the wiseguys. It was an extraordinary gesture on his part to guarantee that he could maintain his independence. "Tony's sister, Mary, didn't tell me too much about it," Derek Boulton said. "Tony didn't talk to me about it and I never raised the subject. I don't know who did the deal. After I became Tony's manager in 1970, I was going over the books. I said to Mary, 'What the hell is that $600,000 for?' She said that was for his previous management, that they got paid off. She never referred to the Mafia. Look, all the jukeboxes were controlled by the mob. Everybody had what Tony called a 'rabbi.' I just don't know who negotiated it and how it came about. CBS wouldn't say what it was for. CBS was quite prepared to give that sum for what I'd call a 'release fee' from his contract. The only way Tony broke with whatever you want to call it was when CBS loaned him that $600,000. The wiseguys must have thought Tony was finished. He had slipped down the ladder. They never did put a high value on him. See, he didn't want to play nightclubs anymore."

Although the Mafia appeared to go along with the $600,000 severance package, the boys may not have been too happy, as things did not end there. There was an ugly incident in 1971. When Bennett performed again at Carnegie Hall on October 9 with Robert Farnon and a fifty-piece orchestra, a stink bomb was planted in the auditorium, emptying out the concert hall in the middle of the performance. (The audience was able to return later.) Bennett has written that he assumed it was one of "the boys" trying to scare him but that it didn't work.

"Bennett was upset," Derek Boulton remembered. "He's got a very strong front. He overrode it all. He overrides a lot. They were trying to wreck our concerts. We went around the country doing proper concerts and ignoring nightclubs. The wiseguys love the control of the liquor. I don't think for one minute they thought I was going to last more than three months. I changed Bennett around. I was a vehicle that drove the bus in a different direction."

Bennett recalled the stink bomb incident at Carnegie Hall in a 2006 interview with the *London Daily Telegraph Magazine*, but mistakenly ascribed it to 1962, his first Carnegie Hall concert, not 1971, when it actually took place. In the process of denying that the wiseguys had ever put pressure on him, he did acknowledge the one incident. "Just once," the article stated, "he says, has he felt a threatening hand on his shoulder. . . . 'During the Carnegie show somebody threw stink bombs into the air-conditioners. They explained to everybody, please step outside and we'll have this cleared immediately. And everybody stayed and we finished the concert. But it's a changing scene now; that's all gone.'"

Equally odious for Bennett was his ongoing conflict with Clive Davis. "Clive Davis never respected Tony for the artist that he was," Derek Boulton told me. "Davis wanted to control everything. He placed Barbra Streisand and Andy Williams above Tony when it came to promotion. He was not the best A&R boss for him. You've got to have chemistry between the two. There was no chemistry there." Davis, in his memoir, contrasted the success he'd had with Johnny Mathis with his struggle with Bennett. He wrote that he had considerably less luck with Tony, and that he had urged Tony to record more contemporary material. Tony always resisted him.

"The best writers in the world, Tony kept telling me, were Gershwin, Richard Rodgers and Harold Arlen; he may have been right. The best performers were Judy Garland, Al Jolson and Jimmy Durante. Again, he certainly could make a case. He felt that his artistry was linked to them and he did not want to compromise it. . . .

"He wouldn't budge. I met with Buddy Howe, who was Chairman of the Board of CMA . . . to ask his help. Then Tony's sister, Mary— who sometimes acted as his manager—called to say that Tony was so emotionally distraught over the problem that he was literally throwing up just thinking of recording this unfamiliar repertoire. . . .

"He kept calling to complain about sales; and this would inevitably lead to arguments about whether he should be recording an album of Rodgers and Hart or Lennon and McCartney. 'I fully respect your artistic integrity,' I said, 'but if you keep accusing us of not promoting you enough, I have no choice but to put on my business hat. You have to *update* your repertoire.' Finally, Tony agreed to try an album of contemporary songs in 1970 [*Tony Sings the Great Hits of Today*].

"With current repertoire, Tony's album sales jumped substantially . . . but he basically returned to his original thinking. His artistry was clearly defined—he just couldn't change.

"After a while the conversations ceased; we were both exhausted."

While recording *Tony Sings the Great Hits of Today*, Bennett literally vomited before the recording session. It is hard to think of another singer who would have such a visceral reaction to betraying his art. Yet Bennett recounts several incidents in his memoir when he threw up when being confronted with singing material he detested. The album itself is one of his least satisfying, and it did not accomplish much careerwise. If anything, it threatened to reduce his core base of fans.

In 1968 Bennett had a great hit with his single "For Once in My Life," recorded three fine albums—*For Once in My Life, Yesterday I Heard the Rain*, and *Snowfall*—and celebrated his twentieth anniversary in show business with a twenty-five-concert tour with Duke Ellington beginning with a sellout at the New York Philharmonic on March 3. Once again, as he had done with Count Basie, Bennett expressed his veneration for Duke Ellington by taking second billing, an almost unprecedented gesture for a singer to do and, on Bennett's part, a spontaneous and absolutely genuine one. He has emphasized over and over again that Ellington has composed more music than anyone in musical history, from ballet suites and tone poems to popular songs and sacred concerts. Bennett told Willis Conover that year, "William Blake said something like 'If you sit on the shoulders of a big man you can see a thousand miles.' That's one way of saying the way I feel whenever I have an opportunity to work with Duke."

The musical trade paper *Billboard* marked Bennett's twentieth anniversary in show business by devoting an entire issue to him on November 30, 1968. Filled with accolades and accounts of Bennett's incredible success, there was no indication that Bennett was not at the top of the entertainment world, no hint of the acrimony of Bennett's relationship with Clive Davis and Columbia or of the turning point he was reaching in his career with the advent of rock culture and the encroaching commercialism of the musical marketplace. There were expressions of love and approbation in ads taken by composers Johnny Mandel, Harry Warren, Jimmy McHugh, Jule Styne, Betty Comden, Harold Arlen, Adolph Green, Cy Coleman, and Carolyn Leigh, as well as Sinatra, Lou Rawls, Judy Garland, Louis Armstrong, Fred Astaire, Duke Ellington, Harry Belafonte, Jackie Gleason, Gil Evans, Stan Getz, Dizzy Gillespie, Barbra Streisand, veteran bandleader Ted Lewis, and Count Basie, writers Alec Wilder and Gunther Schuller, Mitch Miller, Clive Davis, and Howard Richmond, and many photographs of Bennett in performance. A vivid lead article, "20 Years with Tony," was written by Willis Conover, jazz broadcaster for the Voice of America and chairman of the jazz committee of the National Endowment for the Arts music panel, and clearly a Bennett enthusiast. There seemed to be heavy support from Columbia, and the front page was a photo of the cover of Bennett's latest album for Columbia, *Snowfall*.

Conover recounts the ritual of a recording session for *Snowfall* at the church on Thirtieth Street. He writes of Bennett as a singer: "If Tony is a figure of controlled passion in the recording studio, onstage he is electrified. You can almost see the rays shooting from him, like a science-fiction movie. He leaps onto a stage as if he can't wait to sing, and he is singing when he hits the microphone.

"The effect is more than merely gymnastic: the music is coming from every part of his body, and he will silence none of it.

"A friend says, 'Tony is like a boxer. He's always in the ring, always fighting, proving himself in every round, even when everything's under control and at his fingertips.'

"It can be frightening, being so exposed—on a record, or facing a live audience. It's the only way an artist can reach his audience, of course, but the audience can also reach him."

"Pearl Bailey said to me once," Bennett told Conover, "'Sonny boy, it's gonna take you 10 years merely to learn how to walk on stage.'

And that's how long it took me," says Tony. "I don't even have to think about it now; it just happens."

Tony projects the same spontaneity on television. He prepares himself for his TV appearances because "I want to do TV really right—like Fred Astaire," but he believes that "too often a performance is so well rehearsed, so technically perfect, that the fun goes out of it. What you're left with is Muzak."

In October 1969 Bennett appeared with Lena Horne on a Burt Bacharach TV special on NBC. Peter Matz conducted and Joe Soldo was contractor for the show. It would be the start of a series of collaborations between them from 1971 to 1975. The pattern was set on the Kraft show, with the two of them singing four songs together, a solo set by Horne, a solo set by Bennett, and a closing lengthy medley of Harold Arlen songs, including "Ill Wind," "I Got a Right to Sing the Blues," "Any Place I Hang My Hat Is Home," "Paper Moon," "One for My Baby," "Over the Rainbow," "My Shining Hour," "This Time the Dream's On Me," "Get Happy," "Accentuate the Positive," "Last Night When We Were Young," "Right as the Rain," "I've Got the World on a String," "Let's Fall in Love," "That Old Black Magic," "Happiness Is Just a Thing Called Joe," "Stormy Weather," and "Come Rain or Come Shine." A great singer but a steely, icy, and combustible personality, Horne rarely looked at Bennett except in the magnificent closing medley, when she seemed to finally—intermittently—respond to him. Nevertheless, Bennett liked the combination, and would soon organize a duo tour, *Tony & Lena Sing*.

On the surface Bennett was maintaining his career at a steady pace, but he was reeling from the pressure with Clive Davis at Columbia and the separation from Patricia, which had been dragging on for four years. They were unable to reach an understanding. Bennett was served with divorce papers.

At the same time, his relationship with Sandra Grant was a stormy and volatile one, and his problems with her would steadily worsen in the coming years. "Sandy Two, we used to call her," John Bunch recalled. "They had a lot of fights, terrible. One time we were rehearsing, just he and I with a piano. In a suite in the Beverly Hills Hotel. That's where they were staying. She gets mad at him. I'm sitting at the little spinet piano. And she threw something at him. It burst by my head. And I got up and left. I couldn't get into this. I said to him, 'Tony, I'm sorry. I have to leave.' He said, 'Go ahead, John. I'm sorry.'

"There are a million stories about her. We were on a tour with Buddy Rich's band in London. The place was packed. Sandy threatened to go out onstage in the middle of his act. They had a terrible fight and she was going to run out there. She had to be restrained by somebody."

"There was one incident," Geri Tamburello told me, "where Tony was having an altercation with Sandy. She was actually attacking him physically. She was hitting him on the head with the telephone. I wasn't there; my husband, Tony, was there; he saw it. Tony B tried to defend himself."

"Sandy Two got friendly with Gene Kelly," Derek Boulton recalled. "One Christmas, Kelly's Christmas tree caught fire and his house burned down. He goes to live in Bennett's place. Bennett was in New York. Tony says to me, 'I'm feeding Gene Kelly.' Sandy Two made the remark, 'Gene is a gentleman.' Well, no one was gentler and kinder than Tony."

There was one concert triumph after the other: he toured Europe with the Count Basie Orchestra in late 1967. "There are very, very few singers I asked the great musicians in my band to play behind," Basie commented, "and Tony is one of them. But you know what? When we play with Tony, we're not behind him at all! Tony puts us all up front with him! Someday I'm going to find a way to sit in the audience and watch Tony work with the Basie band, just like a fan. Because that's what I am."

There was standing room only at every show at the Palm House, in Chicago, the Waldorf and the Copacabana in New York, the Coconut Grove and the Hollywood Bowl in Los Angeles, the Diplomat in Hollywood, Florida, and Caesars Palace in Las Vegas. All four Carnegie Hall concerts had been sold out in advance. On March 3, 1968, Bennett set a new house record in Lincoln Center's Philharmonic Hall. His tour in England was as big an attraction there as the Beatles were in the United States. There was the command performance for the queen of England in 1965. He sang for the president at the White House and for the prime minister of Japan in 1968 while touring in Japan. Prime Minister and Mrs. Sato sent a wire and flowers to his hotel room. Caesars Palace in Las Vegas signed him to a lifetime contract. He was on the road thirty-seven weeks in 1969, performing two shows a night. He seemed to be simultaneously on top of the world and standing on a fatal precipice.

With all the tumult in his life, Bennett continued to confirm his reputation as "Tony Benefit" by giving endless concerts for good causes. He sang at the Billy Strayhorn Scholarship Fund Concert for Duke Ellington on October 6, 1968.

When I interviewed the late George Siravo, a talented composer and arranger for Bennett and Sinatra, he spoke of Bennett's persona as usually a model of affability, even politesse, and recalled Bennett's past patterns with aggressive women. "Tony Bennett could say, 'I'm going to kill you,' and have a smile on his face. Tony was dating a girl who everybody thought was a high-class hooker from Sherman Oaks," Siravo said. "I used to call her Coke Bottles because she used to hit Tony on the head with them. As beautiful as she was, she was as cold as ice. What he took from that broad!"

In addition to Bennett's divorce battle with Sandy One and escalating pitched battles with Sandy Two, his mother was bedridden with several different kinds of arthritis. Her condition was seriously worsening. He was running back and forth between New York and River Edge, New Jersey, to see her. Each time he was afraid he would never see her again. His relationship with Sandy Two reached some level of stability for a while when their daughter, Joanna, was born in January 1970. Bennett was overjoyed.

In October Bennett recorded another contemporary album, *Tony Bennett's Something*. The album cover was a lovely photo of Bennett cradling Joanna in his arms. It was much closer in spirit to his genuine art than the album he'd made for Clive Davis, *Tony Sings the Great Hits of Today*, the one that caused him to regurgitate. Here he sang the George Harrison song "Something" and "The Long and Winding Road" beautifully and did an outstanding version of "Wave" and Louis Armstrong's immortal hit "What a Wonderful World."

As Bennett told Willis Conover in 1968, "No matter what happens in your personal life, you come out and perform anyway. I don't want people to know my hangups so they can get over theirs. I want them to respond to the performance. Because that's when I'm communicating the essence of my life, not the superficials. A good performance is like good literature; it says the truth, the reality. Sensationalism only distorts things. . . . Offstage, the incongruities are what make life beautiful, it's not the things you expect. But in performances, you must be prepared and consistent." Self-discipline and hard work anchored him. "I believe a man's life is his work," he said to Phil Casey. ". . . Laying off makes me restless. I like to keep up the tempo of my life. I think work is the answer to a lot of things."

At this time Bennett found someone who understood his problems: Derek Boulton, the enormously successful English manager of Robert Farnon, moved from London to New York and became Bennett's manager as well in April 1971. Bennett, who had a faltering pattern with previous managers, was lucky this time. Boulton was a brilliant, convivial, and cheeky character who could stand up to Bennett, love him, take care of him, and help to right his career. Boulton could not have come at a better time: in addition to his problems with Columbia, Bennett was deeply in debt. When I interviewed Boulton in London in the fall of 2009, he was eager to convey how deeply he respected Bennett even though he was highly mindful of his flaws. "I followed Tony into this world six months later," Boulton told me. "Mary, his sister, used to say to me, 'You don't realize it, but you are so much like him.' Not in our looks, but our attitudes toward life.

"When I look at it," Boulton said, "I gave him my life. I helped him at a very important time. I wasn't his savior, but I was very much an influence at a time he needed somebody. He needed somebody to fight his agents, and to fight CBS, where he was being shockingly treated."

As early as 1961 Patricia had been threatening Tony with divorce. They separated in 1965. She had finally sued Bennett for divorce on September 25, 1969, on grounds of adultery and desertion, and charged that he had committed adultery with Sandra Grant on New Year's Eve 1966 and "in the months and years before and after that date." She charged that Bennett left her as early as August 19, 1964, and had "willfully, continuously and obstinately" deserted her. She asked for the custody of their two boys. There were many separations and reconciliations over the years until it was really over in 1971.

One of Boulton's first tasks as Bennett's new manager was helping him actually obtain the divorce. "When it came to helping him get the divorce from Patricia," Boulton recalled, "his sister, Mary, wouldn't move, the priest wouldn't move. He needed badly for someone to help him at the time. I had just begun to manage him. Tony asked me to help him with the divorce.

"I was to go through a deposition. It was the first move toward getting the divorce. Tony said, 'You've got to come over to New Jersey with me.' And off I go with him to Hackensack. 'Would you state your name, sir?' the court official asked me. I answered, 'Derek Nelson Cyril Boulton.' 'Cyril' provoked laughter. Tony said, 'What's funny about that?' They asked me a few questions about what sort of person he was. Very moral, I said; loved his children, loved his family.

"On the way home in the car, I said to Tony, 'Are you going to go ahead with all this?' Tony closed the curtain between Caesar, the driver, and us. He looked me straight in the face. 'Derek,' he said, 'if I do not marry Sandy, I will never be able to look Joanna in the face.' He is a very honorable man.

"And I was there without Tony later for the divorce proceedings. He was in Detroit; he was working in Windsor, the other side of the river in Canada, for six days, and couldn't attend. At that point, he really needed the money. He owed a million, but nobody who worked for him ever told him. He was earning $700,000 gross; how was he ever going to pay it off? He phoned me to go to New Jersey to witness the proceedings. I had to be a bit of a stand-in. Tony said to me, 'Make sure my family's all right.' Which I thought were lovely words from a parting husband. He didn't want their alimony or child support cut. He wanted his family well taken care of. He said if there was any attempt, stop it. The boys were on about twenty-six a year and I think Patricia was getting ninety. So they weren't reduced in any way.

"Danny had long hair, and his mother was stroking the back of his head," Boulton remembered. "Patricia was ideal for Tony. On the occasions when I met her with Danny, she was very charming and very wonderful. To me she was more suited for Tony than anyone. Tony said to me once, 'We fell out of love.' As his sister, Mary, said to me, 'When he's on tour, you never know who he's going to meet. And if you're Italian: bingo.'

"So I had to sit there and watch all that. It was the breakup of a loving Italian family. It was a genuine marriage and a wonderful, real love between them. I was very sad about it. It was one of the saddest things that Tony asked me to do, witness his divorce.

"When the divorce was finalized I called him and said, 'You're divorced.' He said, 'Thank you,' and hung up. They were all—Tony, Patricia, Danny, Daegal—very kind to me. A lovely family. I'm still sorry today it got all screwed up.

"Tony and Patricia should never have parted," Boulton continued. "Why he screwed it up I do not know. Way after they parted, Patricia saw him on television. She said to me, 'Derek, I can see that sadness in his eyes. And it makes me want to cry.'"

Bennett would rarely live in a house of his own again. His other residences have mainly been apartments, and, for many years, adjoining or near Central Park, as he had always wanted.

The early 1970s would be a period of change for Bennett, when, due to Boulton's efforts, he essentially went from nightclubs to concert halls. It would be more in keeping with his personality—he hated the noise, the fights, the clanging of dishes, the rough, abrasive atmosphere of clubs—and would raise his image and stature. "I came at the right time, when Tony needed someone he could trust," Boulton recalled. "He wasn't doing well at Columbia, yet his TV show in London for Thames would soon garner the number-one rating. I felt sorry for him: somebody I admired a great deal—somebody who'd given happiness to people for years and years of his life and not gotten any in return. Very sad. He had that group around him: Phil Braunstein, Buddy Howe, and Jack Katz. Katz was an attorney, very straight man. But Braunstein seemed to want to control his money. I was treading on people's toes, or should I say, stamping on them. And all on Tony's instructions, too. He wanted to be free of them. His finances were a mess. He was in debt for about a million dollars: $600,000 to the tax people, he'd borrowed $600,000 from CBS to buy off his previous management, and he'd only earned $700,000. I had the job of trying to sort it out in a year. Well, I did it in three years, and then I left.

"You see, when I got there, there had been people around Tony trying to tell him how to spend every dollar. There were four people who would sign Tony's checkbooks apart from his sister, Mary—whom he trusted completely—including his accountant Phil Braunstein and Braunstein's son. Braunstein was replaced by David Gotterer; I took his assistant, Frank Stella, to the proceedings with me to make sure there was no monkey business with the money. Tony's son Danny was in court with his mother. 'Do you admit having adultery with [so-and-so]? 'Yes.' 'Do you admit having adultery with someone else?' 'No.' I answered in his place. He told me what to say. The lawyer turned to the judge and said, 'I've got some more [names].' The judge banged his gavel. 'All right,' he said, 'don't make a career out of this. Divorce granted.' They tried to blacken Tony a lot that day, and all he did was make sure his family was all right.

"After I found out the true financial state of Tony's business I went to New York. I had to tell him. I told him at dinner one night. When I said, 'You don't owe 300,000, you owe over a million.' '*What?*' Nobody had told him the truth. He had told me he needed a cleanup job and by God he got one.

"So at the time I got there, there were these four people: sister Mary, who was a lovely soul; Phil Braunstein; Fred Braunstein; and the other Braunstein. Three of them! And I asked Phil why is Tony paying all the airfare up from Florida? He would charge Tony the airfare for all his clients. It was crazy crazy crazy. Phil Braunstein boasted he represented Burt Bacharach, Marlene Dietrich. Then I had him. I said, 'Why are you charging Tony for your fare when you're also coming to town to see Bacharach, Dietrich, Angie Dickinson, and Percy Faith?' He said, 'Dietrich's got no money so I don't charge her.' I said, 'Why should Tony pay the full fare when he's only one of four or five artists you're coming to see?' He took the bill away and gave me back a third of it. I caught the bastard. I'm surprised Mary didn't twig him on it. I've never stolen a penny off of anybody. I did a load of expenses, picked up bills for Tony, and never charged him. And he counteracted by doing some of mine. We had a very close relationship.

"They'd say to him, 'How'd the dago? [day go]? At that time I didn't know what 'dago' meant. And I'm thinking you're taking his money, you can keep your mouth shut and respect him or fuck off. They weren't right for him. I wondered what have I gotten myself into here? And Phil Braunstein took me out to lunch and said, 'He's [Tony] on smoke every day. He's in hopeless debt.' I said, 'I know he's got a problem. You should have sorted it out by now.' Phil didn't like that one. He wanted me to get my ass back to England, wanted me to run away. Bennett was a money-making machine for CAM [Creative Artists Management].

"I said to Tony, 'I have a suggestion. Only you sign the checkbook. You've made a million this year. First time ever.' It worked out he had about $120,000 after everybody was paid. So I made him sign his own checkbook. And I think he spent money on bloody dope, although I never once saw him use a drug in my presence. I'm not a purist at all, but I wanted him right. You never knew what he was going to do tomorrow. Bennett has got a wonderful spirit going. But it was very strange, erratic behavior. He trusted me completely. I honored it. I threw my business up for him and threw my lot in with him completely. I argued with people who said it was a complete waste of time.

"You'll never meet another man like him, that's for sure. He's a one-off. He's got so much to offer us all. Gives so much pleasure. Sinatra and Bennett are both Italian hotheads. Sinatra hated the fact that I got Tony with symphony orchestras. Sinatra said to Tony in an elevator, 'You're singing with symphony orchestras, huh?' Bloody jealous. Tony called me about it and told me. He laughed. He loved it. I took Bennett amongst the arts, away from the booze brigade. I was bloody determined to figure it out."

Sandy Two and Tony were married in December 1971. "The moment she became his wife she took a deep interest in the financial situation," Boulton remembered. "She disgraced him. He used to order her out of the room when we discussed business together. She got in the way: money money money. It was very sad for him. All his life he worked hard, he made millions of people happy. But he wasn't happy himself. How do you account for this?

"When I joined Tony in 1971, Danny and Daegal wouldn't even talk with their father. Danny said to me, 'How would you like to have your father run away when you're eleven and leave you for another

woman?' They were very bitter. Sandy Two wouldn't let him even see
his sons. She had said to me before he married her, 'Whatever you
do, don't bring them up to the apartment.' I said, 'They're his sons.'
'They're not going to come in my home.'

"Tony didn't say anything, but I could see by his face how he felt.
This was at East 68th Street. Tony was playing the Waldorf. He had
the Duke of Windsor suite, which was 33-A in the Towers. It had five
bedrooms, a large lounge. A part of the lounge had a floor brought in
from a French château and a little grand piano. This was where Fred
Astaire used to rehearse with Cole Porter [when Porter and Astaire
worked in *Gay Divorce* together on Broadway in 1932]. I could see
the closeness that was missing between Tony and the boys, which was
wrong. He was still paying out all the time; he was a very good father
like that. But I felt that he needed some love and affection in return.
He never got it from the boys until I brought them together.

"I called up the boys and said, 'Come and see your dad.' One day
between the two nightly shows—he'd done one and the second one
wasn't until midnight; he had three hours to kill—I said to Tony, "I've got
somebody in the spare room for you to see.' 'What?' he said. 'Please come.'
He had his trousers and shirt on, no shoes. 'Who is it?' I said, 'Please come
out. It's Danny and Daegal. They want to see you.' And he went in there,
and there they were. I closed the door. I wasn't part of it. And Sandy Two
ripped into me: 'What the fuck have you brought them here for?' I said,
'Sandy, they are Tony's sons. And it's been eating him up.'

"Tony said to me later that night, 'You brought my boys back to
me. You brought my boys back to me.'

"He saw them from then on. Patricia came to London with the
boys. 'We want to meet the Beatles.' I knew George Martin very well.
They went down to the Beatles' offices with George. They met Paul
McCartney and all of them; they could not have been happier. But it
was very hard for Tony. Because of Sandy.

"After I left Tony, Danny said, 'Will you come to the house for
dinner? I'll come and pick you up.' He came, took me to Englewood.
On the way over he said, 'Derek, what do you think of Sandy?' Being
tactful, I said, 'Not a lot.' He said, 'I hate her guts. She took my daddy
from me when I was eleven.'"

"Divorce smashes everything," Bennett told *Good Housekeeping* many years later, in April 1995. "And it affects everyone—kids as well as grown-ups. One of my few regrets is that I wasn't with my children as much as I would have liked. But I did stay involved with them. I truly tried to be a good father and some of my most wonderful moments were with them. My children are my true joy and blessing. And they understand my need to work."

Bennett's marital troubles coincided with his ambivalent relationship with Columbia. In 1971 Bennett was offered $50,000 a year by the label for a three-year deal. "It wasn't perceived as a lot of money anymore," Gary Marmorstein wrote, "but it was still a risky chunk for a company with a direction that largely precluded jazz singers. Over the course of two decades Bennett had undeniably enriched the label—but he was at heart a jazz singer and sensed he was being increasingly marginalized. On July 8, 1971, Bennett appeared on the *Merv Griffin Show* along with Peggy Lee. While Columbia had promoted Bennett's recent album *Love Story*, with the movie title song its centerpiece, Peggy Lee had more comfortably handled Lieber and Stoller's "Is That All There Is?" and a cover of Bread's "Make It with You." "Capitol Records is going all out with promotion, advertising, etc., for Peggy and we should do likewise for Tony," Columbia producer Teo Macero implored his colleagues. "He is on the verge of leaving the label and I think our action regarding the above will help cement relations. After all, he is a great artist and should be treated as such."

"I have arrived at a point where I don't want to make any concessions just to get ahead," Bennett told the music critic Leonard Feather. "I could very easily get into trouble saleswise, but I'm sorry, I can't do a song unless I feel it. I want to stay with the great songwriting specialists, the Jimmy Van Heusens, the Johnny Mercers, the Harold Arlens. I'm moving more and more toward music, rather than having a company dictate to me. I feel a great audacity toward these IBM machines that tell me, 'This is how we want you to do it, whether you like it or not.' I don't know how long I can get away with it, but it's fun. It's a funny thing. The better the songs I record, the more people seem to like it." Derek Boulton recalled Bennett's passion for good music: "He used to get hold of something, a new song, and exclaim to me, 'Listen to this lyric! Listen to this!'"

Another precipitating factor in the deterioration of Bennett's relationship with Columbia was his friendship with composer Alec Wilder and his determination to record a series of poems Wilder had set to music. *The Children's Plea for Peace* was based on the antiwar poems of the son of Bennetts' British friends Ken and Renee Gordon. The poems dealt with the Vietnam War from the point of view of a child. Wilder composed an octet around the poems and by the time he completed the work, it had music for a full orchestra, a children's chorus, and a narrator: Tony. Columbia thought the piece was too controversial and uncommercial, even though no one at the company had ever heard it.

Columbia's decision brought about Wilder's permanent estrangement from Bennett. Tony had been determined to record it, and waged a battle on its behalf. He walked out of an argument with Clive Davis and other Columbia officials and overheard one of them say, "We gotta get rid of that wop!"

Bennett went to Columbia and said he wanted to terminate his contract. He wanted to make records that were the best he could make, not merely records that sold. The battle got nastier and more personal on Davis's part.

"Clive Davis had done the dirtiest trick in the world on Tony," Derek Boulton told me. "Paramount had made the film of *Love Story*. Before I joined Tony in 1970, Tony recorded the song. Paramount gave him the exclusive rights to make the first record. He goes and records it. In the morning, when they got to do the mixing, Teo Macero goes down around eleven and finds out that Jack Gold, who was head of Columbia West Coast A&R and was a record producer for the label, had taken all of the tapes, not leaving a copy, to Andy Williams on the Coast. Williams got the record out before Tony's. While this is going on, Columbia also got Johnny Mathis to record it. So you've got three boy singers on the CBS label all singing the same song. I think Clive Davis's behavior toward Tony was damaging.

"Then Columbia plugged and pushed Williams's record far more than Tony's. Tony got to about forty on the charts, no more, and Andy

Williams got right into the top ten. Clive Davis did all this. He couldn't stand not being able to control Tony. He wanted to manipulate him. But Tony's character was too strong. You don't destroy what's been your main catalog for two or three decades; that's what Davis did.

"That was not the end of the story," Boulton said. "Columbia still didn't want to lose Tony. They were not dropping him; they wanted to retain him. I went to the CBS lawyer, Walter Dean. We had meetings for two or three hours three or four times a week. These were about giving Tony a new deal. Andy Williams had gotten a deal from them for a label of his own called Barnaby. Williams took other singers on that label, but he had to pay for it all: hire the studio, pay for pressing, everything. Barnaby cost Williams a fortune. I said to Dean, 'We'll do this differently. You give Bennett a label, but not a separate one like Barnaby. Call it Tony Bennett Productions. You give him the studio, you do all the editing, you pay for printing, you give him a straight 10 percent royalty—[which was top royalty in those days]—and no advance. He has to bring the artists in and pay for the recording.' I thought it was a bloody good deal actually, one they'd never done before with anybody. I felt I'd done something wonderful.

"So I got the contract for Tony. It was a thick one; it had the heft of a phone book. I took it up to Tony. Sandy Two was there with him. 'You've won the battle with CBS,' I said. He said, 'What do you mean?' 'There's your contract. You can take five singers on the label of your own choice. They're paying for the printing, recording, the publicity. All you've got to do is put the talent in the studio.' He said, 'Let me look at it.' And he looked at it. He didn't read it. He gets hold of it and he tries to tear it up. And he had so much bloody strength he actually succeeded. Tore it right up. In half! He said, 'I don't trust those mothers.' He could not work with them. He was determined to leave.

"So he wouldn't sign it. Walter Dean had done all the paperwork. Anyway, two or three days later, I took Tony up there to Dean's office. I pretended Tony had lost the contract. They must have known I was playing games. Walter begins, 'I'm so glad you're going to stay with us, Tony.' And then Tony struck right out and socked Walter in the jaw. Knocked him on the floor. Walter had some papers in his hands and they went flying. I had to pick him up with his glasses and everything.

Then I picked the papers up. They were a new contract for Barbra Streisand.

"Tony patted me on the shoulder and said, 'I'm leaving,' and walked out. I stayed with Walter, because I feared a legal action. He wasn't hurt; he was shaken. I went back to my office and wrote an apology to Walter.

"It was a very good deal and Tony blew it."

Bennett made his last record for Columbia, "The Summer Knows," by Michel Legrand and Alan and Marilyn Bergman, at a recording session on November 15, 1971. He had been at the label for twenty-one years.

It was over.

8

A Quality That
Lets You In

On February 19, 1971, a concert took place in London that turned
Tony's career around in England. The orchestra consisted of
ninety musicians, including sixty strings. Robert Farnon conducted,
and John Bunch was his pianist. Bennett received a ten-minute standing ovation. The concert, "Tony Bennett Sings," was televised by
BBC2 in January 1972 and produced by Yvonne Littlewood.

The year 1971 had begun auspiciously for Bennett, with an invita-
tion from the London Philharmonic Orchestra to sing at a benefit at
Royal Albert Hall. It was a special event, as it was the fiftieth anniversary of the London Philharmonic. Derek Boulton, who was associated with the Philharmonic and specialized in concert music, felt that
Bennett was not being promoted in England and initiated the invita-
tion. He was acting as Bennett's contractor and would soon become
his manager later in 1971. "I had asked Tony if he would do the
concert, and he said yes." Boulton had gone to the Philharmonic and
said, "'Why don't you get Tony Bennett?' They said, 'Do you think

it will work?' I said, 'Of course it will work; it's magic.' It happened
during a great postal strike. I stacked my car with fliers and began
with northwest London one night, northeast London the next night,
and southwest London. I was like a postman for a week. I set off
about seven and came home about two. They sold out within a week.
Because if you give Tony a mountain to climb, by golly he'll climb it.
He will climb any mountain you give him."

Writing of the event in the July 1, 1971, issue of *Radio Times*,
Richard Williams noted that Bennett "carries himself with a simple
honesty and strength which have won him the respect of his musician-
peers, as well as that of a huge worldwide audience. Bennett is the
calm eye of the hurricane, a man of immense personal stability—and
because of it he's now welcome anywhere. Bennett's career was never
of the get-rich-quick variety. As befits his humble beginnings, he's
had a long, hard struggle to the top and now that he's there he doesn't
spend all his time letting you know it. He fought hard but he fought
fair, and even in his role as a popular entertainer he's never cared to
compromise his own musical standards to suit what many assume to be
a crucially changing market."

Boulton had arranged it all: the Philharmonic and the TV deal with
the BBC. "I had originally gone to see Bill Cotton, who was head
of BBC Variety and in control of programming," Boulton recalled,
"and told him 'I've got this charity show going with Tony Bennett;
what about televising it?' 'Who the hell wants to see a singer in front
of a bunch of fiddle players for an hour?' he said. I replied, 'I do.'
He said, 'Then you pay for it and I'll get us a deal. If you pay for the
orchestra and the whole thing and give it to us for one or two show-
ings in Britain, the tapes are yours for the world.' I bloody well did.
I thought the least we could do for Tony, who was coming to do
a charity, is to film it and give him the opportunity to be seen. When
I sold it in America with NBC, it got the top rating in New York;
it got a 28 share. You know, I could see more in Tony. His agents in
New York treated him only as a nightclub singer—a very lovely one,
a very successful one. They were quite happy to keep him in nightclubs and collect their money. But I saw him as a supreme concert
artist, and I proved myself right."

Boulton then negotiated a deal for a British TV series called *Tony Bennett from the Talk of the Town* [a famous supper club in London], coproduced with Thames Television. Billy Eckstine, Annie Ross, Cleo Laine, and Sarah Vaughan were among the guest artists. Bennett recorded thirteen shows and they were formatted as six specials. Bennett settled down in a penthouse flat in Grosvenor Square with his new wife, Sandra Grant, and baby daughter, Joanna. Bennett loved Britain and stayed an entire year. He felt that the British didn't pressure him to sing music he disliked and understood the nature of his art in a special way. Bennett went on to give two concerts at the London Palladium on March 26. The box office was sold out in thirty-five minutes.

But his personal life was not as successful as his performing, nor did it have the clarity and perspective. His relationship with his second wife, Sandy Two, would never achieve a level of equanimity. There were constant scenes; some of them were public and some were horrific. Jack Parnell, who conducted the royal command performance for Bennett, told me that "Tony was performing. She stripped in the front row while he sang. She was drunk. Her knickers [panties] came off. She was throwing her clothes on the stage. And he kept singing."

There seemed to be no limits to Sandy Two's erratic behavior. "Before I was with Tony," Boulton told me, "he had wanted Sandy Two out of the way. He had Jack Katz, the attorney, draw up a check for ten thousand dollars on the condition she leave Tony alone. She accepted it. They parted for a week or two or whatever. He came back to her. Then she became pregnant."

Director Abby Mann was close to Bennett at that time and told Robert Sullivan, "He was terribly depressed, at loose ends. His second marriage was breaking up and he was trying to find himself. I was in a divorce at the same time, and we were helping one another get through. We were in Rio, I remember, in a club. This singer started singing in Portuguese. Tony started humming; then it just poured out of him. He was scat-singing away! Everybody was electrified. He wasn't drunk or anything. It was just . . . he was a very unhappy man, and still he sang." It was during this period that Bennett began to paint seriously, and he would apply the same dogged determination to it that he gave to his singing.

Tony had brought Danny and Daegal over to meet the Beatles, and later they came to London for a vacation with their mother (Sandy One). "Phil Braunstein, the accountant, had given Sandy One only a couple of thousand dollars for the trip," Derek Boulton told me. "It was not enough. She said we're going to need more because we're going to Italy. Phil Braunstein said to Tony, 'This is what I can afford.' After that, Tony said to me, 'Fire Phil Braunstein. My family comes first, and I'm going to make sure they do before Sandy Grant [Sandy Two] gets a wooden nickel.' He wanted his two families taken care of.

"So I did fire Phil Braunstein. In defense of Braunstein, Tony didn't have the money to give at the time. So I loaned Tony the money; I sold my house. I was helping a bit, making the deposits on concert halls where we were playing, which turned Tony around. I'm glad I did that. Wherever he went, I doubled his money. Tony gave the boys whatever they wanted. 'They got the money,' I told him. 'Marvelous,' he said, and put the phone down. Those are the things he wanted.

"Tony looked at me at the end of our first year and said, 'You've made me give up dope.' The general atmosphere with Tony was insecure and worried. Tony was continually nervous. He'd wake me up. I'd be the first call of the morning before he got out of bed. You're with him lock, stock, and barrel. But I loved him a lot, and I still do. And if he wanted me, I'd be up there and I wouldn't leave him until ten or eleven or twelve at night. One night I was with him at half past ten. My wife said, 'When are you coming home?' I said, 'Look, I'm with him. I'm going to see it through.'

"When I knew what deep trouble Bennett was in, no way would I leave him. What a bloody mess he was in. He changed his direction, which he wanted and needed."

Bennett returned to the Palladium on October 25, 1971, for a three-week engagement and brought with him John Bunch, drummer John Cocuzzo, and cornetist Ruby Braff. He also costarred with Louis Armstrong at a charity variety gala on October 29 hosted by David Frost and attended by Princess Alexandra.

Bennett expressed his reverence for Armstrong in Gary Giddins's fine documentary, *Satchmo:* "Louis is really the tradition. We haven't caught up to it yet. He created our colloquialism. Every musician that I know of worth in popular music or jazz music is stung by Louis Armstrong. Billie Holiday, if you listen real close, even though it's feminine and it's Billie Holiday, if you listen real close, it's Louis Armstrong's phrasing. . . . You hear Billie, and as much as you love Billie, if you listen real hard, you can hear Louis, it's Louis in there.

"I'll never forget during the '60s revolution, I was in Washington, D.C. On a black radio station. And I mentioned how I loved Louis Armstrong. This defiant black announcer just said to me, 'How dare you say that?' He intimated Louis was an Uncle Tom and was an insult to his race. . . . I didn't get angry, but I just got so frustrated. I just said, 'This is the greatest contributor of American music.' And it kind of cooled him out a little."

Bennett went on to reiterate his main theme: "It's [Armstrong's music] really America's classical music. The bottom line of any country is what did we contribute to the world. And we contributed Louis Armstrong."

As Bennett continued performing in London, Boulton went about consolidating and expanding Bennett's career both there and in America as a concert performer. "That was the end of his twice-nightlies," Boulton told me. "You could see an artist of that caliber and magnitude doesn't want to sing in nightclubs. He had had a bellyful of it, for twenty years. He was ready to evolve. His agent, Buddy Howe of GAC [General Artists Corporation], was a nice man, but he was also looking after Tom Jones and Engelbert Humperdinck. He wasn't, in my opinion, giving Tony the respect and service he deserved.

"We went up to Boston, did concerts there with Buddy Rich at Symphony Hall for two nights running. Sold out. We did a beautiful concert in Carnegie Hall that year. I was most unpopular with the people who wanted him in nightclubs, I can assure you.

"So we went out with Buddy Rich, Woody Herman, and Count Basie more than anyone. We did the Hollywood Bowl with Neal Hefti and the L.A. Philharmonic. Zubin Mehta conducted the first half of the concert. I was so pleased, because Tony had been waiting for this."

Bennett gave a phone interview with the show business gossip columnist of the *New York Post*, Earl Wilson, on May 8, 1972. He told

Wilson: "I got a new manager—Derek Boulton of London—and my whole career is changed. Lena Horne gave me some advice. She said, 'Get a manager that loves you.' I've known Boulton as a friend for twenty years."

Bennett toured the British provinces in 1972 with a big band with John Bunch, Kenny Clare on drums, and Arthur Watts on bass. He began to paint more consistently and studied with John Barnicoat, a professor of art. He also took up tennis due to John Bunch. "One day I was going to play tennis," Bunch remembered, "and I went to Tony's apartment in my tennis outfit. I felt he was kind of looking at me intently. The next day he shows up at my apartment dressed in togs, holding a tennis racket. He's been playing ever since. Now he always gives me credit for getting him started in tennis. I didn't have anything to do with it. He did that on his own. He saw me and that's where he got the idea. He's stayed with the tennis. He kept up with it so consistently. He's got good legs. He can still run around the stage like he always used to. I think it saved him. I think he would say that. He was messing around a lot with drugs."

When Bennett returned to the London Palladium in 1973, James Green, the entertainment editor of the *London Evening News*, likened Bennett's appeal to the great London fire: "A second great fire of London has begun. It was lit at the Palladium by America's Tony Bennett; and the old town caught fire as he swung into action backed by an orchestra of 32, producing a big band sound to remember. . . . There was Bennett, all smiles and eager to please, showing clearly that he was one singer being paid for what he does supremely well. There was an outstanding pianist and musical director, Bernie Leighton [John Bunch had resigned late in 1972, and Bennett replaced him with Leighton for a few months], and behind him all those beautifully drilled musicians, who when not responding to Bennett's jazz feel, were driving him on. Everyone gave one hundred percent, and how often does that happen? Tony Bennett, without saying a dozen words, was making a public declaration of his regard for life, music, lyrics, and audience, as he applauded them and they broke into spontaneous applause of their own. At the end, arms spread like a triumphant sun god, blessing the faithful, he beamed through a standing ovation."

Derek Boulton related to me that Bennett had a decorated plate made of Green's review with Bennett's photograph in the middle. It was on display for a month in the window of Lawlays China Store on Regent Street.

Meanwhile, Bennett was searching for another record company. "Mike Curb, a semi-independent producer, was running MGM," Boulton remembered. "He heard Tony wasn't happy. He said, 'To have a record company, you only need Tony Bennett.' And Tony used that as a four-page ad in *Billboard*. Mike loved Tony." Boulton negotiated a deal with Curb, head of A&R in the American Division of Polygram/MGM. Bennett's albums would be released on MGM/Verve in the United States and on the Philips label in England. "I loved the Mike Curb deal," Derek Boulton told me. "From a tax point of view, MGM was owned by Polydor, which was a German company. To do a deal, Mike gave us sixty thousand dollars on the first record guarantee. Mike pulled out the stops for Tony. We recorded with Don Costa. Mike bent over backwards for him." Curb also was an important recording artist, the director of the popular choral group the Mike Curb Congregation.

"Derek Boulton really was very important at that time," Curb told me. "Because it was a crucial moment in an artist's career when they're going through a down period. We know through our friends and through our artists: the most important time in an artist's life is when they're starting. Then in the middle of their career, when things get a little bit cold, and then toward the end, when people lose interest. It's kind of like a human being: the cycle of being born, the cycle of figuring out what you're going to do with your life, and then the end of your life. You certainly need doctors and mothers to be born if you're going to be brought into the world. And then when you're trying to find your way, you need friends. And then at the end of your life, again, your real relationships emerge. That's sort of what it is in the career of a recording artist.

"Derek's the one that made it happen," Curb continued. "We had Sammy Davis Jr. on the label, and that leads to Tony Bennett. I produced 'Candy Man' with the Mike Curb Congregation, and it didn't hit. Then I signed Sammy Davis. We put him over the same track of 'Candy Man' that the Congregation were on. We even left their voices on it. So we put Sammy singing with the kids, and it was like 'High Hopes' with Frank Sinatra. It went to number one.

"So Tony asked Sammy 'How did you get to number one?' 'I didn't want to record it,' Sammy said, 'but Mike Curb talked me into it.' Sammy asked Tony what he was doing now, and it turned out Tony [was off] Columbia. So I said to Sammy, 'If Tony wants to be signed, we'll do it.' Then Derek called me and said that Tony had talked to Sammy, and also that Derek and Tony had heard positive things about me.

"The other thing that was exciting is that right about the time Tony signs with us, I merged my company with MGM and Verve for just a five-year period. About 1969 Kirk Kerkorian bought MGM and Verve, and he put Jim Aubrey in charge. And there had been all kinds of problems at MGM in New York and they were in effect almost shutting down the label. Then Kerkorian bought the company, and he didn't want to start up a label. I was in California at the time. So he let us merge Verve and MGM with Curb. During that five-year period—1969 to about 1975—I could use the Verve label. I actually used it because Tony loved to be on it; he loved a lot of the great jazz records that Verve had done during the Norman Granz years. I still owned Curb, and of course MGM still owned Verve, but we were actually operating it just like a Curb Records label. So I repackaged fifteen Verve albums, whether it was Wes Montgomery, Ella Fitzgerald, or Stan Getz. One artist that Verve didn't have was Tony Bennett. Sammy Davis had recorded one album for Verve, with Count Basie. And both could now record for Curb.

"Tony was going through a period when he was willing to do some songs that he hadn't done before, like Paul McCartney's 'My Love.' I have never seen an artist in my life who knows how to make a song his own faster than Tony Bennett. Then he also did ''O Sole Mio' in Italian, and he had resisted recording in Italian before. Then he did 'Living Together, Growing Together' by Burt Bacharach and Hal David. In a very short period of time Tony made a really deep body of work with us. I never had more fun working with an artist."

Curb praised Bennett's flexibility and how he expanded his base. "So for those of us who are in the commercial record business, let's face it: if Tony Bennett sings 'My Love,' well, that opens him to a new audience. And of course from my standpoint, it was obvious things weren't working at that time between Tony and Columbia, and we didn't want to be in the position of doing exactly the same thing that Columbia was doing. Or we would have had the same results. So we wanted him to do things like 'My Love.' Because, let's face it, it's a Beatles, McCartney song. But at the same time, Tony was willing to do it; we didn't force him. I mean, he was happy to do it.

"Tony's not the kind of guy that really needs a producer. He doesn't like drums or singing over a track. When you go into a Tony Bennett session, you really don't know what to expect. It's something many a producer has learned the hard way. Tony, the way he makes a record his own, is he does it his own way, at his own tempo. He stops when he wants to stop. And he leads the musicians. Musicians follow him. Even the arrangement: Tony in the studio is going to change it if it doesn't feel right. If he can't make a Tony Bennett record, then he won't record. Because in the studio, Tony Bennett, no matter what the arranger has done, and no matter what the producer has in mind, Tony makes the kind of record that he's going to put his stamp on or he doesn't do it. You don't tell him how to sing and how to sell the song. Because Tony does that himself.

"I always had the feeling that sometimes he would surprise himself. Because he'd start smiling after he heard a take, like he didn't even know he was going to go there. You know what it is: if someone said, 'Describe Tony Bennett,' I'd say, 'He almost has too much talent. No matter what he does with a song, I'm thinking, 'How does he get there? How does he take a song and find notes that no other artist who ever recorded it found?' You know, in life you don't get to work with everybody forever. But when you've had a long career like I've had, the things you remember are not always the biggest hits; it's the biggest moments. Tony never tried to make big hits. What he tried to make was great music."

Bennett had done some of his greatest work in his final albums with Columbia in the early 1970s: *Get Happy/With the London Philharmonic Orchestra*; *The Summer of '42*; *With Love, Tony!*; and *Sunrise, Sunset*. Now he went on to record *The Good Things in Life* (with Robert Farnon) and *Listen Easy* for Mike Curb's label.

Boulton and Bennett had a contentious but affectionate relationship that somehow worked, since Bennett needed a manager who stood up to him. "Derek and Tony used to fight and argue a lot," Bunch said. "When we were doing one-nighters around England, I'd sit in the front seat of the limo with the driver. Real chauffeur style, partition and everything. And they'd be in the back, fighting and yelling at each other. I had to listen to that on the way back from gigs. And it was upsetting to me. We had the window closed, but you could hear them. So Derek got me my own car with a driver."

Bennett and Boulton went to Houston to appear with Count Basie, and encountered the lingering, bestial vestiges of racism. "I didn't realize the South in the seventies was still so antiblack," Boulton recalled. "When we did a date for Anheuser-Busch in Houston, we got up early and left about six forty-five, and from Houston to the airport was about fifty miles. And we passed fields where the crosses were still smoldering. And it made me and Tony sick."

Tony went on to tape a one-hour TV special at the Palladium with Lena Horne. This was the first of the many collaborations with Horne from 1971 through 1975. Bennett and Horne toured England during 1972, and performed the show in the States in 1974 and 1975, including a successful stint at the Minskoff Theater in New York. Horne and Bennett returned to the Palladium again in 1976.

Bennett was determined to become a more skilled painter. He loved impressionism, and as he continued to study with John Barnicoat, he was bolstered by Barnicoat's encouragement to move in that artistic direction. Bennett was ready and open and willing to work hard, to play with form and expand beyond it, and soon he had his first one-man exhibit as a painter at a gallery on Mount Street in London. It was a momentous occasion for him. He exhibited in London again in 2000 in Hampstead Heath. The gallery was at the top of a hill, looking down at the whole city. Bennett was elated by the praise he received in the *Times* of London.

London seems to have been one place where Bennett's creative, artistic horizons expanded in an atmosphere of nurturing, calm, and enlightened discourse. He was very much loved and somehow instantly understood in England. To this day the largest, most sophisticated, and most urbane Bennett fan club—the Tony Bennett Appreciation Society—is in England. The club is presided over by a highly intelligent and sophisticated Londoner, Mark Fox. And it is clear that Bennett's deepest, most personal, and most productive bond with a manager occurred in his relationship with Derek Boulton.

Back in America, Bennett still had the remarkable knack of learning from the most unexpected sources. It was his openness and receptivity that made people befriend him in unique ways. Even Ed Sullivan, the notoriously stiff host of his own Sunday night television show, was moved to give Bennett good advice for a painter. Sullivan, a walker in the city himself, encouraged Bennett to walk around the city and sketch different scenes. Tony sketched skyscrapers, taxicabs, scenes in Central Park. To Bennett's surprise and delight, Sullivan took some of his sketches, blew them up, and created a set of them on the *Ed Sullivan Show* behind Bennett as he sang. Soon the sketches also materialized on the walls in Sullivan's office.

Shortly after John Bunch's departure, Torrie Zito, a leading arranger-conductor, became Bennett's full-time personal musical conductor and accompanist in 1973 and stayed with Bennett until 1979. He'd been writing for him since 1967, when he did his first recording date for him with the songs "For Once in My Life" and "Get Happy." Leading from a jazz foundation, Zito had worked with James Moody's Little Big Band, Herbie Mann, Sinatra, Morgana King, jazz singer Helen Merrill (who became his wife), and Andre Kostelanetz, and had scored John Lennon's *Imagine* album. He also had been on the arranging staff of Skitch Henderson's *Tonight Show* band in the 1960s.

Tony Tamburello had originally brought Torrie to Bennett's attention. "I was doing a record date with Tony," Zito told Will Friedwald, "and he asked me if I would be interested in the road thing with him. So I said I was, and then he hired me." Zito would orchestrate most of three Bennett albums, *For Once in My Life*, *I Gotta Be Me*, and *Yesterday I Heard the Rain*.

In an interview with the British writer Les Tomkins in 1974, Zito said, "The person who is needed here has to fill three requirements, and they're probably in this order: conductor, pianist, and, if possible, writer. . . . And if you have a jazz background, it's fun.

"There are really no restrictions with Tony. Since he's so flexible, and such a capable performer, it gives the accompanist all sorts of leeway. Whatever I can think of to play is fine. Which makes for a very good relationship. Some singers that I've orchestrated for in the past are sort of locked in—they want to hear the same kind of thing all the time. Whereas Tony isn't like that at all. . . . He likes variety, because he performs that way himself.

"You know the wild thing with Sinatra and Bennett is whatever song they do, old or new, the way they sound is such a personal expression. Like Tony takes a Beatles song or something, and it's as if it was never done by anyone else but Tony. The same with Frank. It's the mark of greatness, to be able to do that."

When I met Torrie in 2009, he was deeply ill with emphysema, and would die a few months later. John Bunch would soon follow. "I wrote about eighty arrangements for Tony from the time I started to record with him," Torrie said. "He has a particular love of the lyric, and he's very good at finding material that he likes to do, that nobody knows.

"He's very sensitive. He operates a lot on his feelings. And a good painter. He used to doodle on airplanes. He did a drawing of me once, sitting across from me. He'd draw people in airplanes. He'd look at them and he'd draw.

"I recently saw him on TV singing the national anthem at some big event, a ball game. He sounded great. I mean, just all alone. There's no telling how he keeps his voice like that. It's different from person to person. What happens, happens. He's careful with himself. Eats good food, he does all that. Certainly a spiritual person. He's a good man. He really is. He's something different."

During the worst days of his illness, Bennett hired him for a recording engagement and called him regularly on the phone. "Tony does keep in touch with me. He calls just to see how I am, how I'm going."

In 1973, the year Tony hired Torrie, Derek Boulton was working on a major tour for Bennett and Lena Horne. "When I took Tony over," Boulton said, "I set up a ten-week deal in Vegas: $75,000 a week. That was good money then. That gave him $750,000 basic. Then I did eight or nine weeks in theaters. And I set up the thing with him and Lena Horne from 1973 to 1975. To me she was a superb artist. When I spoke to her manager, Ralph Harris, I thought she was going to want an equal share of the box office. Tony was making about eighty a week. Lena wanted only twenty. Ralph Harris said to me, 'Derek, we'll take twenty.' I said, 'Don't you want to come in on a percentage?' 'No, if you'll give us twenty, I'll accept it. You don't realize how difficult it is for a black artist, Derek.' They just wanted their money. . . . I just had a gut feeling. And it worked. They went out there, and some weeks they were earning by today's money $400,000 a week. If you put quality on, great quality, believe in quality, you will always survive."

Boulton would never forget the wrenching scene outside Horne's dressing room when Sandy Two shouted at Tony about working with Horne, "What do you need that fucking nigger for?" Ralph Harris, Horne's manager, was standing there and would later say to Derek, "That woman is going to drag Tony down."

James Gavin, author of Horne's 2009 biography, *Stormy Weather*, wrote that Horne was sharing double bills because "many promoters doubted her solo drawing power." He noted that when Horne joined Bennett, "his career was far from its peak. . . . His last hits . . . had happened a decade before and in 1971 his longtime label, Columbia, let him go. [Actually Bennett left Columbia, not the other way around.] The sight of him grinning and singing Cole Porter, while wearing a tuxedo and an unflattering toupee, marked him as kitsch; offstage he faced a crumbling second marriage. A cocaine habit compounded his trouble." Gavin quoted Bennett as saying, "That was a tough period for me, very tough."

Gavin wrote of the culmination of the Horne–Bennett tour, their Broadway appearance at the Minskoff Theater, which opened a four-week run on October 30, 1974: "In a musical era that had made Horne and Bennett's middle-age fans feel cast aside, the concert ushered them back to what seemed like the ultimate in class. This was no rote survey of the stars' hits; instead the show focused on the cream of the Great American Songbook, from Arlen to Bacharach. The singers barely spoke, save for a few words at the end: 'Good night, Lena' . . . 'Good night, Tony.'"

Bennett told Gavin that Horne mesmerized him: "I found myself watching her performance every night. I couldn't believe her consistency. To be able to stand next to her and watch her wonderful instincts onstage—she was riveting."

But Horne remained as detached from Bennett as she had been from the onset of their first TV appearances together. "Few viewers, it seemed," Gavin wrote, "noticed her subtle detachment from her costar. During a long Arlen medley, Bennett gazed at her in awe; Horne fixed her glance carefully in the distance. Offstage, she wasn't overly friendly. 'We were just respectful of one another, and it stayed like that,' explained Bennett.

"At the opening-night party at Sardi's," Gavin continued, "columnist Earl Wilson asked Horne about rumors of tension between her and her costar. Horne denied them. 'Tony looks out for me like he really cares about me being happy,' she said. But privately, she didn't hide her annoyance at her second-place billing, and at the fact that she opened the show for Bennett."

"The real cause was much simpler. 'I put the show together,' said Bennett. 'The whole package and the expenses came out of me. Usually in the past if I worked with Count Basie or Duke Ellington, I put their names on top of mine, because I felt it would be incorrect for me not to play second fiddle. But that didn't happen with Lena. I realized the situation, but we never spoke about it.' "

Newsweek wrote, "Tony Bennett, 48, and Lena Horne, 57, are on Broadway together, sharing the billing and the plaudits—though not equally. His name came first on the marquee, in the playbill and in every press-release mention, but she won better notices from the critics." Gavin quotes several unnamed critics: "Tony Bennett found himself in an all but impossible situation. He had to follow Lena Horne." Another praised Horne as "a genuine superstar" while terming Bennett "almost an afterthought." However, one of the finest music critics in the country, Nat Hentoff, jazz critic of the *Village Voice*, took an opposite view, one that was more accurate. (I can attest to this, as I saw Horne and Bennett at the Minskoff.) Hentoff contrasted Bennett's utter sincerity—"I've seldom seen anyone who so enjoys being a performer"—with Horne's coldness. He wrote that her phrasing was exaggerated and that she didn't swing.

"The stage Lena Horne needs to keep pushing her singing to help her voice impersonate buoyancy and passion." Where was the real Lena Horne?

Gavin noted that "clearly Horne had felt trapped in her overriding image as a lady. But she had to maintain it in the tightly directed *Tony & Lena*. Years later, Horne told Jonathan Schwartz about 'this feeling' that struck her during certain performances, when she truly felt the magic happening. She could only remember it occurring during a performance once with Tony Bennett at the Minskoff.

"Bennett," Gavin continued, "whose enthusiasm for his audiences kept them packing his shows even when he'd passed eighty, couldn't understand Horne's pessimism. 'If you're doing well, count your blessings!' he said. "'This business of artists who are unhappy with their lives—it's just incorrect. If you get a break and connect with the public, what is the problem? Anger doesn't work; love is the only thing that works. And when you can arrive at that genuinely, and you learn forgiveness in the proper way, you have a more content life. The other way you're just hurting yourself.'"

Bennett was a little disingenuous in those remarks, since he'd had more than his share of unhappiness and pessimism in his life. Triumph and tragedy always seemed to be waging a war within him. The upbeat image was the one he wanted to convey more and more in his later years. Yet even if that image was rose-colored, in reality he was the antithesis of Horne as a singer and performer. There always was love in what he did, but for Horne singing sometimes seemed like a pitched battle to contain her anger and bitterness.

When the association with Curb and Polygram ended, Columbia urged Bennett to return many times. Bennett refused. According to Will Friedwald, Tony's sister, Mary, said, "My little brother is a typical Calabrese—very hard-headed. Once he gets stuck on an idea, you can't talk him out of it—especially if you cross him."

After leaving Curb, Bennett created a new label, Improv. "When Tony met Bill Hassett, a businessman who was very successful in real estate and owned the Statler-Hilton in Buffalo," Boulton said, "they started the label together."

In his notes for "The Complete Improv Recordings," Will Friedwald writes that "the idea was partially inspired by Frank Sinatra, whose company, Reprise Records, founded in 1960, had been a conspicuous success (Sinatra sold most of his interest in it for three million in 1963) and who encouraged Bennett to start a similar operation." But the true inspiration for the label was the "Panglossian spirit" that Friedwald returned to again in speaking of Bennett: "In Tony Bennett's best of all possible worlds, getting people to appreciate the great works of culture isn't a matter of taste so much as it is of exposure; people will choose good music over bad if you only give them a choice. The reason more people buy Metallica than Louis Armstrong is because they haven't had the chance to hear the latter for themselves. If you present people with the good music, a significant number of them will flock to it. For a few years in the mid-1970s, Tony Bennett put those theories to the test."

Billboard wrote on July 19, 1975, that Jack Rollins, who had become Bennett's manager (a relationship that would last for only a year), became vice president and Richard Roember was appointed general counsel of Improv. The first album would be *Life Is Beautiful* (the title song was by Fred Astaire and Tommy Wolf). Hassett saw Improv as having "a Tiffany's approach—not mass market" and cited as his model the achievements of Norman Granz and Verve Records. "The motivating concept behind Improv," Friedwald wrote, "was that between the combination of Bennett's ongoing popularity, his musical wherewithal, and Hassett's business smarts, they should be able to get a successful record company off the ground. Bennett had plenty of contacts in the recording field, and also recruited his longtime friend, the famous artist Rudolf (Rudy) DeHarak, as art director, and they both knew plenty of musicians." Eventually, Improv would record Jimmy and Marian McPartland, Earl "Fatha" Hines, Bill Evans, the Ruby Braff-George Barnes Quartet, and others.

Friedwald noted that it was Danny Bennett who realized from the outset that Improv's goals were unrealistic. He told Friedwald that "what an independent label can't do on its own was distribute. You can do everything else on your own, but to actually get records into stores, you need a network like only the major labels have."

In 1974 Bennett gave an in-depth interview to Whitney Balliett. Titled "A Quality That Lets You In," it was the best and most important profile of him ever written to that point. Balliett was the dean of jazz music critics and the jazz critic for the *New Yorker*. The piece gave no hint of the roiling turmoil in Bennett's life, but that was certainly due to Bennett's reticence and desire to keep his private life to himself. Balliett noted that Bennett "lives in controlled splendor" with his sons, Danny, who was nineteen, and Daegal, eighteen, four-year old Joanna, and Sandy Two, "a cool, blond, pearl-skinned beauty from Leesville, Louisiana."

The article began with scenes of Bennett painting ("It's just recently that I've regimented myself to paint every day," he told Balliett) and of Sandy Two discussing school for Joanna when they traveled abroad. "There are lycées in Los Angeles and London and Paris," she said, "so if we spend three months in any of those places, she'd have a school. I mean, that's what our lifestyle is."

Balliett wrote that "Bennett has become the most widely admired American popular singer." The source of the article's title is a key quote from Alec Wilder: "There is a quality about [Bennett's singing] that lets you in. Frank Sinatra's singing mesmerizes you. In fact, it gets so symbolic sometimes that you can't make the relationship with him as a man, even though you may know him. Bennett's professionalism doesn't block you off. It even suggests that maybe you'll see him later at the beer parlor." Balliett augments Wilder's comments by addressing Bennett's singing style: calling Bennett "a ceaseless experimenter," Balliett writes, "He can be a belter when reaching rocking fortissimos. He drives a ballad as intensely and intimately as Sinatra. He has been a lilting, glancing jazz singer. He can be a low-key, searching supper-club performer." Referring to his appearance, he notes that "Now, with the disappearance of most of his hair—an occupational hazard that has likewise afflicted Crosby and Sinatra—he wears a variety of stunningly accomplished transformations."

Balliett framed his profile as several days in the life of Bennett: morning, noon, and night of each day. In the afternoon they dined at the Amalfi, Bennett's haunt for many years. "Bennett has the sort of face that is easily sculptured by light," Balliett wrote. "In broad daytime, he tends to look jagged and awkwardly composed: his generous Roman nose booms and his pale green eyes become slits. But the subdued lighting in the Amalfi makes him handsome and compact. His eyes become melancholy and shine darkly, the deep lines that run past his mouth are stoical, and his nose is regal."

Bennett spoke about his musical values, and reading those sentences now, it's clear that he was aesthetically formed in 1950 and has never deviated from his values. When he speaks of these matters with Balliett, he is very expressive and his language soars. It's simply impossible to think of any other singer—not even Sinatra—who speaks nearly so eloquently about his craft. The commercial instinct is there—Bennett is grounded and realistic, not only a dreamer—but he sounds like the genuine, dedicated artist he is.

"It's beautiful not to compromise in what you sing," he told Balliett, "and yet I've done business since I had my first record hit for Coumbia. Hanging out with good songs is the secret. Songs like 'All the Things You Are' and 'East of the Sun' are just the opposite of singing down. . . . I love singing too much to cheat the public. And I can't ever lose that spirit by listening to the money boys, the Broadway wiseguys who used to tell me, 'If you don't sing such-and-such, you'll end up with a class reputation and no bread in the bank.' But if I lost that spirit, my feeling for music would run right out the window. It's this obsolescence thing in America, where cars are made to break down and songs written to last two weeks. But good songs last forever, and I've come to learn that there's a whole group out there in the audience who's studying that with me. There's a greatness in an audience when it gets perfectly still. It becomes a beautiful tribal contact, a delicate, poetic thing. A great song does that. It also works two ways: the performer makes the song work, and the song inspires the performer."

Speaking of giving his musicians the chance to shine, he said, "I've always liked the Billie Holiday tradition of allowing the musicians you're working with to take charge and to solo, and my arrangements are always written that way. Jazz musicians create great warmth and feeling. When they play well, they make *you* sing, too. I've worked with Bobby Hackett and Woody Herman and Duke Ellington and Stan Kenton and Count Basie. You can't beat the perfection of Basie. He even talks the way he plays: one or two words take care of conversation for the month."

Balliet accompanied Bennett when he took Joanna kiting in Central Park's East Meadow. On the way there, Bennett told his driver to stop at a shop specializing in kites. "At the shop," Balliett wrote, "Bennett and one of the cameramen choose a couple of big, semitransparent German kites that look like birds. Bennett is all thumbs, but he manages to get one of the kites assembled by the time the limousine pulls up at Fifth Avenue and Ninety-eighth Street. Joanna sails in the south gate ahead of Bennett and, sensing the expanse in front of her, takes off up the Meadow, her legs going like a sandpiper's. Bennett, laughing and shouting, catches her at One-hundredth Street. . . . There is almost no wind, but Bennett gets the kite twelve feet into the air, and he and Joanna run up the Meadow. The kite crashes. Joanna picks it up and runs south, Bennett galloping after her. They go up the Meadow, down the Meadow, across the Meadow. Joanna maintains her speed, but Bennett begins to puff. . . . He picks up his jacket from the grass and flings it and the kite across one shoulder. Joanna latches on to his index finger and tows him back to the car."

Bennett took Balliett with him to his concert at Alice Tully Hall the next evening, billed as "An Evening with Rodgers and Hart." Tony was appearing with the Ruby Braff–George Barnes Quartet, with whom he would soon record one of his first albums for Improv. Noting Bennett's awkwardness onstage, and deeming it an ultimate plus, Balliett wrote that Bennett's stage manner was "startlingly old-fashioned: he uses a hand mike, and he whips the cord around as though it were a lariat; he half-dances, half-falls across the stage during rhythm numbers; he salutes the audience and points at it. He is clumsy and at the same time delightful." Describing the concert, Balliett wrote:

> He sings twenty-one Rodgers and Hart tunes, and many are memorable. He sings a soft, husky "Blue Moon," and then comes a marvelous, muted Ruby Braff solo. "There's a Small Hotel" is even softer, and Braff and George Barnes react with pianissimo statements. The group, indeed, is impeccable. The solos are beautiful, and the dynamics all anticipate Bennett's. During Braff's solo in "The Most Beautiful Girl in the World," Bennett sits on a stool to the musicians' right, and near the end of "I Wish I Were in Love Again" he forgets his lyrics and soars over the wreckage with some good mumbo-jumbo (it is usually done at top speed) then briefly takes the tempo up, and goes

out sotto voce. He does "I Left My Heart in San Francisco" as an encore. The ovation is long and standing.

After the concert, Balliett got into the limousine again and Bennett settled into a corner of the car. "It's what I used to dream of—a concert in a big hall like Alice Tully," he told Balliett. "But it hasn't all been smoothness since I started doing business. . . . Frank Sinatra came out in *Life* and said I was the greatest singer around. Sophie Tucker once told me, 'Make sure that helium doesn't hit your brain,' but it did, and for several years, to match up to his praise, I overblew, I oversang. But I've found my groove now. I'm solidifying everything, and working toward my own company. You learn how to hold on to money after a while. I like to live well, but I'm not interested in yachts and fancy cars. There are things I'm searching for, but they won't take a day. I'd like to attain a good, keen intellect. Alec Wilder set one of William Blake's poems to music for me, and I was reading Blake last night. Imagine being that talented and feeling so much at the same time!"

Bennett spoke of his hopes for making more movies and having his own regular TV show. Like all good, well-laid plans, some of these would not come to fruition in the coming years. The roller coaster of life, and Bennett's own demons, would intervene. Bennett would not learn how to hold onto money for many years. There would be no more films, nor would he have his own TV show for more than a season. Yet in the long run his achievements and triumphs would outstrip his plans and dreams in ways he never could have imagined.

Tony in Atlantic
City, 1979.

Nick Riggio (second
from left), a longstanding
friend of Tony's,
introduces Tony to Susan
Crow, his future wife,
and her parents, 1982.

Tony at the Columbus Day Parade, New York City, 1982.

John Bennett, Tony's
brother, and Nick
Riggio, 1983.

Tony and Nick Riggio
at the Sunrise Music
Theater, Fort Lauderdale,
Florida, 1987.

Ralph Sharon, Tony's
musical conductor and
accompanist for
many years.

Robert Farnon, famed
British conductor and
arranger, and Danny
Bennett, late 1980s.

Tony Bennett and Tony
Tamburello, brilliant jazz
pianist, vocal coach, and
Tony's closest friend.

9

"A Pure, Simple Thing"

"For a while, as long as he could," Marion Evans told me, "Derek Boulton tried to manage Tony Bennett, which is basically impossible to do. Because Tony's got his own ideas of doing things. Derek eventually gave up and went back to England."

"Tony and I were supposed to be together for one year," Derek Boulton remembered.

Tony's sister, Mary, worked with me in the office the first five months. Tony said to me, "If you stay with me, I want Mary to look after my mother. But I want somebody in the office I can trust."

I knew his mom very well. She lived with her daughter, Mary; Tom Chiappa, Mary's husband; and granddaughter Nina. She worried so much that she was bedridden. In the last year or two of her life, she found the blankets too heavy. I used to pick her up in my arms when they wanted to change the bed, held her, and took her to the window so she could look out. Her daughter, Mary, found her too heavy to carry.

She was always concerned about her son. She was a wonderful lady. They were very close. Tony loved the way she cooked lasagna. Lasagna was the family dish. Whenever I went over there for dinner on a Sunday: lasagna. When we went to Patsy's or anywhere: lasagna.

Tony said to me once, "I'll be a basket case if anything happens to my mother." He didn't believe in a life hereafter. I remember once he was ill, and I put my hands on him and said a prayer. The next day he said, "You did the hocus-pocus on me." That's the mentality he's got.

It was warm, it was friendly. And I made a deal with him. I said, "Tony, I can't do the job in one year." That's when I had to tell him what he owed. Then he turned around to me and said, "Will you promise to stay with me until I'm straight [financially]? I don't want you to leave me. You stay with me until I'm straight, and then it's six months' notice either way from the person who gets pissed off with the other." "Yes, I'll do that," I said. "I've started a serious job; I want to finish it." We shook hands in the car.

I protected him as much as possible. Without being unkind, if there was dogshit on the street and he went for a walk, he would tread in it. He never had anybody looking after him. Tony had people around him who were no bloody good to him at all. Scroungers.

When I got there, it was a wonderful, wonderful first year, just Tony and me. When he started to make money, everybody's jumping in the pool with us. The first time Tony saw Sandy Two was at Dean Martin's house. This was before I was his manager. Whenever Tony went to the Coast to do Dean's show, he stopped at his house. One day Tony was in the steam room, sitting there stone naked, when Sandy Two walks in with a dress three sizes too small and says, "Have you seen Dean?" And he fell for it. Joanna was best part of a year old when I joined him. When Tony was getting married to [Sandy Two], I said "Congratulations" to Tony. "Don't congratulate me. It's another good soldier biting the dust." Those were his exact words. And he went down to the Town Hall and married her.

Things began to change in 1973. Tony would bawl all the musicians out. Once in Vegas at the Hilton he starts bawling out Louis Bellson at the end of the show. Louis had done nothing wrong. I could tell from the expression on Tony's face what was coming. Without his opening his mouth, I could tell what was in his brain. Oh, Christ, after the show he'd go in the dressing room for an hour and all hell would break loose. It would spoil an evening. Packed house, standing ovation, what every artist is looking for. Upset [the musicians] for the night. It was mad. I told him so, too. I told him many times. The first year he was grateful for everything I did. The second year, even better, because he was starting to make money for the first time in his life. The third year, when we were really making money—he made the best part of two million—he was getting mad at everything. He was so self-destructive.

There's a strong affection there, but I don't want to be shouted at every day. When I knew what deep trouble Bennett was in, no way would I leave him. What a bloody mess he was in at the beginning. And he got his freedom. He changed his direction, which he wanted and needed. The only person I ever split with was Tony in the end because he became too bloody heavy. When you look after a person, you throw your lot in with him or you don't get involved.

For the entire three years I was with him, he got about $3.9 million. I got rid of the agent. I promoted the shows. Did everything. It was a great thing until every day became a fight. When I told David Gutterer I was leaving, nobody believed me. I said, "David, I've written him a letter. I'm going to uphold it." I left Tony in the middle of the Bennett-Horne tour. I set it up, and I left. When I left him, he said, "Nobody leaves Tony Bennett! I fire them." He didn't like it at all.

Tony had my life for a few years, and I must say I enjoyed it. I gave up a business that was grossing two and a half million. I was sorry to break up with him. When I left him, he had nine months' solid work, worth about a million pounds in the book. But I did not see going to the Coast, where he had to sing at parties every night for nothing. He was invited for one purpose only: to sing. To give a twenty-minute show for nothing. It was Sandy taking him to all those places. He never got another film offer.

Joe Soldo remembered the after-concert rants of Bennett as well. They had begun fifty years before. And when he attended a Bennett show in recent years, he saw at least a trace of the old insecurity. What he encountered, however, was a milder version of the old Bennett. "After *every* show he had a meeting. And I couldn't get over this: when I was in Cosa Mesa recently—fifty years have passed at least—when the show was over I went backstage with my friends. I went to see Vance [Anderson, Bennett's assistant], Harold Jones [drummer], and Gray Sargent [bassist]. And I know Lee [Musiker, Bennett's musical conductor]. Lee wasn't there. Then minutes later he came in and he said to the bass player, 'You know, on "I Got Rhythm," Tony couldn't feel you coming.' 'I Got Rhythm' is a vamp, and then Tony jumps in. I didn't notice this from being in the audience. But I just thought to myself, my God, he's still having meetings after each show. When the show was over, Lee went into Tony's room. And Tony talked about the show. After every show, he's not sure. I don't know what that stems from. Here it's fifty years later and he's still doing it!"

"Tony tore [drummer] Louis Bellson to shreds that night," Derek Boulton recalled. "On a Saturday night, CBS had a convention. Oh, God, they were cheering Tony, shouting at him as only an American can when they get behind you—more than the English. And they loved him. Loved him a lot. And then—after the show he stood there and gave Bellson a bollocking. Lovely drummer! Lovely drummer! Another night Torrie Zito was playing with Tony in Vegas. And at the end of the first show, Torrie went to the piano book and threw it at him. And walked out. Tony went running after him. Tony can be a bloody bastard, but there's no evil in him at all. Buddy Howe told me Tony gave Dave Peterson a breakdown in Vegas. I remember Buddy saying he put him in the hospital. Buddy said to me, 'One thing about you: Where were you born?' I said, 'Why?' He said, 'You stood up to him.' I said, 'If we'd surrendered to the Italians, we [the English] wouldn't be what we are.' Buddy laughed.

"Tony drove the musicians bloody bananas. I never understood it. It's a big thing after a show. Everybody's praising him. People have given him a standing ovation. Ralph Sharon called him 'Mr. Misery.' That's the real Bennett."

"He was not in great voice one night in San Francisco," a family friend told me. "I was sitting off to the side of the stage. Tony walked by us with Ralph [Sharon] close behind. I got up to see what was up. Suddenly Tony started yelling, pointing his fingers and screaming at Ralph at the top of his lungs. Ralph apologized for nothing. Ralph played great that night, and Tony didn't. Ralph had tears in his eyes, and I saw them! He was treated like a dog. I doubt Ralph will tell you this even if he remembers. He never once complained in all the years that I knew him. This incident took place in a walkway not even ten feet from the last table in the room. Everyone could hear it. It was loud!"

"The song was 'It Had to Be You' one night," another friend told me. "The chord in that song at that point as composed is a diminished chord. Ralph Sharon always played diminished with a major seventh on it with a nice-sounding chord. Tony couldn't hear it that particular night. He accused Ralph of trying to sabotage him, of playing all those minor chords. He said, 'I need an up act. When I come out on the stage I want tumult, I want excitement! I want the show to be upbeat! I want positive! Up! Up!' The capper was, 'Take all the minor chords out of the book!' You had to suppress a laugh at that point. . . . I mean, the songs just don't work without the minor chords. There was a lot of stress. Joe La Barbera's stated objective about working with Tony was to 'support my family and not lose any body parts.' Chronic stress can kill you. Tony was a smart guy, but he was prone to non sequitur and malapropisms and firmly held but wild beliefs. He blamed the demise of his kind of music on the Beatles and the electric bass as the onset of evil. He lived in awe and respect of musicians, but I think he felt uncertain around them."

"Tony is really an instinctive musician," John McDonough told me. "He feels more than he actually knows intellectually. That's sort of the way he functions. But it does sometimes tend to make him uneasy around musicians and conductors. John Bunch told me one story. There was a rehearsal, a sound check. They were conducting the orchestra. It happened to be one of the occasions when Bennett was performing with a full orchestra." McDonough mentioned the famous story told by many musicians of John Bunch's touching his nose. "It's basically just standard musician sign language," McDonough explained. "It means 'Take it from the top.' And Tony apparently noticed the gesture, and felt it was directed at him, and it was a comment on his silhouette, his nose, and he was sensitive about that. Aside from the fact that he'd be sensitive about it, it just surprised me that a man, even a nonmusician, even a nonreading musician, would be in the music business and have done so many recording sessions and not have picked up some of the basic sign language of the conductor. Even if a singer didn't read music, after they've been recording with orchestras for sixty years, you kind of expect that they pick up some of the sign language. Yet everybody I talked to said Tony obviously has no reason to feel insecure, because what he has is unique. I mean, it's what's sustained his career."

There were two sides to Bennett, and the musicians, who worked so closely with him, saw things that were less visible to others. Bennett could be the sweetest of men. Even sitting in on jam sessions of other musicians, he was genuinely enthralled with the music and appreciative of the musicians. But in his own sphere, he could be darkly suspicious and erratic. "When Tony had finished a show," Joe Soldo recalled, "the musicians and Tony got into the elevator, and this new drummer was jingling his change. Ralph Sharon was looking at him and said, 'Don't jingle your change.' And then when they got to the top to go to Tony's dressing room, the guy went to the fruit bowl and started to eat a banana. And Ralph kept shaking his head. To Tony the jingling was saying he was cheap. And the banana was making fun of his nose. So Tony didn't use that drummer anymore."

The greatest paradox about this behavior is that Bennett genuinely loves and esteems musicians, as so many musicians told me. In an interview with the BBC in 2000, he disclosed some extraordinary information about a group of musicians he'd encountered who became world-famous multimillionaires, and how their unique intelligence had moved them in that direction. He mentioned that musicians are often disparaged as pot smokers, but in fact they were the most "authentic, logical" people he knew. He recalled an experience with a group called the Bohemian Grove, an assemblage of presidents and former presidents, businessmen, and other power brokers that met annually in the redwood forests of San Francisco to discuss investments and politics, and to "cut the pie up." They had invited him to sing for them—songs such as "All the Things You Are." He was surprised by the sophistication and selectivity in the songs they asked him to sing, and he questioned them about it. He found out to his amazement that many of them were ex-musicians who had played with the big bands. They had utilized the "mathematics of music" in becoming multimillionaires. Alan Greenspan, who was present, told Tony he had played the saxophone with Henry Jerome's society orchestra.

Bennett also addressed with great feeling the lack of justice in the fate of musicians. He spoke of the contrasting fates of a Paul McCartney at the top of the world and a Lester Young, who received seventy-five dollars for his last performance at a tribute staged for him at Birdland. "There's such a lack of justice!" Bennett said. He went on to say it applied to so many great musicians. There were exceptions like the pianist Teddy Wilson, but most suffered the fate of Woody Herman, a great artist who died bankrupt and was quickly forgotten.

There was the Bennett who loved musicians but sometimes feared them out of his insecurity, and there was the Bennett who loved and deeply respected the audience that made his amazing career possible. He never felt above that audience. They were part of his family.

"Tony was always surrounded by adulation and people who wanted to talk to him," a close friend of Bennett's told me. "He was never dismissive or impolite to fans that would accost him for autographs. As a matter of fact, he was always thankful for their asking him. He's tremendously grateful to the audience. Without them, where is he? The thing that struck me was that the Tony hanging out after a gig when you go to a show with him was quite a different guy than the Tony who was ranting after his show. Part of it was he felt comfortable; he was in a situation where people were coming up and expressing appreciation. He was relaxed and able to enjoy the fruits of his work, basking in the appreciation of others. That fed him; that was important to him. But it

was also important to him to be perceived as a guy who remembered
where he came from. He always wanted to be the singing waiter from
Astoria who got lucky. At times the contrast between that Tony and the
ranting, illogical guy after the show was really quite stark."

Perhaps it was insecurity that motivated Bennett in the 1970s to
introduce his act with a Sinatra tape—or perhaps it was related to John
McDonough's perception of him as being overwhelmed by the praise
of lifelong idols such as Sinatra, Astaire, and Crosby. "Maybe Tony was
really faltering in the early seventies," Gary Giddins told me. "Tony
was at a Playboy club in Miami. And apparently he did this for quite
some time. He had himself introduced by a recording of Sinatra saying, 'Tony Bennett for my money is the best singer in the world.'
And I thought, God, what a lack of self-esteem! He didn't need that.
I thought that's where his insecurity really came out. I found that
bizarre. First of all, there's a sense of getting on your knees before
Sinatra. Which is not appealing for either man. There's a line in *A Man
for All Seasons* where a character says, 'To have to be on your knees is
a terrible thing; but to have to have other people on their knees before
you is even worse.'" Giddins laughed. "And Sinatra was the kind of
person who liked to have people obeying his whims."

Speaking of the Sinatra introduction, Derek Boulton said, "Tony
is the most insecure man in the world. General atmosphere: insecure
and worried.

"And he's publicity-mad. If you have any idea for promotion he'll
wrap you up as though he's a kangaroo and put you there. When we
went to Vegas, I had four flags with his name on a pole in the middle,
and the two on either side. But the air was so thin they didn't start blow-
ing until five o'clock at night. 'Why aren't mine there?' he shouted.
"He was talking about the flag in the middle without his name. Yes,
there was one big flag in the middle but that was the Nevada state
flag. He said to his accountant once, 'How did you make Coca-Cola
famous? By putting its name everywhere. And I want the same.' He's
correct. You've got to admire him for it, because every singer has to
fight his way through. See, he's not out to harm anybody.

"We used to put up posters for Tony at the top of Sixty-second
Street in Manhattan. Sixtieth upwards. Tony lived on Sixty-eighth.

We went up and down every street, Second and Third avenues. Wherever he looked he saw these posters about him. We hit a certain area. We went for a walk where he was going to find them."

Addressing the contradictions in Bennett, Boulton told me, "Tony is a Jekyll and Hyde. He can be the most lovable man on earth. But when Tony wants to let go, he can be very fiery. Lovable and fiery. A terrible temper. He kept it away from the public. Sinatra would row and shout in front of people. Tony's much more careful.

"And then there's his ego: Tony would think, 'Why am I not going to be the pope next year?'" When he had the flat by Grosvenor Square, he used to say to me, 'I want to see in the papers tomorrow morning that Tony Bennett left his apartment and walked across Grosvenor Square.'

"But Bennett cares for people. Some people will get to where they want to get, just treading on people. Not Tony Bennett. Never. Never never never. And he would never turn down a worthwhile charity. The real Bennett is a lovely man. He loves singers and he loves jazz. The musicians, so many of them, although he can have a row with them, love him tremendously. At times he's his own worst enemy. I suspect we all are. I think he's been very cruelly treated in the past. But he came through. He has fought through and he's won."

Thanks to the steps Boulton had taken, Bennett's career remained on the upswing. At the end of 1972, when he returned from England, Bennett received an eighteen-month contract at the Las Vegas Hilton. In May 1973 he had a 109-piece philharmonic orchestra installed in the hotel, with Louis Bellson on drums and orchestrations by Robert Farnon. In between engagements at the Hilton, he went on the road with John Giuffrida on bass, Torrie Zito on piano, Chuck Hughes— and then Joe Cocuzzo—on drums. In late 1974 Bennett also joined forces with the brilliant trumpet player Ruby Braff and two great guitarists, George Barnes and Bucky Pizzarelli, for two concerts at Alice Tully Hall in Manhattan. Bennett went on to record twenty-four Rodgers and Hart songs with Braff and Barnes that became the Improv album *Tony Bennett: The Rodgers and Hart Songbook.*

Sandy Two gave birth to a second daughter, Antonia, on April 7, 1974. At Sandy's urging, they moved to Los Angeles and bought a lavish fifty-eight-hundred-square-foot house, built in 1911, in Beverly

Hills. It included five bedrooms, a guesthouse, maid's quarters, and a poolhouse converted into a music and painting studio. This was to be the beginning of the end of the marriage, and the darkest period in Bennett's life. "Tony loved his music," Derek Boulton told me. "Sandy used to say to me, holding Joanna in her arms, 'He doesn't care about me, he doesn't care about his daughter, he cares about his show.'"

Hollywood's drug style—the heavy use of pot and cocaine—took its toll on Bennett. In conversations with Robert Sullivan, Bennett would liken that period to the song "The Good Life," in which the lyrics say, "you hide all the sadness you feel." "The words of the song really say it's good but also bad," he told Sullivan. "The reality is, it's good and bad. 'Wake up, kiss the good life good-bye.' It's not just about being successful."

In 2006, recalling those years, Bennett related them to the mood of the times in the United States. Speaking to Mick Wood of the *London Daily Telegraph Magazine*, he mentioned the assassinations of Martin Luther King Jr. and Robert Kennedy and the rise of the military-industrial complex. "It was no longer America at that point, and it felt bad," he said. "It was like a hammer hitting glass and everything cracked. It just psyched me out." He spoke of his cocaine addiction as "a little bit of everything." He sighed. "But I never really got hooked. I never got desperate." Bennett has often denied a serious addiction while in Hollywood, but events transpired that contradict his account.

"When I took Tony over," Derek Boulton told me, "I got him straight. But then Tony goes and does a dive when Sandy Two wanted to take over his management. She wanted him out there in Hollywood with Gene Kelly. Tony said to me, 'My children have to call him 'Mister Kelly.' And then Kelly goes out with somebody much younger than her."

The positive part of Bennett's Hollywood experience was getting to know many of his idols, including Cary Grant, Fred Astaire, and Ella Fitzgerald. He and his family spent every Christmas with Fitzgerald, and composer Sammy Cahn lived next door. Astaire would walk by Bennett's house every morning. "He was so graceful," Bennett noted, "he actually looked like he was floating as he strolled by." Bennett encouraged Astaire to write more songs (he was the author of several, including "Not My Girl" and "I'm Building Up to an Awful Letdown," with lyrics by Johnny Mercer). According to Will Friedwald, the result was that Astaire (with Tommy Wolf) wrote "Life Is Beautiful" at that time, and Bennett loved it. He made it the title song of his first album for Improv. The cover of the album is a photo of Bennett embracing his two young daughters: Joanna on his shoulder, Antonia in his arms. Friedwald wrote that the album was "quintessential Tony Bennett—everything about it was bright and optimistic," including the diagonal bars of bright color designed by Rudy De Harak. It was Cary Grant who helped to dissuade Bennett from making more movies. He told Bennett that films would be boring for him, that traveling around the world doing concerts and connecting with people was far more exciting and nourishing to the soul. Grant astonished Bennett when he asked to purchase his painting *South of France* and hung it in his home.

Bennett would never lose his amazement about actually getting to know artists such as Astaire, whom he'd loved from his youth. He never viewed them as celebrities in the abstract, but as great artists, mentors, and friends who graced him with their recognition, friendship, and, to his surprise, praise. They looked upon him as an equal. John McDonough, a noted music critic who has written about Bennett and interviewed him for *Downbeat* and the *Wall Street Journal*, told me that "Tony Bennett is very proud of the fact that his 'schooling' was in the hands of people like Fred Astaire and Frank Sinatra. When he gives interviews, it's curious, because he is a chronic name-dropper. And he's perhaps the biggest singing star alive today. You would think his would be the name other people would drop. But he drops these names into his conversation: 'Fred Astaire told me a great thing once,' or 'I learned a great lesson from Count Basie,' or 'My friend Frank Sinatra used to tell me this.' I think it's a way in which he reaffirms his association with that generation of music that he so admires and that shaped him—and that he has rigorously clung to and defended against considerable challenge over his career. So he's proud of the fact that Fred Astaire might have given him a little tidbit of advice once, and he's taken it very much to heart, because it came from a man whom he idolized.

And Tony likes to remind people that he learned from the best. I think that's one of the messages he's sending out a little bit subliminally."

"Tony loves stories," Jonathan Schwartz told me, "loves to tell stories about people. And his stories are populated by names: 'You know, Judy Garland once told me . . . you know, Louis Armstrong said to me once.' And they're populated by these *amazing* people in American history. He can't somehow yet believe he's in their ranks. He manages to drop names without dropping them. He loves these people, no question."

Many events in the 1970s pointed to Bennett's career resilience. His paintings were displayed beside those of other celebrity painters at an exhibition at Lincoln Center in New York, highlighting his continuing growth as a visual artist. The final Horne-Bennett TV special that was filmed in London, *Tony & Lena*, aired in the United States in April 1974. "The hour is consistently pleasant, frequently superb," wrote John J. O'Connor, television critic of the *New York Times*. "Both singers are, of course, master stylists, possessors of musical taste and distinctive phrasing. And that is precisely, and intelligently, the focus of the program. There is no patter, no cute routines, no nonsense." The American tour of Horne and Bennett followed and concluded late in 1976. In May 1974, Bennett had been awarded an honorary doctorate of music at Berkley College of Music in Boston.

In October of that year, the controversy over the busing of schoolchildren in the city resulted in the stoning of black children and the beatings of blacks. Citing the racial cauldron that was seizing the city, Horne refused to perform her scheduled concerts with Bennett at Symphony Hall. Bennett, of course, was in complete accord with her and canceled the shows.

The serious, debilitating illness of Bennett's beloved mother cast a pall over his entire life that year and for several years to come. Writing the liner notes for his album *Perfectly Frank* many years later in 1992, he would recall one of the many acts of kindness that Sinatra did for him during that period. "The date is October 13, 1974," Tony wrote. "My mom, tragically bedridden, had her entire family around her. We were praying, doing everything to lift her spirits. Her only entertainment was watching television, so we were anxiously tuned into a music special called 'The Main Event.' The performer was Sinatra, 'The Champ,' at Madison Square Garden. We were so enthralled with his performance, Suddenly, in-between two marvelous songs, he belts out that I'm his favorite singer. Taken by surprise, I looked over at my mom. Her eyes opened almost as big as her heart. It was one of the great moments of my life. I'll never forget what he did for me that day. It will remain one of the great moments of my life."

Soon after, Bennett was overjoyed to share the stage with Frank at Gower Champion's tribute to Ira Gershwin. The event took place on July 27, 1975, at the Dorothy Chandler Pavilion of the Los Angeles Music Center. Then, in November 1976, he performed at the Smithsonian Institution before a sold-out crowd. Also that year, Bennett became national spokesman for the United Way for its 1976–77 campaign.

In May 1977, Mayor George Moscone of San Francisco presided at the dedication of Tony Bennett Plaza, in the cobblestoned courtyard of the Mark Hopkins Hotel on Nob Hill, and a street in Golden Gate Heights on the highest hill in San Francisco overlooking the ocean was named Tony Bennett Terrace.

The output of Tony's new label, Improv, was a tremendous source of pride for him during the early 1970s. It included orchestral sessions with Torrie Zito and quartet sessions with the Ruby Braff–George Barnes Quartet. His superb album with Zito, *Life Is Beautiful*, in addition to the great title track by Fred Astaire and Tommy Wolf, contains four new songs and six standards never sung before by Bennett. The new songs include "All Mine," by the veteran songwriting team of Ray Livingston and Jay Evans; "Bridges," by the Brazilian composer Milton Nascimento, with English lyrics by Gene Lees; and Duke Ellington's "Reflections." The marvelous Cole Porter song "Experiment" and the haunting "This Funny World" by Rodgers and Hart are reflections of Bennett's worldview and philosophy. Both are songs that, without being didactic, express serious sentiments—in "Experiment" about the need for openness and tolerance, and in "This Funny World" about cruelty and the lack of understanding in human relations. In the latter song, human beings will "laugh at the things that you strive for." The song is almost a bookend to the Dinah Washington masterpiece

"This Bitter Earth"; both songs are laments for the human condition and have become immortal standards. Two other songs are simply classics: "Lost in the Stars," which Bennett had recorded twice before, on *Tony* and on his Carnegie Hall album. As Friedwald writes, "It's a real concert work, with Bennett starting slowly, almost rubato, backed only by Zito's piano, and building to one of his famous blockbuster climaxes, where he builds to a high note like an Olympic weight lifter hoisting a ton or two. Even when Bennett sings a deep philosophical song about how humanity is essentially abandoned by God . . . it's hard to describe it as depressing. He ends on a note of serenity more than anything else." And finally, there is the torridly swinging "There'll Be Some Changes Made," with three increasingly rapid choruses leading up to a resounding climax.

But the ultimate albums of the Improv period were Bennett's duets with Bill Evans. "By the sixties, especially after his tenure with the Miles Davis Sextet and with his own groundbreaking trio," Bennett wrote, "Bill had become the most-listened-to jazz pianist in the world. He recorded with very few singers, though, so I was surprised when Annie [Ross] suggested that Bill and I work together."

"Bill Evans was an orchestra," Jonathan Schwartz said. "You didn't need any other musicians. What he did at the piano was so wrenching, it was so beautiful, harmonically new at the time. Also he turned out to be a great accompanist for this iconic figure standing next to him."

"He played like the ocean in a storm," Bennett said.

According to Friedwald in his notes for the Improv recordings, the idea of Bennett doing an album with Evans was completely unexpected because of the vastly different personalities of the two men. Bennett is one of the most outgoing communicative musicians; Evans is "one of the most introverted players in the history of jazz." Friedwald went on to write that despite their differences, "the two more than meet each other halfway—Bennett also possessed a reflexive, inwardly-direct quality that he had already allowed to come to the fore . . . and Evans . . . could play as dynamically extroverted as anybody."

The two musicians had met before. They appeared in the same concert at a special jazz party organized by President Kennedy on the White House lawn in 1962, though they played separately. Bennett had been a fan of Evans ever since Evans had worked with Miles Davis's *Kind of Blue* sextet. "I met Bill backstage [at the White House]," Bennett told Friedwald, "and he told me that he liked the songs I picked throughout my career, and that he admired me for sticking with quality songs." Later, when *Billboard* paid tribute to Bennett with an entire issue in 1968, Evans took out an ad and wrote, "Like many instrumentalists, I never was a great vocal fan. But Tony's development has been fantastic, and for the past few years he's been my favorite singer. Tony really has knocked me out more than anybody. The reason is that he has developed through a long, hard process of pure dedication to music and to his own talent. The end result of this type of development is more precious; it has a depth and a quality and a purity that appeal to me."

Bennett and Evans arranged with Bill's manager, Helen Keane, to tape two albums. "Lee Musiker and Torrie Zito told me that during a recording session, Tony would shut the microphone off, go to the edge of the stage, and just sing while Bill played," John Bunch recalled. The first album, *The Tony Bennett/Bill Evans Album*, was released by Fantasy in June 1975; the second, *Tony Bennett & Bill Evans Together Again*, was issued by Improv that September. It was conceived as a very intimate, spontaneous experience. There was no preparation for the first album. "I remember how the intensity of the whole experience kept mounting," Bennett said. Bennett told James Isaacs that he would tell Helen Keane to keep the tape rolling: "I couldn't believe what he was doing, over and over again, each thing was magnificent. Then he'd turn around and say, 'I think we're ready to do one.' We did that for two or three days; we didn't have anyone in the studio except Don Cody, the engineer, Helen, myself, and Bill."

At such a moment of professional crisis in his career, without a major record label and with a contracting market for the music he believed in, with many major artists such as Peggy Lee being bounced from their labels, and with a coalescence of cultural forces ranged against him, a lesser artist might have settled for the lowest common denominator, made commercial records that reflected the musical trends of the day, and desperately looked for a hit. Bennett, of course, chose precisely the opposite route. Having formed his own label, a precarious financial undertaking under any circumstances, he chose to go with even more intimate and soulful music and with an artist who, while revered in the jazz world, was not a star, and hardly a household name. Bennett did not go with Roger Williams or even Erroll Garner. Instead he chose a great artist, Bill Evans, and a relatively esoteric project for the marketplace with very limited distribution prospects (although the first of the two albums was released by the small but established Fantasy label), made two sensational and moving records, and did some of the greatest singing of his life.

And it was deeply significant that a musician of Evans's stature chose to undertake the project with Bennett. "Musicians have nothing to lose by being honest," Eric Comstock told me, "and Evans obviously saw something in Tony that a lot of people didn't see. So it must have been a fifty-fifty thing. And the albums were not about the marketplace at all. It was a totally pure artistic statement on both their parts. There were things that Bill Evans had already recorded and made great records of. And remember they're both busy international stars and have to do all this in a few days. There is always the practical element with these guys. That's what makes the accomplishments of Tony Bennett so astonishing. Because this is a guy being pulled in a zillion directions, and yet he takes the time to make the artistic decision. I'm sure Tony did some of these songs because Bill Evans had recorded them before and already knew them and they could record them in a fairly short time. But it's also a great gesture of respect to Bill to say, 'We're going to do the thing that you've done before.' It's a secure artist who says, 'Let's do that one that you did. We'll make it work.'"

During a radio broadcast, the esteemed WNEW disc jockey William B. Williams asked Evans if working with Bennett was a "jazz sound." Evans responded, "As far as I'm concerned, it is. Occasionally fans will act surprised by the fact that Tony and I have joined together for this particular project, because they tend to see Tony in the superstar pop singer image. But you know, every great jazz musician I know idolizes Tony. From Philly Joe Jones to Miles Davis, you name it. The reason is that Tony is a great musical artist. He puts music first, and has dedicated himself to it. He has great respect for music and musicians, and this comes through, and it's just a joy to work with somebody like that. . . . This is one of the prime experiences of my life."

"Bennett approaches the material on both albums," Friedwald wrote, "with the confident air of the artist who knows he has nothing to prove. The routines are neither overtly fast and swingy nor slow and dramatically draggy, but somewhere right down the middle. . . . Even the verses (some quite rare) that precede many of the tunes have lots of rhythmic feeling. 'Lucky to Be Me,' a 'sequel' of sorts to 'Some Other Time' on the first album . . . sets the mood by establishing a swing feeling that doesn't necessitate a fast tempo.

"Both this and 'Make Someone Happy' give Bennett and Evans the opportunity to examine the melancholy underside of two traditionally peppy, lucky, and happy show tunes. Evans doubles the time on his improvisation on the former, and Bennett's out-chorus is one of many trademark examples of the singer's mastery of dynamics; he knows exactly when and how to gradually turn up the volume on the climac-tic 'build your world around her' and he can take a nondescript phrase like 'stuff of life' and invest it with so much feeling you know exactly what lyricists Comden and Green were thinking. He does the same with all of Alec Wilder's somewhat cryptic lyrics to 'A Child Is Born,' turning the abstract into the concrete. Dynamics are even more crucial here. He increases the impact of the last word ('born') by whispering it at the end of the first chorus, belting it on the second."

"Some Other Time" by Comden and Green on the first Bennett–Bill Evans album is quintessential Bennett—utterly uncommercial, reflective, touching on the precious fleetingness of life, and infused with both melancholy and hopefulness. "There is so much more embracing still to be done, but time is racing." The song is about the eternal need to "catch up some other time." Bennett sings a refrain of "Oh, well" four times to signify wistfully the swift passage of time, how hard it is to encompass all the beauty of life. His voice is rich and deep and vulnerable. The song is perhaps a meditation on his mother's approaching death and his wish to embrace her, for he knew that not much time was left for her. Bennett would travel to the old Bennett home in River Edge often to see her. "Tony would of course come visit often," his niece, Nina Chiappa, remembered, "because my grandmother was bedridden the last five years of her life. Because she lived with us, a lot of relatives came to our home, including Tony. So there was a lot of family life in our home. Every Sunday after Mass was the cooking and the dinners."

Bennett and Evans opened the Newport Jazz Festival at Carnegie Hall in June 1976. John S. Wilson wrote in the *New York Times* that "It was Mr. Bennett's evening and he made the most of it. He was in good voice, strong and sure, pacing his program with a skill that he has mastered brilliantly. He is a superb old-fashioned pop singer." They went on to perform together at the Smithsonian in Washington and on Dutch TV, and recorded a half-hour concert for the Canadian Broadcasting Corporation.

"To this day," Friedwald writes, "Tony remains especially proud of the two Evans albums, often citing them as the most satisfying projects of his long career. Tony says, 'If you can get to a pure, simple thing, it always, it lasts forever. The best records that Nat Cole ever made were with his trio and the best records I ever made are the duos with Ralph Sharon and Bill Evans. We just went in there at two-thirty in the morning and went to work. Just piano and voice, that's all we needed.'"

Bennett connects Evans's addiction and suicidal self-destructiveness to that of comedian Lenny Bruce. Bennett once asked his ex-manager Jack Rollins what he thought of Bruce, who'd also been his client. Rollins replied, "He sinned against his talent." Those words, Bennett has said again and again, changed his life. "If you have a gift, nurture it, don't smash it."

During the last months of recording, Evans was constantly sick and would go back to his room to rest after each recording date. Bennett spoke to Evans for the last time in the spring or summer of 1980. Evans tracked him down and called him. Evans's voice was full of despair. He said that he wanted to tell Tony one final thing, and that was just to think "truth and beauty." He asked Tony to forget about everything else: just concentrate on those two things. It caused Bennett to really focus on his drug problem. He realized that something must be done.

The most comprehensive account of Bennett's experience with Improv and a critical analysis of the recordings can be found in the notes by Will Friedwald in a booklet enclosed with Bennett's four-CD compilation *The Complete Improv Recordings*. "To this day," Friedwald writes, "Bennett refuses to regard his Improv experiment as anything other than a success. 'Oh, man, it was ridiculous,' he says, and then repeats for emphasis, 'It's ridiculous! These guys are crazy to look at Improv as a failure. I had Bill Evans, Earl "Fatha" Hines, Charlie Byrd, Torrie Zito, Jimmy and Marian McPartland, all the greatest musicians. The critics went crazy for the albums; they thought they were the greatest albums ever made. So the company fails because I had some hooligans handling it.'"

Danny Bennett had been right in predicting the outcome. Bill Hassett did not know how to run a record label, and Bennett wound up in debt for $250,000. "The very late '70s turned out to be a disastrous time for Bennett," wrote Friedwald, "but in a sense it became a sort of spiritual and artistic purging" that would lead to Bennett's 1985 comeback. In Bennett's universe, Friedwald wrote, "good things happen to good songs. Bennett, too, would seem naïve if the world didn't keep proving him right, or had he not succeeded beyond his wildest dreams, giving Bennett the opportunity to enjoy what Gary Giddins calls 'the longest last laugh in history.'"

There is no hyperbole in calling the Bennett Improv experiment heroic, for that is what it was. Bennett certainly had access to a wide public relations apparatus, including a vast network of TV shows and wide coverage from the press, and he promoted the albums vigorously, but the lack of viable distribution was Improv's death knell. The label lasted only two years. Yet it was hardly a sidetrack or a career failure; it garnered great critical respect and represented another artistic advance for Bennett. In the long run it would win him even greater fame and applause. But it was a financial disaster. It's hard to conceive of any other artist of Bennett's fame and stature undertaking such a dubious commercial venture; certainly not Sinatra. The entire venture signified Bennett's enormous belief in himself and what he wanted to achieve in his art.

Bennett would not release a single album between 1977 and 1986. "I remember that Tony was considered box-office poison," George Avakian told me. "We talked about doing something, but I didn't have a connection at the time. And people were simply not interested. 'Oh,

Tony Bennett. Everybody has his old records. Who cares?'" These were the bitter, difficult years, even though Bennett kept performing live to sold-out houses.

Tony Bennett marked his fiftieth birthday on August 3, 1976, with a huge celebrity-packed party around the swimming pool at his Beverly Hills home, including such guests as Cary Grant, Fred Astaire, and Johnny Carson. It was, again, an event that seemed to symbolize his great success and his arrival at the pinnacle of show business, while in reality many conflicts were churning just beneath the surface. The words of his great hit "The Good Life" must have been revolving in his head, especially the lyrics about "hiding all the heartaches you feel." Another major event followed when Sinatra invited him to sing with him on his ABC special *Sinatra and Friends* in 1977. Bennett sang the knockout song from *A Chorus Line* "One," and dueted with Sinatra on "My Kind of Town." Another high point occurred with Sinatra when Bennett was playing the Sands in Las Vegas in February 1979. He received a note that Sinatra was listening to his performance at a party on a yacht off the southern coast of France. Sinatra had asked his friends at the Sands to set up a shortwave hookup. In the note, Sinatra requested that Bennett sing Torrie Zito's arrangement of "My Way."

On Thanksgiving night in 1977 came an event that pitched Bennett into a tailspin, a crisis that was long in the making. He was backstage at the Fairmont Hotel in San Francisco when he learned that his mother, his mainstay and bedrock, had died. He hid the news from his audience until the end of his performance. He said later, "She was a great lady and would have wanted it that way. And I wouldn't have wanted to disappoint the audience." He often reflected ruefully on the fact that his mother had been in good health until he kept the promise to himself and to her to buy her a house and enable her to retire as soon as he could afford it. That opportunity had come early with the huge success of "Because of You." Ironically, his mother's sharp physical decline seemed to virtually coincide with his loving gift to her. "Tony's mother adored him," Nina Chiappa recalled. "Of course she loved all of her children. But Tony was a special person to everyone in all of our lives. And still is. I remember that Tony could not handle any death very well. He was too emotionally overcome. It must be hard for him now. Being one of the last ones standing. I mean it gets hard when you get older and most of your colleagues are gone. He was close to Judy Garland and I think that was really difficult for him. And of course when Duke died, I'm sure that was very difficult. Count Basie, and so many people that he was really close with. And Pearl Bailey, he was very close with her as well. Not just from a career standpoint. And so of course his mother—that was tremendous for him."

When his mother died, Bennett bounded into the street and in a grieving frenzy ran for miles. His mother had been everything to him. She'd kept him grounded and focused. He thought he would never get over her death. He felt as if he were going crazy, and he turned more and more recklessly to drugs for relief.

Events were converging: his drug addiction, his crumbling marriage, the loss of his latest manager (Derek Boulton's successor, Jack Rollins, had already quit), and with the collapse of Improv, the loss of a record label. His career was foundering, although he was playing to sold-out houses forty-five weeks a year. Worst of all, Bennett was facing huge debts, an investigation by the IRS over unpaid taxes, and the possible loss of his house as a result of the debts. He publicly recovered from his mother's death, but the depths of depression he was feeling were overwhelming him.

Sinatra seemed to always appear at the most unexpected moments throughout Bennett's career to bolster him and give him encouragement. Once again, as he had done on national television at Madison Square Garden in 1974 when Tony's mother was already seriously ill, Sinatra reached out to Bennett at a time of great sorrow. In July 1978, Bennett was appearing at Harrah's Reno and Sinatra was appearing at Harrah's Reno Convention Center. According to the July 28, 1978, *Nevada State Journal and Reno Evening Gazette*, Sinatra introduced Bennett, who was in the audience, as the only other saloon singer in the world.

Harbingers of the imminent disintegration of his second marriage were several interviews with his wife. In 1976 Sandy Two was asked by Marshall Berges of the *Los Angeles Times* if she was happy, and she responded, "Ask me tomorrow if you want a cheerful answer. . . .

My life seems empty." On the brighter side, she said that she and Bennett were in love, and "I like being married. It's a nice moral life, and it suits me just fine." Later, in an interview in a book by Marilyn Funt that appeared in 1979, *Are You Anybody: Conversations with Wives of Celebrities* (the interview had originally appeared in the *National Enquirer*), Sandra expressed anger over Bennett's not initiating "strong enough action to bring about divorce" from his first wife. Sandy Two also stated: "When I found myself pregnant [for the second time], I wanted him to help me decide whether or not to have an abortion. He has two sons from his previous marriage and I knew he felt our one child was enough and I felt our lifestyle, with all the traveling, made a second child impossible. I wanted to force him to make the decision. He refused, he would not verbalize about it. I had the baby and he was very happy. He loves her very much. His attitude during my pregnancy was very strange, and after she was born I went into a severe depression." The interviewer commented, "It sounds like you're at a turning point or 'the' turning point?" Sandy Two replied, "Well, it is definitely a crisis. I really want the marriage to survive, but it has to survive on new terms. He interferes with me too much. He criticizes results rather than sit down and go through the planning of things. There is never any question of his care when he is home, he is very well attended to, it's just his own negative feelings due to his insecurity."

Bennett has always tended to show more candor in his interviews with the British press. In an interview with BBC2 in 1979, he expressed a bitterness and a personal despair in which he related the decline of good music to the political situation in the United States. "Everything that happened in the sixties," he said, "Kent State, Martin Luther King, two Kennedys, and the Vietnam War . . . well, it didn't just end there. If you do good things, good things come out; and if you do bad things, you have to live with it." The interviewer asked him what this had to do with popular music. "Everything," he said. "An artist goes by what he feels. If he sees nothing but violence, anger, and hate, then he has to record this because he is a victim of his time."

Bennett has often returned to the theme of the feeling of hopefulness he experienced in the United States during the Great Depression when people felt they were building a human society. Poverty did not extinguish the feeling of hopefulness; on the contrary, people banded together to help one another. The level of compassion was deeper. The music of Kern, Berlin, Rodgers, and Gershwin reflected that hopefulness. People cared, and they knew it took time to do things well. In contrast, contemporary society, including music, was based on obsolescence. Nothing lasted. Computerized, electronic musical outputs were designed to prove that the true artist wasn't needed anymore. To Bennett, it was always the artist that counted.

In contrast to this assessment of the effect of the political situation in the United States on popular music, the eternally optimistic side of Bennett asserted itself in an interview with Rick Kogan, "Timeless Tony in a Timeless Land," in the *Chicago Sun-Times* in 1979. Kogan visited Bennett at the Desert Inn in Las Vegas, where he was costarring with Count Basie at the Crystal Room. "There is a good deal of contemporary music that I enjoy," Tony said. "I like Joni Mitchell, Paul McCartney, Stevie Wonder—marvelously talented people. But for the most part I don't care much for rock." It was fifteen minutes before showtime, and Bennett closed his eyes. "At my age," he said, "I've really got to take care of myself. A singer is like a fighter, so I play a lot of tennis. It's keeping me young, but more important, it's keeping my voice in shape, allowing me to sing the way I want to sing." He took a sip of water. "And I want to sing forever."

It continued to be "the best of times, the worst of times." In 1973, *Variety* had reported that the monumental Italian film director Vittorio De Sica was seriously considering directing a film about the life of Bennett, *Two Bits*, with Bennett playing himself in the lead as "a first-generation New Yorker with a tough exterior but a soft center." It had not materialized. In June 1979 he was lauded by the Smithsonian Institution in Washington, D.C., as "one of the nation's living national treasures." Bennett seemed to be everywhere: in 1978 he played himself in a six-part NBC miniseries about the life of Martin Luther King Jr. titled *King*. He taped six specials in London, *Tony Bennett Sings*, with BBC2 and appeared at the Odeon, New Street, in Birmingham in June. Reviewing his appearance at the Odeon, the June 25, 1979, *Evening Mail* wrote that Bennett "was tremendous . . . A vast stage, a cavernous auditorium and only a piano, double bass and drums for support, but Bennett triumphed again. . . . Every word, every nuance is crystal clear. He fully deserves his place among the greatest ballad singers of our time."

Bennett made numerous appearances on American television in 1979, including a three-and-a-half-hour celebration of the Great American Songbook titled *American Pop* on March 17, on PBS on behalf of its "Festival '79" membership drive. Blossom Dearie, Sarah Vaughan, Billy Eckstine, Odetta, Jackie Cain and Roy Kral, George Shearing, Chet Atkins, and vibraphonist Milt Jackson were among his guests. William Gillen, in an article for the Associated Press, wrote that Bennett called his guests "the believers, the artists who kept the legacy of American popular music from being washed away by musical fads in the time since the swing era of the 1930s and '40s." The night before, he touted the program in an appearance on the *Mike Douglas Show*; Bennett sang "Just in Time"; "Lazy Afternoon"; "There Will Never Be Another You" (with a great Bennett growl); "From This Moment On"; and a fresh, slow, and haunting version of "Because of You." He was accompanied by superb tenor saxophonist Harold Land. "The best in the land," Bennett shouted. On May 2, 1979, he appeared on the *Tonight Show* with Johnny Carson and offered tributes to other singers: Sammy Davis Jr. ("I've Gotta Be Me"), Sinatra (a beautiful "Here's That Rainy Day," "Fly Me to the Moon," and a weak, swinging version of "My Way"), and Nat King Cole (a splendid "Nature Boy"). For the latter song, he utilized Cole's actual voice to duet with Cole for the final few bars of the song (surely Bennett's original idea and one that would be utilized by Natalie Cole for her later duet with her father, "Unforgettable").

Bennett returned to the *Mike Douglas Show* on May 14, 1979, for a "mini-concert." Douglas announced that Torrie Zito was in the hospital and that Joe Cocuzzo was conducting. He commented that "You Italians really stick together," and Bennett replied, "Mike, you know a good thing." Unfortunately, Douglas went on to make a denigrating remark: "It's like watching *Godfather 3*." It was rightfully received with a stony silence (and no doubt, silent rage) from Bennett. Bennett went on to sing "Old Devil Moon"; "They All Laughed"; "Fly Me to the

Moon"; "My Favorite Things"; and, with a Chicago string quartet of young musicians, a magnificent version of Billie Holiday's "If You Were Mine." The latter song never appeared as a Bennett recording, yet it deserves to be preserved, like so many of Bennett's lesser-known but great songs. There is so much that awaits discovery.

Will Friedwald has alluded to the difficulty of locating the best of Bennett in his book *Jazz Singing*: "After the watershed year of 1962, which produced his two biggest sellers ('I Left My Heart in San Francisco' and 'Wanna Be Around') as well as his triumphant Carnegie Hall debut, Bennett albums began to lose their identity, whether crass or artsy. 'We had Bennett in the studio all the time then,' one Columbia exec recently told me, 'practically every day.' CBS threw together Bennett LPs almost randomly, mixing up sessions from all over the place, throwing in single releases as well as material already released on other albums. Especially when a hit single came around and Columbia wanted to capitalize on it with an album, they seem to have grabbed whatever pieces of tape marked 'TB' were nearest and threw them on the album master without rhyme or reason."

Bennett returned to the Sands in Vegas for a five week-engagement, followed by two weeks with Count Basie at the Desert Inn. On September 17, 1979, he appeared at the Drury Lane/Water Tower in Chicago at a benefit for the Martin Luther King Jr. Foundation. Coretta Scott King was a guest of honor.

On December 16, 1979, Bennett also made one of his innumerable benefit appearances in New York, at the Hilton at an event honoring the late jazz singer Teddi King. The concert was given for the SLE Foundation of America, a charitable organization seeking a cure for the disease known as SLE or lupus, a chronic inflammatory condition involving the connective tissues, most often affecting women of childbearing age. King had died two years before, at age forty-eight, from the disease. Tony's humanitarian efforts were endless and mostly unknown to the public.

Many of Bennett's admirers feel that his autobiography, *The Good Life*, glosses over some of the difficult realities of his life story. "*The Good Life*, that 'nice guy' thing, is completely sanitized," Gary Giddins told me. "Everybody knows that he had a thing with pills for a while. But the point is, if you're going to do a memoir, it can't just be about how great everybody was. It just rings as phony. Well, he loves that book, but that book is a valentine to himself—even the anecdotes. He really has an understanding of popular culture. And the same thing when I interviewed him about Bing. Privately. The things he said about Bing were just really shrewd and smart. And I didn't feel that the stuff in *The Good Life* was nearly as smart."

In *The Good Life* Bennett only suggests the depths of depression he was experiencing at this time. He tells of his overdose, and ascribes it to the strain of his financial situation and the danger of the IRS starting proceedings to take away his house. Accountants had called him that day and warned him of the situation. He writes that in frustration he "overindulged." Realizing he was in danger, he tried to relax by taking a hot bath, and passed out. In that time he experienced a "near-death experience": a gold light, "a clear yellow peaceful plane" filling him with a warm glow. At that point Sandy Two discovered him, pounded his chest, and saved his life. She rushed him to the hospital.

There is no denying the pain and agony that Bennett was going through, but, as with much of his memoir, there is a holding back, an attempt to shield himself—or the reader—from the pain he was experiencing. It happens so fast and is resolved almost before Bennett is out of the bathtub. "I overindulged"—those are rather odd, euphemistic words for what had apparently transpired. And it's over: he "quickly realized [he] was in trouble" . . . "and tried to calm [himself] down by taking a hot bath." The passage is written in such a way that one finds it difficult to realize that a torturous period of suffering and addiction had resulted in Bennett almost taking his life.

Jerome Helligar, who interviewed Bennett in 1998 for *People*, refers to Bennett's "cocaine-and-marijuana-induced stupor." Nick Duerdon, who interviewed Bennett more recently for the British newspaper the *Independent* (September 20, 2008), spoke to Bennett about his "overdose." Bennett replied, "That's a lie; it never happened. Sure, I did maybe indulge in moderate drug use, but the whole country did back then. You have to remember that this was a time of Martin Luther King being assassinated. Bobby and Jack Kennedy, too [although these events actually happened a decade and more before]. It really smashed America. The whole country went out and did things. We were devastated by what was happening to our people and so we . . . tried drugs. It's the same old routine: you start out on marijuana and then somebody hands you cocaine. If you keep going with that, you die. It stopped."

Denial—or damage control—is woven so completely into Bennett's account in *The Good Life* that it virtually glosses over the reality of a near suicide—and the fact that we could have lost the greatest singer of our time. Much of *The Good Life*, as valuable and moving as it often is, suffers from this same airbrushing of experience, rendering the book an important document that somehow skirts the truth at some critical moments.

Gary Giddins feels the denial only lessens a great artist and a courageous life story. "Anybody who's ever worked on a screenplay knows there has to be something that you overcame. And Tony did. Beginning with poverty, then the pill thing. He was *famous* for that addiction. I used to hear about it from musicians *all the time*. Because jazz musicians are accustomed to all kinds of drugs and shit, but they would say, 'Man, Tony Bennett had one of those reputations the way Stan Getz had in his early years with heroin of just being on stuff all the time.' You know, this makes for a great story. A guy who goes through all of that and then comes out as the only star of his generation who's still performing, at eighty-five! On top. That's the story. And he managed to keep his integrity despite everything. Tony's from another world, and yet he manages to stay afloat."

I asked Will Friedwald why Bennett was so reticent in talking about overcoming his addiction. "I don't know," Friedwald said. "Most of the people of my experience, people that have been through that, are really like serious junkies, like Art Pepper and David Allyn. And they get so into it that the only way they can get out of it is by replacing talking about it for the real thing. So it's like a therapy thing for them, and they get into this wildly confessional thing. I don't think it was that serious for Tony. I don't think it was year in and year out. It wasn't like he was selling—dealing on the streets or stuff like that. I just don't get the impression it was that terrible and life-threatening."

"The real story," said Lenny Triola, manager, producer, and programmer at WNEW-AM for many years, "is how Tony stayed intact musically. I think Tony plays it really cool now, playing it even. Doesn't say much, doesn't say little. Very careful. All smiles, but you know there's a cobra behind that closed door. Look, he came from an era where Sinatra wasn't careful. Frank would say anything he wanted. So did Jimmy Roselli. Tony is always about educating people and educating kids. Educate the kids about how the business was back then. Who ruled Las Vegas, who ruled Atlantic City, and how they ruled all the singers really."

Bennett wrote of his rapid recovery that it took him a couple of weeks to recover. A very quick recovery indeed. Almost unbelievable, in fact. Bennett did not go into rehab. Shortly afterward, Sandra Grant served him with divorce papers. There were bitter feelings, but in the long run Bennett, always a devoted family man, would never forget that Sandy had saved his life and that they had two wonderful daughters from the marriage.

"When Tony left California," Derek Boulton remembered, "he came back to two rooms in New York on Fifty-sixth Street, two blocks from where his office used to be. I was no longer managing him, but we stayed in touch. Tony was very lonely at that time. He woke up, grabbed me on the phone for two hours before he got out of bed. He said, 'Come over.' I'd go over, waste time. He'd be sitting there in his dressing gown. He had a daily maid. He lived well always. He lived very well. But he couldn't get a manager. After we split up, he phoned me three times, the last conversation was for four hours. I'm ashamed to say I was very rude to him. I'd had a fucking bellyful. But I will love and respect him always."

Bennett continued to do well, as always, in clubs, earning $1.8 million for a sixteen-week engagement at the Desert Inn in Las Vegas. He appeared often on the Johnny Carson *Tonight Show* and played himself on *Skag*, an NBC series starring Karl Malden. Meanwhile, Bennett sought to protect his Beverly Hills home from his estranged wife, who was reportedly being seen with Gene Kelly. Bennett, meanwhile, was dating singer Minda Feliciano.

At this time Sandy Two, still living in the Bennett home in Hollywood, filed a palimony suit against Bennett for their five years of living together before their marriage. It failed. If the suit had been successful, she would have received half of all his finances. The final property settlement included the sale of the Bennett home for nearly $1.65 million in 1994.

Bennett finally turned to his sons for help. There have been countless stories of fathers oppressing or saving their sons, but rarely has there been a story of role reversal like the one of Tony Bennett's rescue by his sons, Danny and Daegal. Here the sons took the loving, paternal role and rescued their father at a critical low point in his life. Without a record label, without a manager, living estranged and alone in Manhattan, and about to go bankrupt (he owed $2 million in back taxes), Bennett, in an act of desperation, picked up the phone and called his sons for help. He first spoke to Danny, who turned out to be his redeemer. Danny's perspective was that his father was a pure and great artist, and great art would prevail if people had a chance to hear it. He would make sure that Tony was heard. Danny worked with his father on his finances (explaining, as to a child, that he could not spend more money than he earned), and made sure he did not lose the Hollywood home. The IRS debt was paid off in 1990. He told his father, "Your head is above water now." Tony could not believe it.

By 1999 Danny Bennett was overseeing a nest egg of $15 to $20 million for his father. Today it is many times that sum.

In an article in the *New York Times* (May 2, 1999) titled "Talking Money with Tony Bennett: His Heart's in San Francisco, His Money in His Son's Hands," Geraldine Fabrikant quoted Bennett as saying, "For forty-five years, I had an ax over my head. I was spending more than I was making, on advertising, publicity, and all. . . . I realize how fortunate I am to have someone, in Danny, that is truly looking out for my best interests and not just in it for the money."

And in that regard, as philosophically and psychologically different as father and son were, they were alike. Neither was in it for the money. For Bennett it had always been the art; for Danny it was his love for his father.

Bennett had landed in his son's arms, a story almost unparalleled, unpredictable, totally surprising, humanly compelling, and filled with hopefulness—just like Bennett's music and art. The compass was now set, but also true to Bennett's complex personality, the journey would have many more jolts and conflicts and victories that stun the imagination.

But Danny Bennett had freed his father to do some of the most productive and enduring work of his life.

10

Renaissance

Danny called Tony up and said, "If you make a hundred dollars and you only spend ninety-nine, then you're a buck ahead. But if you make a hundred dollars and spend a hundred and one, you're in trouble." Danny wrote out his father's entire financial predicament on a spreadsheet so he could finally see it clearly.

Danny went on to explain that Tony had spent exactly the same amount that he'd earned that year, leaving nothing for the tax man. He worked out a three-year payment plan with the IRS. Tony, for the first time, would work within a budget.

And so the traditional Italian father role of supreme authority was transferred to the son. Yet for Bennett there appeared to be little strain. As in so many other ways, his was a modern sensibility unusual in many men of his generation and background. Bennett seemed to transcend—float over—some of the usual categories with apparent ease. His was more an artistic—a jazz—sensibility, combined with a hard-edged pragmatism.

Nevertheless, there were underlying moments of conflict with Danny. "I see Tony periodically," Derek Boulton said. "About ten years ago, I was with him in the car. Tony said to me, 'I'm a Leo. I'm a lion. At the moment they've got the lion in a cage. But the lion's going to escape.' He wasn't entirely happy with the setup."

Danny took over in a managerial void. After Jack Rollins's resignation, Gino Empry succeeded him briefly. But Tony was considered unmanageable by many in the musical community. Danny was really a desperate choice. "Danny Bennett must have seemed an odd choice to replace the professional managers," Geraldine Fabrikant wrote. "At the time, he was a twenty-five-year-old punk rocker with long, dyed-blue hair. . . . He had never gone to college, and instead pursued his dream of becoming a rock star. His father, he said, had no objections.

"But it turned out that the son was the mirror image of the father: Tony's talent lay in art, not business, and Danny's lay in business, not art. 'I was always the business manager for the bands I was in,' the son recalled. . . . For more than a decade, the son crunched the numbers and wrote the budgets while the father performed. To revive the singer's career, he marked him as a living American legend, a genial master of his craft."

With Danny as his new manager, Bennett mapped out a new game plan with his son. When Danny asked him what he sought to accomplish, Bennett replied, "I want to do what I do best, nothing more and nothing less. Above all else, I never want to compromise my musical integrity." He wanted to be one of the keepers of the flame, a preserver of the Great American Songbook. Great music, he insisted, transcended generations.

Bennett was reunited with Ralph Sharon when Torrie Zito resigned as musical conductor. The rest of the new trio was comprised of Jon Burr on bass and Butch Miles on drums.

"As the old TV variety shows and nightclubs disappeared," John McDonough wrote in Downbeat (October 2006), "Danny Bennett's basic strategy was to build bridges that could take his father's pop classicism into the new music venues that were emerging in the 1980s. When a minor counter-revolution against the techno-steroids of amplifications began to take hold in a part of the MTV audience, Tony Bennett became a symbol of a new kind of 'unplugged' authenticity that would bring him together with a whole new sector of contemporary performers and their audiences."

It would be a long slog from 1980 to 1986, when Danny's efforts took hold and things began to fully stabilize for Bennett with the recording of his first album in nine years.

Back in New York in 1980, according to Bennett in his memoir, he never wanted to get high again. Some people do not remember it that way. They describe the next five years as ones of intense struggle and conflict for Bennett on many levels. They repeat earlier accounts of Bennett's difficulty with musicians.

"Tony had a lot of unusual ideas about how the rhythm section functioned and what he wanted to hear behind himself," an associate who worked with Bennett in the 1970s and 1980s recalled.

> For example, for the drums to play the hi-hat [what the drummer plays with his left foot] on two and four, that's a standard thing. As a matter of fact, this same dispute was why Joe La Barbera ended up leaving. In the eighties, Tony found that distracting and felt that it interfered with his consonants. But that's how drummers feel that they hold the time together. So there was a kind of intrinsic tension between what Tony wanted and what a drummer believed was the right thing to do. So Butch Miles the drummer left in November 1980. Joe La Barbera had been with Bill Evans during that time, and Bill passed away in the summer of 1980. Joe was on the loose, and he was hired. He stayed for about twelve years. Ultimately it was the hi-hat issue for him, too.

> Offstage Tony was such a personable guy, and he liked to hang out. Created an affable, amiable atmosphere, always had time for people who wanted to talk to him. Had this philosophy that his role was to bring a song to life and express for the inarticulate guys in the street what they couldn't express for themselves. That's what made Tony tick. But onstage, Tony could be very difficult.

> Tony was prone to late-night calls to the guys. By the time he got to me, he'd talked to Ralph Sharon already. He would

swing around to positive, be more aspirational: "We got great stuff coming up." I didn't get the ranting calls. Ralph had to take those; he knew it was part of the job. But it was very costly. Ralph ended up with heart problems, and he appeared to be beaten down. Well, you know everybody is responsible for themselves. Ralph could have said, "Fuck you, Tony." Ralph had plenty of profile; he could have worked in a heartbeat. But Ralph was inherently lazy; rather than make a change like that. I guess he was enmeshed. One cost that it had on Ralph was that physically he began to look beaten down. And he was not using his body efficiently to play the piano. His playing started to sound kind of constrained, cautious. He wanted to play the same thing every night so he could say to Tony, "We did exactly what you want." He played defensive piano.

Tony was a pothead for a long time. There was a guy who was a chronic hanger-on in the dressing room who always showed up with blow. He disappeared from the scene and went to prison. His name was Tony Sabella. We used to do it together. I'd drink wine, smoke shit. Tony Sabella would show up and we'd share. Most of this stuff was after the show. So Tony never really stopped smoking in the period I knew him best. The first word I got from Tony that he was clean was around 1990 or 1991. I got sober myself in 1988. Then I saw Tony at a jazz place on the Upper East Side. I hadn't seen him for some time, and sat and talked with him for a while. I tried to do a little of a nine-step [AA steps]. He said that he was clean and quit using pot. He seemed better, clearer.

Then there were the Mafia drops. I'd heard from Ralph Sharon that in the past, Tony had to make a stop in a few of the cities that we went to. That was basically over by then, but there was one time where I had some direct experience with the wiseguys. We had to go to Wilkes-Barre, Pennsylvania.

The meet was at Tony's place on Fifty-fifth Street. There's a limo waiting there out in front. The limo has two drivers.

Huge guys. Okay, they both sit in front, and we're in the back. Now this gig is a testimonial dinner at a bowling alley. The honoree was a gentleman named Russell Buffalino. [Buffalino was the boss of the northeastern Pennsylvania crime family and a significant influence in Cosa Nostra from 1959 to 1989. He was convicted of extortion on August 8, 1978, and sentenced to four years at Leavenworth. He was later convicted of murder.] So we're going out to play at this affair. This is around 1982. The occasion was Buffalino had just gotten out of Leavenworth after four years. The drivers called him "Uncle Russ." Uncle Russ was cooking goat at a bowling alley. He was the chef; he made a big dinner. He made a big goat stew and pasta. And we go out there—Tony said, "We gotta do this—come on, let's go."

So we go to the bowling alley. They've having the dinner there. We sit down at these long tables with the plastic white and red checkered tablecloths. And these guys come around and they shout, "Oh, Tony!! It's a shame ya missed the head [of the goat]! Tony, Tony, ya missed the head!" Capo D'Agniello [head of the goat].

So we're on the way back. I said to Tony, "Who was that guy Russ?" Tony turns and he says, "Jukeboxes." That's all he said. Ralph told me that Tony stopped all the drops soon after.

One can only imagine the deep discomfort of Bennett, who wanted nothing to do with the wiseguys, in a surreal environment like this. He had no choice. It was a matter of survival. Miraculously, he was able to cut all relations with them within a short span of time.

"Tony made Ralph Sharon a nervous wreck," Derek Boulton said. "The worst thing to do with Ralph is knock his confidence, and Tony did that. Tony did it every night. He made him the whipping boy." A family friend recalled Bennett's scapegoating of Ralph Sharon. "I saw him go at Ralph Sharon at the Fairmont Hotel over nothing," he said. "Chronic abuse. But Ralph, being the man he was, took it. When I tell you the gravity of the situation at the Fairmont in Frisco, the way he yelled at Ralph, in front of me, in front of my wife, it's just incredible.

His Astoria pal, the late Joey Petraglia, told me, 'Don't get too close. Because when you do, you're out.'"

But for every negative account of Bennett's treatment of musicians, there are many positive ones that tell of his humanity and sensitivity toward them. "1998, the year that I was working with Tony on his book," Will Friedwald relates, "was also the first year, I believe, that Gray Sargent, the jazz guitarist, was part of Tony's band. . . . I traveled with Tony to a show in Atlantic City right when Gray had first joined the group. Ralph Sharon was playing piano, of course, and there was a full string orchestra conducted by Vinnie Falcone.

"At the show, Tony assembled the quartet (which until recently had been a trio) onstage; I was standing in the wings, and I don't think Tony or anyone else was fully conscious that I was there. Tony wanted to talk to all four of the guys and Gray in particular, and what he had to say was this: 'Gray, I get the feeling you're holding back," he said. 'It's like you're afraid to put everything you've got into your solos. You're afraid you're going to pull focus from me, and I appreciate that. But don't worry. Don't hold anything back. Your solos are your moment to shine. So don't worry about stealing the spotlight from me. . . . It's not going to happen. The better you play, the better it's going to make me look.'

"I thought that was a wonderful moment to have observed."

An account by an old friend refers to the contradictions of Bennett's personality. "One time I was with my kids. They'd never met Tony. He was walking to a theater, and I approached him. I said, 'Tony, excuse me, I want to introduce you to my kids.' He ripped me apart in front of them. I had my hand in my pocket, and I was jangling change, and he told me what bad luck that was. He embarrassed the hell out of me. Then, another time, he was doing a watercolor in San Francisco. I was with him when he was doing it. He said, 'Here, take it. It's going to be worth money someday.' He knew it. We all get these mixed signals from Bennett."

Whatever the extent of Bennett's problems in the first half of the 1980s with drugs, he was masterful onstage, on TV, and in clubs. After viewing and/or listening to Bennett performances during virtually every month of his career from 1976 through 1985 (thanks to the prodigious efforts of Nick Riggio and his incredible collection of videos, tapes, CDs, cassettes, and DVDs), I have no doubt that Bennett was in complete control of himself while performing—he simply gave peerless performances.

As to the wiseguys' efforts at extortion and coercion of Bennett, his true feelings can be found in a stark and powerful watercolor painting titled *The Underworld*, which was published in his book of artwork in 1996, *What My Heart Has Seen*. The painting, one of his greatest, is a Dantesque vision of bold colors. The upper third of the painting contains a series of menacing, individualized faces of wiseguys in black, orange, and green on a red background, with one man with a mustache in the center staring directly ahead, wearing a half-green, half-black hat and a polka-dot tie, and another, his eyes closed, the right side of his face in black, who appears to be a corpse. The lower portion of the painting contains three rows of skulls, and a gun in the second row is poised with two sets of fingers tightly coiled around it.

Despite his roller-coaster ride, by 1980 many of the more knowledgeable critics were already calling Bennett the logical heir to Sinatra. Prominent WNEW-AM disc jockey Bob Jones told Richard Goldensohn in *Attenzione* (September 1980) that "they think he's inevitable [as a successor]. He's just as inevitable today as Sinatra was when Bing Crosby was everybody's favorite singer. . . . Tony simply reaches people. Some other singers may have better voices from a technical point of view, but they just don't have his ability to touch that human being on the other side of the footlights."

Those who had criticized Bennett at the start, such as John S. Wilson, who'd written a critical review of his 1962 Carnegie Hall debut in the *New York Times* and who had written of Bennett's "husky, limited voice," had long since reassessed their opinions. Wilson praised Bennett as "one of the continuing wonders of the pop music world" who could "let a slow ballad emanate from him like a warm mist."

Bennett himself was sad but unfazed about still not having a major recording contract in 1980. "I try to look at it like somebody in the clothing business might," he told Richard Goldensohn. "I'm in silk and everyone else is in cotton. Sure, it feels lonely and takes longer, but it's also very gratifying." He said, "The songs . . . they're like an onion. You go deeper and deeper into the core of their meaning every time out. How can you get tired of that?" When he was battling Columbia, he had told an interviewer with characteristic clarity, "Every artist has his own dignity. When a record company says, if you don't record this song, you'll lose your job, all they're doing is trying to frighten you into doing something you know you shouldn't be doing."

Bennett also took an acting role in 1980, playing a clown in a network television film titled *A Gift of Love*. The film was produced by the United Way to support its funds appeal. Mario Pellegrini, its producer-director, said he chose Bennett because "we didn't want a slick Hollywood type. We needed sincerity. And that's what Tony Bennett is all about."

The year 1980 also was tough for one of Bennett's greatest champions, Jonathan Schwartz at WNEW-AM. Schwartz had infuriated Frank Sinatra by criticizing the third disc of his three-record album *Trilogy: Past, Present, Future*. While Schwartz had praised the first two records on the album, he had deemed the third one a disaster. Sinatra had prevailed upon the station manager of WNEW to fire Schwartz. It was devastating for Schwartz, who suddenly found himself without a job due to the very person he esteemed most and had promoted on the radio for many years. Bennett quietly called upon his friend and fan Nick Riggio to launch a letter-writing campaign on behalf of Schwartz. "Tony came to me and said, 'Do me a favor. Get everybody that you know that's a fan of mine and have them bombard WNEW.' That's what we did. I had letters sent to WNEW from Belgium, England, Brazil, Poland, Italy, everywhere in the United States," Riggio told me. "Jonathan did get his job back." When I spoke to Schwartz in 2010 about these events, he told me that even though he was close to Tony, Bennett had never told him of what he had done on his behalf.

At a time when he was still feeling estranged and isolated due to his marital breakup, it was a comfort for Bennett to be reunited with his childhood friend, composer-arranger Gene Di Novi, when Tony played the Royal York Hotel's Imperial Room in April 1981. The April 8 *Toronto Star* reported a conversation between the two old friends before the show. Bennett spoke of how melodic the Italian language was and how much affinity the Italians had for music. "It is in our bones . . . our blood," he said. He said he didn't know of any Italian in Italy who couldn't sing beautifully. He encountered them on the streets of Italy and found them open and uninhibited people. He affectionately cited as an example his boyhood buddy: 'There is nobody who knows how to laugh and love, to live more than Gene Di Novi.'"

Di Novi observed that most stars now were really interested only in their careers, but Bennett really felt the music and loved it. Bennett spoke of those who had inspired him as a young artist, from Getz to Tatum to Holiday, and he lamented that the younger generation lacked great mentors. He spoke of the current cultural amnesia: a great history was being ignored. He went on to say that in the mid-1970s, "Everyone sold out. I never saw anything like it."

Di Novi injected a note of optimism and said that young people were beginning to become aware that "something groovy happened before 1960." Bennett agreed, and recalled that Duke Ellington had told him that music came from anywhere: from rock, from classical, anywhere. Tony concluded, "Either it's good or it's bad, there's no in between. It's as simple as that."

Bennett was eager to communicate to young people the beauty of the Great American Songbook. Danny Bennett agreed, and urged his father to tackle the youth market in 1981, a strategy that would soon prove immensely effective in rebuilding Bennett's status. In May Bennett played three hip New York clubs: the Village Vanguard, the Bottom Line, and the supper club Marty's, as well as a concert at Carnegie Hall with a jazz trio, a string quartet, and a thirty-two-piece orchestra, all as benefits for the Police Athletic League. Reviewing Bennett at the Vanguard, John S. Wilson in the May 8 *New York Times* was full of praise. "Initially, it seemed as though this were going to be standard Tony Bennett—the short, hoarsely husky phrases that develop strong rhythmic intensity, the single chorus of a song that grows from casual statement to a shouted climax. But that was not Mr. Bennett's purpose at the Vanguard. . . . As he began to get the feel of the Vanguard, supported by a very responsive audience, his delivery adapted. The pressure drained away from his voice and it took on colors and sensitivity that get lost in the high amplification of a big hall. His singing became smoother, softer and easier as he found the right level for the [small] room and the image of intimacy that Mr. Bennett tries to create in an auditorium became reality. This kind of close contact in which Mr. Bennett does not have to strain to make his points is an ideal setting for the low-keyed, simmering intensity that vitalizes his songs."

As a result of Danny's advice to target a younger audience, Bennett now appeared with David Letterman as well as Johnny Carson. Danny went on to book him on *SCTV*, a Canadian sketch comedy show. Bennett appeared with such innovative younger comedians as John Candy, Catherine O'Hara, and Rick Moranis. He next became an animated special guest on the *Simpsons*. Danny was elated to discover an interview with Bob Guccione Jr., editor of *Spin*, which celebrated the hip spirit of his father. Guccione was asked, "What do you think is the essence of rock 'n' roll?" He replied, "James Brown and Tony Bennett, because they're the essence of cool and that's what it's about." It was exactly the image Danny was seeking to build of Bennett, and there it already was in print from one of the hippest editors of the time.

A vivid glimpse of Bennett (who was fifty-four) during that month was captured by Chet Flippo in his 1981 profile "On the Town with Tony Bennett," which appeared in his book *Everybody Was Kung-Fu Dancing*. Separated from his second wife (she and their two daughters still had the use of the Beverly Hills house) and returning to New York, Bennett was living in a suite at the Park Lane Hotel on West Fifty-seventh Street while waiting to move into his co-op on Fifty-fifth Street. There was no hint that Bennett was disconsolate or depressed. Flippo asked Bennett whether he considered himself Sinatra's successor. "Well," he answered, "they claim that I'm the heir apparent. I don't even know what that means, because we're two different animals. Frank is ten years my elder, and I still have a way to go yet. There are some strong storm warnings that if I just stay healthy it'll get good, it'll start getting *good*." Bennett, Flippo noted, "delivered a strong wink."

Flippo was amazed at the number of times Bennett was stopped for an autograph or a photo as they walked down West Fifty-seventh

Street. Flippo asked why he never had bodyguards or security. "I'll tell you," Bennett replied. "If I walk down the street like this, swaggering, with my shoulders back, everybody will say, 'Hey, Tony, how you doing?' you know, because I'm just walking like a citizen." As they kept walking, Bennett said, "Sinatra used to have to walk underground through the pipes of New York City just to get out of the Paramount Theater after a show. The only way they could get him past the crowds was through the sewers of Manhattan." Bennett shook his head.

Bennett had just returned to New York, and his love and appreciation for the city had been reignited. Asked why he had decided to do a week of benefit shows for the Police Athletic League, he said, "It's really a salute to New York's nightlife. I'm indebted to New York. It's the greatest city because of its vitalness. You can get that in other cities, but you have to search for it. Here, you just walk up the street and see the best paintings in the world. And there are great teachers sprinkled all over this city. It's the greatest place in the world to learn the ropes, to get streetwise, to get this terrific education. Chicago has transformed itself into a cultural center, and San Francisco is America's Paris. But this one is the *big daddy*."

No matter how complicated his life, Bennett continued doing benefits for good causes, almost fifty charity concerts a year—something he'd learned from Sinatra. "Let me tell you something that Tony did for me," Gary Giddins said. "In the eighties John Lewis of the Modern Jazz Quartet and I started the American Jazz Orchestra at Cooper Union. It went on for seven years. And we never had money. We never took salaries, and we were always borrowing. I would say to John, 'We're in trouble here. Let's call Sarah [Vaughan].'" And he would say, 'No, no, we have to save her for a rainy day.' And I would say, 'John, it's pouring.' And he would say, 'It's a big mistake to have famous guest stars because then the audience will start expecting them.' But one night we were doing arrangements we'd gotten that had never been performed before, written by Sy Oliver and Fletcher Henderson. So if you were a serious jazz person, this was pretty exciting stuff to discover. And four or five of the pieces had vocals. We asked Tony and he agreed to do it.

"What I didn't know until the day of the concert was that he was in Brazil! He flew back! Do you know how long a ride that is? That's like twelve hours. And he came from the airport to Cooper Union, sang four or five tunes, wouldn't even accept the little honorarium that we prepared. I just thought that was unbelievable."

Alone and striving to rescue himself from a disastrous time in his life, dislocated and at a career impasse, still without a record label, Bennett drank in the city and it invigorated him and fed him. Here he would sing and paint and love again. The city answered his hunger for creative life and beauty. He would make it.

Speaking to Flippo, Bennett exclaimed, "*Oh*," stood, and thumped the table to emphasize his point. "I've come to the complete conviction that the songs of the nineteen-twenties and thirties in American music are deep, *very*, very deep. I think that one hundred years from now they will become America's classical music—the Richard Rodgerses, the Gershwins, the Kerns—it was an *era*. We were poor in those days, but there was great hope, and this city was building, skyscrapers were going up, everybody felt we were going toward something great. Those songs will *live*. They might be out of fashion, but what is good *is* good and will always be good. People like Harold Arlen, who was *destined*, you know. He wrote 'Somewhere Over the Rainbow,' 'Black Magic,' 'Stormy Weather,' 'One for My Baby.' It's part of our heritage. And I doubt that it's ever going to go out. You just say, 'They can't take that away from me.' It's hard to beat."

Gary Giddins caught Bennett's performance at the Bottom Line and was overwhelmed. He'd had reservations about Bennett in the past and would have them again at an impending Carnegie Hall concert, but he was full of praise about Bennett at the Bottom Line (and would be again later). Giddins wrote about the concert in May 1981 and republished his review in his book, *Rhythm-A-Ning*. Bennett "was everything we've come to expect—charming, friendly, energetic, excitable, emotional; yet he also had a steel grip on his pitch problem, and he was swinging not in the manner of a well-meaning but alienated jazz lover who has to settle for a businessman's bounce, but as a knowing rider with both feet firmly planted in the metric stirrups. . . . He sang 10 first-rate songs. The rhythm section—pianist and music director

Ralph Sharon, bassist Jon Burr, drummer Joe La Barbera—played hard, thanks chiefly to the relentless La Barbera, and Bennett pushed them without faltering. His appealingly bald and husky voice seemed a little dry in the middle register, but he had no problem shooting for firecracker endings and rather obvious but effective embellishments, and even when he reached for something slightly out of grasp (which happened very rarely), he saved himself so quickly that I was willing to applaud the risk.

"Bennett knows how to read a lyric; on some ballads, he's even better at it than Sinatra. Sinatra calls himself a saloon singer though he wouldn't be caught dead singing anyplace smaller than a Vegas ballroom, but Bennett—who'll sing anywhere—really is a saloon singer, in the best way. He's an audience-lover who presents himself as real, unpretentious, part of the crowd. He's too straightforward to impart irony to a lyric, so he conveys meaning with a sense of wonder, using his hands and face for nuance and emphasis; at 'It's hard to conceive it' in 'Body and Soul,' he tapped his noggin and looked like he was having a hard time conceiving it. He can also underline meaning without visual help; there's a marvelous moment at the outset of his recording of 'The Touch of Your Lips' with Bill Evans, when he utters the word 'sweet' as though he were first realizing what sweetness is. On ballads, the big-hearted bellowing voice is honed for dramatic effect, as vowels and phrase endings linger in fuzzy exhalations of breath made especially piquant by contrasting rapier shouts."

Bennett continued to grow as a painter, devoting a large amount of time and concentration to his art. He sketched constantly, in airports, restaurants, limos, hotel rooms, wherever he happened to be. The paintings would evolve out of the sketches, and for many years his apartment in New York City has been filled with paints and easels. He has compiled those sketches and paintings for sixty years into a visual diary of all of his travels, and they are now collected in two fine books of art, *What My Heart Has Seen* (1996) and the more recent *Tony Bennett in the Studio: A Life of Art and Music* (2006), edited by Robert Sullivan. He began to attract wide recognition by the early 1980s and gave an exhibition of his artwork at Tavern on the Green in New York City that garnered wide praise.

In 2005 he spoke to author Jerry Tallmer of his lifelong friendship with Everett Raymond Kinstler and his other art teachers, Charles Reid, Robert Wade, and Basil Baylin, "strung out over several hemispheres, depending on where the singer, who lives out of a suitcase while he performs all over the map, happens to be at any given moment. Bennett also drops in at the Art Students League whenever he can."

One of Bennett's two suitcases, Tallmer wrote, was for his watercolors and brushes. "It's functional for me when I travel," Bennett told Tallmer. "Not messy. Watercolors are like jazz, full of happy accidents. You paint what you see, and if you happen to do a good one, you turn it into an oil when you get home." He said that his own gods were Rembrandt and Velasquez. "Base your work on that," he said, "and you're on your way."

Major music awards were now coming his way: the National Academy of Popular Music, an association of songwriters, gave Bennett a lifetime achievement award. The academy's president, songwriter Sammy Cahn, bestowed the award on Bennett at the annual Songwriters Hall of Fame dinner in Manhattan.

Bennett costarred in a ninety-minute special with Count Basie in March 1982 called *Bennett and Basie Together!* He taped it in Boston with pianist Dave McKenna. Janet Maslin in the *New York Times* wrote that the concert was "buoyant" and that Bennett was in top form. "Bennett's performance [had] incomparable dash and energy." Bennett was Grand Marshal of the Columbus Day parade on Fifth Avenue in October 1982, following in the footsteps of Frank Sinatra and Luciano Pavarotti. In 1983, he gave a fifth royal command performance—a concert in San Francisco for Queen Elizabeth and Prince Philip.

In 1981 the great drummer Joe La Barbera had joined Bennett and would stay with him for eleven years. "Tony used to come into the Village Vanguard quite often to hear Bill Evans," La Barbera told me, "and also to Michael's Pub when I was working with Jimmy Rowles. When Bill passed in 1980, Tony was looking for a drummer around the same time, and my name came up.

"You know Sinatra has been the benchmark, I think, for male baritones for a long time. But Tony's take on it is uniquely his own.

He's got his own *sound* and his own way of phrasing. I think that's what gets him across, but it's the sincerity, too. It's just Tony. If you know the guy, that's just the way he is. The highlights of the show for me were when he would do 'Lost in the Stars' with just Ralph [Sharon].

"He was very particular about his health. He loves tennis. It actually worked out to be an ideal way to stay in shape for someone who travels. Because you don't have to carry a whole lot of gear. Just a racket and some shoes, shorts. Minimal. Being Tony Bennett, he knew all the tennis pros in all of the cities. So wherever we went, it was guaranteed we were either going to get a lesson or we were going to play with somebody. When I was first starting to play, we were in Florida. He calls me and says, 'Hey, we're going to play some doubles this afternoon. Meet me down at the court at three o'clock.' I showed up and our doubles partners were Tony Trabert and Virginia Wade. It's like sending a kid that just got a tenor on the bandstand with Coltrane.

"And Tony was never big on entourage, period. Our whole thing for the whole time I was with him consisted of, at the most, six people. It was the rhythm section and a sound guy and Tony. That was it. Sound guy/road manager. And I think that's the way he liked it. He knows he can stand alone.

"No bodyguards, no nothing. He hated that kind of stuff. You've got to give him credit for being able to have this business on his own terms. Instead of going that other route, where you have all this insulation between you and the fans. He just never left the street. Tony Bennett can walk down the streets of New York anytime he wants and people are always going to want to say hello. But they're going to be respectful, too, and they're not going to intrude on him beyond a certain point. They're going to ask for an autograph and say, 'How you doin'?' and that's it. I think it's because he's always been down there. That's why someone in the audience can relate to him so easily. If you were sitting in the audience and listening to Sinatra, in the back of your mind, maybe all of that other baggage is connected as well beside the great performance. Such as you've got fifteen bodyguards."

As he reached the mid-1980s Bennett's painting was increasingly playing a major role in his life. When he gave a two-week engagement at the Westwood Playhouse in Los Angeles in August 1985, he also gave an exhibit of his lithographs and paintings in the lobby. A full exhibition would be held September 6–9 in the Art Expo at the Los Angeles Convention Center.

Meanwhile, Danny was actively seeking to find a recording contract for his father. His efforts came to fruition in the best possible way. Danny had been approached by Italian producer Ettore Stratta, who was based in the United States and a producer for Sony. Stratta told him that Mickey Eischner, head of A&R (artists and repertoire) at Columbia, wanted to do an album with Bennett. Columbia was unwilling to invest money in Bennett, but Stratta had an investor who wanted to back the album financially. Danny and Stratta worked out an agreement in 1985; Stratta would be the arranger and conductor of the album. Now, after fourteen years, Bennett was reconciled with Columbia, and both Danny and Daegal were now involved in management and production.

The reconciliation with Columbia was an entirely new arrangement. Bennett would have complete artistic control, from the recording engineer to the final mix of the album. Every aspect of production was completed before the album was delivered to Columbia for pressing and distribution. As Will Friedwald wrote, "It would be on his own terms, enabling him to call his own shots and giving him the right and the responsibility to sing songs straight from his heart. And the only pressure he needed to worry about was actually the worst of all—that which came from within."

The result was *The Art of Excellence*, one of the greatest albums of Bennett's career. Stratta located the great Argentinian orchestrator Jorge Calandrelli, who has over the years received twenty-four Grammy nominations, for the album, and Calandrelli would be involved with Bennett's next eight albums as well.

"One day Ettore Stratta calls and says Tony hasn't recorded an album for almost ten years," Calandrelli told me. "Ettore says he's going to approach him with the idea of doing an album of gorgeous songs and he wants to do it in London with an orchestra and he wants me to do the arrangements. Tony liked the idea a lot, heard some of the things I had done, loved my arrangements, and thought I sounded

like the right guy for the project. I wanted to meet him. Then I flew
to Atlantic City to meet Tony.

"There was an incredible coincidence involved with that album.
Tony told me he was going to be sending me a cassette with a list of
songs for the album. When I got it and started listening, all of a sudden, wait a minute, that's my song on it! It was a song I had composed
in Argentina at least ten years before: 'When Love Was All We Had.'
I composed the melody, and the lyrics were by an Argentinian, Sergio
Mihanovic. At that time I had said to Sergio, 'This song would be so
great for Tony Bennett.' At that moment, that was like an impossible
dream. So Sergio wrote the lyrics and recorded the song in English
for an album in Argentina. I forgot completely about the song. All of
a sudden when I listened to the cassette, there it was. There was no
title; it said 'Untitled Song.' No composer was listed.

"I called Tony and told him it was my song. He said, 'Oh, my gosh,
I'm so glad you told me. We had no idea who the songwriters were.'

"I said, 'How did that song get on the cassette? How did the song
get in your hands?' And he told me an amazing story. When he was
performing in Brazil, a woman approached him and gave him a cassette
and told him it was of songs by her husband. The woman was Sergio's
wife, who happened to be in Rio de Janeiro. Tony took that cassette
with him. You know what the likelihood would be that he would
never have listened to it. But eventually he played it. When he started
listening, among those twenty songs, he fell in love with 'When Love
Was All We Had.' He had said, 'The day I record a new album, I want
to record that song.' When he told me that, it was so amazing. I was
thrilled and he was thrilled, too.

"Then after we recorded the album in London, we presented it
at Radio City Music Hall in concert in 1986 and I conducted the
orchestra. The way he introduced me as a conductor was by telling
the story: 'I once met this girl in Rio . . . she gave me a cassette . . . the
composer is my conductor, Jorge Calandrelli.'

"The whole experience of working on the album was magical for
me, because I had always loved Tony since the first time I heard 'The
Shadow of Your Smile.' So we went to London and recorded with
a sixty-piece orchestra with the Ralph Sharon Trio; Joe La Barbera, a

wonderful drummer; the bass was Paul Langosch. We had almost like a symphony orchestra. Ettore decided to make Danny coproducer, because he had been so involved.

"Tony had sent me a cassette of the songs he wanted for the album. Not the arrangements, but just the songs. He would have a lead sheet. With that, I would write the arrangements. Then he first heard my arrangements live in London when we started rehearsing the orchestra. At that time we didn't do demos or anything. He would listen right there, and he liked it so much, he said, 'Jorge, I love that. Let's do it.' And he would start singing like he had sung that arrangement a hundred times. But that was the first time he had ever heard it.

"The Ray Charles duet 'Everybody Has the Blues' was a different thing. I went to that session and I wrote that arrangement. Danny and Daegal had come up with the idea of a duet out of the blue. I didn't even know beforehand it was going to be Ray Charles; I heard the song sung by Tony. Then they decided to invite Ray, and he heard it and loved it."

Bennett shared his passion for art with Calendrelli. "Tony would call me in New York and tell me he wanted to take me with him to show me the paintings he loved, like the Frick collection," Calendrelli told me, "and a Latin Museum of Art uptown, which had his favorite painting by an Impressionist from Spain. When he arrived at that museum, there was a security guard who said the museum was closed. 'Oh, my gosh,' Tony said, 'I don't believe it. I want to show the maestro.' (He calls me 'the maestro.') All of a sudden the guard realized it was Tony Bennett. He said, 'Excuse me, Mr. Bennett.' He calls the curator to the phone. He said he would be there in ten minutes. So the curator came and opened the museum for us. And he went with us through all the paintings and explaining them. These things that happen to Tony are things that don't happen every day."

Calandrelli gave another example of Bennett's stature and the private doors that open for him. "Tony calls me and says, 'I want to take you to the Library of Congress.' So he picked me up and we went there. They were waiting for him at the library, and they showed us the paintings and the books. He said, 'The maestro would like to see some music.' They took us to one of those endless halls with musical scores, and he said to me, 'Would you like to see some original scores? Who are your favorite composers?' I said, 'Stravinsky, Ravel, Debussy, and Copland.' And they started showing me originals. They had the original 'Rite of Spring' written by hand by Stravinsky. I saw Ravel's 'Daphnis and Chloe.' And one of Copland's scores. So the whole experience with Tony was incredible, because he would take you everywhere, and wherever we went at the Library of Congress, there were open doors."

The cover of the album, shot by Annie Leibovitz, is an outdoor picture of Bennett in a sweatshirt with the letter "B" and a leather jacket and the World Trade Center in the background. *The Art of Excellence* is an almost uninterrupted flow of greatness, a release of creative expression on recording that was denied Bennett for nine years. It has balance, passion, joy, romance, and endless artistic surprises. This is a new Bennett intertwined with the old; the depths of maturity and interpretation burnish each song—new wine mixed with old. "After a Salinger-like silence of nine years, Tony Bennett released an album . . . that grows taller each time it's played," Jonathan Schwartz wrote. "*The Art of Excellence* is one of those 'Wee Small Hours' flukes of nature—letter perfect, immune to even the slightest jab, a remarkable, ongoing success. Two super-duper Tony Bennett ballads are included . . . 'How Do You Keep the Music Playing?' and 'Why Do People Fall in Love?' Also, a haunting 'I Got Lost in Her Arms' (there is simply no better version anywhere at all). 'What Are You Afraid Of?' is the slyest of all of Tony's songs, and easily the wittiest."

Lenny Triola, who also considers the album a masterpiece, is critical of the way it has been obscured. "Some of his best work was on that album," Triola told me. "Surely the best before his comeback. Nobody talks about it. And then *Astoria*. Truly tremendous records. *The Art of Excellence* was one of the great records to come out. And everybody's forgotten it. Calandrelli, Stratta, it's Ralph, it's Paul Langosch on bass. A hell of an album. It's just amazing how we don't even talk about these things anymore."

In "I Got Lost in Her Arms," Bennett takes an old Irving Berlin song (from *Annie Get Your Gun*) and makes it the most romantic and convincing love story I've ever heard. I felt myself reeling and falling into the vortex as he sang, "It was dark in her arms, and I lost my way." This is a sublime artist realizing the full intention of the composer and, as Sinatra said, "probably a little more."

Bennett's voice on the album is deeper and darker. Sometimes it is a whisper. It has the depth, huskiness, and maturity of late Sinatra, the sense of the hard-won wisdom of a lifetime, but while Sinatra's voice would decline dramatically, Bennett's seems to have weathered the years well. Each song contains its own Bennett inventiveness, and Bennett's customary big windup is sometimes exchanged here for a gentle denouement, including "When Love Was All We Had," and, if anything, the result is even more effective. Marilyn and Alan Bergman's "Why Do People Fall in Love?" originated with Sinatra. He sang it at the Hollywood Bowl and, addressing Tony in the audience, said, "Tony: you should sing this song!" The song has the heartbeat of romance, and Bennett, as always, enunciates the lyrics in unpredictable, startling ways. On "The second she walked in" he breathlessly emphasizes "second"—and we live the moment with him. When he asks if "There is some power in touch that sends a crazy rush running through my soul," he emphasizes "touch" and "crazy rush," and most of all "soul," when he both holds the note for a long time and raises it higher and higher. He similarly emphasizes "needing" on "But here I am needing someone," holding the note, and "the everlasting fear" of losing this love. Bennett segues into a few bars of another song, "People," near the end, and concludes with two spontaneous touches: When he sings "People fall in love," he adds, "Ah!" as a sigh, and finally, he sings from the other song, "People who need people," and then "When they fall in love," he holds "love," the last note of the song, raising it higher and higher in crescendo.

Bennett sings "Moments Like This" in exactly one chorus, repeating only the last two lines. The song is lighter in tone, for the singer knows that as thrilling as the moment is and however he longs for more, the experience is just one of "all your affairs . . . But at moments like this: who cares?" Here Bennett practices his credo of prolonging the length of the song for only as long as is needed: no more, no less. If one chorus will do it (plus two lines in this case), it's a done deal.

"What Are You Afraid Of?" is even more playful, although as always with Bennett, passion and romance are the basic motifs. The singer is trying to persuade his girl to hang out a little more: what is she afraid of? The gang is gone, the fire is bright, and it's time to dim the lights and "put Sinatra on." If anything happens, "blame it on the stereo . . ." and, again, Sinatra mischievously peeps up with the phrase "All the way." The seduction is conducted lightly, expertly, and the singer knows exactly what he is doing. Bennett brings it all home with the final line: "Do it one more time . . ." and the perfect touch: "Mmmm."

James Taylor's "Everybody Has the Blues" is the first Ray Charles–Tony Bennett duet (Danny and Daegal's idea), and it is pure joy. An absolute romp, it treats the blues so merrily that the gentle, ironic, mocking tone belies the bad news the lyrics convey. Tony begins, "Hey, Ray, I feel so sad, I guess you're thinking nobody ever felt so bad before." Ray replies, "Oh, come on, Tony, join the club!" And they're off and running. It's back and forth, Tony playing innocent, brother Ray the wiseguy. Then Charles rips into the piano, with Tony's "Uh-huh!" in the background, and "Tell them the way it is, Ray." The effect is playful, celebratory, and raw—it's real. And there's no doubt Ray and Tony love each other's company. After we are told that even JR on Dallas and TV anchorpeople get the blues, the song ends with a piano note, a finger flick, a chord, and a final flick of the finger. It's heaven.

"Tony, when he goes into the studio, he just sings, alive," Calandrelli said of that recording session. "Right there. There's no editing, no punching in. Nothing. What you hear is what he did. It's absolutely pure. Honest, straight ahead. Never, ever, do we use the devices, the alto-tuner, never. He didn't even want to use headphones. He doesn't like them. The reason you use headphones in the studio is that you don't get leakage in your voice track from the orchestra. Tony said, 'I don't care about that. I want to sing live.' And we created a stage in the studio where Tony's singing in front of the whole orchestra and the trio and me conducting, and he has two monitors where you can listen to his singing without having to use headphones."

As to the Calandrelli song "When Love Was All We Had," who else but Bennett would have had the *aliveness*, ten years before, to respond to the lyricist's wife in Rio de Janeiro, take the cassette she offered of the untitled, unknown song her husband had written, carry it with him to America, listen to it, remember it, and choose it, not yet knowing the lyrics, for the first album he would record in almost ten years? And mail it to the very composer of the melody of the song!

People magazine reviewed the album in 1986 :

Bennett is 59, so the youthful bombast that sometimes lends a histrionic touch to his early hits is dissipated. On this, his first LP in 10 years, Bennett sings with a knowing, easy confidence, in a voice that has lost none of its texture and is at least as musical as it was when he was young. He and co-producers Ettore Stratta and Danny Bennett . . . have also come up with an extraordinarily involving set of songs.

The release of the album was accompanied by Bennett's first concert at Radio City Music hall, launching *The Art of Excellence* tour. Brian Chin, writing in the May 12, 1986, *New York Post*, observed:

Bennett was the personification of mastery. "I came here to sing," he announced as he took the stage, and sing he did, flawlessly. Tributes to Radio City's film history, and to the songs of Duke Ellington, Fred Astaire, Charlie Chaplin, and Walt Disney, provided a varied palette of pop, jazz and blues that Bennett used to create a rich landscape of American songwriting. Out of the variety, almost every number had to be counted a highlight. But the most astonishing of them might have been the delivery of *Sophisticated Lady* with his excellent rhythm trio— without any amplification at all. . . . "How Do You Keep the Music Playing?" and his own favorite, "Why Do People Fall in Love?.," were movingly delivered, with the bravura and brio that Bennett brings to all his songs—but also, crucially, with sensitivity to the expressiveness of the lyric lines.

Handling his material with that consummate balance, he sent away the audience in bliss over the singer and the songs as well. Bennett's engagement at Radio City Music Hall also included an exhibit in the lobby of his oil portraits of Judy Garland, Charlie Chaplin, Fred Astaire and Cary Grant and a street scene of Radio City. It was his first art exhibit in New York.

Bennett's longtime relationship with Susan Crow, whom he'd been introduced to in 1982 by his number one fan and, at one time, close friend Nick Riggio, was consolidated in these years. It was a relationship that seemed to stabilize Bennett's life, bringing him a new level of peace and happiness. Crow, who graduated from Columbia University, was teaching social studies at the LaGuardia High School of Music & Art and Performing Arts. "Susan is a great lady," the singer Margaret Whiting told me. "She's a woman who can travel on her own, very independent, very beautiful. She's a teacher. And Tony likes that. There were always women around him, but he's smart, he didn't want that. She's the perfect one."

"Susan has had a very positive influence on Tony," Nina Chiappa said in 2010. "I think that the time he's been with Susan, he's been extremely happy and very content in his life. From the time he was with her, he really grew internally and evolved into a more peaceful kind of person. I think she's been just a really lovely woman. She is another person like my mother who has wanted to pursue her education and career. And has a sense of independence about her. Tony and Susan used to go to lectures together, so that they had a common interest in that regard. I think that the school [the Frank Sinatra School of the Arts] was their joint effort, and what a wonderful thing, exploring the arts, that came out of the two of them being together. I'm really proud of them. I just don't know that he would have done that on his own. But Susan being involved as a teacher, I think a combination of their efforts together really made that happen."

Bennett toured London in November 1986. His appearance at Royal Festival Hall was reviewed in *Variety* on November 19:

While some of his contemporaries are searching for the notes, Tony Bennett, at 60, remains in full voice. He's as sharp as ever and retains all the old power. This concert, fifth of six on a British tour, pulled a capacity crowd of 2,500 and hundreds were turned away. . . .

Bennett came on, unannounced, to limn a clutch of songs. This without pause or interruption for a solid 100 minutes. It was clear from the start that Bennett's vocal cords and stylish handling of a lyric are undiminished. . . . Bennett's lasting appeal, the voice aside, is that he never seems bored, not even by "San Francisco." He loves musicians, treats lyrics with respect, lives and acts out his numbers, and communicates an unsophisticated excitement to the audience.

He is a classic example of the entertainer who honestly thinks he has the best seat in the house. And his patent desire to please convinces the rest that they have the second best seat.

In 1987 Bennett recorded his fifty-first album for Columbia, another one of his very best: a tribute to the music of Irving Berlin titled *Bennett/Berlin*. "It's like I'm a different singer on every track, using a different concept," he told Larry Kart in the November 8 *Chicago Tribune*. "And every take of every track was different, too. I consider that my craft now, to be instantaneous with what I'm thinking. Whatever the atmosphere is at the moment, I just sing it." He had questioned whether he should do the album. "I'd never thought of Berlin's songs as my meat," he said. "I've always considered myself a Harold Arlen man, because I'm a dramatic singer and he was such a dramatic writer. Anything Arlen wrote, I can do and feel very good about it. Berlin, I realize now, is a people writer. He gave us that great melody stuff—the silver lining, Fred Astaire used to call it. On one side is the elevator music, the other side is cacophonous, and in between there's a silver lining of straight, caring songs that are just right."

Bennett performed "When I Lost You," a song Berlin wrote in 1912 after the death of his first wife, a cappella, with sorrow and sadness, but also with the strength, the sense of endurance that he brings to darker material. "All of My Life," a plea for emotional directness, is almost a definition of the way he practices his craft. He was backed by the great tenor saxophonist Dexter Gordon. Gordon also appeared on "White Christmas," and Dizzy Gillespie joined him for "The Song Is Ended" and "Russian Lullaby," while guitarist George Benson appeared on "Cheek to Cheek." The album is marked by total spontaneity: on "Cheek to Cheek" Benson hums a wordless vocal while playing, and suddenly breaks into a gravelly, Louis Armstrong sound, laughing along with it. The album climaxes with an intense "Let's Face the Music and Dance," Bennett singing out of tempo, with only Ralph Sharon accompanying him. Bennett reads social significance into the lyrics of songs he chooses; just as "Just in Time" was the appropriate song to sing when demonstrating at Selma, Alabama, "Let's Face the Music and Dance" was about the Depression, and he told Jonathan Schwartz that he sang "Dancing in the Dark" with the George W. Bush years in mind.

The Art of Excellence and Bennett/Berlin, like the forthcoming Astoria and Playin' with My Friends, are simply great albums—to my mind, Bennett's highest achievements so far in the latter stage of his career. They were so great, so uncharacteristic of the musical times that they failed to make much of a commercial impact. As Francis Davis wrote in the Atlantic, "Bennett has become the best singer of his kind, but he must sometimes feel like an ambassador from a country that's fallen off the map." Still, these albums critically paved the way for what was to come. Despite the massive cacophonous din around him, Bennett was being heard and seen.

Bennett had never appeared in concert with Sinatra, and in 1988 had urged his friend Frankie Randall, a singer and entertainment director of the Golden Nugget who was like a son to Sinatra, to see if Randall could prevail on Sinatra to do a concert with Bennett in Atlantic City. Sinatra was reluctant (according to Randall, he called Bennett a wonderful singer but a "lox" onstage), but Randall persisted, and Sinatra eventually agreed. Thanks to Nick Riggio, I have a videotape of the event.

The concert took place at Bally's Grand on September 3, 1988. Bennett was sixty-two; Sinatra, seventy-two. It was interesting to watch the body language. The two men walked out on the stage rather stiffly and uneventfully, but it was clear this was a historic moment. Bennett appeared in a white jacket, black bow tie, and black pants; Sinatra, in a tuxedo. The Oedipal nature of the proceedings may have been hinted at by Sinatra calling him "young man" (just one time). Once, he also addressed Frank Sinatra Jr., conductor of the orchestra, as "son." Bennett, the heir apparent, was eager and smiling, obviously thrilled to be there beside the old man at last, Sinatra a bit grudging and stern. There were two separate sets by the two men, followed by a concert by the two together. Sinatra obviously regarded it as a test, a duel. Nobody was kidding around. But he rose to the occasion and really did his best. He was very well prepared and he warmed to the concert as he realized he was holding his own. He was starting to slide in those years.

Bennett, accompanied by Ralph Sharon, Paul Langosch, and Joe La Barbera, began with a swinging version of "Because of You," followed by "As Time Goes By" and "The Girl I Love." He appeared a bit awkward at first, but quickly grew in confidence. Paying tribute to Irving Berlin and his one-hundredth birthday that year, he did a beautiful version of "I Got Lost in Her Arms." The gestures were standard Bennett; when he sang "How I felt as I fell, I can't recall," he put his hand to his heart and shook his head. Then he sang "When I Lost You" a cappella. He went on to another tribute medley to Fred Astaire, including a vigorous and buoyant "Cheek to Cheek," and wound up with a medley of his own hits, "Stranger in Paradise" and "Who Can I Turn To?" He appeared very confident indeed by the end of the set.

Bennett introduced "the king of the entertainment world." And then there was Sinatra standing there, saying about Bennett, "How'd you like to follow him?"—a real tribute. Sinatra began with a shaky "Mack the Knife" but grew in strength with "Come Rain or Come Shine," "Summer Wind," and "For Once in My Life." Like Bennett, he always paid tribute to the composers and, unlike Bennett, also to the arrangers: Harold Arlen, Johnny Mercer, Don Costa, and especially

Nelson Riddle. He paid tribute to Rodgers and Hart with "My Heart Stood Still" and "It Never Entered My Mind." He concluded with "The Gal That Got Away," "Witchcraft," "My Way," and "One for My Baby." It was the time of his career when he was forgetting lyrics (he even alluded to it), but it was clear he was working very hard to avoid any major gaffes for this "main event" in his life. He did gallantly, and more—he was terrific.

Now the two men were onstage together, and they traded their trademark hits. Frank did "Just in Time," Tony did "In the Wee Small Hours"; Frank did "Maybe This Time" and Tony did "I've Got the World on a String."

Bennett always showed great respect for Sinatra, but when Sinatra did so—by expressing obvious pleasure at Bennett's singing—it was especially moving. They sang "The Lady Is a Tramp" together. Frank paused and said, "And now the prettiest song in the library [catalog] sung by the prettiest singer and the prettiest guy I know"—that was Frank's tough/tender way of saying he loved this paisano—and Bennett sang "San Francisco." Sinatra brought it all home with "New York, New York," Bennett joining in at the end. And that was it. Someone in the audience gave Sinatra a bouquet; Sinatra bent down to pick it up, took a flower from it, and placed it in Bennett's lapel. He ended it with a handshake, no kisses, no hugs.

But there was a lot of feeling there, including rivalry and respect. "I am sure," Vinnie Falcone, Bennett's musical conductor at one time, told me, "that that concert is one of the highlights of Tony's life."

By the late 1980s Bennett was frequently seen on *Late Night with David Letterman*, bantering with the superhip Paul Shaffer, who accompanied him on the piano. Danny's efforts at burnishing his father's image were slowly taking hold. By 1989 Bennett, discouraged by the limited sales of his new albums (although *The Art of Excellence* had sold 150,000 units, a respectable figure but probably not by Bennett's demanding lights), was considering leaving Columbia again. He was dissuaded by its new president, Don Lenner, who recognized Bennett's value and urged him to stick it out and to return to the "concept album" formats that were effective in Bennett's early career and fundamentally decisive to Sinatra's throughout his life.

The Sinatra–Bennett concert was probably the seminal event of the last years of the decade for Bennett. It was a promising time. Danny was making headway with both his father's career and his financial problems. Bennett had a solid, loving relationship with Susan Crow, and he was back at Columbia where he belonged, recording again and making magnificent albums.

As to the concert, Bennett had stood beside the master with grace, poise, and on serene equal ground. They were different singers, and there was no question of imitation or comparison. Both of them forgot their fears as they sang, caught up in their own gifts, in the electricity, the power, the joyousness, and the historic nature of the occasion.

Sinatra was in no mood to pass any torch; that was for sure. And he had no reason to. He remained great. But he plucked the flower from the bouquet he'd been given by a fan and carefully, conscientiously—it was awkward to do as both men were still moving to the music—placed it in Tony's lapel.

For Sinatra, that was love.

Bennett opened Rainbow and Stars, a new cabaret and supper club on the sixty-fifth floor of the RCA Building in Manhattan, in January 1989. Stephen Holden wrote eloquently of Bennett's performance in the January 9 *New York Times*:

Tony Bennett, as much as any other pop singer of his generation, symbolizes continuity in a city where it often seems nothing was meant to last. His mixture of street wise toughness, a starry-eyed romanticism and punchy sincerity also gives musical expression to a time-honored image of New York as a place wherewithal you have only to scratch someone's hardened surface to discover an unexpected reservoir of integrity, loyalty and decency.

Even at the start of his career, there was the hint of a rasp in his passionate bel canto singing. Now that rasp is a central element of his voice; he has adjusted his style to suit a vocal sound that is no longer seamlessly caressing but jagged and complex. . . . Mr. Bennett, much like the contemporary Frank Sinatra, searches for the basic essence of a lyric and punches down on key words that simultaneously distill his interpretation and rhythmically recharge the music. It's a kind of expressing shorthand.

While Mr. Bennett's style of swinging may be similar to Mr. Sinatra's, the attitude he projects is very different. Mr. Sinatra's exhortations often have a combative edge. For him, going on in the face of diminishing powers means fighting the future. Mr. Bennett's point of view is more accepting of the inevitable and grateful for the good times . . . even his most aggressive exclamations felt benign. And they all reiterated the same message: cherish the preciousness of the moment.

Near the end of the show came a sentimental gesture that only a performer with Mr. Bennett's aura of genuine innocence and humility could have carried off. Putting down the microphone, he sang "Fly Me to the Moon" as a love song to the audience, lingering dreamily over the song's last three words, "I love you." That kind of ingenuousness and belief in pop music is what sets Mr. Bennett apart from the male lounge singers of comparable talent—some younger than he—who cynically go through the motions. Mr. Bennett remains pure in heart; he has kept the faith.

"Bennett's comeback after 1986 was such a joy for him, it was so invigorating for him," Jorge Calandrelli said. "He already had had a fantastic career. So this was all over again, but even better than before. And his voice: I think the maturity of interpretation, and the spontaneity, it just keeps getting better. When he performs, when he gets to the moment of truth, he's completely concentrated on what he's doing. Totally focused, and every time he sings it's like it would be his first or his last time. I remember talking to him when suddenly he said we should take his recordings seriously because they're documents. He's documenting things for history, for the future generations. And amazingly, during his comeback, I recall when he did a show in

Los Angeles at the Hollywood Bowl. The average age was between twenty-five and fifty, so much younger than the crowd you would expect. The way he phrased the lyrics, it's an amazing experience for them, because they've never heard anything like it ever. Because many of today's acts are so fabricated, it's all like a million overdubs in the studio until they get it right. They're not even real artists.

"I think that the honesty of what he does, that's what people get."

11

A Partially Hidden Legacy

By the early 1990s, the demons were receding in Tony Bennett's life. He was clear of drugs, he had a top-drawer booking agency, William Morris, and a first-rate agent, Rob Heller. And most importantly, he had Danny and Daegal. Bennett was on the way to becoming a true superstar, even bigger than he had been in his prime. His *Perfectly Frank* album went gold in 1992, selling more than half a million copies, and he starred with the Red Hot Chili Peppers in 1993 on the MTV Music Awards. A lot of it had to do with Danny. Danny had seen early on that video was going to be the next platform, and he positioned Tony for that. Soon he got him into the rotation at MTV that would open him up to a whole new generation.

Danny and Daegal were an ideal team for Tony. "Daegal's an excellent engineer," an anonymous source said. "Unassuming, quietly competent, not really voluble. He's a quiet guy with a quick sense of humor. Tremendous competence. Really good ears. He does a hell of a job running that studio."

In the same period, Bennett's artwork reached a level of excellence that revealed him as a real painter of substance with a body of work of eight hundred paintings. He was enormously elated when his first museum show was held at the Butler Institute of American Art in Youngstown, Ohio, in 1994, and his painting *Homage to Hockney* was included in their permanent collection. It was significant that he decided to sign his paintings with his given name, Anthony Dominick Benedetto. Bennett's work achieved real depth, and an artbook of his paintings, *What My Heart Has Seen*, with an introduction by Ralph Sharon, was published by Rizzoli in 1996. It is revelatory.

New York Yellow Cab No. 1 is one of his best-known paintings. It is highly impressionistic and quintessentially New York. Against a background of trees (conveyed by vivid navy-blue blotches) and buildings (expressed by vertical blurs), yellow cabs in visible motion swish down a nighttime Manhattan avenue. An American flag and a few lights in windows provide the only real contrast to the pervading dark blues and bright yellows.

Sedona expresses in striking swaths of pure color Bennett's emotional reaction to this imposing country scene. A mass of bright orange rising from lower right to top center, with a few expressive black markings, is the face of the nearest mountain in a range that recedes in oranges, blacks, and reds. The side and the back of the mountain are black, and a blue sky overhangs the whole. Several small buildings blocked loosely in oranges, browns, and greens lurk at the foot of the mountain, and rough greenery and cacti hold down the front corners.

The Plaza, painted a block from Bennett's home just inside southern Central Park, shows a magnificent gray Plaza Hotel with moldings of verdigris rising out of the park's trees, the largest mass in the paintings, beautifully rendered in impressionistic blotches of dark green, light green, yellow, and an accent of orange. In the foreground, one of the park's arched stone bridges, with a red-orange underside, spans a small creek, and yellow ground and green grass anchor the right corner. Bennett always dreamed of a studio that would catch the afternoon light so he could paint it over and over, and he found it when he moved to Central Park South.

Sunday in Central Park is a large oil-on-canvas that uses almost pure chiaroscuro (dark and light) to express sunlight and shadows, the joy and vitality, and his love of the park and of all the people who love it. Unusual for having no large, unbroken areas, the painting jumps with happiness. The foreground is horizontal stripes of gray, white, and black punctuated by bicycles and carriages, a stoplight, and a monument. The background is an abstract impression of trees in black and white dots and swirls. Only occasional accents of red, orange, and yellow punch through the pure shadow and sunlight of the painting.

Some of Bennett's most emotional and striking paintings are of musicians he knew and loved. *Louis Armstrong*, in scratchboard and gouache, is one of many Bennett did of the great musician, one of which Armstrong hung in his study in front of his desk. This painting shows a minimal evocation of the right half of Armstrong's face in white highlights on a dark background. The rest of the background is vivid, vertical strokes of brown, black, red, and yellow. The names of some of Armstrong's songs (including "What a Wonderful World" and "Basin Street Blues") are printed randomly in white at the top.

Ted Curson shows the musician's hands, face, and trumpet expressed dynamically with vivid strokes against a black background.

Candido Camero, a small, intense watercolor on paper, captures the drummer's intensity directly in a vivid Indian red on his arms, his head, and on a horizontal stripe against a black background with three huge Congo drums in pale yellow in the foreground.

In *James Moody*, Bennett shows the artist playing a saxophone, to which he later added an aborigine-type background of white dots and dark swaths, as he felt it was "the only type of painting that looks like music."

Bennett also did hundreds of outstanding pencil sketches, many of musicians (such as Stevie Wonder and again, Candido). In a minimum of incredibly expressive pencil or pen strokes, he captures the emotional essence and soul of each musician.

In 1989, Sinatra's pianist Vinnie Falcone had become Bennett's musical conductor and would be with him intermittently through the 1990s. "Joe La Barbera called me," Falcone told me.

Ralph Sharon had gotten ill. I had known Tony because of my association with Sinatra. So I went out on the road with him. It was a great pleasure and a great honor, because I love Tony and I think the world of him.

It's difficult to explain what it's like to accompany someone who has such command of the material. It's a feeling, an aura; it's something that comes over you. In the case of Tony, there's such a connection between you at the piano and the artist, it becomes a situation where you may feed off what he is doing and he may feed off what you are doing, and if it's right and it's together, it becomes artistically wonderful.

Tony has remained pretty much down to earth. He married Susan last year [2007], whom I've known for many, many years. He's always treated her, as far as I could see, with great respect. She's a wonderful girl, and I think they're very happy together. I think he's reached a point in his life where all the good things have come together.

Tony's been very generous to me over the years. He's given me paintings. He's done sketches of me when we've been together. He's come to listen to me play when we've been in town and I do an afternoon jazz gig. He'll come and do a sketch and give it to me. He's given me other paintings of his, including one of Sinatra that I treasure. One night I went to work, and he had on a bow tie and a handkerchief in his tuxedo, which were just knockouts. I said, "Boy, Tony, where did you get those? They're wonderful." Two days later he gives me a box; I opened it up, and he had bought them for me. That's the kind of relationship I've had with him, and I love him dearly.

Tony has been a beacon. Thank God he has finally been recognized for the genius, the giant that he is. And when nice guys finish first, ahh! Boy, it happens so infrequently, it's wonderful when it does.

His daughter Antonia and I have a long relationship. Many years ago, he asked me to coach her a little bit. Over the years when Antonia has an engagement, she'll sometimes call me to play for her. When Tony was at the Golden Nugget here in Las Vegas, she would be hired and sing in the lounge, and I would play for her. And then after Tony's show, he and Lee Musiker and the rest of the guys would come into the room and listen for the rest of the show. So it was like a love-in. Tony's very aware—he's discussed this with me—of not spoiling his kids. He wants them to make it on their own. He's very wise. That's the Old World Italian belief that you raise your children, your children love you, but you make them learn that they've got to become adults and be responsible for themselves.

I think that as he has gotten older, his voice has gotten better. Just like Sinatra. You see, I met Sinatra when he was sixty years old. And I was with him until he was well into his seventies. Even though the voice wasn't as pure as it was when he was young, there was so much more depth and understanding. And Tony, too. Tony's got that thing now where it's just so real when he sings. The range gets lower as you get older anyway. There may be a little gravel here and there that there didn't used to be. You may not be able to do certain technical things with your voice that you did before. But that's not what singing is about. I mean, some of the people that were the greatest singers of our time—Louis Armstrong and Jimmy Durante—they didn't have any voice at all. If you know anything about interpretative singing, the voice is important, but the interpretation is more important. When you hear Louis or Durante sing—or remember Moms Mabley? No voice at all, but that woman could make you cry. She was incredible. The warmth and the understanding of the lyric; the story that you're telling. The Sinatras and the Bennetts are different from the rest; they know what it is that they're singing. And they understand how to tell the story and make it reachable to the people for whom they're performing. I think Tony recognizes—I know Sinatra did because he told me so—the great gift that they were given and the success that they've had with that gift, which is God-given, and I think they are very thankful for it.

> Tony has gotten stronger and, in my view, more artistic, in
> the past twenty years than the previous sixty.

For many, one of the strongest albums Bennett has ever made is
his 1989 *Astoria*. *Astoria* is a return to the concept album format that
Bennett had done so beautifully in his early years. *Astoria* is the portrait of an artist, Bennett's autobiography in song. The front and back
covers were Danny Bennett's inspirations. The front shows Tony as
a young man just returned from the war standing in front of his apartment in Astoria; the back shows him in the present day. He is clad
in a suit in both pictures. The covers together invoke the mood of
bittersweet nostalgia (laced with triumph) of a life recollected with
serenity and joy.

Astoria, a deeply personal album, movingly tracks the stages of
a life from the yearning of a young man for love and success, staring at
the lights of Manhattan from his hometown street in Astoria. Charles de
Forest's "When Do the Bells Ring for Me?" sets the tone for the album,
expressing the feelings the young Bennett had. Beneath a picture of the
youthful Bennett and his mother, Anna, standing by a brick building,
Bennett writes in the liner notes, "This song reminds me of the many
hours I spent as a boy walking on the banks of the East River while
admiring the spectacular view of the most powerful city in the world.
I would often wonder if I really had what it takes to make a difference in
my life and under what circumstances my 'big break' would come."

Bennett's voice is older in this album, lower and deeper, full of intro-
spection and maturity. The song opens with bells chiming and Bennett's
voice almost whispery. "Those who say wake up, feel life," he sings,
emphasizing "wake up." "Show me those arms"—longingly stretching
the last word, evoking the image of welcoming arms—"that say welcome
to real life!"—again he emphasizes "welcome to real life" with passion—
"and I'll stay, I'll stay." Tired of parties and party girls, he sings, "I want
more and more," "I want someone to want more of me." He sings
plaintively, "Here am I, where is she?," holding the last note and raising
it high, and then asks with deep need and longing when his chance will
come and when the bells will ring for him. It's no wonder that the song
has become a showstopper at almost every Bennett concert.

The album almost bursts with vitality and deep feeling. It is both universal and specific in location, for Astoria—the sense of home— hovers everywhere in the geography of its theme. (There also are snap- shots in the liner notes of Tony as a little boy with sister Mary and brother John, of Tony at ten, and of an adolescent Tony in Astoria Park.) "I Was Lost, I Was Drifting" by Kaper and Gannon depicts the state of indecision, of soul-searching, of a young man adrift, just back from the war. Bennett sings it with tenderness and gentle feeling. An old vaudeville song by Gus Kahn and Harry Woods, "A Little Street Where Old Friends Meet," is a perfect change of pace, a "That Old Gang of Mine" song, replete with nostalgia, playfulness, and atmos- phere. Bennett proclaims that the street he grew up on was just as good as any street in the world; the implications are that those who dwell there are as good as the next guy, and that he'd rather be there than anywhere else in the world. (Of course, Bennett made his way out of it relentlessly and ferociously, but he will never relinquish his loyalty to those who stayed behind.)

He recalls that his first job was as a singing waiter, "waiting on tables and taking requests for songs. I would go back to the kitchen where two Irish waiters would teach me the song, then go back out into the dining room and perform for an extra tip. Truly, one of my most enjoyable jobs." The street, he sings, may seem to the outsider "sort of old and tumbledown, but it means a lot to folks in my home- town." And whether he's rich or down and out, he still feels as wel- come as the flowers in May. And, typically Bennett, he takes the old vaudeville song and brings it up a notch with a final bluesy, buoyant riff; it's not Basin Street, or even Easy Street, he concedes, but that's okay with him. Going up the scale, he sings, "It's-just-a–little–street– where-old-friends meet!" Three single piano chords bring it home.

Bennett does a magnificent "The Girl I Love" by the Gershwins, and a song that Carmen MacRae had given him (originally sung by Billie Holiday), "It's Like Reaching for the Moon." A tale of longing and hopefulness, deeply romantic, it is one of the original standouts of the album. Bennett goes on to Ogden Nash and Kurt Weill's "Speak Low" and Kern and Hammerstein's "The Folks That Live on the Hill." "Antonia," by Bob Wells and Jack Segal, is a lovely tribute to Bennett's daughter Antonia and to the joys of parenthood. And really, there are no words for the Ralph Sharon and Jorge Calendrelli arrangement of two songs together, "A Weaver of Dreams/There Will Never Be Another You." They are odes to young love, a subject Bennett never grows too old to speak of with authenticity.

"Body and Soul," "Where Do You Go from Love?" (Charles de Forest), and Bennett's original hit, "The Boulevard of Broken Dreams," by Harry Warren and Al Dubin, are splendidly rendered by Bennett. "Where Did the Magic Go?" by Jack Erickson and B. Weed is a very personal statement for Bennett about the heyday of American popular music in which he pays tribute to Ella, Bing, Benny Goodman, Basie, Stan Kenton, Frank, and Jule Styne. "Great music never dies," Tony sings. In the liner notes, he writes: "I hope the answer to the question posed in the song's title is true forever—the magic lives on in our hearts." The final song, "I've Come Home Again," also by Charles de Forest, is the culminating high point of the album, just a single chorus, a song of fulfillment, a triumphant statement of Bennett's return to where it all began. "All those wondrous dreams," he sings, "were a prayer still unanswered." Since then, "I've touched a star or two . . . tomorrow, if I try, even brighter stars and prayers will be answered." The song is the bookend, the answer, to the album's first song, "When Do the Bells Ring for Me?"

The dreams of a lifetime were answered for Charles de Forest with the appearance of this album. It was Tony Bennett who saw the beauty in de Forest's music. "Charles worked in saloons pretty much uninterrupted for forty-four years," singer Eric Comstock recalled. "Five to six nights a week. Usually, especially during the end, Mafia dives.

"Then he played a great place called Diva in the East Eighties. Tony and Annie Ross would come in to see him. After a date, Tony would go and unwind and go to where Charles was working and sit at the piano with him. Charles would sing some forgotten Hollywood song by Mercer and McHugh. Charles would do an esoteric Berlin song. And Tony would say, 'Oh! Is that Berlin? Oh! I wish I'd known of that for my Berlin album.' And it would be a serious reaction. Not like a superstar who's slumming at this *gavone* dive. It would be an artist with another artist whom he admires very much. That's the way Tony would react. What a mensch! Charles told me all this.

"So that's when Tony said, 'I'm going to record your songs.' Charles had had lots of people promising to record him, including Judy Garland.

"But Tony came through. Charles was at Tony's recording sessions: 'When Do the Bells Ring for Me?,' 'Where Do You Go for Love?,' and 'I've Come Home Again.' And Tony sang these songs on the Johnny Carson show and on a telethon. Charles lived to see this all happen."

Astoria was nominated for a 1991 Grammy as "Best Jazz Vocal," and Bennett performed "When Do the Bells Ring for Me?" on the televised broadcast of the awards ceremony.

There is no question that Bennett's voice on that album has a more limited range, but it hardly matters at all; he sounds more moving than ever. "Bennett had the good sense to have the parts of a song transposed down half a tone regularly," Derek Boulton told me. "In fact, there were four arrangements of 'San Francisco,' and each one went down half a tone as he got older." *Perfectly Frank*, Bennett's tribute to Sinatra, was conceived as his first real commercial opportunity, and Sony/Columbia quickly fell in line and promoted it properly. Bennett enlisted Sinatra's pianist Bill Miller and consulted with Sinatra's old friend Frank Military, the head of Warner-Chappell Music and a major figure in the music business. Bennett also brought back his brilliant engineer Frank Laico to take part in the record. The results were huge: the album was a gold record, and Bennett received his first Grammy since 1962. Sinatra invited Bennett to sing "New York, New York" on his 1993 *Frank Sinatra Duets*. Sinatra was never present for the album; he prerecorded his songs, and his guest artists prerecorded their parts, singing along with a disembodied Sinatra voice.

Bennett busted out in his great *Playin' with My Friends: Bennett Sings the Blues* in 2001. Here, unlike Sinatra's album of duets, was spontaneity and life. Bennett recorded it with three generations of singers from pop, rock, and blues, many with ties to jazz and country. "Frank Sinatra, who later called him the best singer in the business, pegged Tony Bennett at the start of his career with a phrase too colorful to print here," Gary Giddins wrote in the November 18, *New York Times*, "implying he had a brass neck, nerves of steel, colossal chutzpah—that kind of thing. Sinatra was probably thinking of Mr. Bennett's dynamic, over-the-top attack and vocal range, but he proved more discerning than he knew.

"Two decades later, the remark might have also referred to Mr. Bennett's challenging repertory; heart-on-sleeve emotionalism; actorly inflection of lyrics; or stubborn idealism. . . . Indeed, it's impossible to survey Mr. Bennett's astonishing 51 years of recordings—capped this month with the almost ridiculously ambitious *Playin' with My Friends: Bennett Sings the Blues*—and not marvel at the guy's sheer moxie . . .

"The blues have never been a core part of Mr. Bennett's repertory, but as the song says, he has a right to sing them. He is so comfortable with who he is that he can approach them as he does other songs, with no need to growl, groan or posture; a song is a song, even when it's just 12 bars long. . . . Mr. Bennett was in rare form . . . and the gems beam with pleasure. . . . Mr. Bennett, swinging with easy assurance, mines every lyric for meaning, and when he really lets loose, as he does on almost every track, you can still hear the nerviness that impressed Sinatra half a century ago."

Forty Years: The Artistry of Tony Bennett—A 4-CD Compilation was issued by Columbia in 1991, and reissued in 2004 under the title *Fifty Years*. A magnificent collection of eighty-seven of Bennett's best records, it constitutes the best introduction to Bennett available thus far. For most singers, this would be the definitive compendium. But Bennett has made so many great records that this collection can be considered a fine introduction, but much more is needed. At present, only eight of Bennett's greatest albums of the 1950s and 1960s are in print on compact disc. Since a limited number of songs from some of these albums are included on *Fifty Years*, the public is being deprived of some of the best popular music ever recorded.

The inevitable result must be that with all of Bennett's renown, the full magnitude of his achievements is barely known. It is a mystery why Columbia does not rerelease these albums. Among the masterpieces are *Hometown, My Town*; *Long Ago and Far Away*; *My Heart Sings*; *I've Gotta Be Me*; *A Time for Love*; *Life Is Beautiful*; *For Once in My Life*; *Cloud 7*; *Tony*; and *The Beat of My Heart* (the latter three, Tony's very first albums, have been reissued together on a British edition, which can be found in some record stores). Add to that such unavailable albums as *The Very Thought of You, Love Story, Snowfall/The Tony Bennett Christmas Album, Tony Makes It Happen, This Is All I Ask, Mr. Broadway, Tony Sings for Two, A String of Harold Arlen, Alone Together, To My Wonderful One*, and *Songs for the Jet Set*—and that's just the beginning. And we're talking about masterpieces. Jonathan Schwartz has told me that there are about 180 Bennett records that have *never* been issued and are still awaiting the light of day. For the present, then, *Fifty Years* constitutes the best available Bennett compendium.

By the early 1990s the awards flooded in and kept coming. He had been a Grammy nominee for fourteen years and won almost all of them. Then there had been a long silence after 1963, when "I Left My Heart in San Francisco" was Record of the Year and Bennett won Best Male Solo Vocal Performance for that song. Thirty years later, in 1993, *Perfectly Frank* won for Best Traditional Pop Vocal Performance.

The dimensions of Bennett's work—his music and his art— somehow still elude us despite his fame. Tony Bennett is actually world-famous for only a small proportion of his actual achievements. He still has a partially hidden legacy.

Bennett would go on to record albums that were tributes to performers he esteemed, including Fred Astaire (*Steppin' Out*, 1993), Billie Holiday (*Tony Bennett on Holiday*, 1997), Duke Ellington (*Tony Bennett Sings Ellington: Hot and Cool*, 1999) and Louis Armstrong (*A Wonderful World*, 2002), and to some of his favorite female singers (*Here's to the Ladies,* 1995). He also recorded two duet albums—*Playin' with My Friends* (1991) and *Duets* (2006)—and the marvelous children's album *The Playground* (1998), on which he sang a song his father had sung to him when he was a boy, "My Mom" (undoubtedly singing about Tony's grandmother),with utmost simplicity and beauty. The song (by the veteran songwriter Walter Donaldson) had long disappeared and had haunted Bennett for years.

From the start of their collaboration, Tony and Danny had the same goal in mind. As Will Friedwald wrote, "Tony wanted to bring the best music that he knew—the music that he had been singing all his life, the music of Gershwin and Basie, of Bobby Hackett and Cy Coleman—to the greatest number of people. The two Bennetts achieved this by gradually making Tony seem hip to the twenty-something and thirty-something audience."

"Tony abhorred demographics," Danny Bennett told the *New York Times*. "He believed he could play to the whole family. I told him that in order to do that, you have to go to them." By the early 1990s Bennett clearly had MTV in sight as a way of penetrating the youth market. Trip Gabriel wrote in the *New York Times* that Bennett "has all the hallmarks of classic cool, including a vocal style that is controlled, suggesting banked passion." He had already filmed a commercial for the "I Want My MTV" campaign and wanted to maintain momentum. He asked Danny to pitch a video tribute to Fred Astaire. MTV invited Bennett to perform on their annual video music awards show with Flea and Anthony Kiedis of the Red Hot Chili Peppers—they would dress in traditional clothes and Bennett would wear sunglasses and dress like them. Bennett's appearance was a hit, and the Astaire tribute, *Steppin' Out*, was featured on MTV's *Buzz Bin*. He also appeared with the Smashing Pumpkins at a series of alternative rock Christmas shows.

When he appeared on WHSF, a rock radio station in Washington, D.C., at its Christmas festival in 1992, five thousand screaming kids cheered "Tony! Tony! Tony!" The amazing thing was that he had changed nothing about his music or his persona; he was just himself, and the kids were coming to him.

MTV then offered Bennett the opportunity to appear on its most desirable show, *MTV Unplugged*, which had already featured Eric Clapton, Nirvana, Bob Dylan, and Paul McCartney in front of live audiences. The program was taped on April 12, 1994. *Entertainment Weekly* was present and noted on June 3 that "not long ago Bennett was a walking punch line." Elvis Costello told the magazine that "the people that watch TV are curious about him, but it's not because he's had to do anything modern. . . . Make no mistake, this is not about kitsch but about a singer who's emotional and sincere, and that's the truest kind of style. It's as if he were already modern and the rest of us are just catching up with him."

Bennett was caught up in the euphoria of a dream come true, but stopped to reflect on how things might have turned out differently for him. "Bennett was thinking about Kurt Cobain," the magazine wrote.

Years ago, if Bennett had kept up the wild pace, "I wouldn't be around. I would not be around." He paused. "That kid dying, it really moved me, that suicide. Because that shouldn't have happened."

The evening was a triumph, and was the second-most-watched event in the history of the program. What is perhaps most impressive was that Bennett didn't change a second of his act. Dressed in an executive blue suit, blue shirt, and tie, he did not pander to his audience. He stood there calmly, sometimes with one hand in his pocket, sometimes with his arms crossed. It was not their music, but they treated him with respect and they applauded wildly. He was not a relic to them, not a novelty. They were not going to run out and buy his records, but they knew they were in the presence of someone of great value, a last link. As always he paid tribute to his musicians, pianist Ralph Sharon, drummer Clayton Cameron, and bassist Doug Richeson. He still shouted "thief" as in "Time is a thief" on "Speak Low." He ended a medley of "The Good Life" and "I Wanna Be Around" with a Satchmo growl of "Oh, yeah!" that was pitch-perfect. Following the program, Danny was asked how he had devised such a winning strategy for his father. He had thought about it a lot, he said, and decided that Tony "was a man who transcends age." He was right.

Bennett was astonished with the reception. "I'm not sure what did it, really," he told Robert Sullivan. "It's been crazy, this whole thing with the kids, the young generation. Danny did all that. He said, 'Just trust me, Dad.'

"All of a sudden, kids!

"What I know is, I sing the way I always sang. And I know that these kids are the most enthusiastic fans I've had in my entire career."

MTV Unplugged became the biggest-selling album of Bennett's career, and in January 1995 the program was nominated for three Grammys, including Album of the Year—which it won. It was the culmination of Bennett's efforts over a period of forty-five years. He had accomplished all this without compromising his music in any way. On top of that, he now had complete artistic freedom to express himself fully, and the ax of financial fear was no longer poised over his head. At sixty-eight years old, he was truly a free man at the top of his game.

No wonder Bennett spreads joy and happiness wherever he goes to this day. He radiates the sense of accomplishment granted to few people at any point in history. And he finally has a solid, stable marriage. "I love Susan," the composer Johnny Mandel told me. "She's great. She's the perfect girl for him. There's a mutual respect there, which there has to be. If she's just a clinging vine, it's no good. One out of three is okay."

As a result of his escalating success, Bennett created a program with Sony Music Entertainment called *Live by Request* on the A&E cable network, showcasing prominent singers. *Live by Request* was a hit and won an Emmy in 1996. More than 1.5 million viewers called in to Bennett requesting songs when he starred in the first show.

And due to his success with his father, Danny Bennett had been named one of the top one hundred marketers of 1994 by *Advertising Age*. Tony Bennett was popping up everywhere: he performed at halftime at the Super Bowl and sang the national anthem in Albert Brooks's baseball comedy, *The Scout*. In 1995 New York, Los Angeles, and San Francisco celebrated "Tony Bennett Day." In 1996 Tony was a guest on *Charlie Rose* and on *Muppets Tonight*.

"The money followed the restored magic," Geraldine Fabrikant wrote in the *New York Times* in 1999. "Today, Mr. Bennett makes an estimated 100 live performances a year, earning $50,000 or so a concert, or about $5 million. An avid artist, he sells his paintings and drawings for up to $80,000 apiece. His son, intent on marketing his father's image wherever it will sell, has plans for Tony Bennett furniture, Tony Bennett sheets and Tony Bennett towels. Then there are the royalties from more than four decades of recorded music, and even a commercial or two.

"It is Danny Bennett, in consultation with brokers at Gruntal & Company and Salomon Smith Barney, who decides how to invest his father's money; his father's only rule is a ban on tobacco and chemical stocks. About 70 percent of the singer's portfolio is currently in tax-free municipal bonds—conservative, income-generating investments not unusual for someone his age. The remainder is in an array of stocks. Once a month, father and son go over a printout of the investments and other financial details."

The *Times* reporter noted that Bennett's lifestyle continued to be modest for a celebrity, despite dressing well and flying first class. His apartment was rented; he rejected a country place, preferring the lively city streets—and Susan Crow was a schoolteacher.

"'On the stage, Tony is remarkably intellectually agile, though he does not have anywhere near the vocal range or improvisational gift of Ella and Mel Tormé,' said Jonathan Schwartz. 'Tony has the confidence in this part of himself. But one of the things that Tony has known all his life are his limitations.'

"Whether such a perception of himself reflects humility, as his son believes, or insecurity, as Mr. Schwartz believes, it has freed him to throw his energies into his art. In that sense, Mr. Schwartz said, it has provided a boost to his career. 'If Tony's low self-esteem had been higher, it is entirely possible the music would have been lower, fused as it would have been with arrogance and self,' Mr. Schwartz said."

The *Times* article dealt in depth with the financial arrangements Danny had carved out with his father and the way in which he had resuscitated his father's career. Tony's disdain for money was deeply ingrained in him, and it was linked to his reverence for art. He told the reporter that in the 1950s and 1960s "one of the touches of class that singers had was they never spoke about money." The focus was on music, and "whoever did the best job rose to the top. Fred, Ella, they were the best," he said, referring to Astaire and Fitzgerald. "Integrity was as important as money. If you just make money, so what?" Bennett went on to his favorite example, the one he'd given Will Friedwald: "It's like the Chinese say about paper money: the rats eat it."

Bennett illustrated his point with a fuzzy memory of a written account of a jam session in Harlem at the Blue Note with Fats Waller. "Waller just came down and wrote that song ["Ain't Misbehavin'"] on a paper bag. He was paid two bottles of gin. The song became a great Broadway musical and made millions."

Clearly this was not the kind of person who knew how best to financially navigate a career. The reporter commented, "Better to have somebody overseeing his portfolio who cares about his money as much as about his talent—somebody, in short, like his son."

In 1996, the *Times* reported, Danny moved about 30 percent of Bennett's money into such winning stocks as Bristol-Myers Squibb, Merck, Spring, and Viacom, and some that were less successful. He invested in the Internet as well, buying Amazon.com and Yahoo stock for himself and Microsoft for his father.

Bennett cited his own investment triumph. "Years ago, he says, he was approached by his friend John W. Kluge, former director of WNEW-AM and the billionaire founder of the company then known as Metromedia Inc. . . . 'Do you ever buy stocks?' Mr. Bennett recalled. 'I said, "Not really." He said, 'Buy my stock.' So Mr. Bennett did, sometime around 1970, and held on to it until Mr. Kluge called him one day in the mid-'80s and advised him to sell. 'I had $5,000 worth of stock at $3 a share. It ended up being $350 a share,' a gain of 11,567 percent.

"While once a person had to have a million dollars to retire nicely, today the level is a 'tenmillionaire,' the younger Mr. Bennett said. It appears that his father has passed that mark."

The Bennett juggernaut had become unstoppable, and yet its underlying motivation remained not the thirst for money but the reverence for art. Bennett told Matthew Hoffman, "Through song and art, I can communicate what I believe is the essence of life—truth and beauty. In my time, I've seen both go out of style, but they always come back in vogue again. . . . It's not just that I want to sing. I have to. The heroes of my life, Duke Ellington, Basie, and Fred Astaire, they just kept working until the day they died. So will I."

In that statement were echoes of remarks Joe Williams, Louis Armstrong, and Bill Evans had made to him over the years. Bennett, the eternal learner, had imprinted them in his heart. His commitment was the source of his longevity; his selflessness and integrity kept him young and striving. Perhaps that was what the audience at MTV instinctively understood. There was no fountain of youth. There was only Bennett.

Tony, 1997.

Tony in the studio,
1997.

Tony and Robert
Farnon, 1997.

Tony and the Backstreet Boys, 1998.

Derek Boulton in London, 2009.

Mark Fox, head of the Tony Bennett Appreciation Society in London, Antonia Bennett, and Mark's wife, Margaret, at Royal Albert Hall, London, 2010. Sinatra looks on in the photo behind them.

Tony and Ralph Sharon, early 2000s.

12

The Next Century

Tony Bennett jumped into the next century with little or no diminution of energy or joy. It was, simply, a second, new life he was
leading, even more exciting and rewarding than the first had been. He
looked as if he could not believe his good fortune, but he had earned
every inch of it, time and time again. And he finally found the natural
high he had been always been seeking: the high of life.

The new century brought him new triumphs that lifted him higher
and higher. What gave it its particular luster was that Bennett never
retired on his laurels; he kept striving, surging, reaching. Jonathan
Schwartz probably caught one aspect of Bennett when he said that
Tony's insecurities drove him to greater and greater heights of achievement. That would explain a lot: his tirades against his musicians after
triumphant concerts, his addictions, his fears and doubts, the abuse
he took from some girlfriends and his second wife. He was a simple man, a complex man, a kind and sweet man, a selfish and cold
man, a vindictive or a forgiving man, a sexually voracious man, a saint
and a sinner.

He earned everything he had achieved the hard way. Few singers had ever worked as hard to achieve their goals. Critical to understanding Bennett's success is his intense focus. "Tony kept his love of the music and the painting," Johnny Mandel said. "That's his center, and it's the best center there is. The world is what's screwed up, and you have to come to that realization. What you do and what you are: you have to have your center and system of values, because everything else is going nuts. Once you realize that, and all the people that are telling you things 'for your own good,' they're the ones that are wrong. With few exceptions. And Tony had to realize that. And that's what keeps him sane."

The world's insanity intruded in the most horrific way on September 11, 2001, at the World Trade Center in New York City, at the Pentagon in Washington, D.C., and in a field in Shanksville, Pennsylvania. Bennett kept his thoughts to himself for a while, although his feelings were expressed at his concert at Radio City Music Hall on September 29. According to Mark Rotella in his book, *Amore*, Tony did not mention the attacks, but he sang "I've Come Home Again," and when he concluded the song he said simply, "I'm from a little town called Astoria." He paused and said, "You know, I gotta tell you . . . I love this city." The audience stood, applauded, and cheered.

Life went on. The new century was Bennett's; he seemed to own it. But now he seemed to finally know what he had, and to have banished some of his worst fears. He'd given special performances for nine presidents; when he'd had a ruptured hernia in December 1996 while visiting President Clinton, Clinton rushed him to the hospital and provided the services of his private surgeon. He had lived to see the election of the first black president, and it fortified and inspired him. *Billboard* announced that year that it would present Madonna with a Lifetime Achievement Award. She pouted that she would appear only if her favorite singer, Tony Bennett, presented the award to her. He happily agreed.

He liked the rich, too, and the rich liked him. He was comfortable with them, with the powerful, the executives, and the CEOs. British royalty adored him. He'd performed for Queen Elizabeth II in 2002 and for the queen and Nelson Mandela at Royal Albert Hall in 1996;

he'd given a royal command performance in 1995; the list goes on and on. Yet he doesn't cultivate the rich and is not a social climber. He has scores of friends who are obscure painters, musicians, artists.

In 2002 Bennett ended his working relationship with his pianist and musical director Ralph Sharon, a relationship that had spanned forty years. Sharon began working with Bennett in 1958, split with him in 1966, and reunited with him in 1979. It was a very traumatic split for Sharon, if not for Bennett.

For some who regard Bennett critically and think he is totally self-centered, his parting with Sharon is characteristic of a merciless streak in his personality, a tendency to use people and thoughtlessly abandon them without a moment's regret. Others think that Bennett merely acted rationally and understandably—that Sharon was less agile and that it was time for Bennett to end the long professional relationship. There is no doubt that Bennett was genuinely dissatisfied with Sharon.

"Ralph had phoned Tony to say he was taking the following week off to have an operation," Derek Boulton told me, "to have a lump taken off his back. He goes into the hospital on a Monday, the operation's Tuesday, Wednesday they told him he's great and they're going to discharge him Thursday. He phones Tony and says, 'I'm okay, I'm back.' Tony says, 'Well, I want to keep the guy that I've got. Let's leave it at that.' And he puts the phone down on him."

"I'm sure Ralph is depressed," a friend of the family told me. "I've heard terrible reports from others that know him very well. Bennett went out to Denver last year. Evidently he tried to mend fences a bit. But it hasn't worked. Ralph will never gain his self-esteem back. I've heard that Ralph is afraid to pick up the phone because it may be Tony."

"While they were working together," Derek Boulton said, "Tony made Ralph a nervous wreck. He destroyed Ralph."

"Tony would do miserable things to Ralph," Vinnie Falcone said.

"Ralph Sharon made him," Jack Parnell told me. "Tony was quite nasty to Ralph. It didn't seem like the real him. I was most surprised that the guy who more or less made him was treated that way. Ralph was so good and so right for Tony."

Not everyone agrees with this version of events. Some feel that it was time for Ralph to go. "The only thing I can tell you," Joe Soldo said,

is that Ralph was okay when Tony was just on radio, and on record dates. Because first of all Ralph doesn't read that well. And on record dates he was never the leader. It was either Marion Evans, Torrie Zito, or Pat Williams. Because when you do a record date, the fellow that writes the arrangements, he's the leader. And a lot of times arrangements would be written, and Tony would go on the road using those arrangements. Ralph would play his own chords that would not go with the written arrangements. Because I remember doing a show in L.A., the Century Plaza, and Vinnie Falcone was the conductor. And Tony said to Vinnie, "Gee, those strings don't sound good." And Vinnie had to explain, "The strings are right. There's nothing wrong with them. But Ralph's playing different chords."

So that was the problem. I saw Ralph recently. He said that Tony called him recently and said, "I made a mistake. You were great for me." Ralph felt very good about it. See, the other problem was when Tony did anything with a symphony, Ralph just couldn't handle it. He just wasn't a good conductor for the symphony.

So I don't think it was a one-way thing. The first time Ralph left Tony, in 1966, he went with Robert Goulet. And when I met him backstage in Vegas in 1979, when he was back with Tony, I said "You're back!" And he said, "I didn't get enough the first time."

When we worked in Orange County, Ralph lived not too far from where I lived. And I gave him a lift down to the job. And he told me, "When the concert's over, Joe, park your car close to the stage entrance." And I said, "Okay, fine." So I did. And then I helped him pack the music up. And he said, "Let's do it real fast." I didn't know what was going on; I wondered why we were rushing. We'd just played an hour and a half concert, let's relax. No. "Pack up, hurry." So we got in the car and I said, "What's going on?" And Ralph said, "I know Tony's going to want a meet about the show. And I've had enough meetings." So we just left. He wanted to get away.

Well, Tony firing Ralph—it probably was cruel, maybe the way Tony handled it. But from what I understand, there was always that problem when they did something with a large orchestra. You know, Ralph is the first to admit that he's not a very good conductor.

Ralph told me that Tony said they're both around the same age—Ralph's a little older—and Tony said he needed someone younger, with more energy. I think that is kind of the truth.

"Bennett always fights with his accompanist, it seems," Johnny Mandel recalled. "He had many. He finally cut Ralph Sharon—well, Ralph really was well past his prime. And Tony kept him on. But I guess Ralph expected to be kept on forever. And it's not like that. Because he wasn't at the top of his form at the end. Whereas Tony is."

According to Derek Boulton, Bennett always had a ravenous, consuming ambition. He sang "If I Ruled the World," and Sammy Davis Jr. said to him, "What do you mean, 'If'?" This second chapter in his life is the exact consummation of his lifelong desires—what he had sought for himself all along. Tony wanted his name in lights everywhere, Derek had told me. "I placed in a playbill all the quotes about him from Buddy Rich, Judy Garland, Dean Martin, Sinatra. When I printed that, he opened it in his home one day, put it in front of him, put his feet up, and spent twelve hours reading it. And the following day, the same thing." Today Bennett's status is not merely an elevated one; it really transcends normal categories of what constitutes success. He is more than a singer, a painter, or a personality now; he is an icon, an untouchable. At the same time, his elevated status is belied by his extremely modest, humble manner—the tricks of the trade that he has mastered—he can crinkle his eyes, shake his head in bewilderment, hold up his clasped hands in triumph, look around with astonishment at the adoring throngs of admirers—which evokes even more adoration—just as cunningly as Ronald Reagan ever did.

Success follows him everywhere. Perhaps one of his greatest successes of all was his marriage to Susan Crow in a private civil ceremony on June 21, 2007. She has chosen to be called Susan Crow Benedetto. Mario and Matilda Cuomo were the witnesses. They had been together for twenty years, years in which Bennett had finally achieved a level of inner peace. In 2006 he had told Mitch Albom, "It's funny. When I was 14, I would put on a pair of roller skates and skate all day. All over Queens. Sometimes over the bridge, up into Harlem and back. I loved it. I was content. And, strangely enough, at my age right now, I feel like I'm on those skates again. A certain contentment has settled over me."

Extraordinary events continued to happen. "We did Bill Clinton's inaugural," Jorge Calandrelli recalled. "And we also did the Democratic National Convention in 2008. And at his age, it is remarkable that this man can perform the way he does. His physical condition belies his age. And in the past fifteen years Tony has reached the pinnacle of success that he should have had all his life. He was always in the shadow of Sinatra. But of course he busted out of that long before Mr. Sinatra passed on. That's why I'm so pleased he's getting the accolades now. Because he's deserved them his whole life."

Bennett has lived a relatively privileged, affluent life—a wealthy existence, despite the debts—since 1950, and it has only been increased manyfold in the new century. Yet he does not have butlers and maids fluttering around him. He lives comparatively simply—for a rich and famous celebrity. As he told Mitch Albom in *Parade* in 2006, "I don't own a car or a boat. I don't own a house. I'm on a perpetual vacation. I stay in a perpetual creative zone at all times." While credit must be given to Danny Bennett, keep in mind that Tony's gargantuan ambition from the start, his own responsibility in engineering this ascent to even greater heights, must be critical. Yet he has seemed remarkably immune to its uglier temptations. What kept him sane was his art, his credo of excellence, his refusal to betray his roots. The streets always beckoned, where he found subjects to paint, beautiful things to contemplate, people to respond to and who fed him with their praise and their love. Everyone I talked to seemed to have an account of seeing him walking down the street or strolling or painting in the park. He was and is an accessible man.

"He's right down the street from me," Margaret Whiting told me in 2010. "We're pretty good friends, and he sings like a beaver. I've never heard anybody sing like that. It's the intimacy of the voice. He calls to you. I mean, he's about the greatest singer around. There's nobody like him. At least not today. I walk up the street and I bump into him. And we'll kind of saunter along for a block or two.

"And Tony goes out to the park and he paints. I've seen him. I don't ever go near him. I don't want to interrupt him."

A feisty dissenter on the subject of Bennett is Lenny Triola. Triola launched into a little diatribe clearly based on his love and respect for—and consequent disappointment with—the current Bennett incarnation. His is a harsh assessment, and it's a minority one.

I go back with Tony to WNEW, when he used to come in and sit and talk in the library. Always cool, and thanking us for playing his music. A few times he called into the station, he called into the library. Because I did all the programming. He called up and chatted. I played every single record of his. You could come up with five hundred tunes. And that's only what we had on the wall.

Tony is the American classic singer in the tradition of the great old days, the saloon singer, but he seems to be so careful now. It's the image. What he says about every singer on *American Idol*. "She reminds me of Ella or Billie Holiday. It's wonderful, like Bing Crosby." You know he doesn't mean that. He's on all the shows and tree lightings. He shows up everywhere and it's the same: "Everybody's wonderful."

Tony's calling k.d. lang another Billie Holiday, or Judy Garland: there's something wrong in that. You would never hear Sinatra say that. I think he respected the audience more. Look, I do enjoy Tony's music. I love the records. But I just think there's not the real guy there. I think there's guys that have been out there long enough on the street to know that's not the whole story, that "everything is beautiful, it's marvelous; I love it."

Tony's recent records are disappointing. This is the guy who recorded with Bill Evans. This is the guy who recorded with the Basie band for the first time. This is the guy who did *Love*

Story, and the *Movie Song Album*, and *Songs for the Jet Set,* and those wonderful things with Robert Farnon, "The End of a Love Affair" with John Bunch on piano. It makes no sense. A body of work this big, you have a second career, you're here, and you do work that doesn't balance out. Those were great albums in the eighties: *Art of Excellence, Astoria, Playin' with My Friends*.

Look at the *Perfectly Frank* album and the others. Here you're saluting Frank Sinatra and you're playing it safe. The audience doesn't know. It's like everybody just discovered Tony Bennett. But if you pick up one of the other earlier records, those great records of his, you begin to see, wow! There's *The Many Moods of Tony*, where Bobby Hackett's "The Very Thought of You," and "I'll Be Around," is gorgeous stuff; it's Bobby Hackett with Tony Bennett! Then you put out these trio things, even the Basie band on his last Christmas record; that's not the Basie band we know, it's watered-down, too. The wonderful one was the original Christmas album, *Snowfall*, with Robert Farnon. It's a classic. Bennett is a man with a body of work that's so wonderful. So what he's doing now? How could he not know, man?

Anthony DiFlorio, noted journalist, public service director, and broadcaster at WHAT-AM in Philadelphia, is another dissenter: "Danny is trying to reinvent Tony as a great entertainer. He's a great singer. He's not a multimedia guy. He was very true to himself in his loyalty to the great standards. You can't think of any memorable quips from Tony. The repackaging of him and the rewriting of history makes him into an entertainment icon that he obviously wasn't. The fact he is a great singer should be sufficient."

A more positive assessment (and a widely held one) is given by Jonathan Schwartz, who lives a block from Tony. When I visited Schwartz at his apartment, Tony had just called. Jonathan's picture had been in the newspaper, and Tony wanted his permission to do a painting from it.

"I'm always thinking lovingly about Tony," Schwartz said. "We talk to each other on the phone a lot. I met him in the mid-seventies, 1973 or 1974. And then we became friends. Occasionally he would come over to my studio in Carnegie Hall. And I'd play for him, and he would sing. One night he came with the second Sandy, who was just a problem. I mean, you could hear them coming down the hall, she was yelling in some way. There was a girl with me, and she asked, 'What's that?' I said, 'That's Tony and his wife.'

"I had an operation last November. And he came over here one day and sat for a couple of hours. He wanted me to hear a live version of 'Boulevard of Broken Dreams' from Vegas that he had performed a few weeks earlier. It was wonderful. I was just grateful for his reassuring company."

I said to Jonathan that sometimes I thought Tony was a singer who loved to sing more than any other singer. "I've got to feel that that may very well be the case," Jonathan replied. "Because he *loves* singing. He just loves singing. It's not that he loves to hear his own voice. It's that he loves to hear songs sung. And if he's the one to sing the song, so be it.

"I think that Tony's a very gentle man. And I don't think he's totally confident of Tony Bennett. Overall. Sometimes when he gets huge applause, you'll see an expression on his face that says, 'Oh, I don't believe it. My God.' Well, I believe that's real. And this would be after a forty-one-song performance, just impeccable."

"Are we experiencing," I asked Jonathan, "the literal full emergence of Tony from Sinatra's shadow? He seems to grow in stature every minute."

"Yes, he does. But so does Sinatra. Sinatra is everywhere. Neither one of them has diminished. Both of them have grown."

"But it was like, there's always Tony Bennett," I said, "*but* there's Sinatra. And now I feel this sense of power and strength, that he seems to have fully emerged."

"They both have."

"Because there's no one else," I added.

"That's right. On that level. And it's interesting: I don't think that Crosby really survived. It's not moving singing. But these two guys: it's a different story entirely. I think he'll sing as long as he can. His voice is holding up. Not as fabulously as one would want. But it's still there."

The most miraculous fact about Tony in 2011 was that he could still sing beautifully at eighty-five. "He's got the chops," Will Friedwald said. "It's not like he can't sing anymore. It's not like every note has to be rationed. His leftovers are better than most people's prime choices."

But mortality had to be in the air in the first decade of the new century for a man of Tony's age, and it had been for a long time. It made each day more miraculous and precious for him.

"This is a complex day for me," Tony told drama critic Jerry Tallmer in October 2005 in *Thrive Magazine*, seven months after his sister's death. "My brother died last night. He wants his ashes put in the East River."

Actually, Tony's brother, John, was still alive, but in the process of dying, and it was real and painful enough to Tony to express it that way. "He had every kind of illness you can imagine," Tony said, "and came back, and back, and back. He was feeling great, down there in Jupiter, Florida, and then he had a terrible headache and a massive stroke and his heart stopped. Last night. He's on wires right now; they're going to pull the plug on him."

He paused and said, "This is a funny year for me. My sister, Mary Chiappa, died seven months ago, very peacefully, of pancreatic cancer. My daughters, nieces, nephews, all went to see her. Lots of love there. A gorgeous lady."

The interview, one of the most intimate with Bennett, was held in his painting studio in his Central Park South apartment. That August night he was working on a canvas of "Venice at Night."

He told Tallmer that the Smithsonian Institution had taken his huge painting of Central Park, with the public filing into the park, into its permanent collection. It was a great moment for him.

Bennett gave an account of his life and spoke movingly of Louis Armstrong, who is never far from his mind. "Well, Armstrong is the Source, you know. He invented swing. See, swing is not a category. It's an American musical language. Strictly American. Nobody else knows how to do it. Swing was an expression of optimism coming out of the Depression, a determination to pull everybody up by their bootstraps, make things work, and it did work.

"Armstrong influenced Billie Holiday, Sinatra, everybody. He invented scat singing. He invented bebop. Dizzy Gillespie said, 'Without Louis Armstrong, there is no me.'"

"Some years back," Tallmer wrote, he and Bennett "spent a morning being driven around Queens while Bennett searched for the house of his boyhood. He never did find it, and we ended up standing on the Queens edge of the East River, staring over at the skyline of Manhattan just as Anthony Dominick Benedetto in his teens had more than once longingly done from more or less the same exact point on the waterside.

"Now, six and a half decades later than that adolescence, high up in an apartment house on the Manhattan side of the East River, a reflective Tony Bennett said, 'My father used to swim in that water; that was when it wasn't polluted.'"

Tony mentioned his age and said, "Remember Joe Venuti? Great jazz violinist. The older he got, the better he got. I met him once in front of P. J.'s [P. J. Clarke's]. He told me, 'You don't know it yet, but you'll be singing when you're a hundred years old.' I don't know how my life will work out, but if I could live long enough, I'd want to still be right in there singing without a wobble."

13

The Singing Waiter

Teo Macero, a close friend of Tony's and a record producer at Columbia, passed in 2008. Dee Anthony, Tony's manager in the 1950s, died in 2009. In 2010 John Bunch, Torrie Zito, and Mitch Miller followed. And then, in August, Derek Boulton. When Tony heard of Derek's deteriorating health, he tracked Derek down and called him at his home in London and then at the hospice where he spent his last days.

But Bennett, deeply saddened at these losses, seemed to be flourishing in his own life. He was still everywhere. He showed up at George Avakian's ninetieth birthday celebration. He continued to get up and perform spontaneously at the concerts of performers he esteemed. He sold the masters of his records to Sony/Columbia for $10 million. He appeared all over the world in 2010: London, Canada, and throughout the United States.

The refashioning of Tony's image that Danny Bennett undertook in the 1980s has intensified with the years. It is a carefully controlled image. "Danny runs a tight shop," a friend told me. Today Bennett appears cuddly, paternal, ever-smiling, unthreatening, hardly the hot, sexy, combustible personality of the past. At the same time, miraculously, he seems hip to the twentysomething and thirtysomething audience. Part of the change is based in reality: age, a solid marriage, sobriety, serenity, and amazement and joy at a career even more successful and triumphant than the first. Unconditional love wherever he goes. And while Bennett has really always been hip, part of it is skillful reinvention. Refreshing, then, to have him quoted candidly in the British press in 2010 as claiming a little nastily that Rod Stewart "sang like a woman." Bennett continued to let himself go more in Britain when speaking to journalists. The most important and inspiring part of this story is that with his ever-widening acceptance and popularity, Bennett has achieved his desperately sought-after goal of bringing good music to as wide and as young an audience as possible, so that it will survive into the future. That is what counts most to him.

In an interview with Mick Brown at the time of the release of *Duets* in the *London Daily Telegraph* magazine (August 5, 2006) that caught the latter-day Bennett shrewdly, Brown said, "He regrets that he's getting old, he says, 'but I don't *feel* old. I have more commitment and passion now than I did when I was younger, and a wisdom sets in, you know? You learn what to leave out. It's the same with painting. And even more so now, I'm not compromising whatsoever.'"

The article has an eventual note of candor and irony:

Everything in Tony Bennett's life is wonderful. "I am," he says, "a very happy man." He is 80 and feels he could live to 100. Each morning, he rises with a smile and practices his scales in front of the shaving-mirror.

He sings, he paints. "I have no desire for a vacation. I'm on a perpetual vacation." If the weather is fine, he will take a stroll. Here, in London, a city he loves, he steps out of his hotel into Park Lane and people greet him like an old friend: "It's just so . . . lifting."

Bennett smiles his basking-shark smile. His skin is the color of copper, his profile ruggedly Roman; even the silvered plume of his toupee has aged gracefully. He speaks softly, his voice barely rising above a whisper, so you have to lean in close to hear what he is saying—the quiet authority of the Don. . . .

Bennett is not, and never has been, a fan of rock music—he once condemned the Rolling Stones for fostering "juvenile delinquency." But he is shrewd enough to recognize the marketing value of aligning himself with a generation of younger stars, and enough the diplomat to be effusive in his praise of his collaborators on *Duets*. Sting? "I *love* Sting." Bono? "I *love* Bono." McCartney? "Paul is the nicest person and most talented person I've ever met." [When he first looked at the Beatles he said,] That guy in the middle—he's got it. And that was Paul McCartney.

Bennett, a man who cherishes artistry above all else, tacitly acknowledged that *Duets* was "a commercial album." But he considers the project with a kind of incredulity none the less—not so much, perhaps, that he would be singing "I Wanna Be Around" with Bono, but that at the age of 80 he should still be around to sing it at all.

Bennett also recalled his years in World War II, and how they made him a pacifist. He spoke of the revival of war movies and "fear and frightening feelings" in the United States. "This business of machoism is ridiculous. I'm not interested in that." He paused. "I search for truth and beauty in what I do."

Duets: An American Classic, Bennett's album of collaborations that was issued in 2006, has the virtue of not seeming like an uninspired, ghostly reenactment of past hits, a quality that permeated Sinatra's duet albums.

"On *Duets* Tony's voice was to me in incredibly better shape, sounding better than ever," Jorge Calandrelli recalled. "Not only that, but what was really unbelievable was his stamina. We got to London for a portion of the album, and after the jet lag, the trio was kind of tired. We were going to do George Michael at Abbey Road. And Tony, who had gone through everything with us, shows up early next morning: 'Hello, good morning,' and we were dragging our feet. And he was already eighty years old."

Today he sounds better than ever. Singer Carol Sloane has known him since they were both at Columbia in the 1960s. She dated him several times. "Going into a deli with Tony was really a circus," she recalled. "Everything sort of stops. He is so approachable. He never made special demands, never a male diva thing. He's just . . . he's our Tony. He goes to all those jazz spots, and it's clear that he's come out of respect for the artist who's there. That's a bit of generosity that is often lacking.

"At the beginning, with that great lung power he had, I think he just had it in his genes. That full-strength voice was appealing, but he got more and more into jazz. He picks material that he knows he loves, and therefore he's able to very easily express the essence of the song. The self-confidence comes with, after all these years, knowing when you walk out onstage, you get this enormous wave of affection and acceptance and anticipation of your glorious voice. That is built into his every performance and has been for a very long time. I hear all the reflection of what he himself has gone through. Everything of this man's life experience. He always had the goods, but now it's burnished. It's like a painting that has been there for a while. It has some signs of age, of endurance. It's a love affair that goes on. Judy Garland had it; Jolson, Ella had it. He doesn't come out demanding anything. He comes out and says, 'I'm giving.'"

John McDonough came to know Bennett when he covered recording dates for *Duets* for *Downbeat* in 2006. He concurs with Calandrelli on Bennett's amazing constitution. "Tony's been blessed with good genes, a good constitution, and he's aged very well," McDonough told me.

I mean, no one ever knows how they're going to be when they get into their seventies and eighties. He's fortunate enough to be in very good shape. I think he sort of survives today because he's the last of a breed, the last representative of a kind of an era.

Most of the experience I've had with Tony was covering the album. The idea of the album was basically to redo some of his old hits with other performers. But then they came to "San Francisco." That was so completely his own song that a lot of the important vocalists they might want to have would be a little reluctant to cramp Tony's territory. So they decided to go the route of the instrumental accompanist. They finally chose Herbie Hancock. Apparently Tony had very happy memories of doing some spontaneous stuff with him for Columbia back in 1964. So they arranged for Hancock to come in, and he was going to accompany Tony on that. There would just be the two of them.

The recording session was something of a disaster. Two days later I got a call from Sylvia Weiner, Tony's assistant, telling me that the session had been scrapped and they were going to do it with somebody else. And they ended up with Bill Charlap. Keep in mind that the session with Hancock was a very, very cordial session. There were no bad words, there were no expressions of temperament.

But Herbie went into the studio, sat down at the piano, and they started to do the song. They went through about eleven or twelve takes of it. And some were breakdowns. In at least two cases, Tony would sing the first chorus, then Herbie would come in and solo. And Herbie seemed to lose his way halfway through his sixteen or thirty-two bars, and he'd stop the take. And then they'd resume: they'd start from the top or start from a certain point. And it was not going well. I think Herbie had just not prepared properly for the session. I don't think he had familiarized himself enough with the song, so that he could bring to the session some sense of how to interpret the piece. Nobody was saying out loud that it wasn't going well. The producer, Phil Ramone, by about the ninth or tenth take, said to Tony through the box, "I think we've got enough; we can put together a good take." But I don't think it was Tony's idea to create a version of the song by cherry-picking from all those takes. So they had all this stuff that they recorded, and Ramone thought he could work with it.

But Tony was disappointed. He wasn't saying it, but he obviously, based on subsequent developments, realized things that he wasn't saying out loud. After they finished recording, they came back into the control room and there were handshakes and hugs all around. Tony presented Herbie with a lithograph of one of his paintings, signed.

I got the call that the decision had been made to scrap the session. So then they rescheduled it and I went out again, and he did it with Bill Charlap [who had also played for Bennett live on a number of occasions and had more experience with him] and they did it in about two or three takes. But Charlap had done his homework.

And Tony sort of took me into a little anteroom between the control room and the studio. He said, "You know, I just wanted to tell you that I've never been so disappointed with a session in my life. I had such high expectations. But Herbie has just gotten to the point where I can't understand what he's doing. He seemed to lose the essence of the piece when he started to play. It just seemed to evaporate."

Neither person wanted to deal with the awkwardness of it. So they just went through it and were cordial and warm and polite to each other, but they realized that it just didn't happen.

The wrap session for *Duets* was held at Bennett Studios in Englewood, New Jersey, a converted Erie-Lackawanna freight station. Daegal Bennett had created the studio from scratch. The album would include duets with Chris Botti, Elvis Costello, Bono, the Dixie Chicks, Barbra Streisand, James Taylor, Paul McCartney, k.d. lang, Michael Bublé, George Michael, Sting, Elton John, Diana Krall, Billy Joel, and, towering over all of them for his duet with Tony on "For Once in My Life," Stevie Wonder. As McDonough wrote in his October 2006 *Downbeat* piece, Bennett had "insisted that each performance be an old-fashioned, face-to-face, acoustic collaboration (although some postproduction orchestra parts were added). It's not the way some of these artists work." (Bennett's 2000 blues album, *Playin' with My Friends,* also contained live duets. He made a point to distinguish both of these albums from the Sinatra duet albums. Sinatra's albums were totally overdubbed and spliced; Bennett's were totally live and in person. Some elements of the accompaniment were modified later, but on both albums, Bennett and his guests were singing live, together, to each other simultaneously. The "duet" part of the tracks was real.)

McDonough reported that Bennett stood around chatting amiably with the musicians while waiting for pianist Bill Charlap, who was delayed, to arrive. As he frequently does, Bennett stressed the enduring nature of his music. "Certain songs are what I call pop art songs," he said, "like 'Lazy Afternoon' and 'Sleeping Bee.' They're well written and have the kind of craft that will last. After everything floats away, they'll stay at the top.

"'I always consider myself a catalogue artist, you know,' he says with some pride. 'It never just sells right away. Over time it develops a steady cumulative sales volume. The category that I'm in in the Grammys is traditional pop, which is a way of saying it's going to last and not become obsolete or be forgotten in six months or a year.' It's a point he makes in every interview and is the core of his values."

Stephen Holden offered a critical assessment of Bennett upon his eightieth birthday, in 2006, in the *New York Times* (August 2, 2006). Referring to Bennett's invoking Louis Armstrong ("You were right, Pops") at the conclusion of "It's a Wonderful World," Holden commented, "This gentle burst of affirmation melts your heart and reminds you that sincerity, a mode of expression that has been twisted, trampled, co-opted and corrupted in countless ways by the false intimacy of television, still exists in American popular culture. It can even salvage 'trees of green,' 'skies of blue' and 'clouds of white' from the junk heap of pop inanity."

He wrote of Bennett that "he retained the innocence and joie de vivre of his youth. Disappointment is not in his vocabulary. We don't go to him for psychological complexity, but for refreshment and reassurance that life is good. . . . Gratitude and joy, gruffness and beauty balance each other perfectly in singing that has grown more rhythmically acute with each passing year."

Bennett had spoken to Mick Brown about his search for truth and beauty in that interview in the *London Daily Telegraph* in 2006. In September 2009, the Frank Sinatra School of the Arts, a public school of 640 students founded by Bennett in 2001, opened in its new building in Astoria, and its construction was part of the culmination of Bennett's search. It was the realization of a long-held dream for Bennett and his wife, Susan, who is its vice principal. The school had been operating in space borrowed from other schools, and Tony and Susan wanted a brighter, more creative space. (Susan had formerly taught social studies at LaGuardia High School of Music & Art and Performing Arts.) They had lobbied city officials for years until Bennett's foundation Exploring the Arts (ETA), a public charity, finally received about $78 million. An additional $4.25 million was provided by private donors. ETA had been founded in 1999 to support programs that "teach young artists to embrace true craft over the cult of fame that pervades our culture." ETA provides the students with college scholarships, master artists, and an apprenticeship program. They are placed in the program as paid interns in arts organizations with professional artists.

"We're the opposite of instant fame," Bennett told Greg Toppo of *USA Today*. "We want to teach the students quality and to do things that will last forever." They had founded it in partnership with the New York City Department of Education. It was situated in Tony's hometown of Astoria, Queens, at the Kaufman Astoria Studios complex, just blocks from where he had lived as a boy in his grandparents' two-family house at 23–81 32nd Street. The land for the school had been donated by Peter F. Vallone Sr., then the Speaker of the New York City Council, and George Kaufman of Kaufman Astoria Studios, site of the legendary soundstage where hundreds of movies and TV shows had been produced since the 1920s. It was a perfect setting for a school of the arts.

Bennett had originally written to potential supporters that his interest in such a school had been sparked some years ago in Chicago when he'd visited a public school in which an abandoned vest-pocket park was taken over and cleared by the school; murals were painted, and the students put on performances for the community. "This showed me," he wrote to potential sponsors, "how powerfully the arts could be used for a community's well-being. The school I envision would stress community service . . . where the kids could practice their craft. I would like students to know at the outset that fame and celebrity are not the true goals of the arts. The true artist is at the service of a rigorous arts and academic program . . . and his craft.

"I also see a school where artists and entertainers themselves are intimately involved. . . . Through the years, beginning with his Academy Award–winning performance in *The House I Live In*, it was always Frank Sinatra's desire to help children receive a quality education involving the arts. I can think of no better way to remember, celebrate, and honor my best friend and colleague, the great performer and entertainer Frank Sinatra, than to create a wonderful, vibrant school in his name."

In October 2009, I visited the school. Mayor Michael Bloomberg and actor John Stamos were presenting awards for arts and culture. I retraced Tony's boyhood steps, taking the N train to Ditmars Boulevard, walking down the bustling, traditional working-class streets of Astoria with its row houses, restaurants, and cafés. The Italian and Greek population had now expanded to include citizens from Egypt, Morocco, and Brazil. These were all Tony's people, Tony's kind of town. I visited Tony's favorite restaurant for thirty-six years, Piccola Venezia, where his corner table is marked with a shiny metal plate that reads TONY BENNETT CORNER.

Approaching the sleek new five-story school, I was met by eager students on every corner directing me to it. Their smiling, joyous faces told me instantly how thrilled they were to be there. Entering the dazzling building, I noted the fresh scent of varnish, the openness, the brightness, the yellow colors, the spaciousness. The sign on top of the Tony Bennett Concert Hall read THE FRANK SINATRA SCHOOL OF THE ARTS, FOUNDED BY TONY BENNETT. All the music that was piped in was by Sinatra. There was a mural of Sinatra, his jacket slung over his shoulder, standing on the Triborough Bridge. (Asked why he hadn't named the school the Tony Bennett School, Tony replied, "Because Frank's the master.")

The school offers dance, music, drama, film, and fine arts programs in state-of-the-art classrooms, dance and music studios with a recording booth, and a media center with film editing equipment.

Christopher P. Halloran, of the Polshek Partnership architecture firm and an architect of the building, told me, "It was great having Tony here. He was an inspiration even to the contractors. I mean, they got excited about it when they saw him. He came to the site often.

He came here as soon as we had floors, and we were like, well, there's no elevator here yet or anything like that. He was pretty much like, 'Do you know how much I have to work out to sing for two hours straight?' He said, 'Come on. We're going to the top.' So we brought him up to the top. He walked up.

"We probably see Tony every couple of months. He attends and performs at the graduation. And from what we hear, he does go to all the classes. He's keeping a careful eye on everything. It gets the children so excited. It's great to see his inspiration here. The kids really dig it.

"It's not for show, it's the real thing. He's giving back, and he's actually there to give back. So it's not just his name on a program."

There is a glass wall etched with the names of hundreds of artists, which was shining in the moonlight as I entered. "Tony gave us a list of names," Halloran said. "These are all performing artists, composers, ballet, actors, singers, songwriters." I saw the names of Dean Martin, Louis Prima, Milt Hinton, John Bunch, Lena Horne, Paul Robeson, Jimmy Durante, Ray Charles, Duke Ellington, Judy Garland, Dinah Washington, Count Basie, Buster Keaton, George Burns, Gracie Allen, Woody Herman, and Billy Strayhorn. There were dozens more.

"We wanted the kids to see someone performing in art forms other than their own, since the programs are separate. That's why we cut the windows on top. Even if you're just passing by you can just peer in. You can look inside the studios, choral and orchestra. Each one has a recording studio over in the corner. In the hallways and lobby you can hear music coming from all the studios. Actors in the city would kill for spaces like this."

The architect points out the art gallery, the dance studio, the gym. There was light everywhere, even in the gym. "All those are translucent panels to let light in," Halloran said. "Normally in gyms you don't put too much direct light, because then you can't see anything when it shines on the wood. We have high-tech features in the theater. We have a full fly gallery in the back that goes all the way up; we have a loading gallery. It's a full-service theater. It is so high-tech, all the stuff that they have. We have one of those ceiling panels that opens up, and it's just more lighting that will come in. They have a full control room in the back on the first floor. And the way they have it now up and running, they pretty much press a button, and they have everything set."

But at the center of everything was Bennett: his spirit and his actual physical presence. "When Bennett strolls onto the school's rooftop amphitheater to greet students on lunch break," Greg Toppo wrote in the September 21, 2009, *USA Today*, "a crowd jumps up to meet him, tearing sheets of paper from notebooks and offering them up for autographs. 'He's an icon,' says Eleni Broutzas, a drama major. 'He's a legend.' She inches patiently through the crowd and presents Bennett with a purple spiral notebook. He uses a black marker to pen a tiny, neatly lettered autograph on the cover. Broutzas walks away clutching it to her chest. 'It's going in a frame on my wall,' she says."

I spoke to Hannah Speiller, a senior drama student in her fourth year. "I absolutely adore that man," she said. "First of all, I didn't think I would be able to go to a performing arts school, because I got turned down with my other school, LaGuardia. So I came, and all the students who were part of the auditioning process were really like happy and helpful. They were really excited about you coming. One of the first things they said when you got in was, 'We don't tolerate any name-calling, any bullying here.' And it was the students who were saying this. There was such like a great feeling. But the fact that Tony Bennett comes around, asks how you are, comes to performances. He comes around at least once or twice every month, sometimes more. But he's at performances, he stops in your classrooms to check on you. He's just like a heartwarming guy, and he reminds you of a fatherlike figure where he's just very open and you can start any conversation with him you want. But with this school, I think he's honestly given me the best years so far of my life."

"Tony Bennett and his wife, Susan, walk through the brand-new halls . . . and still marvel at all the details they notice for the first time," Glenn Gamboa wrote in the November 26, 2009, *Newsday*. "'It goes there,' Susan says, pointing at a print of Bennett's painting of Abraham Lincoln that greets visitors to the public high school's library. Bennett nods, but his eyes are drawn to the rest of the room, painted a bright yellow and flooded with light. 'There isn't one dark room in this building,' says Bennett, who helped design, with his wife, nearly every detail of the school. . . . 'It stops the children from feeling sleepy and lethargic.'"

Speaking to Corey Kilgannon in the June 26, 2009, *New York Times*, Bennett pointed out Riccardo's by the Bridge catering hall and said he'd worked as a singing waiter there. He then recalled his own school, the High School of Industrial Arts: "'We went to lunch and the ceiling fell down on the desks,' he said. "We would have been smashed—that's how terrible the building was.' He surveyed the space with a satisfied look and announced, 'That won't happen here.'"

The article is suffused with Bennett's obvious pride. "Mr. Bennett tested the acoustics in the impressive space," Kilgannon wrote, "which were designed with the help of Tom Young, a longtime sound engineer for both himself and Sinatra. From the stage, Mr. Bennett barked a husky note—'Bah!'—out into the empty theater. Then he clapped his hands repeatedly to show how the notes leap out into the space but do not echo and linger long.

"'It's a perfect concert hall,' he pronounced."

Bennett's work was not done. On September 15, 2010, he announced an expansion of the program to seven public schools in New York so more students could attend schools that offered arts education. Five of the schools are part of the Urban Assembly, a nonprofit group that coordinates a network of small public schools in New York that are arts-related. Its student population is about 94 percent black and Hispanic. Susan Crow Benedetto told the *Wall Street Journal* on September 17 that she and her husband wanted to make sure that more low-income children had the opportunity to develop artistic skills. "We hear from these kids that really had all sorts of struggles and this is the first opportunity in their family to finish high school and attend college," she said.

"It's all about longevity and not fame," Bennett commented. "It's anti-fame," he added. "It's all about learning the craft" in a way that could be sustained over a lifetime.

Tony and Susan were the recipients of ASCAP's Foundation Champion Award in December 2010 for strengthening the arts in public education by founding both the school and Exploring the Arts.

"Most artists aren't particularly good at intellectualizing their own work," John McDonough told me. "They feel it more than they understand it. John Lahr alluded to that in his essay about his father, Bert, and *Waiting for Godot*. It's a complicated play and it's not what it seems to be. And he wrote his father felt it more than he understood it. That sort of gets to the heart of the way I think a lot of artists approach their craft. I think Tony is one of those great instinctive performers, a combination of instinct, of talent, of experience over a period of time. Over his career he found out what worked and what didn't. When I interviewed him, he didn't want any alternate takes of his recordings issued. This is fairly characteristic, I think, of a lot of performers. Tony was once asked on *60 Minutes* if he still does scales. And he said yes. And the interviewer asked, 'Would you do some for us?' And Tony just sort of looked at him, as if to say, 'Are you kidding? No! That's inside stuff; that's private; that's practice stuff.' That's the sort of thing the artist doesn't share with his audience.

"Tony is just kind of a regular guy. There's nothing that's fascinating about him. If you went up to him, he'd probably be glad to shake your hand. You wouldn't be intimidated, because there's nothing really there that is intimidating. There's not a lot of mystery there with Tony Bennett. He's a great singer, but he's not a fascinating person. This has given him the kind of freedom to be his own musical self. He doesn't have to shape his music to conform to some manufactured persona that has grown up around him."

McDonough gets Bennett; he understands that Bennett's high standards and idealism haven't altered whatsoever in fifty-two years. "He is still in awe of the standards, still suspicious of fast-buck commercialism, and still ready to make another jazz album.

"His basic paradigms have not shifted. But he has to reconcile this inner Tony Bennett with the one who at eighty is 'counting his blessings' to have just signed a multimillion-dollar record contract with Sony and seems delighted to be fellow-traveling with some of the hottest ticket performers on the contemporary scene.

"But if you look closely, even allowing for an imperfect world and a few compromises, you find the inner Bennett has prevailed largely on his own terms. Now that he essentially produces himself, he no longer has to do the musical bidding of Mitch Miller or Clive Davis. He has sought out the major contemporary artists who are most in tune with his temperament (such as Diana Krall and k.d. lang especially, who has become to Bennett what Clooney was to Bing Crosby) and brought them into his realm, rather than vice versa. And his albums of the last twenty years have had an almost hermitic integrity. Moreover, he now owns (through RPM Productions, the management company set up by his son Danny) all his old Columbia masters in a partnership with Sony. This not only gives him control of his present catalog, but his legacy as well."

"I'm like the Erroll Garner of singers," Bennett said to McDonough about his musical training. "He couldn't read a note of music. Neither did Sinatra or Perry Como. [But] I can hear every note in a philharmonic orchestra. I can hear if something's off. I'm also a melody man. Édouard Manet was a great painter before the Impressionists. His attitude was when you paint, just paint what you see. If you don't get it, do it over. He said all the rest is humbug. So I'm stuck on the melody. I like people to know what I'm singing about."

Tony Bennett can still say with utmost simplicity that if he had been a singing waiter for the rest of his life, he would have been happy. Jimmy Lategano can understand that.

It was Jimmy, a haunting and undiscovered singer and a singing waiter at Arturo's, a last vibrant repository of the New York we love, who had stood with his tray at Arturo's and watched Tony the nights Tony came to sing and pay homage to his mentor, Bobby Pratt, in the last days of Bobby's life.

"I get a kick," Jimmy says, "out of what Tony said about being content if he'd remained a singing waiter. I've been very happy at what I do. It's like the Billy Joel song—'What are you doing there, great piano man?' When people hear me sing, they say to me, 'Why are you here [at Arturo's]? Do you sing on Broadway?' 'No, no, no.' I tell them, 'well, I like what I do, and I'm like a chipmunk in a forest. This is my neck of the woods. And I really love my tree.'"

Jimmy and I are seated together, listening to Tony's records. Like many people, he knows Tony's music but doesn't *really* know it. So I play some of my favorites—early, middle, and late Tony.

Jimmy is stunned. He says, "For Tony still to be doing it after all these years! And so happy to be doing it. It's inspiring for all of us who are anonymous. Any one of us who devotes so much of our life to something we love has something in common with Tony Bennett.

"Once I got into trouble and had to make my living singing with a guitar or banjo on the street corners of New York, in front of museums and in Central Park. Winter was coming on, and I was really nervous about trying to survive.

"What I learned was to find a song that tells a story I love. Whether you're onstage or on a street corner, the core of the passion is always the size of a tiny mustard seed. The best way to get that experience is to go out on a street corner, in a park, or just walk into a room of people. It's like you say, 'Oh wow, I've just remembered something that's so important—listen to this story. You won't believe what just happened.' Everybody stops and says, 'What is it?' And you say, 'You've got to hear this. This is for you.'

"And there's Tony. Tony comes out onstage. With Tony it makes no difference if there's no instruments or if there's an orchestra with violins, or just a piano. The audience is just riveted. That's street talk. He is a street singer. He can do it with his passion. He can do it with his voice alone."

We come to the end. But is it the end? When it comes to Anthony Dominick Benedetto, there is clearly no end in sight. This is the story of the endless evolution of a man who, since he was a boy in a white suit on the Triboro Bridge, has been making history. It's musical history, but it transcends one genre, and not only because Bennett became an astoundingly good painter as well. He has recorded hundreds and hundreds of songs, many of which are masterpieces (including many of the unknown ones). He is a vaudevillian, a popular singer, a jazz man, a raconteur. He has brought happiness to millions, as Derek Boulton said to me time and again. He can be unfairly regarded as a selfish man because he has been so maniacally committed to his art, but in that art there is the core of selflessness and generosity. This is a man whose commitment to uplift—even in the meaning he gives to each song—is paramount. Then there is the school he has created and built, named not after himself but after the man he considers the "master," Sinatra. And he is right. Sinatra *is* the master of singers.

But Bennett? Bennett is a transcendent singer, but also an entertainer, a painter, an educator, a troubadour, a messenger of hope and optimism, and a loyal and faithful servant to the regular guy on the street. He is our street singer, our true democratic spirit, our messenger of hope. Bennett is not only eighty-five, he has spent those eighty-five years devouring, celebrating, observing life. Bennett is one of the few who can be a young man at eighty-five. His procreative life's work never ceases. He is one of those creatures outside of time, and not readily explainable. Genetically he is a puzzle. His father died at forty-one; his mother endured a premature old age plagued by five kinds of arthritis.

At the start of October 2010 Bennett appeared in the jazz magazine *Downbeat*. Bennett spoke in depth about the death at eighty-seven of jazz photographer Herman Leonard, whose photographs hang all over Bennett's studio. Implicit in the article was Bennett's commitment on every level to music, encompassing jazz, pop, everything of merit in between, and art.

Bennett had known Leonard for fifty years. Leonard had been assigned to photograph Bennett when he first started at Columbia. Bennett revealed that one of his paintings was inspired by a Leonard picture of Charlie Parker playing. There were strings of colorful dots floating around the image of Parker. "I'm trying to get aboriginal pointillism, like lots of notes," Bennett said.

An indication of Bennett's power and influence—but also his compassion and generosity—can be seen in the help he gave to Leonard during Hurricane Katrina. Herman had called him from New Orleans. "His negatives were on the top floor of his building, and the water was going up," Bennett told writer Michael Bourne. "The National Guard wouldn't let anyone in that area. He called me and said, 'I don't know what I'm going to do. I'm going to lose all my negatives, all the years of work.' So I called [former] President Clinton and told him the problem. He got it done."

In summing up Leonard's life, Bennett might have been offering a portrait of himself as well. "He knew what he wanted to do, and he did it," Bennett said. "He loved New Orleans, so he painted—he photographed New Orleans. He was a true artist. He went toward what he loved. He understood jazz, and he took the greatest photographs anyone ever took of Erroll Garner, Duke Ellington, Louis Armstrong. I've never met anyone more spontaneous. He makes it look so effortless. It's like a Charlie Parker solo. Or a Count Basie beat. His timing was impeccable."

The man seems to never rest. Judy Garland, in a moment of clarity and pungent insightfulness that sometimes illumined her, said, "He is a *Tony Bennett*, and there isn't any resemblance to anyone else. There's just one."

It makes sense that he would carry a pen and sketchpad with him, not only because he paints all the time, but also because he watches all the time. He is curiously impassive to fame, fortune, wealth—all the things he has also craved and achieved, especially in recent years. The art is what matters. Perhaps with advancing years he has become more at peace, but there's been no diminution of his passion, his humanity, his commitment, his ardor for life. And there is this curious humbleness and modesty, showing up at little jazz clubs, getting up and performing, relating to struggling jazz artists. And walking the streets—the most vulnerable activity for a superstar. Who in the world would attack Tony Bennett? It's simply unthinkable. And this school: spend minutes there and you realize you are in the presence of a miraculous thing.

The truth of the matter is that any full-scale examination of the dimensions of Bennett's career leads to an inevitable conclusion: before that examination was launched, there was only Sinatra.

Now there are Sinatra and Bennett.

Tony Bennett has crashed through the generations, holding on to the love and passion he knew as a child; the beauty he saw in his mother, his uncles and aunts with their banjos, mandolins, and guitars singing and playing to him in Astoria Gardens, the lemon trees of Italy in their eyes; and especially the vision of his father, passionately singing on a hillside. It was music, music everywhere, along with the faces, the radiant moments. It was indelible and precious to him. Like Sinatra, he loved the music, cultivating it and honoring it. Unlike Sinatra, he brought a particular simplicity, openness, sweetness, and vulnerability to it, letting his heart speak freely.

Held aloft by his indomitable spirit, by his children, and by the love of his life, Susan, he surged into the twenty-first century.

At the dawn of his eighty-fifth year, opening his door, he takes his easel and canvas or sketch pad, and crosses over to Central Park to paint. Later, he sings.

ACKNOWLEDGMENTS

I am grateful to Jonathan Schwartz for his brilliant insights and for keeping the flame alive; to Will Friedwald, author of the monumental *A Biographical Guide to the Great Jazz and Pop Singers*, for reading a draft of the text and offering priceless commentary and assistance; to Hana Lane, whose editing was like stardust; to Donna Brodie, Executive Director of the Writers Room, for providing a writers' safe haven; and for the memory of Arturo Giunta, maestro of Arturo's Restaurant, the embodiment of Italian soul for me for thirty years and counting.

I am grateful beyond words to Derek Boulton, who was Tony Bennett's manager from 1971 to 1974 and who opened many critical doors into Tony for me. He said, "When you meet Tony, you will love him and he will love you." He departed on August 6, 2010. I will miss him for the rest of my life.

A big thank-you to Nick Riggio, who has been Tony's number-one fan since the 1950s. He sent me scores of Bennett's CDs, DVDs, newspaper clippings, playbills, tapes, and videos of Tony's concerts around the world. I have never met anyone more selfless and indefatigable in his devotion to an artist; and to Mark Fox, who has been the urbane and dedicated president of the Tony Bennett Appreciation Society in London, the largest Bennett fan club in the world, for twenty-two years.

And my deep appreciation to those who spoke with me or provided critical help in other ways that deepened my understanding of a living legend: Nina Chiappa, Nancy Balliett, Will Balliett, Gary Giddins, John Bunch, Jorge Calendrelli, Vinnie Falcone, Joe La Barbera, Torrie Zito, John Simko, Jimmy Scalia, George Avakian, Marion Evans, Johnny Mandel, Sid Bernstein, Ervin Drake, Eugene di Novi, Rudy Van Gelder, George Shearing, Annie Ross, Jerry Tallmer, Eric Comstock, Dale Lind, Terry Teachout, Jim Lowe, Casey Schwartz, Rob Waldman, Les Davis, Jim de Julio, Carol Sloane, John McDonough, Anthony DiFlorio, Jack Parnell, Yvonne Littlewood, Father John Morley, Patty Thunell, Geri Tamburello, Bobby Margillo, John di Martino, Mike Curb, Jimmy Lategano, Ed Hurst, Paul Hefti, Frank Wess, Margaret Whiting, Bernie Ilson, David Patrick Stearns, Richard Budgen, Christopher P. Halloran, Bobby Rozario, Carmel Malin, Roger Schore, Helen Rogers, Pavel Solakhyan, Michael Brockman, Carol del Monte, James Gavin, Gary Marmorstein, George del Monte, Stan Edwards, Christine Vallance, James Green, Graham Pass, Roy Durso, Dennis Bono, Ray Gelato, Andy Alfieri, Barbara Maier Gustern, Ross Giunta, Lisa Giunta, Scottie Giunta, Steven Schrader, Demarys Vazquez, Ellen Martin, Robert Greenwald, Eugene Allen, Brad Stone, Ted Grossman, Lloyd Weatherford, Jeff Weatherford, Dale Lind, Douglas Rogers, Mary-Beth Holland, Danny Betesh, Eddie Bert, Beth Herstein, Santo Romano, Judith Liss, Eva Fogelman, Jerome Chanes, Jack Simpson, Anthony Scalia, Jeff Courtney, Eric Wilson, Mike Feder, Elaine Evans, Jerry Weinstein, John Capotorto, Lisa Montanerelli, Bill Miller, Phoebe Jacobs, Phil Leshin, and Hitomi Tanaka.

APPENDIX

AWARDS, ALBUMS, AND SONGS

Grammy Awards

1963: Record of the Year: "I Left My Heart in San Francisco"

1963: Best Male Solo Record Performance

1993: Best Traditional Pop Vocal Performance: *Perfectly Frank*

1994: Best Traditional Pop Vocal Performance: *Steppin' Out*

1995: Best Traditional Pop Vocal Performance: *MTV Unplugged*

1997: Best Traditional Vocal Performance: *Here's to the Ladies*

1998: Best Traditional Pop Vocal Performance: *Tony Bennett on Holiday*

2000: Best Traditional Pop Vocal Performance: *Tony Bennett Sings Ellington: Hot and Cool*

2001: Lifetime Achievement Award

2003: Best Traditional Pop Vocal Album: *Playin' with My Friends: Bennett Sings the Blues*

2004: Best Traditional Pop Vocal Album: *A Wonderful World* (shared with k.d. lang)

2006: Best Traditional Pop Vocal Album: *The Art of Romance*

2006: Best Pop Collaboration with Vocals: *For Once in My Life* (shared with Stevie Wonder)

2007: Best Traditional Pop Vocal Album: *Duets: An American Classic*

Other Special Awards and Honors

1969: New York City's Bronze Medallion

1996: Primetime Emmy Awards: Outstanding Performance for a Variety Music Program: *Live by Request*

1996: Cable Ace Awards: Performance in a Music Special or Series

328

1997: Inducted into the Big Band and Jazz Hall of Fame

1998: Juvenile Diabetes Research Foundation: Humanitarian of the Year Award

2000: United Nations Citizen of the World Award

2000: American Cancer Society Humanitarian Award

2000: Library of Congress: Living Legend Award

2001: George Washington University: Honorary Doctor of Music Degree

2002: The King Center: Salute to Greatness Award

2002: ASCAP: Pied Piper Lifetime Achievement Award

2003: Songwriters Hall of Fame: Towering Song Award and Towering Performance Award

2005: Kennedy Center for the Performing Arts Honoree

2006: National Endowment for the Arts: Jazz Master

2006: ASCAP: Legacy Award

2006: *Billboard:* Century Award

2006: United Nations High Commission for Refugees Humanitarian Award

2007: Inductee in Civil Rights Walk of Fame

2007: Primetime Emmy Award for Individual Performance in a Variety or Music Program: *Tony Bennett: An American Classic Star on the Hollywood Walk of Fame*

The Best of Tony's Albums: A Selected List

Cloud 7: unavailable (1955: Columbia)

Tony: unavailable (1957: Columbia)

The Beat of My Heart: unavailable (1957: Columbia)

Blue Velvet (1958: Columbia)

Long Ago and Far Away: unavailable (1958: Columbia)

In Person! Tony Bennett, Count Basie and His Orchestra (1959: Columbia)

Hometown, My Town: unavailable (1959: Columbia)

To My Wonderful One: unavailable (1960: Columbia)

Alone Together: unavailable (1960: Columbia)

Tony Bennett Sings a String of Harold Arlen: unavailable (1961: Columbia)

Bennett-Basie: Strike Up the Band (1961: Roulette)

Tony Sings for Two: unavailable (1961: Columbia)

My Heart Sings: unavailable (1961: Columbia)

Mr. Broadway: unavailable (1962: Columbia)

I Left My Heart in San Francisco (1962: Columbia)

Tony Bennett at Carnegie Hall (1962: Columbia)

I Wanna Be Around (1963: Columbia)

This Is All I Ask: unavailable (1963: Columbia)

The Many Moods of Tony: unavailable (1964: Columbia)

When Lights Are Low: unavailable (1964: Columbia)

If I Ruled the World/Songs for the Jet Set (1965: Columbia)

The Movie Song Album (1966: Columbia)

A Time for Love: unavailable (1966: Columbia)
Tony Makes It Happen: unavailable (1967: Columbia)
For Once in My Life: unavailable (1967: Columbia)
Yesterday I Heard the Rain: unavailable (1968: Columbia)
Snowfall: unavailable (1968: Columbia)
I've Gotta Be Me: unavailable (1969: Columbia)
Something: unavailable (1970: Columbia)
Get Happy (1971: Columbia)
The Very Thought of You: unavailable (1971: Columbia)
Love Story: unavailable (1971: Columbia)
With Love: unavailable (1972: Columbia)
Listen Easy (1973: Phillips)
Tony!: unavailable (1973: Columbia)
Tony Bennett Sings 10 Rodgers & Hart Songs (1973: Improv)
Tony Bennett Sings More Great Rodgers & Hart (1973: Improv)
Life Is Beautiful (1975: Improv)
The Tony Bennett/Bill Evans Album (1975: Fantasy)
Let's Fall in Love with the Songs of Harold Arlen and Cy Coleman (1975: Columbia)
Tony Bennett & Bill Evans Together Again (1977: Concord)
The McPartlands and Friends Make Magnificent Music (1977: Improv)
The Art of Excellence: unavailable (1986: Columbia)
Tony Bennett: Jazz (1987: Columbia)
Bennett/Berlin (1987: Columbia)
Astoria: Portrait of the Artist: unavailable (1989: Columbia)
Steppin' Out (1993: Columbia)
MTV Unplugged (1994: Columbia)
Here's to the Ladies (1995: Columbia)
Tony Bennett on Holiday (1997: Columbia)
The Playground: unavailable (1998: Columbia)
Tony Bennett Sings Ellington: Hot & Cool (1999: Columbia)
The Ultimate Tony Bennett (2000: Columbia)
Playin' with My Friends: Bennett Sings the Blues (2001: Columbia)
The Essential Tony Bennett (2002: Columbia)
Fifty Years: The Artistry of Tony Bennett (2004: Columbia)
The Art of Romance (2004: Columbia)
Duets: An American Classic (2006: Columbia)

The Best of Tony's Less Famous Songs

"He Loves and She Loves"
"People" (version on *Tony Bennett's Greatest Hits, Vol. IV*)
"Climb Every Mountain" (version on *Tony Bennett at Carnegie Hall*)
"Some of These Days"

"Limehouse Blues"

"A Pretty Girl Is Like a Melody" (never recorded; only in concert and on the
    Tonight Show)

"All That Love Went to Waste"

"Yesterday I Heard the Rain"

"Somebody"

"Country Girl"

"The Kid's a Dreamer"

"Fool of Fools"

"I Do Not Know a Day I Did Not Love You"

"Wave"

"Street of Dreams"

"I Fall in Love Too Easily"

"Till"

"True Blue Lou"

"It Was Written in the Stars"

"This Time the Dream's On Me"

"Moments Like This"

"What Are You Afraid Of?"

"It Amazes Me"

"Everybody Has the Blues" (with Ray Charles)

"How Do You Keep the Music Playing?"

"When Love Was All We Had"

"Life Is Beautiful"

"Forget the Woman"

"I Got Lost in Her Arms"

"City of the Angels"

"The Day You Leave Me"

"A Sleepin' Bee"

"I'm Through with Love"

"All of My Life"

"Dancing in the Dark"

"When I Lost You"

"Let's Face the Music and Dance"

"When Do the Bells Ring for Me?"

"I Was Lost, I Was Drifting"

"This Funny World"

"It Was You"

"God Bless the Child"

"My Ideal"

"Solitude"

"A Little Street Where Old Friends Meet"

"The Gal That Got Away"

"It's Like Reaching for the Moon"

"Where Do You Go from Love?"

"I've Come Home Again"

"Spring in Manhattan"

"Penthouse Serenade"

"Tell Her It's Snowing"

"I'll Be Seeing You"

"A Foggy Day"

"Here's That Rainy Day"

"My Love Went to London"

"Poor Butterfly"

"Moonlight in Vermont"

"My Mom"

"Spring Is Here"

"Young and Foolish"

"I Concentrate on You"

"Days of Wine and Roses"

"You Must Believe in Spring"

"My Ideal"

"Cloudy Morning"

"Time after Time"

"The Girl I Love"

"A Weaver of Dreams"

"There Will Never Be Another You"

"Indian Summer"

"One"

"All of Me"

"But Beautiful" (Bill Charlap album *Stardust*)

"When I Lost You"

"All of My Life"

"Moments Like This"

"My Foolish Heart"

"I Used to Be Color Blind"

"There'll Be Some Changes Made"

"When My Ship Comes In"

"The Very Thought of You"

"Don't Wait Too Long"

"When Joanna Loved Me"

"I Guess I'll Have to Change My Plans"

"It Had to Be You"

"My Funny Valentine"

BIBLIOGRAPHY

Aaron, Arthur. *Not Just the Beatles: The Autobiography of Sid Bernstein*. New Jersey: Jacques & Flusster, 2000.

Abzug, Robert H. *Inside the Vicious Heart: Americans and the Liberation of Nazi Concentration Camps*. New York: Oxford University Press, 1985.

Bakish, David. *Jimmy Durante: His Show Business Career, with an Annotated Filmography and Discography*. Jefferson, N.C.: McFarland, 1995.

Balliett, Whitney. "A Quality That Lets You In," *The New Yorker*, January 7, 1974. This profile appears in Balliett's *American Singers: Twenty-seven Portraits in Song*. New York: Oxford University Press, 1988. Copyright Nancy Balliett, 2011.

Bennett, Tony. *What My Heart Has Seen*. New York: Rizzoli, 1996.

Bennett, Tony, and Will Friedwald. *The Good Life*. New York: Pocket Books, 1998.

Bennett, Tony, and Robert Sullivan. *Tony Bennett in the Studio: A Life of Art and Music*. New York: Sterling, 2007.

Branch, Taylor. *Pillar of Fire: America in the King Years 1963–65*. New York: Simon & Schuster, 1998.

Burke, Patrick. *Come and Hear the Truth: Jazz and Race on 52nd Street*. Chicago: University of Chicago Press, 2008.

Cateura, Linda Brandi, ed. *Growing Up Italian: Grandfather's Fig Tree and Other Stories*. New York: William Morrow, 1987.

Cuomo, Mario. *Reason to Believe: A Keen Assessment of Who We Are and an Inspiring Vision of What We Could Be*. New York: Touchstone, 1996.

Damone, Vic, with David Chanoff. *Singing Was the Easy Part*. New York: St. Martin's Press, 2009.

Dannen, Fredric. *Hit Men: Power Brokers and Fast Money inside the Music Business*. New York: Vintage Books, 1991.

Di Donato, Pietro. *Christ in Concrete*. New York: Signet, 1993.

Falcone, Vincent, and Bob Popyk. *Frankly Just between Us: My Life Conducting Frank Sinatra's Music*. Wisconsin: Hal Leonard, 2005.

Flippo, Chet. *Everybody Was Kung-Fu Dancing: Chronicles of the Lionized and the Notorious.* New York: St. Martin's Press, 1991.

Friedwald, Will. *A Biographical Guide to the Great Jazz and Pop Singers.* New York: Pantheon, 2010.

————. *Jazz Singing: America's Great Voices from Bessie Smith to Bebop and Beyond.* London: Quartet Books, 1991.

————. *Sinatra! The Song Is You: A Singer's Art.* New York: Da Capo Press, 1997.

————. *Stardust Melodies: A Biography of 12 of America's Most Popular Songs.* New York: Pantheon, 2002.

Furia, Philip. *Skylark: The Life and Times of Johnny Mercer.* New York: St. Martin's Press, 2003.

Gambino, Richard. *Blood of My Blood: The Dilemma of the Italian-Americans.* New York: Guernica, 2002.

Gavin, James. *Stormy Weather: The Life of Lena Horne.* New York: Atria Books, 2009.

Giddins, Gary. *Rhythm-a-ning: Jazz Tradition and Innovation.* New York: Oxford University Press, 1985.

————. *Weather Bird: Jazz at the Dawn of Its Second Century.* New York: Oxford University Press, 2004.

Hajdu, David. *Heroes and Villains: Essays on Music, Movies, Comics, and Culture.* New York: Di Capo Press, 2009.

Hemming, Roy, and Hajdu, David. *Discovering Great Singers of Classic Pop: A New Listener's Guide to the Sounds and Lives of the Top Performers and Their Recordings, Movies, and Videographies, and Recommendations for Collectors.* New York: Haymarket Press, 1991.

Hentoff, Nat. *At the Jazz Band Ball: Sixty Years on the Jazz Scene.* Berkeley: University of California Press, 2010.

Hoffman, Matthew. *Tony Bennett: The Best Is Yet to Come.* New York: MetroBooks, 1997.

Kaplan, James. *Frank: The Voice.* New York: Doubleday, 2010.

Levin, Meyer. *In Search: An Autobiography.* New York: Paperback Library, 1950.

Lewis, John. *Walking with the Wind: A Memoir of the Movement.* New York: Harcourt Brace, 1998.

Mangione, Jerre. *Mount Allegro: A Memoir of Italian American Life.* Syracuse, N.Y.: Syracuse University Press, 1998.

Mangione, Jerre, and Ben Morreale. *La Storia: Five Centuries of the Italian American Experience.* New York: Harper Perennial, 1993.

Marmorstein, Gary. *The Label: The Story of Columbia Records.* New York: Da Capo Press, 2007.

Rotella, Mark. *Amore: The Story of Italian American Song.* New York: Farrar, Straus & Giroux, 2010.

Schwartz, Jonathan. *All in Good Time: A Memoir.* New York: Random House, 2004.

————. *The Man Who Knew Cary Grant.* New York: Plume, 1989.

Shearing, George. *Lullaby of Birdland: The Autobiography of George Shearing.* New York: Continuum, 2004.

Sheed, Wilfrid. *The House That George Built: With a Little Help from Irving, Cole, and a Crew of About Fifty.* New York: Random House, 2009.

Zuccotti, Susan. *The Italians and the Holocaust: Persecution, Rescue, Survival.* New York: Basic Books, 1987.

INDEX

NOTE: Page numbers in *italics* indicate photos.